SUPER SIMPLE
PSYCHOLOGY

Senior editor Amanda Wyatt
Senior art editor Emma Clayton
Project editors Penny Arlon, Edward Aves, Jolyon Goddard,
Ben Morgan, Scarlett O'Hara, Sharon Thorn
Editorial assistant Maddi Oakley
Designers Amy Child, Karen Constanti, Laura Gardner,
Tory Gordon-Harris, Hoa Luc, Anna Pond, Rhys Thomas
Illustrators Gus Scott, Dan Crisp, Aparajita Sen
Picture researcher Shubhdeep Kaur
Managing editor Rachel Fox
Managing art editor Owen Peyton Jones
Production editor Gillian Reid
Producer Joss Moore
Project jacket designer Juhi Sheth
DTP Designer Deepak Mittal
Senior Jackets Coordinator Priyanka Sharma Saddi
Jackets design development manager Sophia MTT
Publisher Andrew Macintyre
Art director Karen Self
Associate publishing director Liz Wheeler
Publishing director Jonathan Metcalf
Authors Tom Buxton-Cope, Ali Abbas, Dr Stacey Bedwell, Mo Hunter,
Dr Penny March, Joelie McCrary, Prof. Martyn Standage
Consultants Tom Buxton-Cope, Catherine Collin, Dr Joseph Swope

First published in Great Britain in 2024 by
Dorling Kindersley Limited
20 Vauxhall Bridge Road,
London, SW1V 2SA

The authorised representative in the EEA is
Dorling Kindersley Verlag GmbH. Arnulfstr. 124, 80636 Munich, Germany

Copyright © 2024 Dorling Kindersley Limited
A Penguin Random House Company
10 9 8 7 6 5 4 3 2
008–331880–August/2024

A CIP catalogue record for this book
is available from the British Library.
ISBN: 978-0-2415-6987-0

Printed and bound in China

www.dk.com

This book was made with Forest
Stewardship Council™ certified
paper – one small step in DK's
commitment to a sustainable future.
Learn more at www.dk.com/uk/
information/sustainability

DK

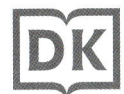

SUPER SIMPLE PSYCHOLOGY

THE ULTIMATE BITESIZE STUDY GUIDE

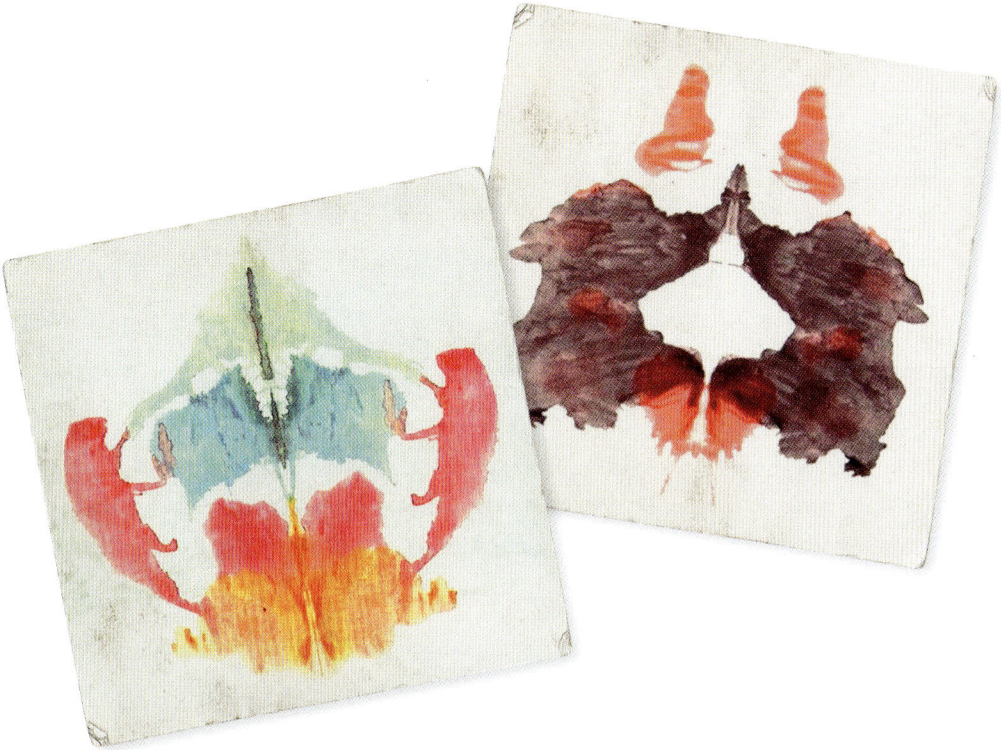

Contents

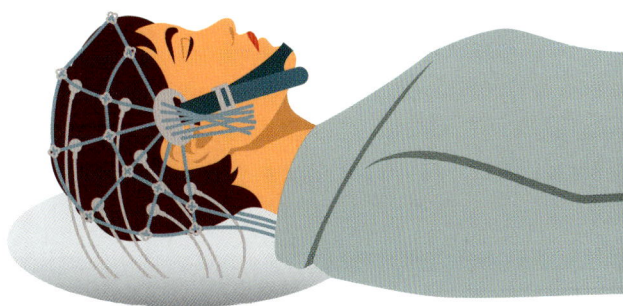

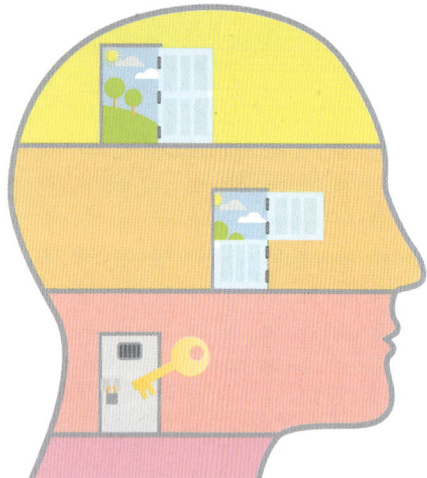

Chapter 12: Emotion

Chapter 13: Clinical psychology: psychological disorders

Chapter 14: Clinical psychology: treating psychological disorders

Chapter 15: Social psychology

Chapter 16: Criminal psychology

Chapter 17: Issues and debates

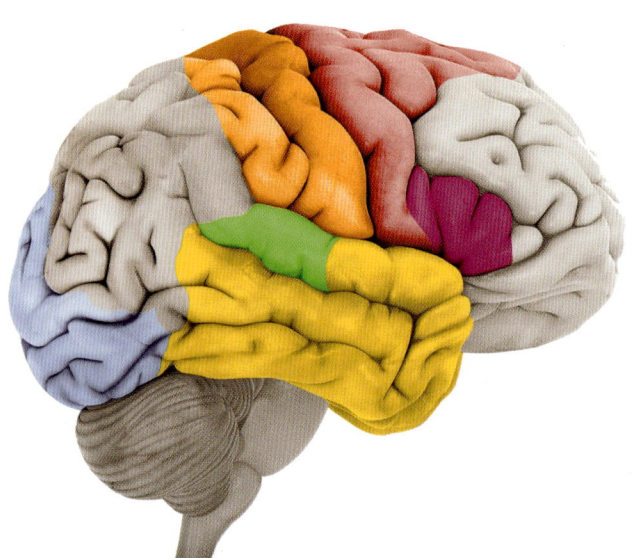

Chapter 1
Scientific foundations

The history of psychology

Psychology is the scientific study of the mind and how it influences behaviour. Interest in the mind dates back to the ancient Greek philosophers — the word psychology comes from the Greek word *psyche*, meaning soul and mind. However, psychology only became a distinct subject in the 1870s, when psychologists began to apply scientific methods to their research.

Key facts

- ✓ Psychology — the scientific study of the mind and behaviour — emerged as a distinct discipline in the 1870s.
- ✓ Approaches to psychology are known as paradigms.
- ✓ Paradigm shifts occur when old approaches are replaced by new research and ideas.

Founder of psychology
German physiologist Wilhelm Wundt sets up the first psychology laboratory in Leipzig, Germany. He asks participants to report on their mind while focusing on a stimulus, such as a ticking metronome. His technique is known as introspection.

Behaviour analysis
The Behaviour of Organisms is published, in which US psychologist B.F. Skinner describes his experiments with rats and reveals how rewards and punishments can affect behaviour. Skinner becomes an influential figure of the behaviourist approach.

1879   **1895**   **1897**   **1938**

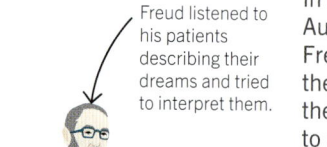

Freud listened to his patients describing their dreams and tried to interpret them.

The psychodynamic approach
In his book *Studies on Hysteria*, Austrian neurologist Sigmund Freud presents studies of his therapy patients. He develops the psychodynamic approach to psychology, which focuses on exploration of the unconscious mind.

The behaviourist approach
Russian physiologist Ivan Pavlov tests dogs' responses to food and a ringing bell. He shows that dogs learn new behaviours by forming associations. His experiments later inspire the behaviourist approach to psychology, which focuses on observable behaviours rather than the mind.

🔍 Changing approaches to psychology

Early psychologists, such as Wundt and Freud, had their own approaches to psychology, known as paradigms. Their theories shaped mainstream psychology of the time. New research, however, can challenge the dominant paradigm, resulting in a shift of ideas. Paradigm shifts do not mean everything from before is rejected though, and modern psychology often draws on multiple approaches.

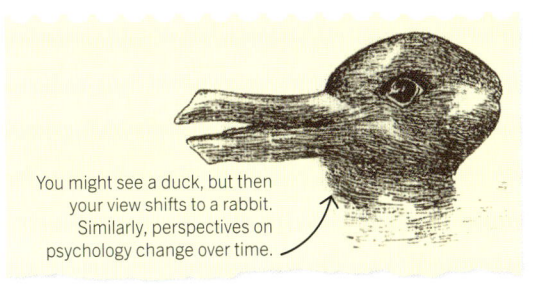

You might see a duck, but then your view shifts to a rabbit. Similarly, perspectives on psychology change over time.

The humanistic approach
US psychologist Abraham Maslow proposes the hierarchy of needs — the idea that basic human needs must be satisfied before anything else. It marks the emergence of the humanistic approach, which looks at the whole person, not just the mind or behaviour.

- Self-actualization
- Self-esteem
- Love and belonging
- Safety
- Physiological needs (such as food and water)

Cognitive neuroscience
Discoveries by cognitive and biological psychologists show how the two approaches can work together. This leads to a fusion of approaches and the emergence of cognitive neuroscience: the study of the biology of mental processes, such as thinking and memory.

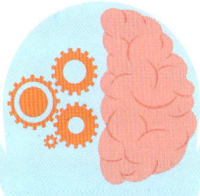

1943   1950s and 1960s   1980s   1990s

The cognitive approach
Advances in technology lead psychologists to find similarities between human mental processes and computers. Cognitive psychologists propose theoretical models of memory using words typically associated with computing.

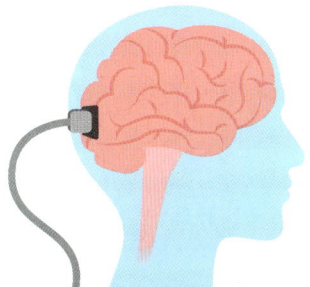

The biological approach
New brain-scanning technologies enable psychologists to see and measure brain activity for the first time. The biological approach to psychology is established as psychologists learn more about how genes, neurotransmitters, and hormones affect the brain and body.

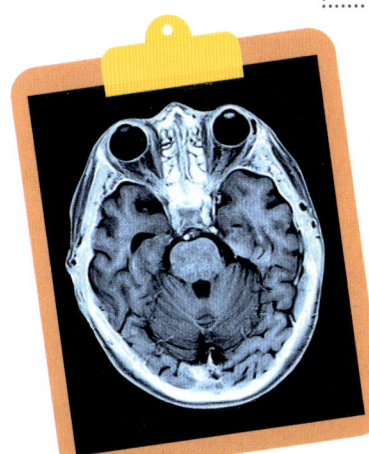

The origins of psychology

German physiologist Wilhelm Wundt is often called the founder of experimental psychology. In 1879, he opened the first psychology laboratory to study the mind and behaviour in controlled conditions. By developing a scientific, evidence-based approach to studying the mind, Wundt moved psychology away from its philosophical roots and turned it into its own separate discipline.

Key facts

✓ Wundt opened the first laboratory for studying the mind and behaviour in controlled conditions.

✓ Wundt pioneered a scientific, evidence-based approach to the study of the mind.

✓ He used a process of introspection to reflect on how an environmental stimulus affects a person's mind.

Introspection

Wundt wanted to analyse the human mind, but the only mind a person can access is their own. To overcome this challenge, he developed a process called introspection. He trained participants to record their thoughts in a standardized way so that he could look for patterns. Wundt's study was the first scientific analysis of the mind.

Participant

The participant recorded their findings for Wundt to analyse.

1. Focus
Wundt asked participants to consider their mental processes while focusing on a stimulus, such as a ticking metronome. All participants had the same amount of time and watched the same object.

2. Reflect and record
Participants recorded the mental processes they experienced while focusing on the stimulus. They broke them down into categories such as thoughts, sensations, and feelings.

3. Compare and analyse
The responses were compared. By analysing different reactions to the same stimulus, Wundt could identify patterns and propose theories about the mind, using the participants' direct responses as evidence.

Empiricism

Wundt was an empiricist – he used the empirical method to develop his theories about the mind, which he based on the reports of participants. The empirical method uses techniques that produce evidence based on direct experience. It seeks to report on the world as it really is, using evidence, rather than relying on unsupported beliefs.

Advertising leads us to believe that burgers look like this...

But in reality, most burgers look like this.

Belief

Evidence

The science of psychology

Psychology is the scientific study of the mind and behaviour. Like all scientists, psychologists aim to collect evidence in an objective way so that conclusions are not distorted by bias. The scientific method relies on forming tentative theories (hypotheses) that can be tested by gathering evidence. This approach allows scientists to check one another's findings, building knowledge. Psychologists collect evidence using five main research methods.

Key facts

✓ The five research methods in psychology are experimental, correlation, surveys and questionnaires, observational, and case studies.

✓ Scientific theories should be falsifiable, which means they can be tested and potentially proved wrong.

Method	Qualitative or quantitative	Procedure	Advantages	Disadvantages
Experimental (see page 14)	Quantitative	Manipulate one variable (independent variable) and measure effect on another (dependent variable)	Most scientific method and the only way to establish cause and effect	Not always practical or ethical; results of lab experiments may not generalize to real world
Correlational (see page 23)	Quantitative	Calculate strength of association between two related variables	May work where an experiment is not possible; useful for detecting patterns in data	Cannot demonstrate cause and effect as confounding variables are not controlled
Surveys and questionnaires (see page 26)	Both	Participants interviewed or fill in forms	Easy to collect large amounts of data from many participants	No control of variables; results may be inaccurate or unrepresentative
Observational (see page 25)	Both	Observing behaviour in a natural setting	Can study behaviour that cannot be manipulated experimentally	No control of variables; results prone to bias; difficult to generalize to other cases
Case studies (see page 29)	Qualitative	Studying one person in detail	Only a single participant needed	No control of variables; small sample size; difficult to generalize to other cases

Falsifiability

The philosopher Karl Popper argued that a theory can only be considered scientific if it is possible to test it and potentially prove it wrong, or "falsify" it. Scientists try to falsify their own theories by testing them, usually in experiments. This is very different from amassing one-sided evidence to support an opinion, as a lawyer might do. If a theory survives many tests it may be accepted as fact, but it can never be proven true beyond doubt. Popper explained this using a metaphorical theory that all swans are white. This is impossible to prove because a single non-white swan would refute it – as happened when Europeans discovered black swans in Australia.

The scientific method

All kinds of scientific research depend on a process called the scientific method. Only by following this process can scientists reach objective conclusions about the world based on evidence rather than opinion or hearsay.

Key facts

- ✓ Scientific research depends on the scientific method.
- ✓ The scientific method allows scientists to make objective conclusions based on evidence.
- ✓ A testable (falsifiable) hypothesis is an essential part of the scientific method.
- ✓ Cause and effect can be established by manipulating variables in an experiment.

Testing a hypothesis

A key part of the scientific method is the formation of a testable hypothesis — a tentative idea that can be tested and potentially proven false by experiment or observation. In an experiment, the hypothesis is tested by manipulating variables, which makes it possible to establish cause and effect.

1. Observation

Research often begins with observation. For example, a psychologist might observe that students score poorly in IQ tests after getting little sleep the previous night.

5. Peer review

The results are written up in a scientific paper to be published. However, before publication can go ahead, the paper is evaluated by experts in the field to ensure it meets the standards of the scientific community. This process is called peer review.

6. Repetition

After publication, other scientists may repeat the experiment. If they obtain similar results, the hypothesis gains support. After extensive testing, a hypothesis may eventually become accepted as a fact or as a part of a wider scientific theory.

2. Hypothesis

A testable hypothesis is formed. This often proposes a relationship between two variables, one dependent on the other. For instance, the hypothesis might be that IQ test results depend on length of sleep the previous night.

4. Conclusion

The data is analysed to see if the hypothesis is supported. This forms the conclusion. A hypothesis can be supported by the evidence or rejected as untrue, but it can never be proven true beyond doubt.

3. Experiment

To test the hypothesis, an experiment is carried out. The hypothesis predicts that IQ score (the dependent variable) will fall after reduced sleep, so IQ tests are performed after deliberately shortening sleep time (the independent variable). All other variables are controlled.

Working with variables

A variable is anything that can vary, from a person's height or IQ to their social status. In experiments, psychologists systematically manipulate one variable to see if it has a measurable effect on another. This must be done under carefully controlled conditions, which means that other variables are controlled to prevent them from affecting the results.

Key facts

✓ The variable that is manipulated is called the independent variable.

✓ The variable that is measured to obtain results is the dependent variable.

✓ All other variables are called extraneous.

✓ Confounding variables are extraneous variables that aren't controlled.

Types of variable

The variable that is manipulated in an experiment is called the independent variable, while the variable that is measured to find any effect is the dependent variable. All other variables are called extraneous and are held constant ("standardized" or "controlled") by the way the experiment is designed and conducted. An extraneous variable that isn't controlled and might distort the results is called a confounding variable.

Independent variable
Could listening to music improve maths skills? In an example experiment, students are split into two groups and given a maths test. Listening to music versus silence is the independent variable.

Dependent variable
The dependent variable is the maths test score. Researchers compare the scores of the two groups to see if music has an effect.

Extraneous variables
All other variables, such as music volume, how long the test lasts, and so on, are kept constant. However, a confounding variable, such as music preference, might be difficult to control.

Sources of error

Demand characteristics
Sometimes participants guess the purpose of a study and try to give the "right" or "wrong" answers in an attempt to please the researcher or sabotage the research. Such sources of confounding variables are called demand characteristics.

The stereotype threat
Exposure to negative stereotypes just before a test can affect a participant's performance. For example, one study found that women performed worse than men in a maths test after being told that men usually do better. When participants were told gender makes no difference, women and men did equally well.

Investigator effects
Researchers may consciously or unconsciously introduce confounding variables into a study. Their gender, accent, or tone of voice can all affect how participants might respond. Sources of error caused by researchers (which also include experimenter bias) are called investigator effects.

Types of hypothesis

When scientists write up a research report after an experiment, they usually begin by stating their aims and hypotheses. The aim of an experiment is a general statement about its purpose. The hypothesis is a more specific, testable statement about how changing one variable might affect another variable. Clearly stated aims and hypotheses are an essential part of good research.

Key facts

✓ A hypothesis is a testable statement or prediction.

✓ The experimental hypothesis predicts an effect; the null hypothesis predicts no effect.

✓ An experimental hypothesis may be directional (predicts either an increase or decrease) or non-directional (predicts a change in either direction).

Null hypothesis

The null hypothesis (H_0) is a statement that there is no relationship between the variables being studied. For example, in a study on the effect of a new drug on memory, the null hypothesis might be that the drug makes no significant difference to results obtained in a memory test. Scientists often want to disprove the null hypothesis.

Experimental hypothesis

The experimental (or alternative) hypothesis (H_1) contradicts the null hypothesis. This hypothesis predicts that the independent variable (such as taking an experimental drug) will have a significant effect on the dependent variable (memory test score). The word "significant" indicates that a statistical analysis is carried out to show whether the results obtained would be unlikely to happen by chance alone.

Directional hypothesis

An experimental hypothesis that specifies a change in a particular direction is called a directional or one-tailed hypothesis. For instance, the hypothesis might predict that a new drug will improve memory. Researchers often use a directional hypothesis when past research suggests results will go that way.

Non-directional hypothesis

A hypothesis that merely predicts a change without specifying an increase or decrease is called a non-directional or two-tailed hypothesis. A non-directional hypothesis makes it easier to detect an effect, but interpreting the results is more challenging if they go against expectations.

🔍 Operationalizing variables

To ensure that a hypothesis is testable and therefore scientific, it is often necessary for psychologists to "operationalize" variables. This means transforming an abstract or complex trait into a measurable quantity so that numerical data can be collected. For example, socioeconomic status might be operationalized by using a person's income, and anxiety level might be operationalized by a standardized anxiety questionnaire.

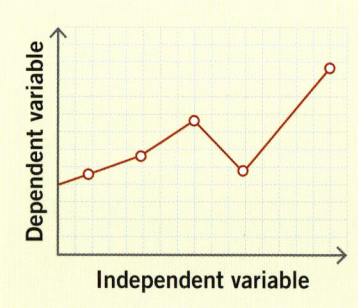

Types of experiment

It is not always possible to carry out psychology experiments under perfectly controlled laboratory conditions. Sometimes it is impractical, impossible, or unethical to manipulate key variables, making other experimental approaches necessary. Each type of experiment has different strengths and weaknesses.

Key facts

✓ Lab experiments are carried out under controlled conditions.

✓ Field experiments are carried out in the real world.

✓ Longitudinal studies take place over long periods.

✓ Cross-sectional studies are snapshots of one point in time.

Laboratory experiments
Laboratory experiments allow precise control of variables, making it possible to draw objective conclusions about cause and effect. They have high internal validity (see page 18) and are repeatable, allowing other scientists to verify them. However, results may not generalize to real-world settings if participants do not act naturally or if operationalized variables (see page 16) do not reflect their real-world counterparts.

Field experiments
Also called real-world experiments, these studies are carried out in everyday settings. The independent variable can be manipulated, but other variables may be more difficult to control than in laboratory experiments. The results have high ecological validity, which means they can be generalized to the real world more easily than lab experiment results.

Natural experiments
In a natural experiment, the independent variable varies naturally and the study compares groups that differ in exposure to it. For instance, a natural experiment might investigate the effect of pollution on mental health by comparing people exposed to high and low levels. Participants cannot be randomly allocated to experimental conditions, so such studies are also called quasi-experiments. The independent variable cannot be manipulated, and findings are only correlational.

🔎 Pilot studies

Before a large or expensive research project goes ahead, a psychologist might carry out a pilot study. Pilot studies check for flaws in the experiment design or procedure. For instance, participants might be asked whether they guessed what aspect of personality a questionnaire was attempting to measure. If they did, the questionnaire could be changed before the real study.

🔎 Longitudinal and cross-sectional

Longitudinal studies measure changes in the same people over long periods. Such studies are time-consuming and participants may drop out. An alternative is a cross-sectional study, which compares people of different ages at one point in time. The drawback of this approach is that confounding variables can occur, as people of different ages grew up in different decades.

Validity

In order for psychologists to draw credible conclusions from their research, it is crucial that the results of studies have what we call validity. Validity means accuracy. If a test has validity, it accurately measures what it claims to test. For example, an IQ test is valid if the results match those of other trusted measures of intelligence. Validity can be internal or external.

Key facts

✓ Validity means accuracy.

✓ To ensure internal validity, scientific studies must be carried out in an objective way under controlled conditions.

✓ External validity means results can be generalized to other settings.

Internal validity
Scientific studies must be carried out under carefully controlled conditions to achieve internal validity. Most science experiments are tests to find out if one variable affects another. For example, an experiment might explore whether sleep deprivation affects reaction times. Valid conclusions about cause and effect can only be drawn if other variables are controlled (held constant). If an experiment is well designed, it has high internal validity.

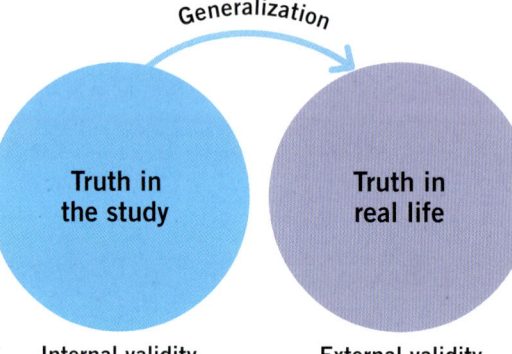

Generalization

Truth in the study

Internal validity

Truth in real life

External validity

External validity
Lab experiments take place under unnatural conditions that may not correspond to real-world settings. A study only has external validity if results can be generalized to other situations. Ecological validity means the results generalize to the real world. Population validity means results apply to other kinds of people, and temporal validity means results apply to other times.

🔍 Assessing validity and credibility

The simplest way to assess validity is a subjective judgment: does the study seem valid on the face of it (face validity)? A more rigorous approach is to check if results correlate well with other tests. If a new test correlates with another test considered to be a "gold standard", the new test has what's known as concurrent validity. Validity can be improved by using consistent procedures across all study participants (standardization) and by randomly allocating participants to conditions (randomization), among other control measures. As well as assessing the validity of quantitative studies, psychologists must also assess the credibility (believability) of qualitative research, such as interviews and case studies. Credibility is the degree to which the study gives a true picture of the perceptions and opinions of participants.

1. Is the test valid on the face of it? ✅

2. Do results correlate with other trusted tests? ✅

3. Were experimental methods standardized? ✅

4. Are all sources of bias avoided? ✅

Reliability

As well as trying to ensure validity (see page 18) in research studies, psychologists strive for reliability. A test is reliable if it consistently produces the same or similar results when repeated. For example, if you complete the same personality test on two occasions and get similar scores, the test is probably reliable.

Key facts

✓ A test is reliable if it consistently produces the same or similar results when repeated.

✓ A test can be reliable without being valid.

✓ Ways of assessing reliability include test-retest, split-half, and inter-observer.

Comparing reliability and validity

Reliability is a concern in many areas of psychology, including experiments, questionnaires, surveys, and the diagnosis of disease. A test can be reliable without being valid. For example, a thermometer that consistently underestimates temperature by 5 degrees will produce repeatable results, even though they're wrong. Psychologists strive for both reliability and validity.

The visual metaphor of a dartboard is often used to explain reliability and validity. Each black dot here might be the result of a repeated IQ test, for example.

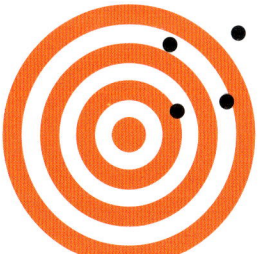
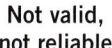

Not valid, not reliable

Reliable but not valid

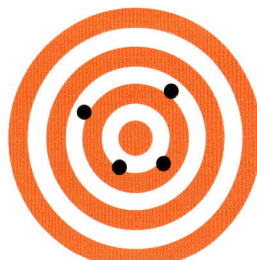

Valid but not reliable

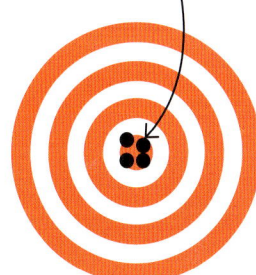

Valid and reliable

🔍 Assessing reliability

Reliability can be assessed in several ways. The test-retest method involves giving the same test to the same participants on different occasions. If the results correlate well, the test is reliable. The split-half method divides a test randomly into two halves (such as odd-numbered and even-numbered questions) to check whether the two halves correlate (internal reliability). A third method is to see if a test produces the same results when carried out by different observers (inter-observer reliability). For instance, if different health practitioners reach the same diagnosis of a patient by following the same diagnostic criteria, then that diagnostic protocol is reliable. Reliability can be improved by using consistent forms of measurement and clearly defined behavioural categories.

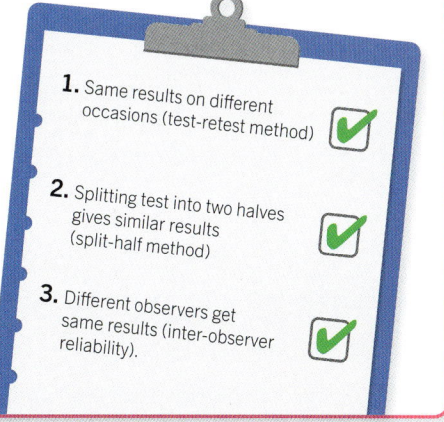

1. Same results on different occasions (test-retest method) ✓

2. Splitting test into two halves gives similar results (split-half method) ✓

3. Different observers get same results (inter-observer reliability). ✓

Sampling techniques

When conducting research, it is impractical to study everybody in a population. Instead, psychologists select a smaller, representative group known as a sample, and the findings of the research are generalized to the wider population. A perfectly representative sample is difficult to achieve as most sampling techniques result in bias, which means some people are ignored in favour of others.

Key facts

✓ Samples are smaller groups taken from a larger target population.

✓ Samples are intended to be representative of the larger target population.

✓ Sampling techniques vary in how accurately they represent the target population and how convenient they are to organize.

Opportunity sampling

This technique, also known as a convenience sampling, involves picking anyone willing to take part; for example, by approaching people in the street. It is quick to organize, but the people available may not be representative of the wider population. Researchers might also happen to approach certain types of people, leading to selection bias.

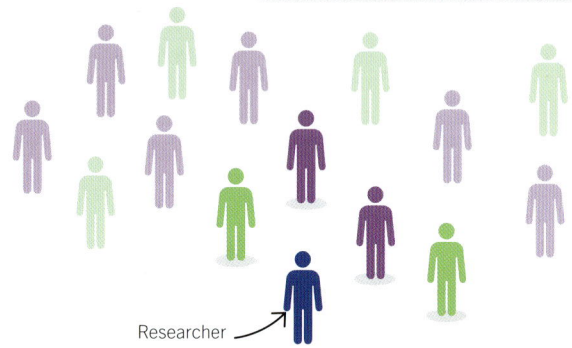

Researcher

Volunteer sampling

This technique involves selecting people who volunteer to take part in a study; for example, by responding to an advert. It is useful when the target population is rare (people with a rare illness, for instance). Volunteers tend to be more motivated than non-volunteers, making the sample biased towards a certain type of person.

Random sampling

Choosing people randomly is the best way to create an unbiased, representative sample. For example, everyone in the population is numbered, and participants are chosen by a lottery method, such as drawing numbers from a hat. Small samples are prone to chance variations that make them unrepresentative, but this issue is reduced if the sample is large.

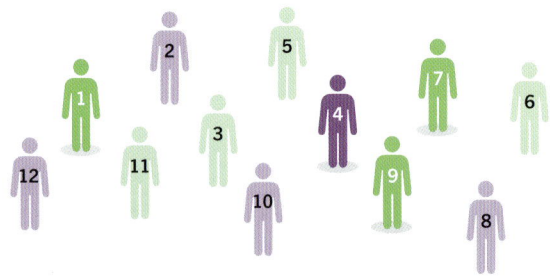

Purposive sampling

This technique involves choosing participants intentionally because of their particular characteristics, which are of interest to the researcher. The sample may be as small as one person.

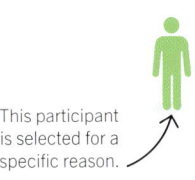
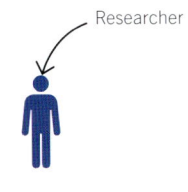

Researcher

This participant is selected for a specific reason.

Bias in sampling

- **Researcher bias** is when the researcher's opinions or beliefs influence the research conclusions.
- **Participant bias** is when the participant acts in the way they think the researcher expects them to act.
- **Sampling bias** is when the sample does not represent the target population.

Stratified sampling

This technique involves creating subgroups, whose size reflects their frequency in the population, then randomly selecting a proportional number of people from each group. It is highly representative, but involves a lot of organization.

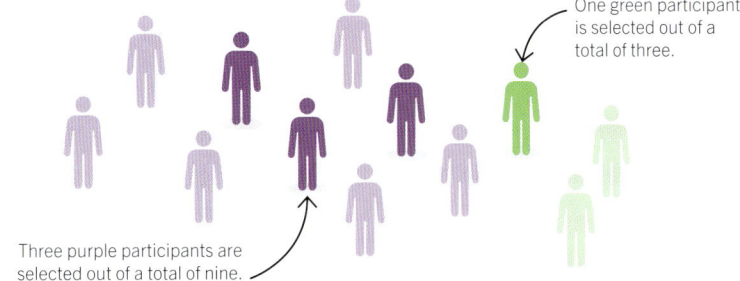

One green participant is selected out of a total of three.

Three purple participants are selected out of a total of nine.

Systematic sampling

This technique selects people by their position in a list; for example, by choosing every *n*th name in a list arranged in alphabetical order. It avoids researcher bias as the researcher does not choose the participants.

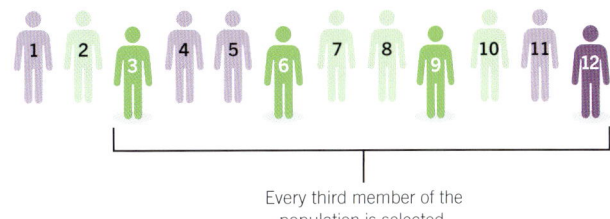

Every third member of the population is selected.

Snowball sampling

Researchers may use existing participants to help them find other potential people to take part in research. This can be a useful way of accessing hard-to-reach populations or when carrying out research into sensitive topics.

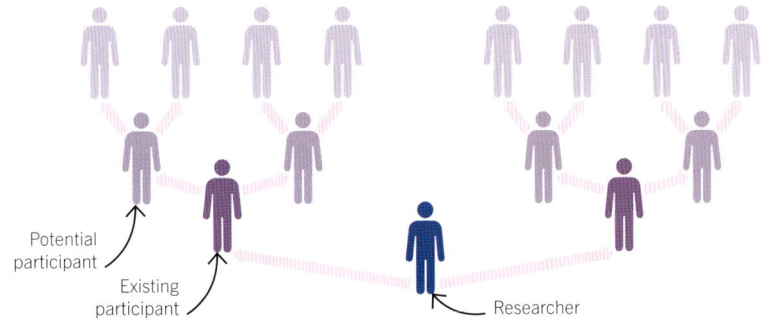

Potential participant

Existing participant

Researcher

Experimental design

Psychology experiments must be carefully designed so that extraneous variables don't affect the data and lead to invalid conclusions. An important aspect of design is the way participants are assigned (allocated) to the different conditions (treatments) in an experiment, such as receiving an experimental drug or an inert placebo. Three common experimental designs are independent groups design, matched pairs design, and repeated measures design.

Key facts

✓ In independent groups design, participants are randomly assigned to different groups.

✓ Matched pairs design controls for variables like age by pairing participants of similar ages before assigning them to different groups.

✓ Repeated measures design exposes each participant to both experimental conditions.

Independent groups (independent measures)
Participants are randomly assigned to two independent groups; for instance, by flipping a coin. This method is often used in drug trials, with one group given an experimental drug and the other (the control group) given an inert placebo, but otherwise treated identically. The independent groups design avoids selection bias, but small samples are prone to chance variations in variables like age or occupation, so large samples are needed.

 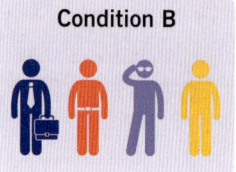

Matched pairs
Participants are first put in pairs that match according to variables such as age or occupation. Pairs are then randomly split between two study groups, so that each person in group A has an equivalent in group B. This method reduces the effect of extraneous variables such as age or occupation, allowing for smaller sample sizes than independent groups design.

 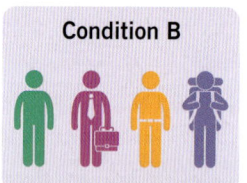

Repeated measures
Every participant is exposed to both experimental conditions. For instance, in a study of the effect of caffeine on reaction time, each participant would be tested twice: once after taking caffeine and again after taking a placebo. The repeated measures design requires fewer participants than independent groups, but the order in which tests are performed can affect the results (order effects).

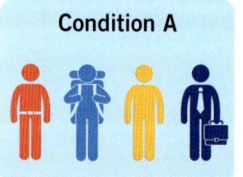 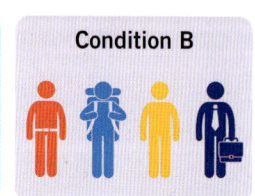

🔍 Counterbalancing

In experiments using repeated measures, participants may become fatigued, bored, or more skilled between the first and second tests, causing order effects. A technique called counterbalancing is needed to remove this confounding variable. If there are two experimental conditions, half the participants are exposed to condition A first and half to condition B first.

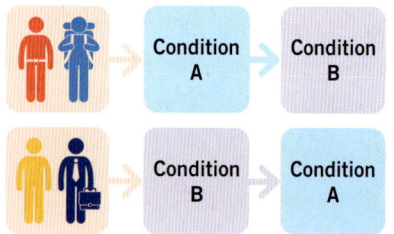

Correlations

A correlational study looks for an association between variables. Graphs called scattergrams (scatter plots) are used to display the results and make patterns easier to spot. They show the strength of a correlation and whether it is positive or negative.

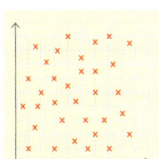

Key facts

✓ If a change in one variable is associated with a change in another, the variables are correlated.

✓ Correlations can be positive or negative and can vary in strength.

✓ The coefficient of correlation ranges from −1 to 1.

Positive correlation

If one variable increases as the other does, the correlation is positive. The example below shows a positive correlation between test performance and sleep time the previous night.

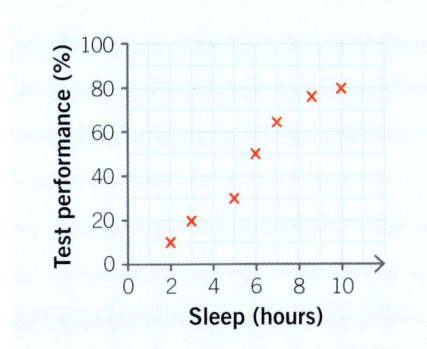

Negative correlation

This is when the value of one variable falls as the other rises. For example, performance in a cognitive test declines with increasing blood alcohol level. Negative correlation is also called inverse correlation.

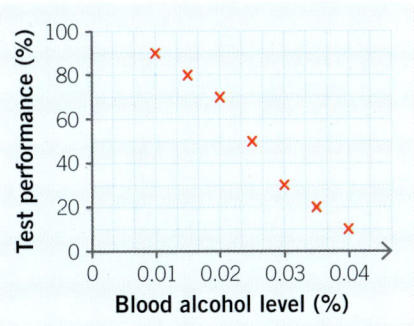

Correlation patterns

The arrangement of data on a scattergram shows the strength and direction of correlation. Randomly scattered points show no correlation; a clear linear pattern shows strong correlation. Note that correlation between variables does not show that one causes the other.

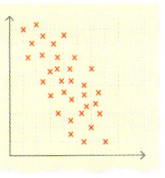
Zero correlation

Weak negative correlation

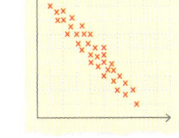
Strong negative correlation

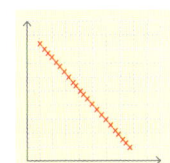
Perfect negative correlation

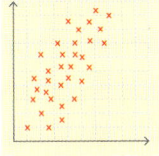
Weak positive correlation

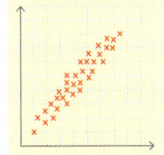
Strong positive correlation

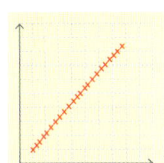
Perfect positive correlation

🔍 Coefficient of correlation

Strength and direction of correlation can also be calculated and expressed as a number: the coefficient of correlation. For example, −0.9 is a strong negative correlation, whereas 0.1 is a weak positive correlation.

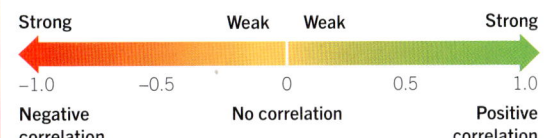

Correlation and causation

A correlation between two variables does not demonstrate cause and effect. A change in one of the variables *might* cause the change in the other, but sometimes a third, unknown variable is at work. To establish causation, a scientific experiment needs to be conducted, with all relevant variables controlled and measured.

Key facts

✓ A correlation between variables does not demonstrate causation.

✓ Causation can only be established by using an experimental method.

✓ In an experiment, relevant variables are controlled and measured.

Establishing causation

Sunburn frequency is correlated with ice-cream sales, but does ice cream cause sunburn or is another variable involved? To find out, a controlled experiment could be carried out. Volunteers are randomly assigned to two groups, only one of which is given ice cream. Ice cream consumption is the independent variable. Rates of sunburn (the dependent variable) are later measured. All other variables, such as sun exposure, are controlled (held constant). If more sunburn occurs in those given ice cream, it suggests a potential causative link. If not, another variable must cause the correlation.

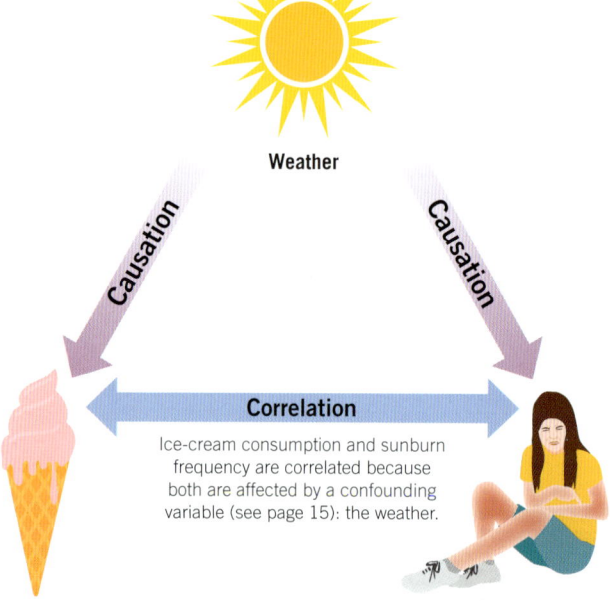

Weather

Causation

Causation

Correlation

Ice-cream consumption and sunburn frequency are correlated because both are affected by a confounding variable (see page 15): the weather.

Ice cream eaten

Sunburn frequency

🔍 Smoking and mental health

Psychologists often want to establish causation, but it is not always possible. For example, rates of smoking are correlated with levels of psychological distress associated with mental illness. We don't know whether mental illness increases uptake of smoking; smoking causes mental illness; or other factors are at work. An experiment to establish causation is difficult to design in this case because asking people to smoke, which is harmful, would be unethical.

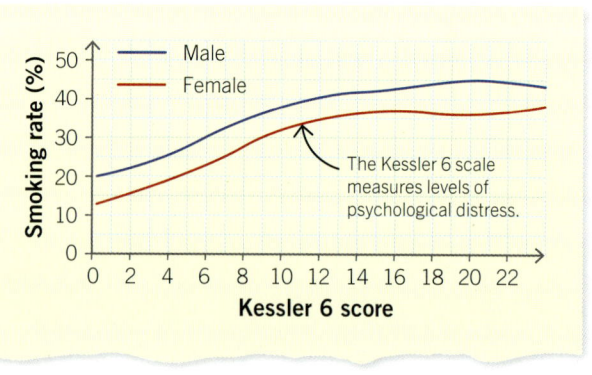

The Kessler 6 scale measures levels of psychological distress.

Observational techniques

Watching carefully how people behave, mostly in natural settings, is called observation. It is used by researchers trained to look for specific behaviours, such as conflict, play, and cooperation, and it can generate both qualitative and quantitative data. Observation is open to bias because researchers may vary in how they interpret what they see. There are different observational techniques.

Key facts

✓ Observation allows researchers to watch behaviours, often in natural settings.

✓ Observation can be used to collect qualitative and/or quantitative data.

✓ There are different observational techniques, in which observers can be more or less involved with the participants.

Participant observation
The researcher joins in with the group being observed, participating in their activities. They observe from within the social context (setting) being studied.

Non-participant observation
The researcher observes from a distance, outside the social context being studied. They do not interact with the group under observation.

Naturalistic observation
The researcher enters the participants' natural environment, such as their home or school, and does not influence their behaviour in any way.

Controlled observation
The researcher watches the participants in a controlled environment, such as a laboratory. They control the conditions of the study.

Overt observation
The researcher makes the participants aware that they are being observed. The observer may or may not participate in the activities.

Covert observation
The researcher is undercover (in a laboratory they may be behind a screen) and the participants are unaware they are being observed.

Questionnaires

Questionnaires are sets of questions given to participants to answer. They can be filled in online or on paper, or conducted over the phone or face to face. Questionnaires are useful for collecting large amounts of data, including attitudes, feelings, facts, and opinions. Disadvantages include a lack of in-depth information about experiences, the possibility of leading questions, and the potential for biased samples. Questionnaires and interviews (see page 28) are also known as self-report techniques.

Key facts

✓ Questionnaires are sets of questions given to participants.

✓ Quick and easy to administer, questionnaires can be filled in online or on paper, or conducted over the phone or face to face.

✓ Questionnaires are useful for obtaining a large volume or wide range of data.

Open and closed questions

There are two types of question in a questionnaire: open and closed questions. Often, a questionnaire uses both to collect data. This is useful as it means both quantitative and qualitative data can be obtained.

Open questions
Questions that cannot be answered with a simple yes or no are known as open questions. These require the participant to respond in their own words and elaborate on their points. They typically produce qualitative data.

How do you usually deal with stress?

What would change your life for the better?

Closed questions
Questions that have a fixed set of answers or options are known as closed questions. These include yes or no, true or false, multiple choice, and rating scale questions, such as the Likert scale. They typically produce quantitative data.

You always walk to school. True or false?

On a scale of 1 to 10, how happy are you today?

🔍 Open questions

Advantages:
- Allow participants to respond freely in their own words rather than by set answers.
- Allow for diverse responses, which may produce unexpected findings.
- Allow for more in-depth information, which may involve the participants' feelings and opinions.
- Allow for capturing data that cannot be categorized into a set number of answers or as a scale.

Disadvantages:
- Can be time-consuming for participants, requiring effort and motivation.
- May produce a biased sample if only people willing to put in the time take part.
- Can be challenging and costly to analyse and interpret.
- Can produce low-quality or irrelevant data if the questions and/or answers are too vague or broad.

🔍 Closed questions

Advantages:
- Narrow the focus and restrict the participant to a predetermined set of responses.
- Generate standardized data in a consistent format that can be easily compared.
- Easy and quick to answer.

Disadvantages:
- Can limit the range and depth of responses.
- Important information may be missed if not captured by the options.
- Participants' responses may be influenced by leading questions.
- Can force the respondent to choose an answer they don't necessarily agree with.

Questionnaire design

Many researchers use closed questions to assess psychological phenomena. There is a range of closed question types to choose from when designing questionnaires, including multiple choice, rank order, and Likert scale questions.

Multiple choice
A multiple choice question requires the participant to choose one or more options from a limited list of choices.

Please select your age group:

☐ 18–24 years old
☐ 25–34 years old
☑ 35–44 years old
☐ 45–54 years old
☐ 55+ years old

Advantages:
- Intuitive and easy to use.
- Quick and simple to answer.
- Generates data that can be easily analysed and compared.
- Ensures participants provide the information that the researcher wants from them.

Disadvantages:
- Does not provide deeper insight into the reasons behind why participants have answered in the way they have.
- Can limit the participants in their answers – they may not be able to find a suitable answer from the list.

Rank order
A rank order question requires the participant to organize a list in order, usually order of preference, such as most preferred to least preferred.

Rank the features that are the most important to you when choosing a new phone:

Battery life	3 ∨
Appearance	1 ∨
Cost	4 ∨
Camera quality	2 ∨

Advantages:
- Generates standardized data in a consistent format that can be easily compared.
- Easy to understand and use.

Disadvantages:
- Does not reveal the reasons why participants rank items in the order they do.
- Multiple items cannot be given the same rating, even if they are regarded as of equal importance.
- Order bias may cause participants to rank early items in the list more positively than later ones.

Likert scale
This scale indicates a person's level of agreement to statements on a five- or seven-point rating scale.

How did you feel about your lunch today?

| Very unsatisfied | Unsatisfied | Neutral | Satisfied | Very satisfied |

Advantages:
- Quick to complete.
- High response rate.
- Easily comparable data.

Disadvantages:
- Participants may put the response they think they should, rather than what they genuinely think.
- The questions can become repetitive, resulting in participants becoming bored and responding inaccurately.
- A limited choice may result in answers being given that are not a true reflection of feelings.

Interviews

An interview is a conversation in which an interviewer aims to obtain targeted (specific) information from one or more participants. The information is usually about a person's experiences, feelings, or ideas. Questions can be open, which participants answer by choosing their own words, or closed, which participants answer by choosing from a fixed set of answers, such as yes or no.

Key facts

✓ An interview is a method of obtaining targeted information from one or more participants.

✓ Interviews are most commonly used in qualitative research to gain detailed data.

✓ An interviewer's characteristics may influence participants' responses.

Types of interview
In psychology studies, the data collected is usually qualitative (detailed notes or recordings) but may sometimes be quantitative (numerical). Interviews vary in their structure and the number of participants.

Unstructured interviews do not follow predetermined questions. This type of interview is most similar to a natural conversation. The direction of the conversation is led entirely by the discussion itself and what the participant says. This approach is often used early on in a study to establish a positive relationship between interviewer and participant.

Semi-structured interviews follow an interview schedule, to steer the discussion towards specific topics of interest. The semi-structured nature allows the interviewer to ask specific questions, while giving them the flexibility to follow up on points to gain more detailed data.

Structured interviews strictly follow an interview protocol. This approach does not allow any deviation from the set questions. Structured interviews are particularly useful if time is limited.

Focus groups are interviews in which an interviewer selects a group of people to talk openly about one or more topics. The interviewer guides the conversation, keeping it focused. This type of interview allows interviewers to gather high-quality data that includes different views on different subjects.

🔍 Interviewer characteristics

Interviewing is a skill. One of the goals is to help the participant to relax so they reveal more information. However, the interviewer's characteristics, such as age, sex, gender, or race, may influence participants' responses.

Case studies

A case study is an in-depth investigation of an individual, group, institution, or event. It can include a mixture of qualitative and quantitative data, and psychologists make use of a range of methods (such as interviews and psychological tests) and sources (such as historical and medical records) to investigate their chosen case study. One of psychology's most famous case studies is that of Phineas Gage, a railway worker from New Hampshire, USA.

Key facts

✓ A case study is an in-depth investigation of a individual, group, institution, or event.

✓ Psychologists use a range of methods and sources to gather data.

✓ Case studies include both qualitative and quantitative data.

Case study: Phineas Gage

In 1848, US railway worker Phineas Gage suffered serious brain damage after an accidental explosion at work caused a metal rod to shoot through his head and out the other side. While it was miraculous that Gage survived, it was reported after the accident that his personality had significantly changed. The case was perhaps the first to suggest that damage to specific parts of someone's brain could cause changes to their personality. Gage died in 1860, 12 years after his accident.

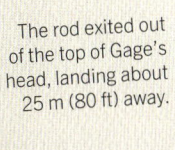

The rod exited out of the top of Gage's head, landing about 25 m (80 ft) away.

The metal rod passed behind the eye through the left side of the brain.

Testimony of doctor and friends

Dr J.M. Harlow, who supervised, treated, and studied Gage from the day of the accident, reported that he had become far more impulsive and aggressive after the event. Before his injury, Gage was described as having a "well-balanced mind", but afterwards his friends claimed that he was "no longer Gage".

Describing data

It often helps to summarize data by calculating measures of central tendency (averages) or measures of dispersion (how widely spread the data are). There are three kinds of average: mean, median, and mode. Measures of spread include range (the difference between lowest and highest values) and standard deviation (a measure of average distance from mean).

Key facts

✓ Mean, median, and mode are different forms of average (measures of central tendency).

✓ Median works better than mean when data are skewed or contain outliers.

✓ Measures of spread include range and standard deviation.

Mean
To calculate the mean, divide the sum of all values in a dataset by the number of values. Calculating the mean ensures that all data are represented, but means can be distorted by outliers (extreme scores).

$$\frac{18 + 24 + 21 + 22 + 23 + 22 + 11 + 19}{8} = \frac{160}{8} = \mathbf{20}$$

Median
The median is the value in the middle when numbers are arranged in order. It is often a better representation of the central or average value when a dataset has outliers or is skewed.

11, 18, 19, **21, 22**, 22, 23, 24

21.5 — If you have an even number of values, the median is the mean of the two middle values.

Mode
The most common value is the mode. This is useful for qualitative rather than numerical data, such as for describing the most common medical condition in a population of patients.

11, 18, 19, 21, **22, 22**, 23, 24

22 appears most often.

🔍 Measures of dispersion

It's often useful to know how widely spread data are. The simplest measure of spread is the range, which is the difference between the highest and lowest values. A more informative measure is the standard deviation, which is a kind of average distance from the mean. In a normal (bell-shaped) distribution, 68 per cent of values are within one standard deviation of the mean. A small standard deviation means data are tightly clustered around the mean.

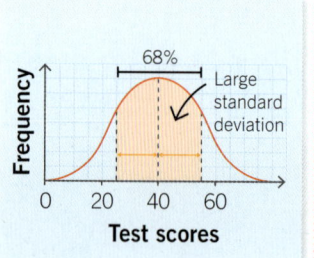

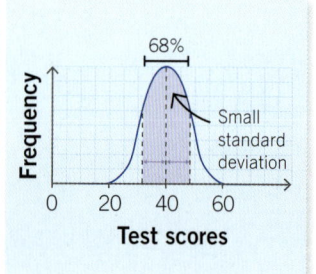

Visualizing data

Presenting data visually, as in a graph or chart, can make findings easier to interpret. Graphs and charts can show a pattern or trend that may not be obvious when looking at the data. They may also reveal interactions between variables and the nature of any relationship.

Key facts

✓ Bar charts are used for data divided into discrete categories.

✓ Histograms are used for continuous data.

✓ Line graphs are used for representing data that changes over time.

✓ Scattergrams are used to show correlation.

Bar chart
These charts are used when a variable consists of discrete (separate) categories. The categories are put on the x-axis, and their frequencies are put on the y-axis. In the example below, the experiences of men and women in dreams are compared.

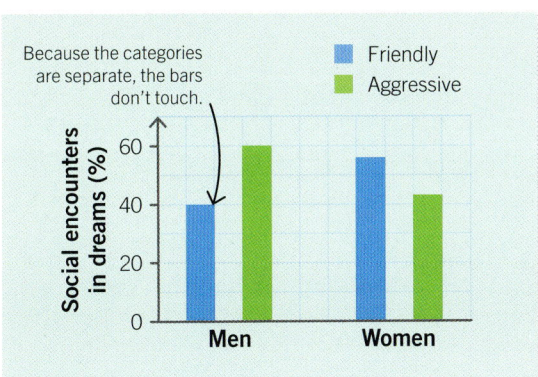

Histogram
Histograms resemble bar charts but the variable on the x-axis is continuous, which means data can take any value across a range of numbers. The bars may vary in width. The y-axis shows frequency density, and the area of each bar represents frequency.

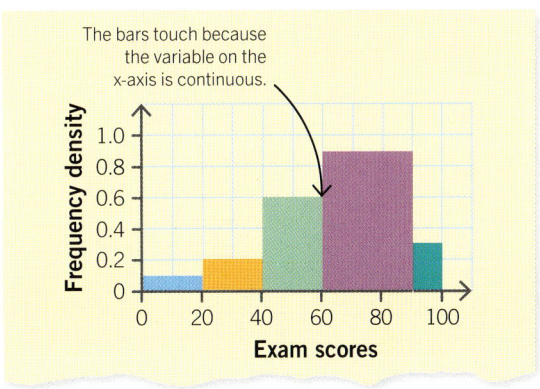

Line graph
A line graph shows the relationship between two variables that vary continuously. These graphs are often used to show how something changes over time. This example shows the effect of a drug, with a second line for a placebo (inert substance).

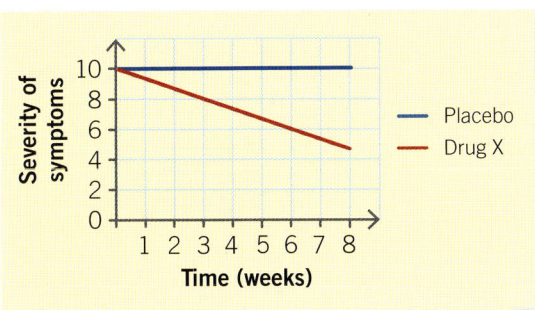

Scattergram
This kind of graph (also called a scatter graph or scatter plot) explores whether two variables are correlated. The data points (x's below) are plotted on the graph. If they form a clear pattern, a line of best fit may be drawn to show the trend.

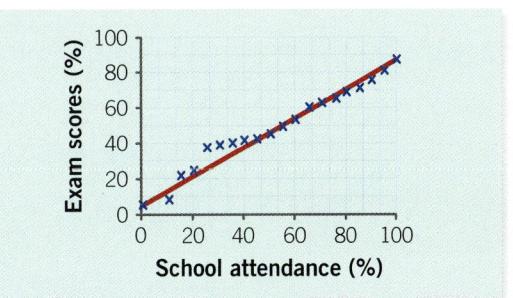

Distributions

When a characteristic can be quantified (measured numerically), the data can be plotted on a frequency graph. The distribution is the visual display that can be analysed to find a pattern. There are two types of distribution: normal and skewed.

Key facts

✓ A normal distribution is a symmetrical spread of frequency data, with most people's scores gathered in the middle or "peak" of the scale.

✓ A skewed distribution occurs when there is a higher frequency of people on one side of the scale than the other.

Normal distribution

When the spread of frequency data is symmetrical and forms a bell-shaped curve, it is known as a normal distribution. Most scores are clustered in the middle of the scale, with progressively fewer on either side. Plotting the IQ scores of a group of people on a frequency graph shows that most people score around 100, with progressively fewer people having very low or very high IQ scores. A normal distribution is "unimodal", which means it has one peak. Some distributions have two peaks and are called "bimodal". This occurs when there are two distinct groups within the data.

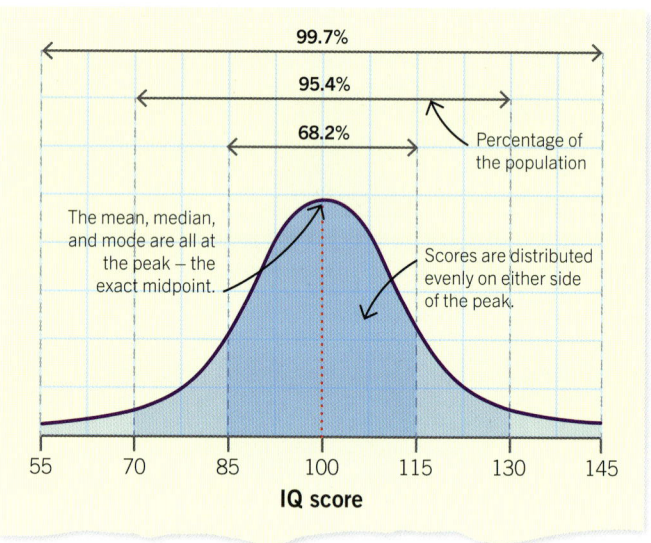

Skewed distribution

A skewed distribution occurs when frequency data is not symmetrically spread on either side of the peak. A lack of symmetry means there is a higher frequency of people on one side of the scale than the other.

Skewed distributions can either be positive or negative. The mode (most common score) is still at the peak, but extreme scores drag the mean (average score) and the median (middle score) away from the peak.

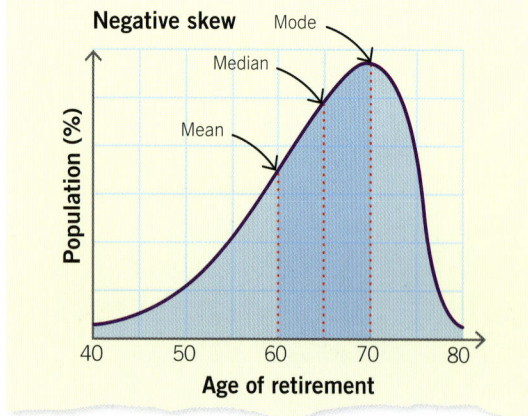

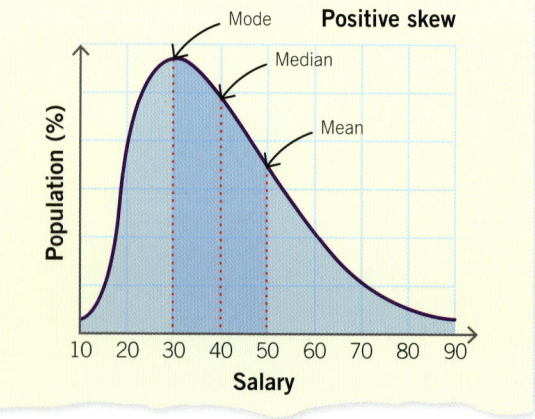

Significance tests

When psychologists collect data from an experiment, they need to know if the results provide evidence of a real effect or are merely due to chance. To find out, a statistical significance test is carried out. If the results would be less than 5% likely to happen by chance alone, then the experiment is statistically significant at the 5% level. A statistically significant result provides evidence that the effect is real.

Taste test

Imagine a test to find out if a new ingredient in cola affects its taste. Thirty tasters are each given three unlabelled samples to taste and asked to identify the odd one out, which has the ingredient. If the ingredient has no effect, an average of 10 people will pick the odd one out by chance. If the ingredient does affect taste, significantly more than 10 people will pick it. The probability of at least 15 people picking the odd one out by chance is 5% (calculated using what statisticians call the binomial distribution), so a result of 15 or more is statistically significant at the 5% level.

Key facts

✓ A statistical significance test is carried out to find out if data from an experiment provides evidence of a real effect.

✓ If results are significant at the 5% level, their probability of occurring by chance alone is under 5%.

✓ If an experiment produces a statistically significant result, the null hypothesis is rejected and the alternative hypothesis is supported.

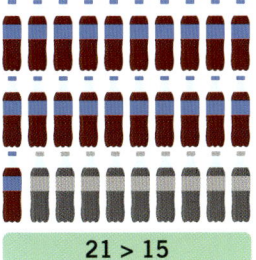

21 > 15

21 out of 30 people identify the new cola

✔ **Statistically significant**
21 people choose the cola with the new ingredient. The probability of this many people choosing it by chance alone is less than 5%, so this result is significant at the 5% ($p \leq 0.05$) level. The experiment's null hypothesis ("the new ingredient has no effect") is rejected, and the experimental hypothesis ("the new ingredient changes the taste") is supported.

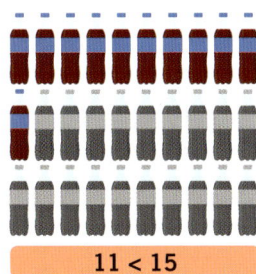

11 < 15

11 out of 30 people identify the new cola

✘ **Not significant**
Only 11 people choose the cola with the new ingredient, which is fewer than the critical number of 15. The probability of 11 or more people choosing it by chance alone is greater than 5%, so this result is not significant at the 5% level. The null hypothesis is supported as there is no evidence that the new ingredient affects the drink's taste.

🔍 Type 1 and type 2 errors

• **Type 1 errors** are errors of optimism, where a false hypothesis is accepted. They are also called false positives.

• **Type 2 errors** are errors of pessimism, where a true hypothesis is rejected. They are also known as false negatives.

You're pregnant!

Type 1 error (false positive)

You aren't pregnant.

Type 2 error (false negative)

Ethics of research

In the past, research in psychology involved experiments on people or animals that would be considered unethical today. Psychologists must now gain official approval for experiments and must follow ethical and legal guidelines that protect the health and dignity of those involved. These guidelines cover consent, right to withdraw, deception, protection from harm, and confidentiality.

Informed consent
Researchers must obtain consent from participants (or parents of children) after providing enough information about the aims and methods to allow for an informed decision. Participants can only give consent if mentally competent and not under the influence of alcohol or drugs.

Right to withdraw
Participants must be told that they have a right to withdraw from a study (or withdraw their data from a study) at any point and without needing to give an explanation.

Protection from harm
Researchers have a duty of care to protect study participants at all times from harm, whether physical or mental. The research must pose no greater risk of harm than ordinary activities.

Deception
Withholding information or misleading participants must be avoided unless this is an essential part of the experimental design, as in a blind drug trial. If deception does occur, participants must be told afterwards in a debriefing. It is sometimes necessary to obtain presumptive consent in advance, which means asking people of similar backgrounds to the participants whether they would object to participating.

Confidentiality
The identity and personal details of participants must remain confidential, and published research should use numbers rather than names to represent individuals. Only essential data about participants can be collected. This data must be securely stored and accessible only to those that need it.

📌 Key facts

✓ Psychologists must follow guidelines and must gain official approval when conducting research.

✓ Researchers must obtain informed consent from all participants.

✓ Participants must be given the right to withdraw.

✓ Participants must be protected from all forms of physical and mental harm.

✓ Deception must be avoided unless it is essential.

🔎 Animal experiments

Strict regulations now govern the use of animals in scientific research, to protect their welfare. Experimenters must demonstrate that any animal experiments have a clear scientific justification. The animals must be legally obtained from licensed suppliers, housed in humane conditions, and any suffering caused by experimental procedures must be minimized. The use of primates (monkeys and apes) is permitted only if no other alternatives are available.

Types of psychologist

Psychologists work in a wide variety of areas, including research, government, business, law, health, sports, and teaching. They tend to specialize in one of more than 20 subfields (research areas) of psychology. Some are listed below.

Clinical psychologists diagnose and treat people with psychological disorders. They work in a wide range of settings, including schools, hospitals, and prisons.

Cognitive psychologists focus on mental processes, such as thinking, perception, memory, language, decision-making, and problem-solving.

Community psychologists look after public health. They help communities to deal with mental health issues by improving the environments in which people live.

Counselling psychologists help to improve the mental health and wellbeing of people struggling to cope with trauma or major life changes.

Developmental psychologists focus on age-related behaviour and how this changes over time. They often work in areas such as childcare and education.

Educational psychologists focus on how people learn and how learning can be tested. They may develop new teaching methods to enhance the learning process.

Environmental psychologists look at how people are influenced by their environments. They also study how we shape these environments.

Experimental psychologists work in an academic setting, investigating a variety of human behaviours. Areas of research include learning, motivation, and language.

Forensic psychologists work in the field of law. They study criminal behaviour, and may aid in crime investigations, assessments, and jury selections.

Health psychologists try to help people to live healthier lives. Some assist people in managing chronic illnesses; for example, by stopping smoking.

Industrial and organizational psychologists investigate people in the working environment. They aim to optimize productivity and workers' wellbeing.

Neuropsychologists are clinical psychologists who specialize in treating and rehabilitating people with brain damage and neurodegenerative disease.

Psychometric psychologists devise and interpret psychological tests for use in a variety of settings, such as schools, universities, and government agencies.

Social psychologists investigate how people interact. Topics of study include leadership, aggression, and group behaviour.

Sport psychologists work with athletes to improve their preparation, performance, and wellbeing. They help them to cope with the pressures of high-level sport.

Chapter 2
Biological bases of behaviour

The nervous system

The human nervous system is a complex network of billions of neurons (nerve cells). Neurons carry messages between the brain and spinal cord and to the rest of the body. The brain is the control centre of the nervous system. It controls basic functions such as breathing, as well as complex processes such as thinking.

Key facts

✓ The nervous system is a network of billions of neurons that allows all parts of the body to communicate.

✓ The nervous system is made up of the central nervous system (CNS) and the peripheral nervous system (PNS).

✓ The CNS consists of the brain and spinal cord and the PNS consists of all other neurons in the body.

Divisions of the nervous system

There are two main parts of the nervous system, each with specific functions. The central nervous system (CNS) is made up of the brain and spinal cord, and the peripheral nervous system (PNS) is made up of all the neurons that branch out from the spinal cord and connect to all parts of the body.

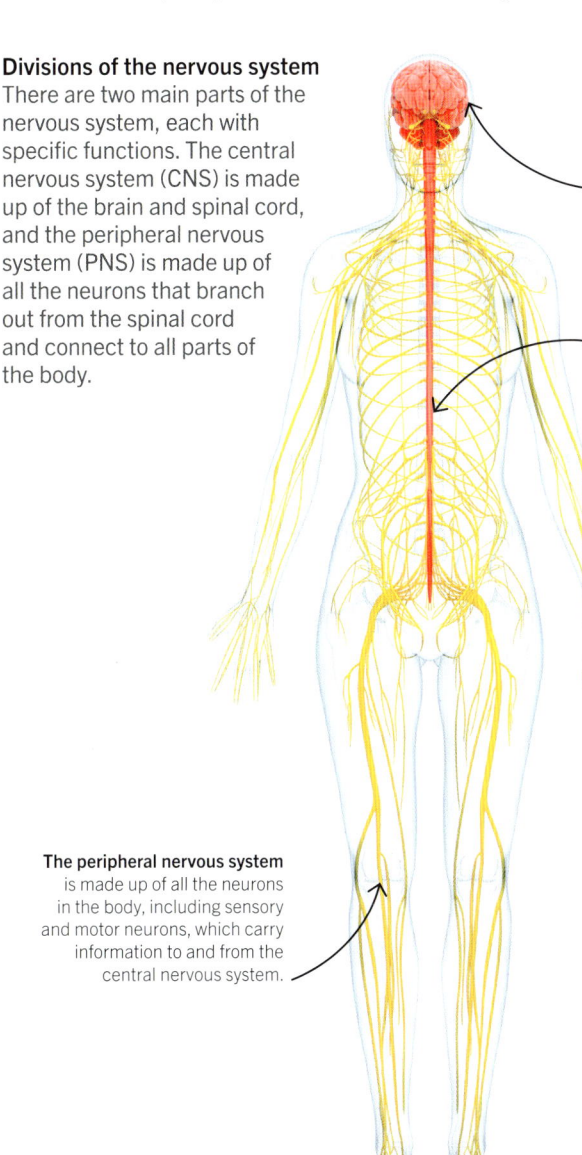

The brain is the organ that controls thought, emotion, memory, touch, movement, vision, breathing, and every process that regulates the body.

The spinal cord is an extension of the brain, and it is responsible for relaying information between the brain and the rest of the body.

Central nervous system

The peripheral nervous system is made up of all the neurons in the body, including sensory and motor neurons, which carry information to and from the central nervous system.

How the nervous system works

Sensory receptors detect changes in the environment, both inside and outside the body. This sensory input is sent to the brain via the spinal cord in the form of electrical signals, and the brain determines the correct response. The brain then sends signals to effectors, such as muscles, which produce the response (motor output).

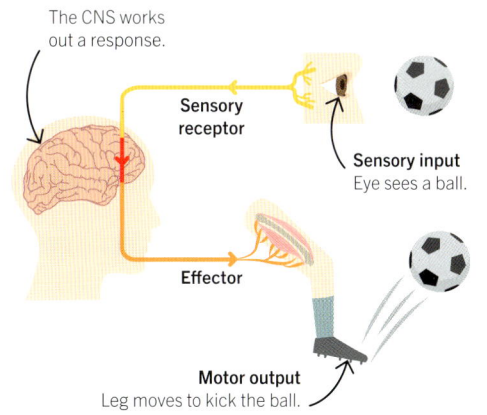

The CNS works out a response.

Sensory receptor

Sensory input
Eye sees a ball.

Effector

Motor output
Leg moves to kick the ball.

The peripheral nervous system

While the brain and spinal cord make up the central nervous system (CNS), all other nerve cells in the body make up the peripheral nervous system. The peripheral nervous system carries signals between the body and the CNS. These include incoming sensory signals from sense organs and outgoing motor signals that tell muscles and other organs how to react.

Key facts

- ✓ The peripheral nervous system is the part of the nervous system outside the brain and spinal cord.
- ✓ The peripheral nervous system is divided into the somatic (voluntary) and autonomic (involuntary) systems.
- ✓ The autonomic system is divided into the sympathetic and parasympathetic nervous systems.

Peripheral nervous system
The body's information highway, the peripheral nervous system is connected to every organ, gland, and muscle cell. It has two major divisions.

Sympathetic nervous system
This branch of the autonomic nervous system gets the body ready for physical action.

Somatic nervous system
This division controls voluntary actions, which we consciously control. Most sensory signals also travel via the somatic nervous system.

Autonomic nervous system
This division regulates involuntary functions like heart rate, breathing, and digestion. It is further divided into two systems with opposite effects.

Parasympathetic nervous system
This branch calms the body down and prepares it for rest, reversing the effects of the sympathetic nervous system.

🔍 Comparing the sympathetic and parasympathetic nervous systems

The sympathetic and parasympathetic nervous systems control the same parts of the body but have opposite effects. Sympathetic nerve signals promote the fight-or-flight response, while parasympathetic signals promote what is sometimes called the rest-and-digest response. Parasympathetic signals usually reduce activity, with one exception: they make the digestive system more active.

Sympathetic	Parasympathetic
Pupils dilated	Pupils constricted
Fast breathing	Slow breathing
Increased heart rate	Decreased heart rate
Digestion paused	Digestion active

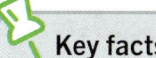

Neurons

The cells that make up the nervous system are called neurons. They carry information around the body and brain as high-speed electrical signals called nerve impulses. Neurons connect to each other at junctions called synapses, where chemicals called neurotransmitters transfer signals from one cell to the next.

Neuron structure
A neuron has a cell body housing a nucleus, and long, slender branches that carry electrical impulses. Incoming electrical signals travel along branches called dendrites. Outgoing electrical signals travel along a single branch called an axon. When the signal reaches the end of the axon (axon terminal), it triggers the release of neurotransmitters that travel across a synapse to the next neuron. There are three main types of neuron.

Key facts

✓ Neurons are cells that make up the nervous system.

✓ There are three main types of neuron: sensory, motor, and relay.

✓ Synapses are junctions between neurons.

✓ Reflex actions are sudden, involuntary responses controlled by reflex arcs.

Sensory neurons
These neurons are found in sense organs and throughout the body. They detect stimuli and typically respond by sending electrical signals to the spinal cord and brain (central nervous system).

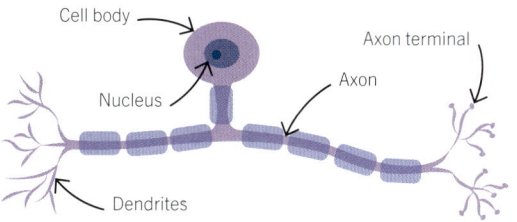

Relay neurons (interneurons)
Most of the neurons in the brain and spinal cord are relay neurons. They communicate with sensory and motor neurons and form complex circuits within the brain, doing most mental processing.

Motor neurons
These neurons carry signals from the central nervous system to effector organs, such as muscles or glands. Motor signals trigger a physical response; for example, contracting a muscle to make the body move.

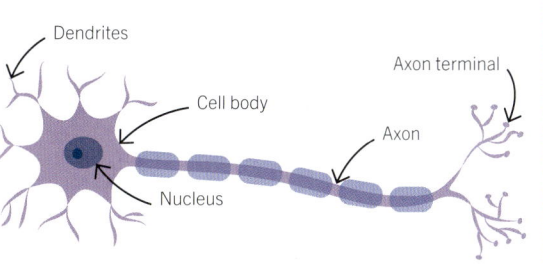

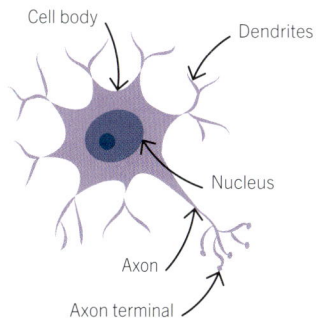

🔍 Reflex arc

Reflex actions are sudden, involuntary responses, such as withdrawing a hand from pain. They are controlled by a simple neural pathway called a reflex arc. For instance, if a sensory neuron detects pain, it sends an electrical signal via its axon to a relay neuron (a type of interneuron) in the spinal cord. The relay neuron passes the signal to a motor neuron, which triggers contraction of a muscle. This rapid circuit allows the body to react quickly, without waiting for the brain.

1. Stimulus A sharp cactus spine pricks a finger.

2. Sensory neuron A pain receptor (a type of sensory neuron) sends a signal to the spinal cord.

5. Response The hand pulls back as the muscle contracts.

4. Motor neuron The motor neuron sends a signal to a muscle.

3. Relay neuron The signal is relayed to a motor neuron.

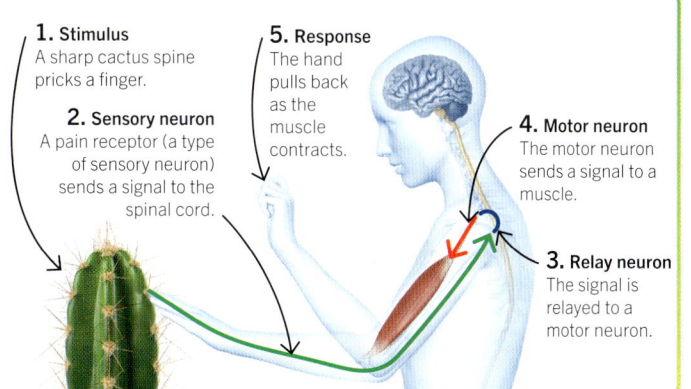

Nerve impulses

Neurons use electrical signals to communicate with each other. Tiny pulses of electricity – called action potentials or nerve impulses – rush from one end of a neuron to the other at speeds of up to 320 kph (200 mph). When electrical signals reach the end of a neuron, they trigger the release of chemical neurotransmitters, which pass the signal across synapses (gaps) to connected neurons.

Key facts

✓ Neurons communicate by generating high-speed electrical signals called action potentials.

✓ Action potentials are created by gates and pumps in neuron cell membranes.

✓ An action potential is an "all or none" process.

Action potential

Like batteries, neurons use chemical reactions to store electric charge. While a neuron is resting, positively charged sodium ions are pumped outside it, creating a net positive charge outside the cell and a net negative charge inside. When a neuron fires, gates open in the cell membrane, allowing sodium ions to rush inside, attracted by the opposite charge. A sudden loss of charge rushes through the cell – an action potential.

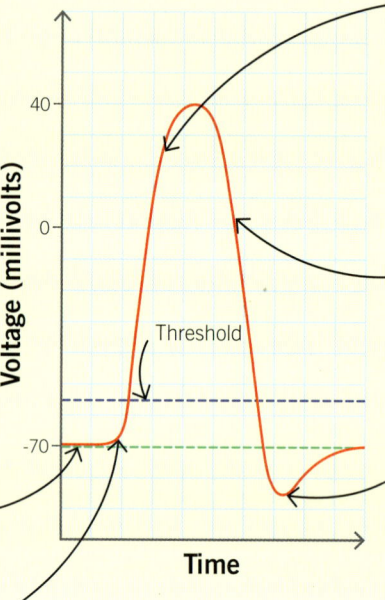

1. Resting potential: at rest, the neuron's interior is negatively charged and the exterior is positive. This difference is called the resting potential.

2. Excitation: incoming signals from other neurons make the cell's interior more positive. If the voltage rises above a certain threshold, the neuron fires.

3. Depolarization: gates open in the cell membrane at one end of the neuron, allowing positive ions to flood in. This part of the cell rapidly depolarizes, and the interior briefly becomes positive. The change causes more gates to open nearby. As a result, a wave of depolarization rushes along the cell, like a chain of dominoes falling.

4. Repolarization: after the wave passes, sodium gates close and pumps in the cell membrane begin pushing positive ions outside the cell again. The cell's interior returns to being negatively charged.

5. Refractory period: following repolarization, the charge inside the cell briefly falls below the normal resting potential. The neuron is temporarily unable to produce an action potential. This is called the refractory period.

All or none

The action potential is sometimes called an "all or none" process. This means that, like a gun, a neuron either fully fires or doesn't fire at all. If incoming signals are not strong enough to cross the threshold, the neuron doesn't fire. If the threshold is crossed, a full action potential occurs. A strong sensory stimulus doesn't make a neuron fire more strongly, but it can trigger more neurons to fire.

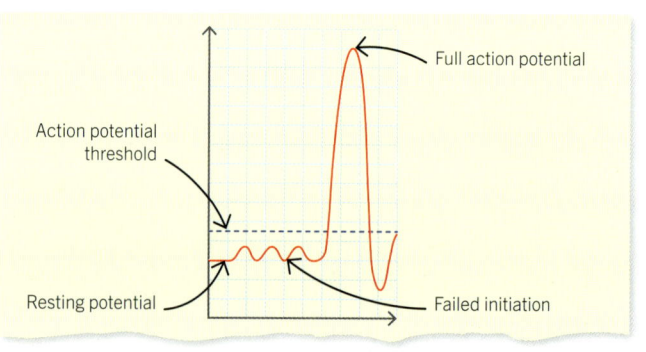

Synaptic transmission

Neurons communicate at junctions called synapses. When an electrical signal reaches a synapse, neurotransmitter molecules are released and cross a gap to the next cell. This chemical message may either excite or inhibit the receiving cell. If a receiving neuron receives sufficient excitatory signals (either from multiple synapses or in rapid succession from one), a new electrical signal may be triggered. The process of adding incoming signals is called summation.

Key facts

✓ Neurons communicate at junctions called synapses.

✓ Neurotransmitter molecules cross synapses to pass on signals.

✓ Neurotransmitters may excite or inhibit the post-synaptic neuron.

✓ Summation is the process by which synaptic signals combine to trigger or not trigger an action potential in the next neuron.

Synapses
A synapse is a gap between the axon terminal of one cell and the dendrite of the next cell. Neurons can have thousands of synapses, each of which usually connects to a different neuron.

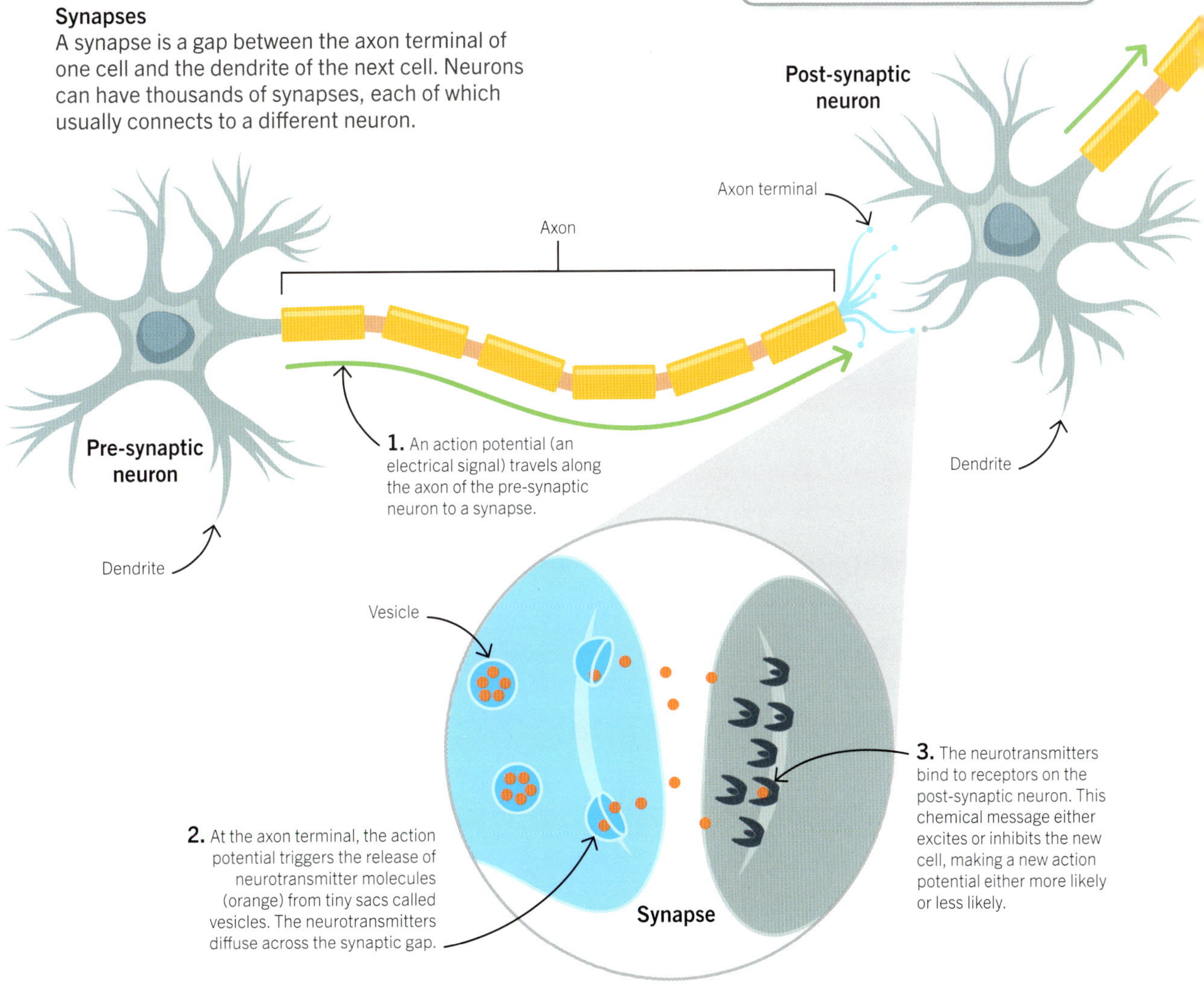

Post-synaptic neuron

Axon terminal

Axon

Pre-synaptic neuron

Dendrite

Dendrite

1. An action potential (an electrical signal) travels along the axon of the pre-synaptic neuron to a synapse.

Vesicle

3. The neurotransmitters bind to receptors on the post-synaptic neuron. This chemical message either excites or inhibits the new cell, making a new action potential either more likely or less likely.

2. At the axon terminal, the action potential triggers the release of neurotransmitter molecules (orange) from tiny sacs called vesicles. The neurotransmitters diffuse across the synaptic gap.

Synapse

Neurotransmitters

Neurotransmitters are messenger chemicals that cross the gaps in synapses (junctions between neurons) to pass on signals. There are many types of neurotransmitter, each of which can affect our emotions, memories, or moods in different ways. Drugs that affect mental states often work by altering neurotransmitter function.

Key facts

✓ Neurotransmitters are messenger chemicals that cross synapses to pass on signals.

✓ Neurotransmitters can be excitatory, inhibitory, or both.

✓ Drugs that affect mental states often work by altering neurotransmitter function.

Excitation and inhibition

Some neurotransmitters are excitatory, which means they make the receiving neuron more likely to generate a new action potential (electrical signal). Others are inhibitory (they make the receiving neuron less likely to fire), and some act in both ways. When a neuron receives excitatory and inhibitory inputs at once, the likelihood of it firing is determined by the sum of the inputs (summation).

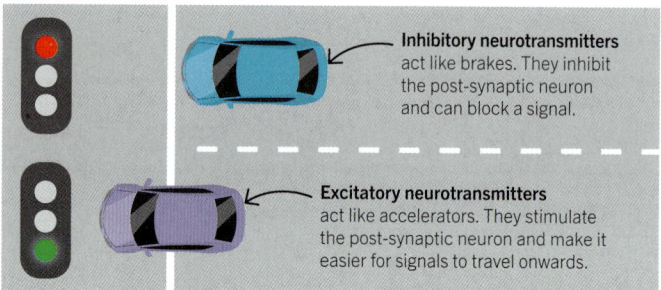

Inhibitory neurotransmitters act like brakes. They inhibit the post-synaptic neuron and can block a signal.

Excitatory neurotransmitters act like accelerators. They stimulate the post-synaptic neuron and make it easier for signals to travel onwards.

Major neurotransmitters	Usual effect	Key functions	Examples of dysfunction
Acetylcholine	Mostly excitatory	Attention, learning, memory, and muscle control.	Imbalances linked to Alzheimer's disease and Parkinson's disease.
Dopamine	Excitatory or inhibitory	Pleasure, motivation, mood, sleep, and learning.	Excess linked to psychosis; deficiency linked to Parkinson's disease.
Endorphins	Excitatory	Pleasure and the alleviation of pain and distress.	Low levels linked to anxiety, depression, and physical pain.
GABA (Gamma-aminobutyric acid)	Inhibitory	Motor control, vision, and regulation of neural activity.	Higher levels improve focus and lower levels are linked to anxiety.
Glutamate	Excitatory	Memory and learning. The most common neurotransmitter.	Reduced glutamate associated with poor concentration or focus. High levels linked to migraines.
Noradrenaline (norepinephrine)	Excitatory	Arousal, cognitive function, and stress reactions. Vital in the fight-or-flight response.	Low levels linked to lethargy, low blood pressure, and memory problems.
Serotonin	Inhibitory	Sleep cycle, digestion, and emotional wellbeing.	Low levels linked to depression. Some antidepressants work by raising serotonin levels in synapses.

How drugs work

Psychiatric drugs and other drugs that act on the nervous system often work by altering the way neurotransmitters function, leading to changes in the excitation or inhibition of neurons. Drugs that increase a neurotransmitter's effects are called agonists. Drugs that reduce a neurotransmitter's effects are called antagonists.

Key facts

✓ Drugs that act on the nervous system often work by altering the way neurotransmitters function.

✓ Agonist drugs work by increasing production of neurotransmitters, blocking their reuptake in synapses, or mimicking them.

✓ Antagonist drugs inhibit production of neurotransmitters or block their receptors.

Agonists

Agonist drugs work in several ways. They may increase production of a neurotransmitter, block its reuptake in synapses, or mimic its effect by binding to the same receptor. Nicotine is an agonist that mimics the neurotransmitter acetylcholine by binding to its receptors. This leads to an increase in levels of the neurotransmitter dopamine, which can lead to addiction.

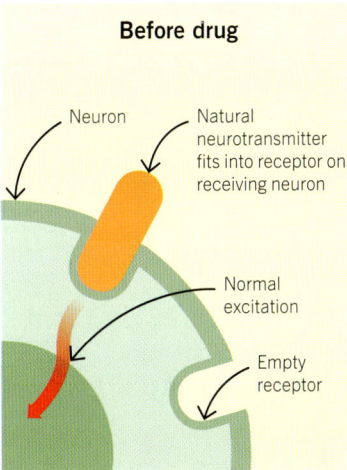

Before drug

Neuron

Natural neurotransmitter fits into receptor on receiving neuron

Normal excitation

Empty receptor

After drug

Agonist drug binds to receptor, mimicking neurotransmitter

Increased excitation

Antagonists

These drugs prevent neurotransmitters from working normally, usually by inhibiting their production or by binding to their receptors without exciting the post-synaptic neuron. Psychosis is associated with excess levels of the neurotransmitter dopamine. Antipsychotic drugs called dopamine antagonists relieve symptoms by blocking dopamine receptors, preventing dopamine from influencing the post-synaptic neuron.

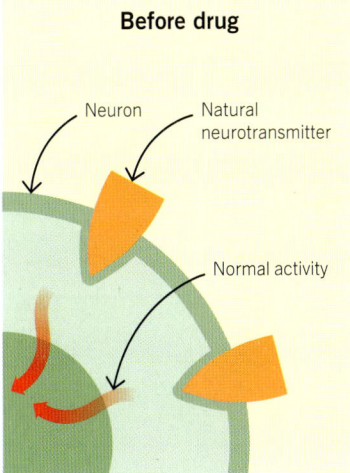

Before drug

Neuron

Natural neurotransmitter

Normal activity

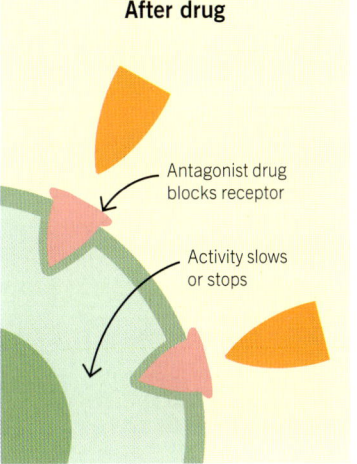

After drug

Antagonist drug blocks receptor

Activity slows or stops

The brain

About the size of two clenched fists, the human brain is a soft, pinkish-grey organ that fits tightly in the skull. Its largest part is the outer region, the cerebrum. Compared to other animals, humans have an unusually large cerebrum with a more deeply folded surface (the cerebral cortex). The folds enlarge the surface area available for neural connections, increasing the brain's processing power. Within and under the cerebrum are more primitive structures similar to those of other animals.

Key facts

- ✓ The largest part of the brain is the cerebrum. Its folded surface is called the cerebral cortex.
- ✓ Many brain structures exist as symmetrical left and right pairs.
- ✓ The brainstem controls vital functions like breathing, heart rate, and sleep.

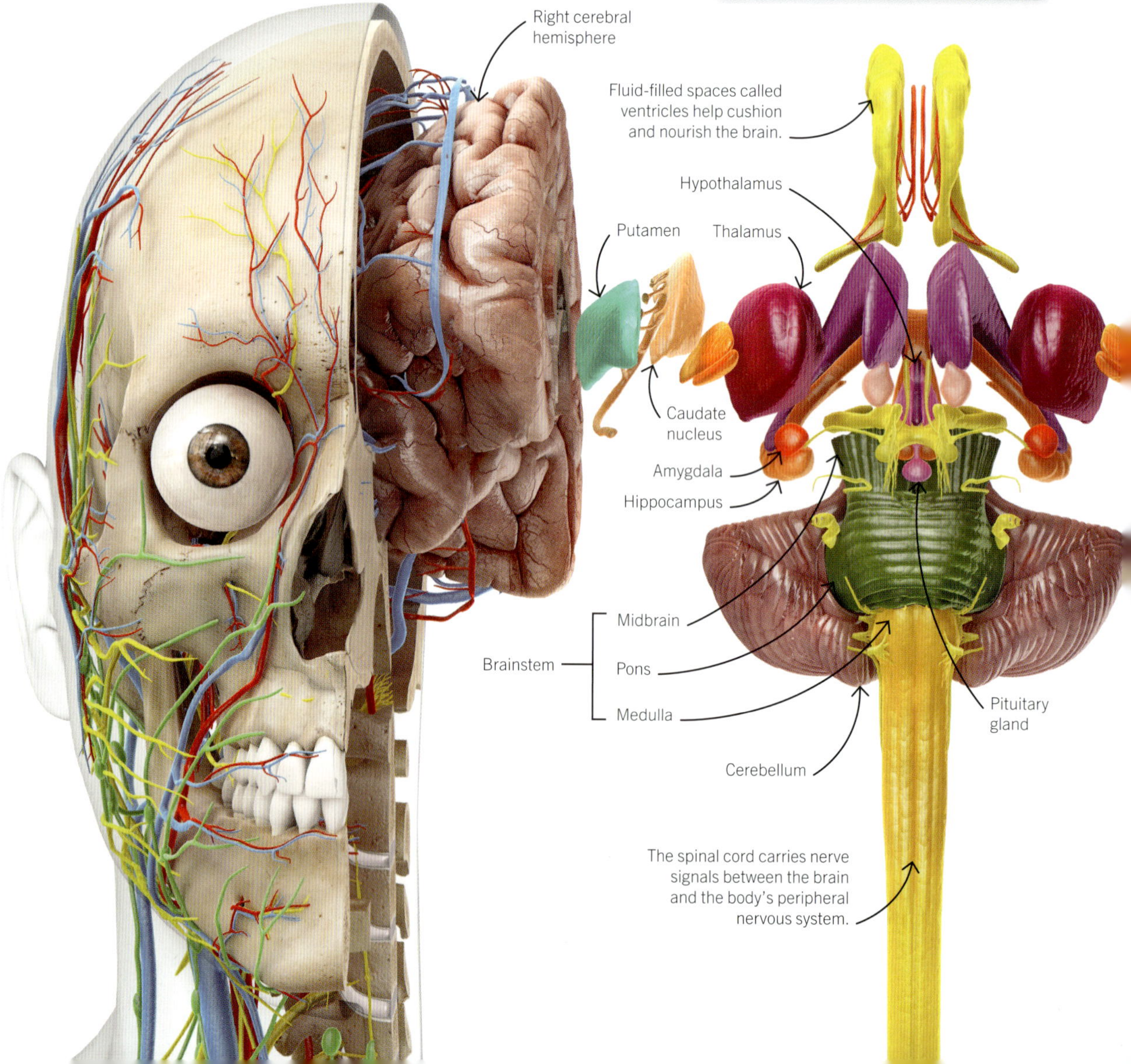

Right cerebral hemisphere

Fluid-filled spaces called ventricles help cushion and nourish the brain.

Hypothalamus

Putamen

Thalamus

Caudate nucleus

Amygdala

Hippocampus

Brainstem

Midbrain

Pons

Medulla

Pituitary gland

Cerebellum

The spinal cord carries nerve signals between the brain and the body's peripheral nervous system.

Hemispheres

Like many other organs (kidneys, lungs, eyes, and so on), most brain structures exist as left and right pairs. This arrangement means that if part of the brain is damaged, the opposite side can often take over its role. The cerebrum is divided into two nearly symmetrical halves called cerebral hemispheres. Most higher mental functions are spread across both hemispheres, but some functions are lateralized. The right hemisphere controls the left side of the body, and the left hemisphere controls the right side.

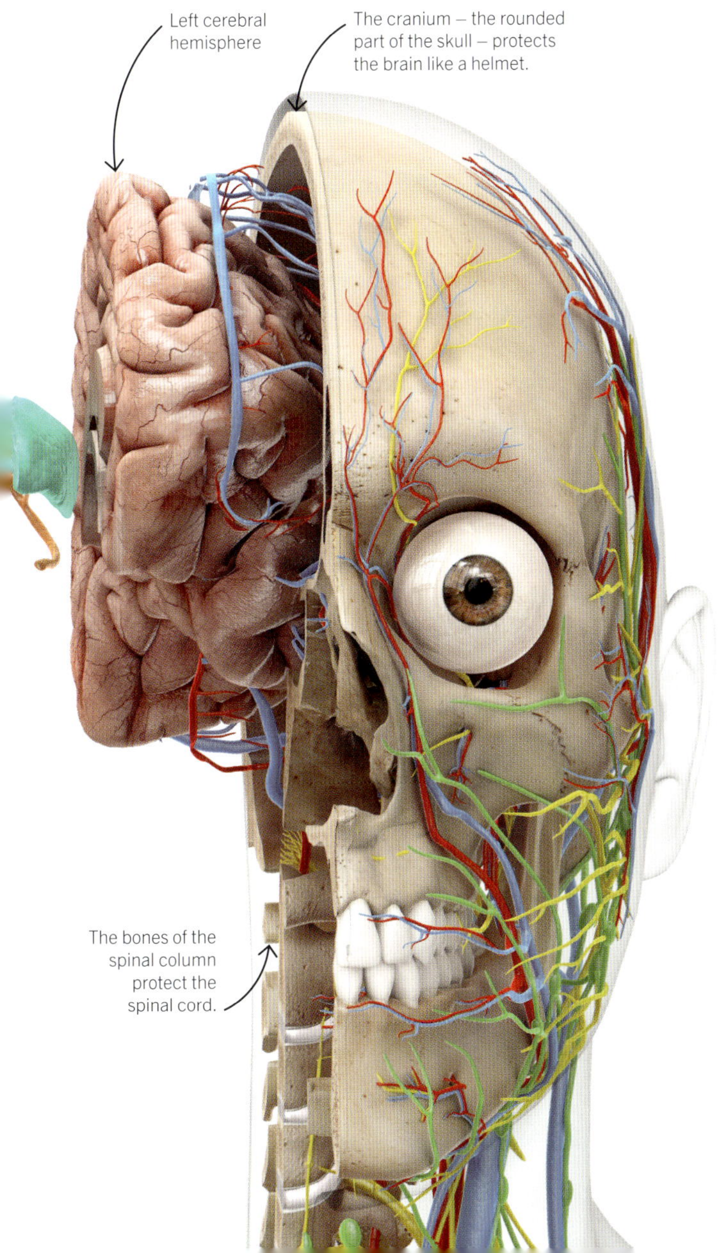

Left cerebral hemisphere

The cranium – the rounded part of the skull – protects the brain like a helmet.

The bones of the spinal column protect the spinal cord.

Top and bottom

Viewed from above, the brain's cerebral cortex has a deeply folded appearance, like a walnut. The folds ("sulci") divide the cortex into distinct regions called lobes, which have differing functions. For example, the frontal lobes are particularly important in thinking ahead and suppressing urges, among other functions. Seen from below, more primitive structures such as the brainstem are visible. The brainstem plays a critical role, maintaining unconscious but vital functions such as breathing, heart rate, and sleep.

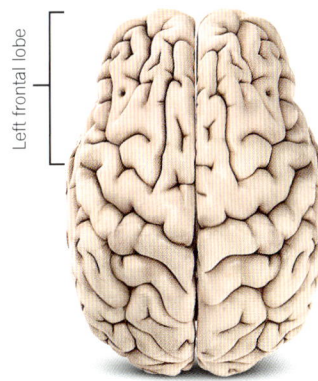

Left frontal lobe

From above

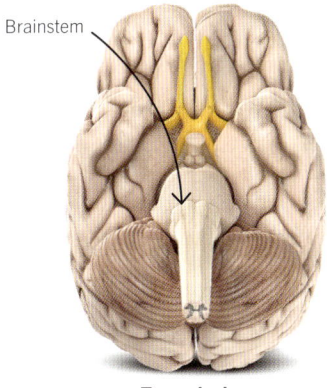

Brainstem

From below

Brain imaging

There are many ways to visualize the human brain, both anatomically and functionally. Different methods and equipment allow researchers and clinicians to study the living brain in different contexts. Some methods allow us to see brain structure while others allow us to see real-time brain activity.

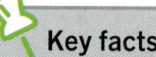

Key facts

✓ Brain scanning (imaging) techniques are used both to diagnose disease and to study healthy brain function.

✓ EEG and ERP measure electrical activity in the outer part of the brain.

CT scan

Computed tomography (CT) scanning involves sending multiple X-rays through the brain and combining the data on a computer to create a 3D model that can be cross-sectioned at any angle. It is useful for imaging bones, tumours, and blood clots.

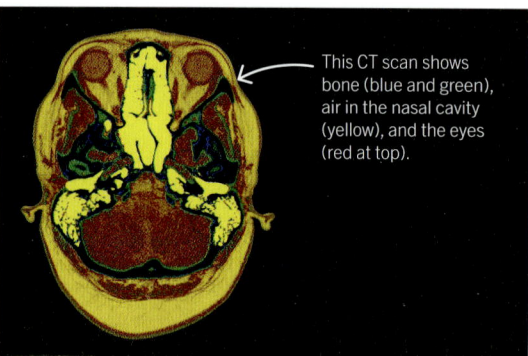

This CT scan shows bone (blue and green), air in the nasal cavity (yellow), and the eyes (red at top).

PET scan

Positron emission tomography (PET) reveals which parts of the brain are most active by detecting radioactively labelled glucose injected before the test. The images are crude but useful for studying brain function in real time.

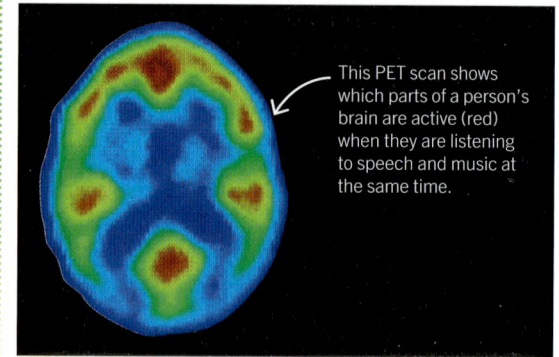

This PET scan shows which parts of a person's brain are active (red) when they are listening to speech and music at the same time.

MRI scan

Magnetic resonance imaging (MRI) scans give clearer images of soft tissues than CT scans. The scanner uses electromagnets and bursts of radio waves to make hydrogen atoms in water and fat emit radio signals, which are then used to build images.

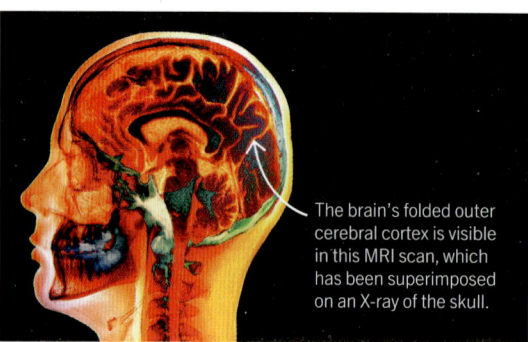

The brain's folded outer cerebral cortex is visible in this MRI scan, which has been superimposed on an X-ray of the skull.

fMRI

Functional MRI (fMRI) is a variation of MRI used to visualize function. The scanner detects radio signals from oxygen-carrying haemoglobin molecules in the blood, creating real-time images of active areas of the brain while the subject performs specific tasks.

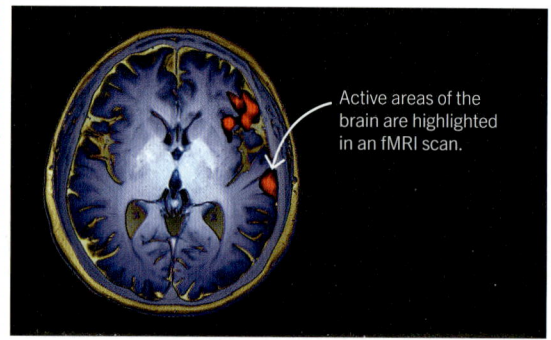

Active areas of the brain are highlighted in an fMRI scan.

EEG

Electroencephalography (EEG) machines use electrodes on the scalp to detect faint electrical signals from the outermost part of the brain. The resulting rhythmic patterns are called brainwaves and are used to study sleep or diagnose conditions such as epilepsy or coma.

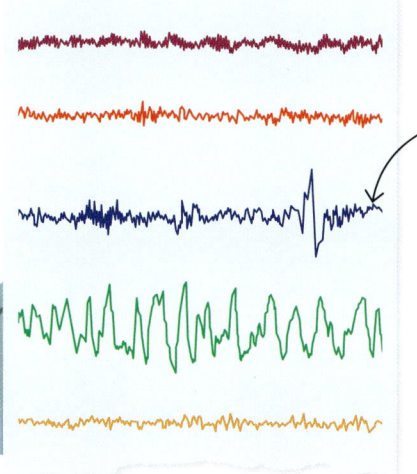

These brainwave patterns from an EEG machine show different stages of the sleep cycle.

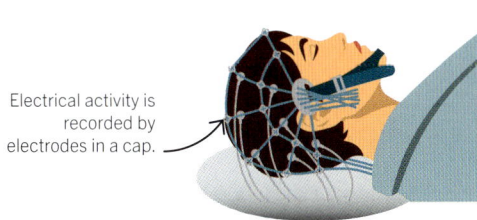

Electrical activity is recorded by electrodes in a cap.

ERPs

An ERP (event-related potential) is a graph of electrical activity in the brain made by an EEG machine in response to a specific stimulus (event), such as a sight or sound. Raw EEG data contains a lot of random variation (noise), which needs to be removed to detect a clear signal. This is done by repeating a trial several times and averaging the result.

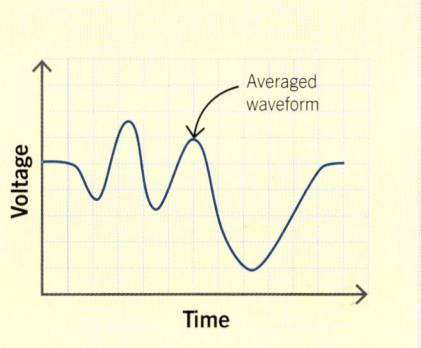

Trial 1

Trial 2

Trial 3

Averaged waveform

Voltage

Time

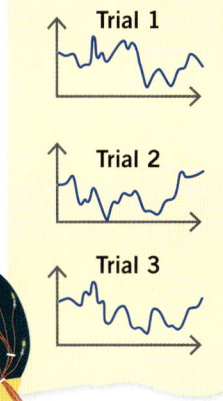

🔍 The injured brain

In the past, studying brains with damage or disease during a postmortem was the principal way of investigating how different parts of the brain function. Today, other techniques can be used to study the function of healthy brains in real time, but studies of injured and diseased brain tissue remain important. These PET scans compare a brain affected by Alzheimer's disease to a healthy brain. The healthy brain shows a higher level of metabolic activity (red) in the cortex.

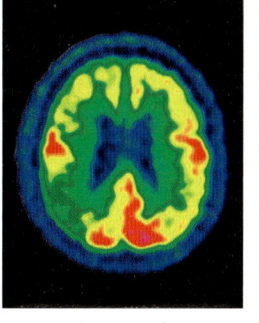

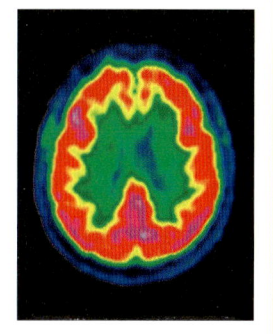

Alzheimer's disease   **Healthy brain**

The brainstem

The brainstem is at the base of the brain, where the spinal cord meets the cerebrum (the main part of the brain). It acts as a control centre for several involuntary but vital life-support functions, including heartbeat, breathing, and temperature control. It also controls certain involuntary reflexes, such as swallowing and vomiting, and plays a role in vision, hearing, balance, and the sleep–wake cycle. Even minor damage to the brainstem can have serious consequences. More extensive damage can cause comas and brain death.

Key facts

✓ The brainstem controls vital functions, including heartbeat, and breathing.

✓ The brainstem connects the brain to the spinal cord.

✓ The three parts of the brainstem are the pons, medulla oblongata, and midbrain.

✓ Damage to the brainstem can have severe consequences.

Parts of the brainstem
The brainstem lies under the complex structures of the limbic system (see page 49). It has three parts: the pons (metencephalon); the medulla oblongata (myelencephalon); and the midbrain (mesencephalon).

The midbrain is involved in regulating motor function and is important in vision and hearing. It is made up of smaller structures, including the tectum, which controls eye movement, and the tegmentum, which controls consciousness and arousal.

The pons is involved in various unconscious actions, including the sleep–wake cycle and breathing.

The medulla oblongata regulates heart rate, blood pressure, and other involuntary functions. It is the link between the spinal cord and brain.

Spinal cord

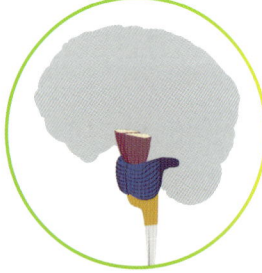

Location in the brain
The brainstem is near the bottom of the brain, at the back of the skull. It connects the brain at the cerebrum to the spinal cord.

The limbic system

Deep inside the brain is the limbic system — a set of complex structures that process powerful emotions, including the fight-or-flight response. The limbic system is sometimes called the emotional brain. It also plays a key role in memory, helping in the formation of long-term memories, especially those associated with emotional states (mood-congruent memories).

Key facts

✓ The limbic system processes emotional responses.

✓ The main structures of the limbic system are the hypothalamus, hippocampus, and amygdala.

✓ The amygdala plays a major role in fear, anxiety, and aggression.

Location in the brain
The limbic system is in the centre of the brain, above the brainstem.

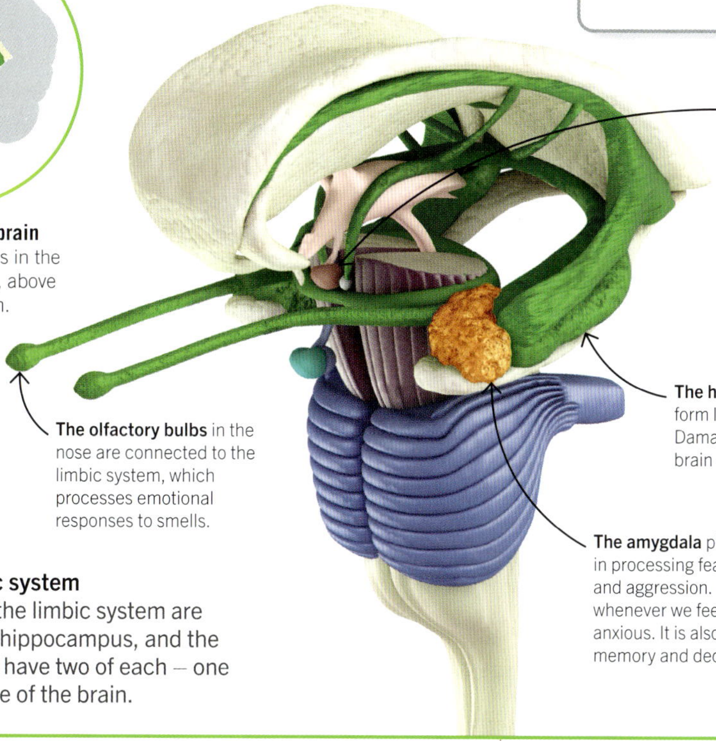

The hypothalamus helps control many involuntary functions, including hunger, thirst, and temperature. It also regulates hormone release through a connection to the hormone-secreting pituitary gland beneath it.

The olfactory bulbs in the nose are connected to the limbic system, which processes emotional responses to smells.

The hippocampus helps us form long-term memories. Damage to this part of the brain causes amnesia.

The amygdala plays a primary role in processing fear, anxiety, anger, and aggression. It becomes active whenever we feel threatened or anxious. It is also involved in memory and decision-making.

Parts of the limbic system
The main parts of the limbic system are the amygdala, the hippocampus, and the hypothalamus. We have two of each — one in each hemisphere of the brain.

The threat response

The amygdala acts as an alarm system, triggering the body's fight-or-flight response whenever it detects a potential threat — even before we become consciously aware of the nature of the threat. Overactivity of the amygdala has been implicated in psychological disorders involving anxiety, including generalized anxiety disorder, obsessive compulsive disorder, phobias, and post-traumatic stress disorder. Damage to the amygdala can also impair emotional function, reducing a person's ability to empathize or read social cues.

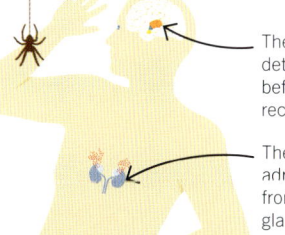

The limbic system detects danger even before the visual cortex recognizes the object.

The hormone adrenaline is released from the adrenal glands, preparing the body for action.

The cortex

The cortex is the outer layer of the brain. It is where many of the high-level functions of the brain, such as decision-making, language, and creativity, are processed. The surface of the cortex has many folds to give it a large surface area, which means greater processing power.

The localization of function

Specific functions (such as language, vision, and hearing) are thought to be located in specific areas in the brain — a theory known as the localization of function. The brain is split into two equally sized halves called hemispheres. In general, the right hemisphere controls activity on the left of the body and the left hemisphere controls activity on the body's right side. This principle is known as contralateral organization.

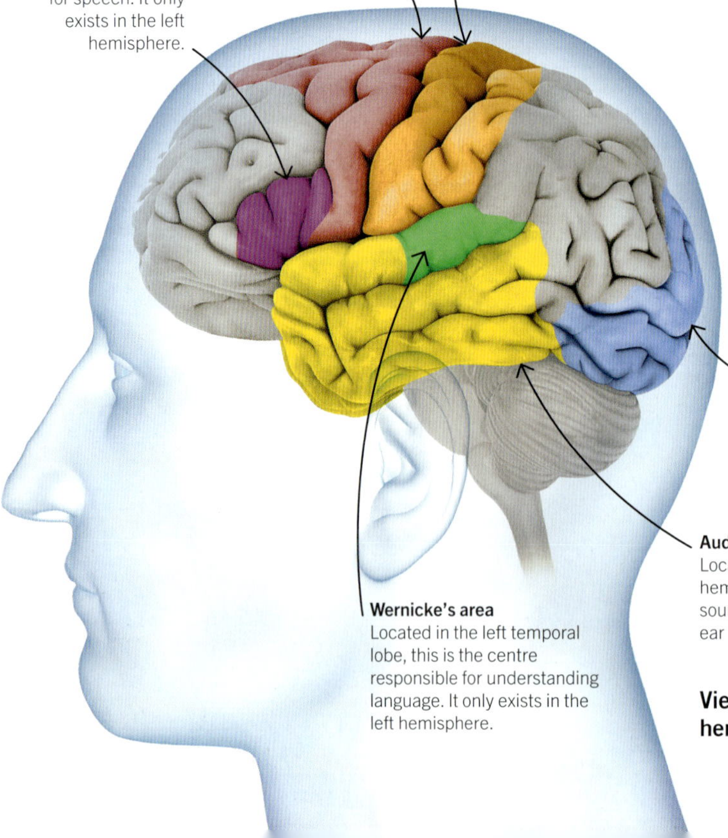

Key facts

✓ The cortex is the outer layer of the brain, where many high-level functions are processed.

✓ Specific functions are thought to have specific locations, a theory known as localization of function.

Brain lobes

Each hemisphere has four major regions known as lobes. Each lobe has a different function. The lobes are separated by deep grooves known as sulci.

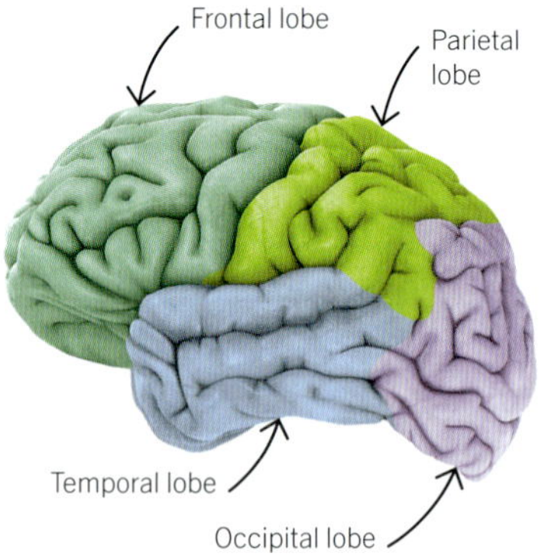

Frontal lobe

Parietal lobe

Temporal lobe

Occipital lobe

View of left hemisphere

The motor cortex
Located at the back of the frontal lobe in both hemispheres, each area controls voluntary movement in the opposite side of the body.

Broca's area
Located in the left frontal lobe, this area is responsible for speech. It only exists in the left hemisphere.

Somatosensory cortex
Located at the front of the parietal lobes in both hemispheres, each area processes sensory information from the skin on the opposite side of the body.

Visual cortex
Located in the occipital lobes at the back of the brain in both hemispheres, each visual cortex processes visual information from the visual field on the opposite side of the body.

Auditory cortex
Located in the temporal lobes in both hemispheres, each area processes sound-based information from the ear on the opposite side of the head.

Wernicke's area
Located in the left temporal lobe, this is the centre responsible for understanding language. It only exists in the left hemisphere.

View of left hemisphere

Split-brain research

The corpus callosum is a band of fibres that connects the two hemispheres of the brain, allowing communication between them. In the 1960s, US neurobiologist Roger Sperry studied patients whose corpus callosum had been cut for medical reasons. He gave them different tasks involving images, words, and objects. The results of Sperry's experiments revealed what happens when the two halves of the brain cannot communicate.

Key facts

✓ The corpus callosum connects the two hemispheres of the brain.

✓ If the corpus callosum is cut the brain's two hemispheres cannot communicate.

✓ Sperry carried out experiments on patients with a severed corpus callosum.

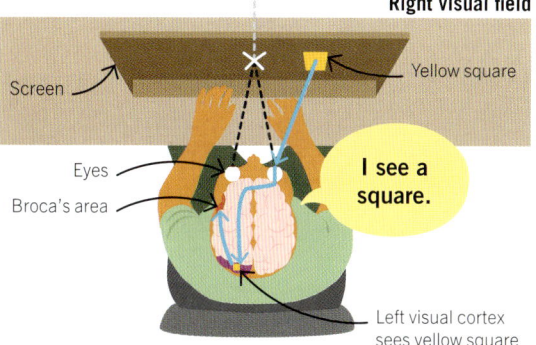

Task 1
The patient focused on a cross in front of them while an image was displayed in their right visual field. Images in the right visual field are processed in the left hemisphere, where Broca's area (responsible for speech) is also located, so the patient could describe verbally what they saw.

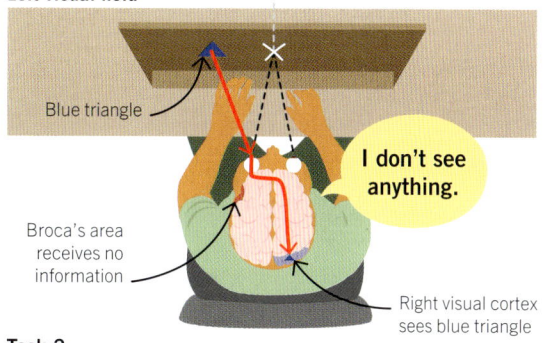

Task 2
The patient was shown an image in their left visual field. Images in the left visual field are processed in the right hemisphere. The patient could not describe the image verbally – information about it could not pass from the right visual cortex to Broca's area in the left hemisphere.

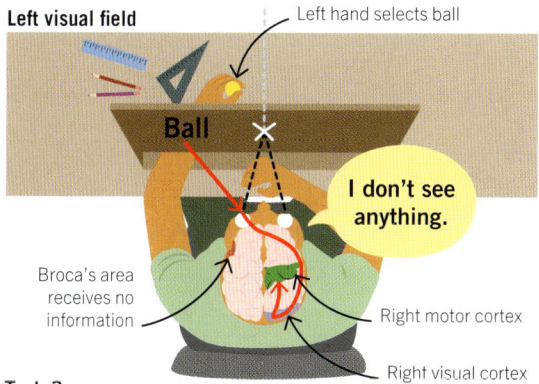

Task 3
The patient was shown a word ("ball") in their left visual field. They selected the ball from behind the screen with their left hand as the right visual cortex sees the word and instructs the right motor cortex, which controls the left hand. But they could not say "ball", as Broca's area is in the left hemisphere.

Task 4
The patient was shown two words. They drew the word in the left visual field ("tree") and said the word in the right visual field ("cat"). The right visual cortex saw "tree" and told the right motor cortex to draw. The left visual cortex saw "cat" and sent it to Broca's area. The patient said "cat".

Neuroplasticity

Although the brain is fully developed by early adulthood, neurons retain the ability to create new connections (synapses) or prune underused ones throughout life, reorganizing the brain's neural networks. This dynamic process is called neural plasticity and it supports learning, especially in early life, when the brain is at its most plastic. Neuroplasticity also enables damaged brains to recover lost function.

Key facts

✓ Neuroplasticity is the brain's ability to form new neural networks by making new synapses.

✓ Functional plasticity allows the brain to re-map functions to new areas.

✓ Synaptic pruning removes unused synapses.

Functional plasticity

Neuroplasticity allows the brain to re-map functions to entirely new areas. This is known as functional plasticity and allows people to make a dramatic recovery after brain injury. For example, strokes (when a blockage or bleed in a blood vessel damages part of the brain) can severely impair speech or the ability to walk, but these lost functions can be recovered with practice as undamaged parts of the brain rewire to compensate. Functional plasticity is also seen in the brains of deaf and blind people, where parts of the cerebral cortex normally dedicated to hearing or vision are repurposed to process other senses, enhancing them.

Occupational therapy
After a brain injury, patients with disabilities often receive occupational therapy to help them regain lost motor skills needed for everyday activities.

🔍 Synaptic pruning

In the first few years of life, a baby's brain generates around 15,000 synapses per neuron. That number halves by adulthood through a process called synaptic pruning. Synapses that are seldom used are removed, while connections that are used frequently are strengthened, making information processing more efficient. Synaptic pruning happens throughout life but the process is most active at two key stages of development: early childhood and adolescence.

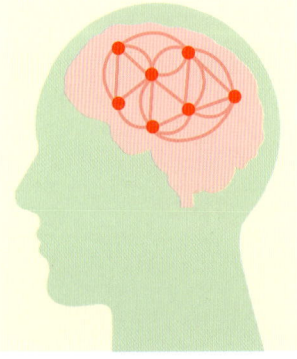

Before synaptic pruning

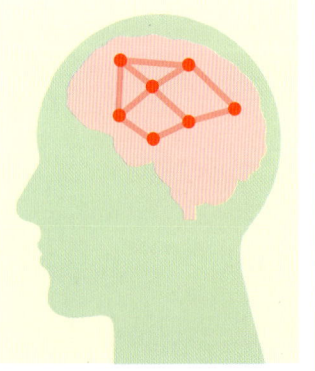

After synaptic pruning

The endocrine system

The endocrine system is a network of organs called glands, which release hormones (chemical messengers) into the bloodstream to control and coordinate bodily functions. Blood transports the hormones to target organs, where they trigger a response. Changing hormone levels affect how hungry or full we feel, help us to fall asleep and wake up, and play an important role in the menstrual cycle and reproduction.

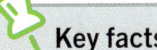

Key facts

✓ The endocrine system is a network of glands that release hormones, which control and coordinate bodily functions.

✓ Hormones help to control a range of functions, including hunger, sleeping and waking, and reproduction.

✓ Different glands release different hormones, and each hormone has a different effect.

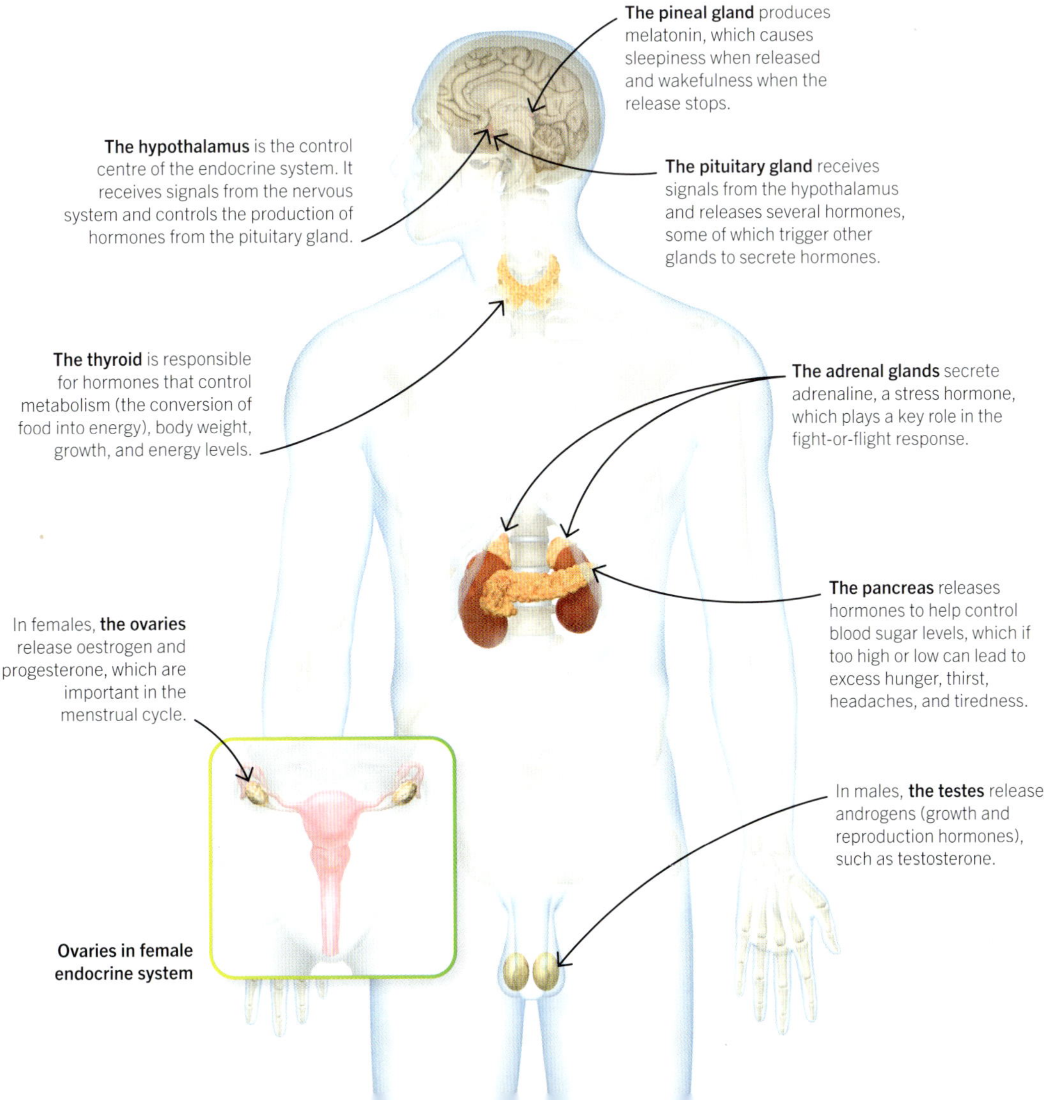

The pineal gland produces melatonin, which causes sleepiness when released and wakefulness when the release stops.

The hypothalamus is the control centre of the endocrine system. It receives signals from the nervous system and controls the production of hormones from the pituitary gland.

The pituitary gland receives signals from the hypothalamus and releases several hormones, some of which trigger other glands to secrete hormones.

The thyroid is responsible for hormones that control metabolism (the conversion of food into energy), body weight, growth, and energy levels.

The adrenal glands secrete adrenaline, a stress hormone, which plays a key role in the fight-or-flight response.

In females, **the ovaries** release oestrogen and progesterone, which are important in the menstrual cycle.

The pancreas releases hormones to help control blood sugar levels, which if too high or low can lead to excess hunger, thirst, headaches, and tiredness.

In males, **the testes** release androgens (growth and reproduction hormones), such as testosterone.

Ovaries in female endocrine system

Biological rhythms

Biological rhythms are repeating cycles of biological or psychological activity. Circadian rhythms last 24 hours, while ultradian rhythms are shorter and infradian rhythms are longer. All these rhythms can affect a person's mood and behaviour. Disruptions, such as jet lag, can have an adverse effect on health.

Key facts

✓ Biological rhythms are repeating cycles of biological or psychological activity.

✓ The three types are circadian, ultradian, and infradian.

✓ Disruptions to biological rhythms affect health.

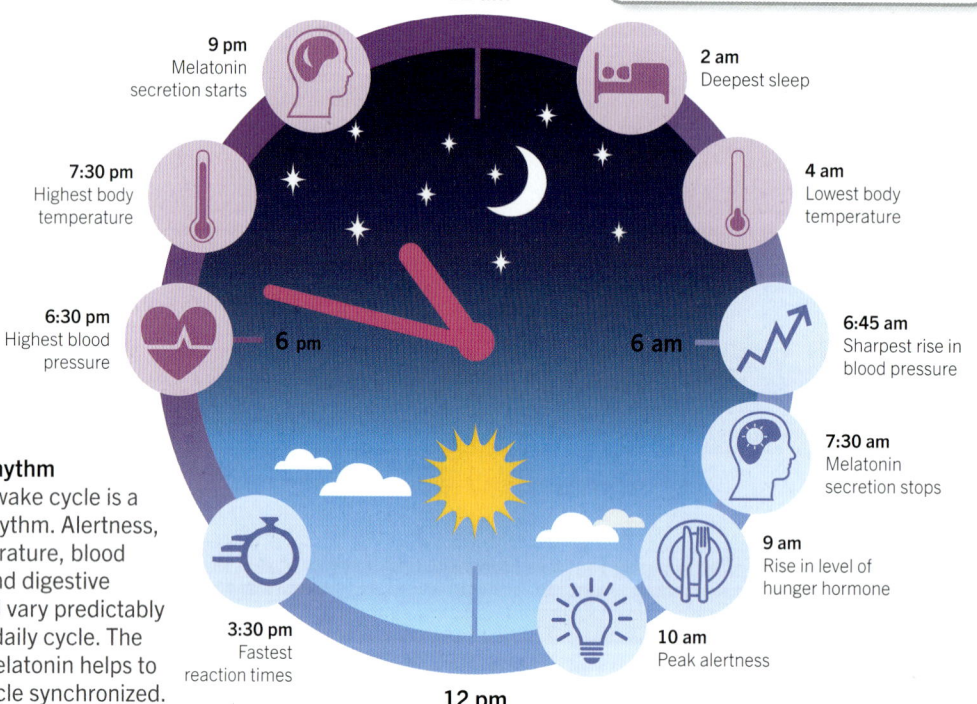

12 am

9 pm
Melatonin secretion starts

2 am
Deepest sleep

7:30 pm
Highest body temperature

4 am
Lowest body temperature

6:30 pm
Highest blood pressure

6 pm

6 am

6:45 am
Sharpest rise in blood pressure

7:30 am
Melatonin secretion stops

9 am
Rise in level of hunger hormone

3:30 pm
Fastest reaction times

10 am
Peak alertness

12 pm

Circadian rhythm
The sleep—wake cycle is a circadian rhythm. Alertness, body temperature, blood pressure, and digestive functions all vary predictably during this daily cycle. The hormone melatonin helps to keep the cycle synchronized.

Endogenous pacemaker

Biological rhythms are set both by external (exogenous) factors, such as daylight, and internal (endogenous) controls. The circadian rhythm is controlled by the suprachiasmatic nucleus in the brain. This natural pacemaker receives input about daylight from the eyes and sends signals to the pineal gland, which produces and releases melatonin.

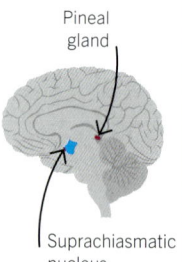

Pineal gland

Suprachiasmatic nucleus

Ultradian and infradian rhythms

Ultradian rhythms
Cycles repeated several times a day, such as the cycle of different sleep stages, are ultradian rhythms.

Infradian rhythms
Cycles that take longer than a day, such as the menstrual cycle, are infradian rhythms.

The sleeping brain

Psychologists are not sure what the brain does during sleep, but studies show that it is essential for our physical and mental health. When we sleep and how much we sleep changes with age, with older people needing less. The brain is still active during sleep and cycles through stages of varying activity.

Stages of sleep

Studies of brain waves (patterns of electrical activity) show that we pass through distinct stages as we sleep. These stages follow a cycle that repeats four to five times a night. The sleep cycle is an example of an ultradian rhythm (a biological cycle shorter than 24 hours).

Key facts

✓ Sleep is essential for health.

✓ A sleeping person passes through a repeating cycle of different sleep stages with distinctive brain waves.

✓ Most dreaming occurs during REM (rapid eye movement) sleep.

✓ The sleep cycle is an example of an ultradian rhythm.

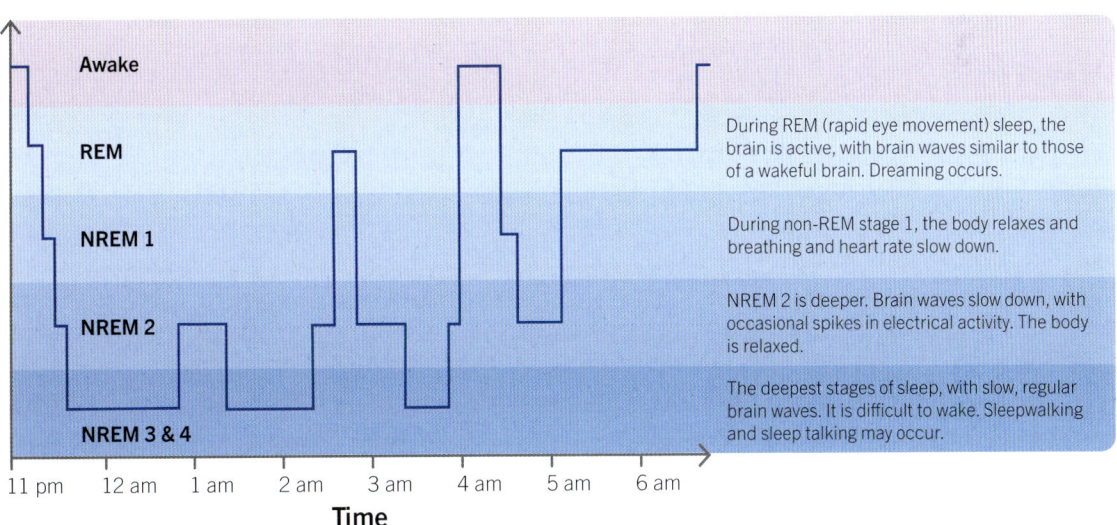

During REM (rapid eye movement) sleep, the brain is active, with brain waves similar to those of a wakeful brain. Dreaming occurs.

During non-REM stage 1, the body relaxes and breathing and heart rate slow down.

NREM 2 is deeper. Brain waves slow down, with occasional spikes in electrical activity. The body is relaxed.

The deepest stages of sleep, with slow, regular brain waves. It is difficult to wake. Sleepwalking and sleep talking may occur.

🔍 Studying sleep

Sleep is difficult to study. There is little to observe from the outside, and an unconscious person cannot communicate. After waking, we remember little. However, psychologists can monitor activity in the brain or body during sleep to diagnose sleep disorders. There are three main methods.

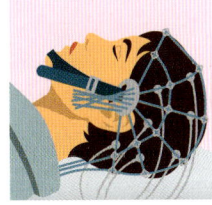

Electroencephalogram
Small sensors attached to the scalp pick up rhythmic patterns of electricity in the brain (brain waves).

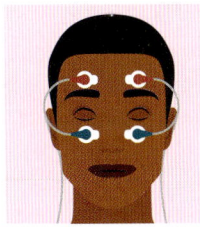

Electrooculogram
This device measures eye movements during REM sleep. These can be compared to reports of dreams after waking.

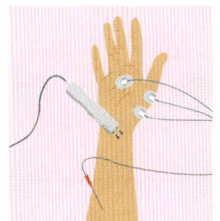

Electromyogram
Muscle activity can be detected with an electromyogram. During REM sleep, muscles are inactive.

Genes and heritability

The genes you inherit from your parents determine many of your physical characteristics, such as eye colour and how curly your hair is. Other characteristics, from your adult height and weight to your personality and intelligence, are influenced by genes but not determined by them. Scientists use a measure called heritability to assess how much of the variation in a group of people for a particular trait can be attributed to genes (nature) rather than environment (nurture).

Key facts

✓ Genes are chemical instructions encoded in DNA.

✓ Genes determine some characteristics but merely influence others.

✓ Heritability is the percentage of variation in a group of people for a trait that can be attributed to genes rather than environment.

Genes and DNA

Genes are chemical instructions encoded in the molecule DNA. You have around 25,000 genes. A complete set is found in every cell nucleus in your body, stored on 46 chromosomes (23 from your mother and 23 from your father). A gene is a section of DNA with a particular sequence of four chemicals called bases (A, G, C, and T). Most genes carry the code to build a protein molecule, but some act as switches to turn other genes on or off. A person's genotype is the combination of genes they carry that influence a particular trait; phenotype is the observable trait affected by those genes.

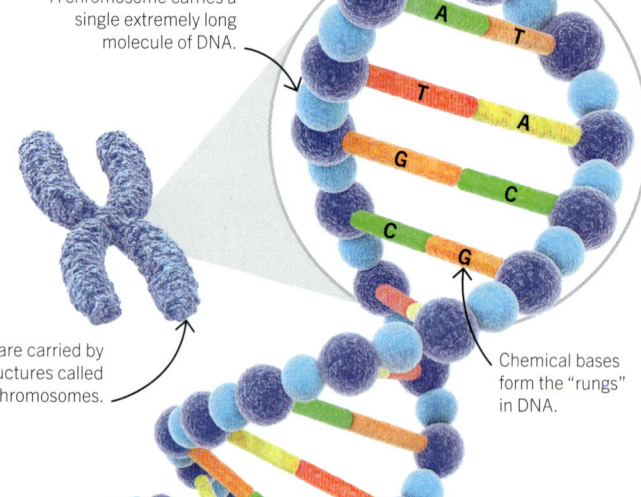

A chromosome carries a single extremely long molecule of DNA.

Genes are carried by structures called chromosomes.

Chemical bases form the "rungs" in DNA.

🔍 Heritability

Psychologists can measure heritability by studying identical twins, who share all their genes (see page 57), or adopted siblings, who share none. Heritability is often expressed as a percentage. For instance, a study might find that the IQ of a study group has a heritability of 50 per cent, which means that 50 per cent of the variation in the group is caused by differences in their genes. It is important to note that heritability applies only to groups of people and not to individuals. Moreover, it is not fixed or immutable. In studies of people drawn from very similar environments, for instance, heritability is higher because environmental differences contribute less to variation.

Low heritability ⟵   ⟶ **High heritability**

| Religion | IQ | Hair colour |
| Language | Personality traits | Height |

Twin studies

Psychological characteristics are influenced by the genes you inherit and the environment you grow up in, but which matters more? Twin studies and other family studies can help answer the question by comparing people with different degrees of genetic similarity. Monozygotic (identical) twins share all of their genes. Dizygotic (fraternal) twins and ordinary siblings share half their genes, and adopted siblings share none of their genes.

Key facts

✓ Genes and the environment influence psychological characteristics.

✓ Monozygotic twins share the same genes, whereas dizygotic twins only share half their genes.

✓ Twin studies allow scientists to determine the relative impact of genes and the environment on a specific characteristic.

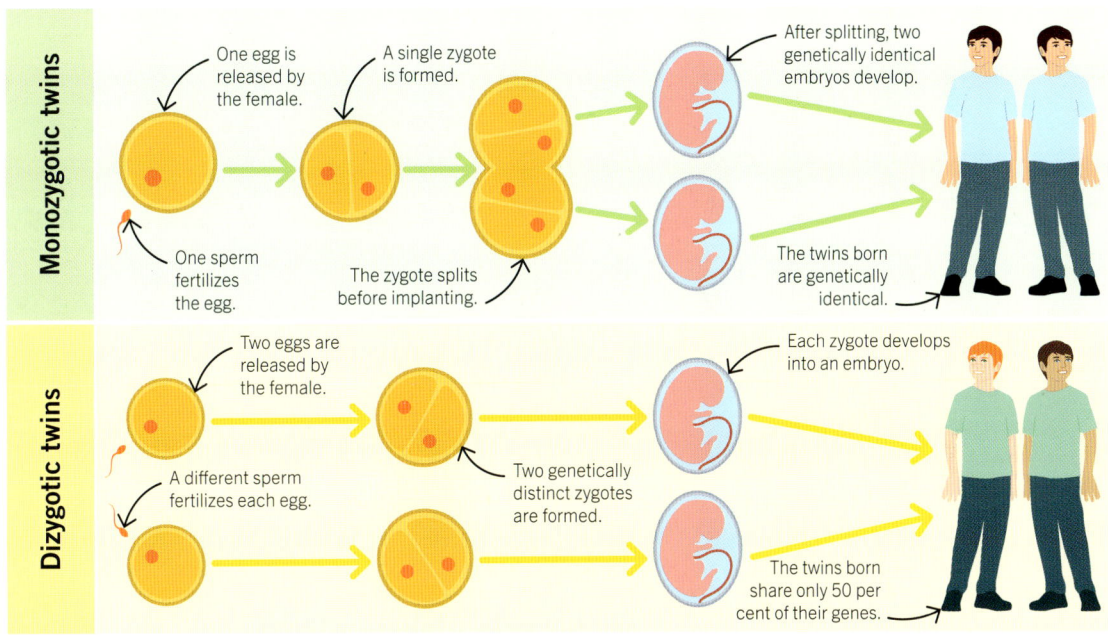

Monozygotic twins: One egg is released by the female. A single zygote is formed. One sperm fertilizes the egg. The zygote splits before implanting. After splitting, two genetically identical embryos develop. The twins born are genetically identical.

Dizygotic twins: Two eggs are released by the female. A different sperm fertilizes each egg. Two genetically distinct zygotes are formed. Each zygote develops into an embryo. The twins born share only 50 per cent of their genes.

🔍 Concordance rates

In a study involving many pairs of twins, the percentage of twins who share the same trait is the concordance rate. For example, the concordance rate for eye colour in monozygotic twins is nearly 100 per cent. By comparing the concordance rates of monozygotic and dizygotic twins for a characteristic, scientists can work out how important genes are. If the concordance rate is higher in monozygotic than dizygotic twins, genes are an important factor. A smaller difference in concordance rates suggests the environment plays a larger part than genes.

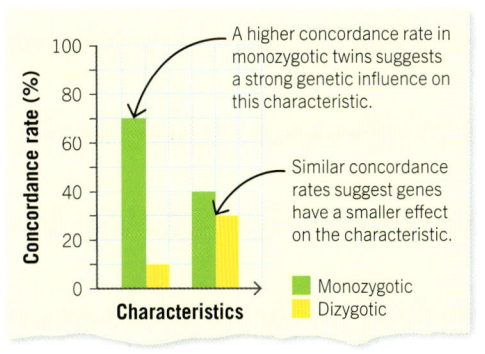

A higher concordance rate in monozygotic twins suggests a strong genetic influence on this characteristic.

Similar concordance rates suggest genes have a smaller effect on the characteristic.

Monozygotic Dizygotic

Chapter 3
Sensation and perception

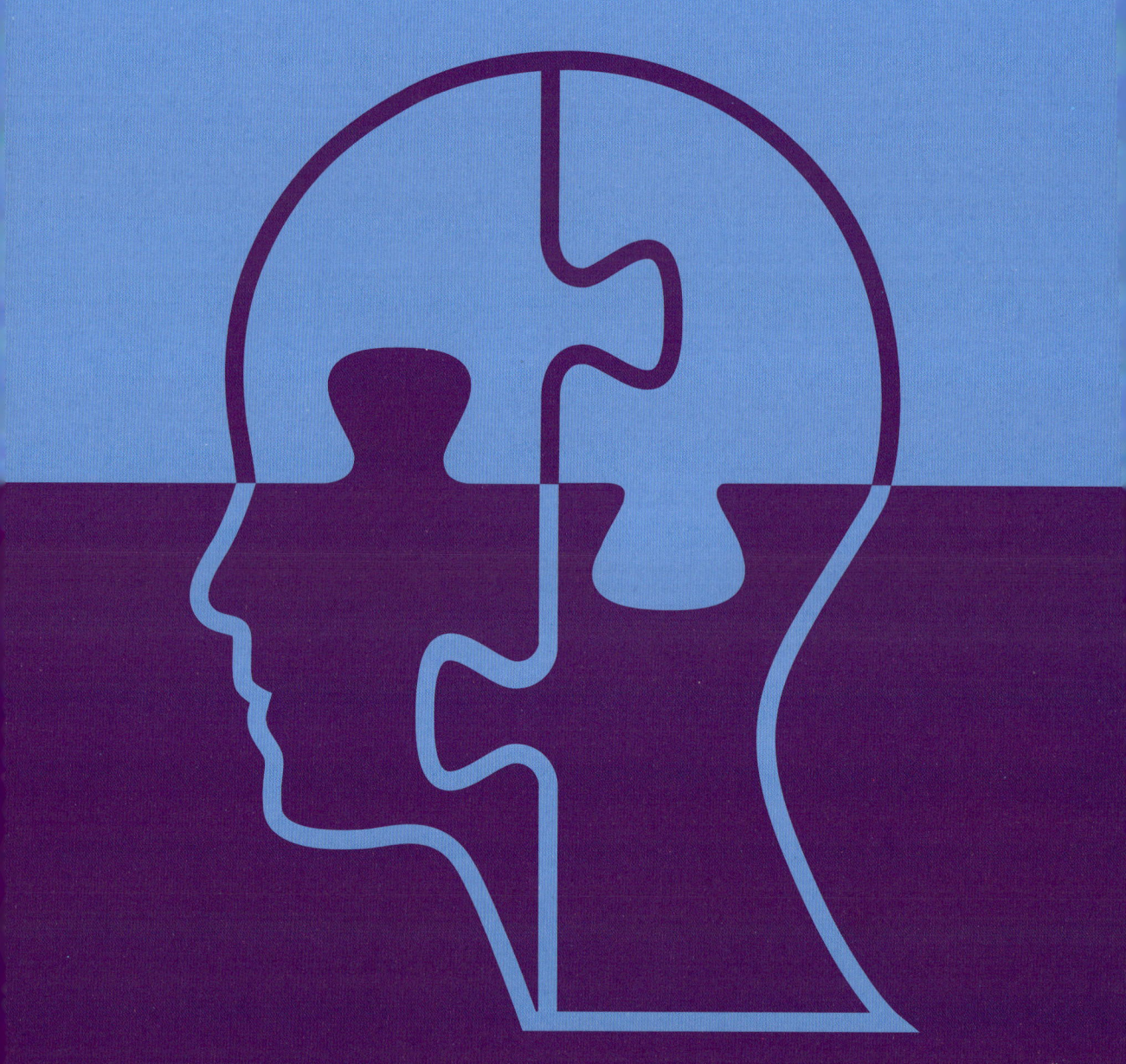

Sensation and perception

Sensation is the process of taking in information about the world or about the body's inner state through sense organs, such as eyes, ears, and touch receptors. Perception, which takes place in the brain, gives meaning to this sensory information by combining it with input from our experiences and expectations.

Key facts

✓ Sensation occurs when sensory organs detect stimuli and pass this information to the brain.

✓ Perception occurs when the brain receives the information and makes sense of it.

✓ There are more than five senses, and each is processed in a different part of the brain.

2. Sensation
Sensory organs detect stimuli, such as the scent, appearance, and texture of a flower. These organs then generate nerve signals.

4. Perception
The brain processes the signals and makes sense of them. For example, it interprets the sight, scent, and touch signals to create a perception of a rose.

1. Stimulus
A stimulus is anything that could trigger a response, such as a rose.

3. Neural impulses
Information from sensory organs, such as touch receptors in the hand, is transmitted to the brain as electrical signals along sensory neurons.

🔎 Human senses

People have more than five senses. As well as sensing light, sound, smell, taste, and touch with our major sense organs, we can also sense motion, gravity, temperature, pain, and the positions and state of our muscles and joints (proprioception).

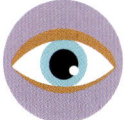
Visual
(Sight)

Auditory
(Hearing)

Olfactory
(Smell)

Gustatory
(Taste)

Vestibular
(Balance)

Tactile
(Touch)

Proprioceptive
(Body awareness)

Processing information

There are two main methods the brain uses to process information about external stimuli, known as bottom-up and top-down processing. The two combine to create our experience of the world.

Key facts

✓ We use two main processes to interpret external stimuli: bottom-up and top-down.

✓ Bottom-up processing starts with the stimulus, using sensory input to perceive it.

✓ Top-down processing starts with prior knowledge of the stimulus, using experience and expectation to perceive it.

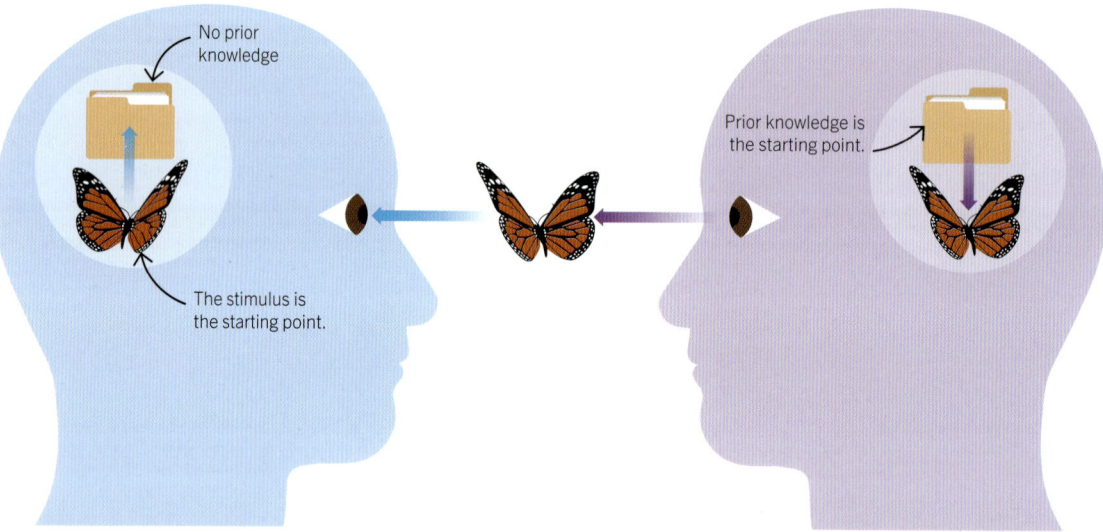

No prior knowledge

The stimulus is the starting point.

Prior knowledge is the starting point.

Bottom-up processing
This type of processing begins outside of the body. The brain analyses the raw sensory information it receives about an external stimulus, such as a large, colourful butterfly, and uses this information to interpret and perceive it.

Top-down processing
This type of processing begins inside the body, and is based on prior knowledge. It applies what we already know about a stimulus in order to interpret it. The knowledge, experience, and expectations we have of something influence how we perceive it.

🔍 Jumbled sentences

We use top-down processing when reading. The brain uses shortcuts gained from prior knowledge to read words as a whole, rather than working through them letter-by-letter. This is why it is still possible to read a sentence in which the letters of each word are mixed up. Similarly, optical illusions work because we often see what we expect to see, even if that isn't what's actually there.

Tihs snetnece si esay ot raed.

Selective attention

Attention can be defined as consciously processing specific information at the expense of other information, which is ignored. Every day we are bombarded constantly by sensory information, so it is essential to work out what to pay attention to and what can be filtered out — an ability known as selective attention.

Key facts

✓ Selective attention is the ability to focus on relevant information and ignore irrelevant information.

✓ Inattentional blindness is when a person focuses entirely on one stimulus, and fails to notice another more obvious stimulus.

The cocktail-party effect

Have you ever been in a room full of people chatting loudly, perhaps at a party or in a busy restaurant, and managed to hear someone quietly say your name in conversation despite all the noise? This ability to hear, or "select", information relevant to you is known as the cocktail-party effect. It is an example of selective attention.

... as I was saying to Emma...

I heard my name – I wonder what they are talking about...

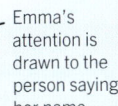

Emma's attention is drawn to the person saying her name.

🔍 Inattentional blindness

When concentrating hard on a piece of sensory input we may neglect to notice another more obvious stimulus – a phenomenon known as inattentional blindness. US psychologists Christopher Chabris and Daniel Simons (1999) asked participants to watch a video and count the number of times a basketball was passed between a group. A person in a gorilla suit walks through the group, but, focused on counting the passes, half of the participants failed to notice.

Anatomy of the eye

Like a camera, the human eye focuses incoming light to create a sharp image on a light-sensitive surface, which reacts by generating an electrical signal. The eye focuses light in two stages: first with the transparent cornea at the front, and then with an adjustable lens behind the pupil. Images are captured on a layer of tissue called the retina. By combining signals from both eyes, the brain creates a 3D image.

Key facts

- ✓ The eye focuses light to create an image.
- ✓ Transduction is the conversion of a sensory stimulus, such as light energy, into an electrical signal.
- ✓ Cone cells detect colours, and rod cells detect faint light.

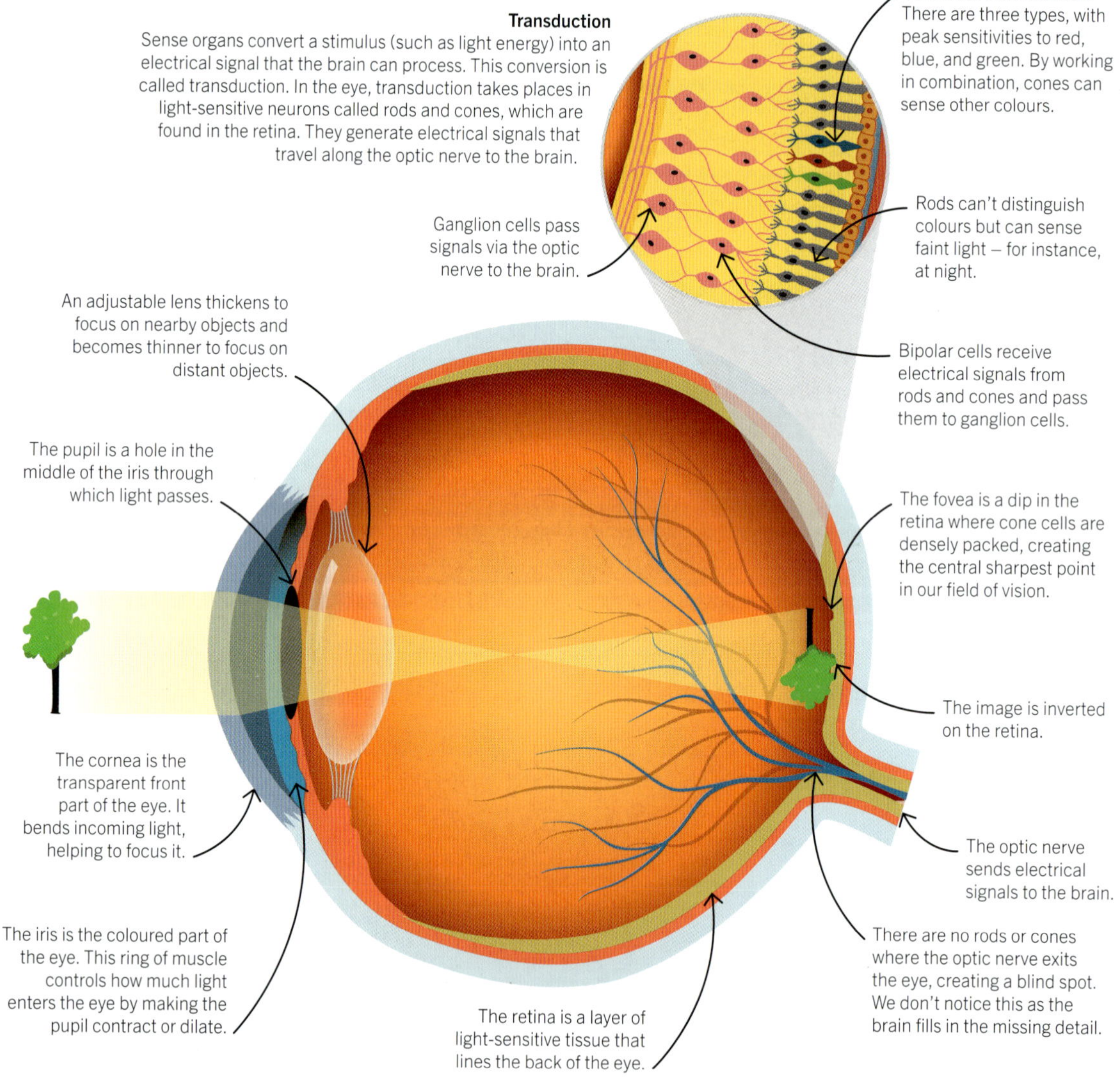

Transduction
Sense organs convert a stimulus (such as light energy) into an electrical signal that the brain can process. This conversion is called transduction. In the eye, transduction takes places in light-sensitive neurons called rods and cones, which are found in the retina. They generate electrical signals that travel along the optic nerve to the brain.

Cone cells detect colour. There are three types, with peak sensitivities to red, blue, and green. By working in combination, cones can sense other colours.

Ganglion cells pass signals via the optic nerve to the brain.

Rods can't distinguish colours but can sense faint light – for instance, at night.

Bipolar cells receive electrical signals from rods and cones and pass them to ganglion cells.

An adjustable lens thickens to focus on nearby objects and becomes thinner to focus on distant objects.

The pupil is a hole in the middle of the iris through which light passes.

The fovea is a dip in the retina where cone cells are densely packed, creating the central sharpest point in our field of vision.

The cornea is the transparent front part of the eye. It bends incoming light, helping to focus it.

The image is inverted on the retina.

The optic nerve sends electrical signals to the brain.

The iris is the coloured part of the eye. This ring of muscle controls how much light enters the eye by making the pupil contract or dilate.

There are no rods or cones where the optic nerve exits the eye, creating a blind spot. We don't notice this as the brain fills in the missing detail.

The retina is a layer of light-sensitive tissue that lines the back of the eye.

Light

The visible spectrum of light our eyes can see makes up just a part of the larger electromagnetic spectrum. All forms of electromagnetic radiation travel as waves of energy, with shorter waves carrying more energy.

Electromagnetic spectrum

Electromagnetic waves vary from radio waves (with wavelengths up to hundreds of kilometres long) to gamma rays (with wavelengths smaller than atoms). We see visible light of varying wavelengths as different colours. Red light, for example, has a longer wavelength than blue light.

Key facts

✓ Light is a form of electromagnetic radiation.

✓ The electromagnetic spectrum includes invisible forms of radiation as well as visible light.

✓ All types of electromagnetic radiation have a particular wavelength or range of wavelengths.

✓ We see different wavelengths of visible light as different colours.

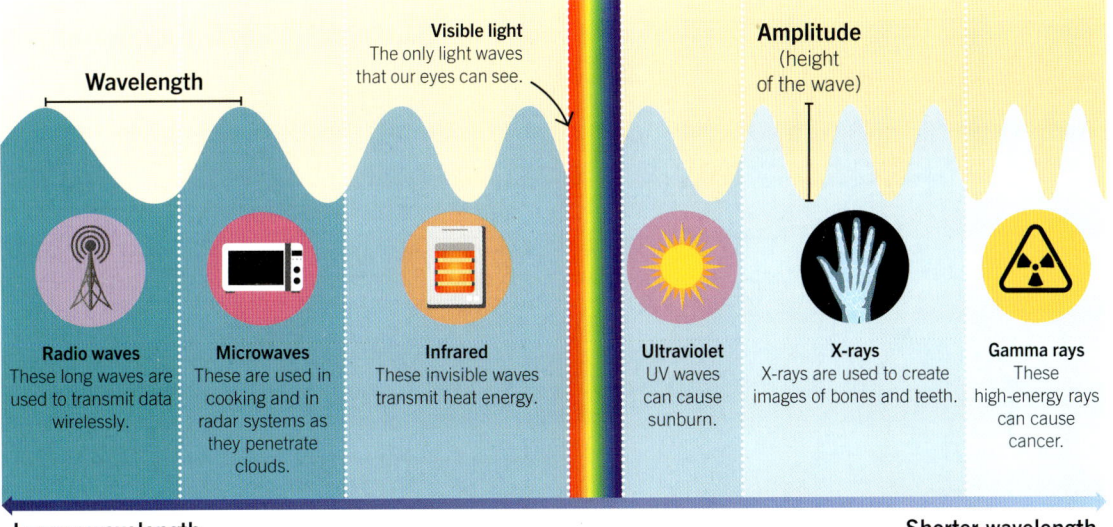

Wavelength

Visible light
The only light waves that our eyes can see.

Amplitude
(height of the wave)

Radio waves
These long waves are used to transmit data wirelessly.

Microwaves
These are used in cooking and in radar systems as they penetrate clouds.

Infrared
These invisible waves transmit heat energy.

Ultraviolet
UV waves can cause sunburn.

X-rays
X-rays are used to create images of bones and teeth.

Gamma rays
These high-energy rays can cause cancer.

Longer wavelength   Shorter wavelength

🔍 Why we see colours

White light is a mixture of all the colours in the visible spectrum. When light strikes an object, some colours are absorbed and others are reflected. The colour we see depends on which wavelengths are being reflected.

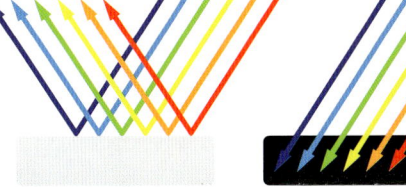

White object
All the colours in the spectrum are reflected, so the object appears white.

Black object
All colours are absorbed. Little or no light is reflected, so the object looks black.

Coloured object
A green object absorbs all wavelengths of visible light except green.

Colour vision

We perceive different wavelengths of visible light as different colours. Longer wavelengths look red, for instance, whereas shorter wavelengths are blue. This colour system relies on three types of cone cell (colour-sensitive cell) in the eye. By working together, the three cone cell types can discriminate millions of different colours. However, some people have limited colour perception due to defects in their cone cells. This condition is called colour blindness.

Trichromatic theory of colour
According to the trichromatic (Young–Helmholtz) theory of colour, colours are detected by three types of cone cell that have peak sensitivities to three primary colours: red, blue, and green. Because their sensitivities overlap, cone cells can also detect other colours by working in tandem. For instance, true yellow light is detected when the red and green cones are activated together. As a result, we also perceive yellow when red and green light are mixed together, since this stimulates the same cone cells. Colour screens exploit this by using red, blue, and green pixels to simulate every other colour.

Key facts

✓ We perceive visible light of different wavelengths as different colours.

✓ The trichromatic theory states that all the colours we perceive are generated by three types of cone cell, with peak sensitivities to red, blue, and green.

✓ Colours can be simulated by mixing red, blue, and green light.

✓ Colour blindness is an impairment of colour vision.

Colour blindness

Most cases of colour blindness are caused by inheritance of a mutation in a gene needed to make functional cone cells. In red–green colour blindness (the most common form), people have difficulty distinguishing certain shades of red and green. The condition is diagnosed by an Ishihara test, which involves trying to see numbers in patterns of coloured dots.

If you can't see the number eight, you may have red–green colour blindness.

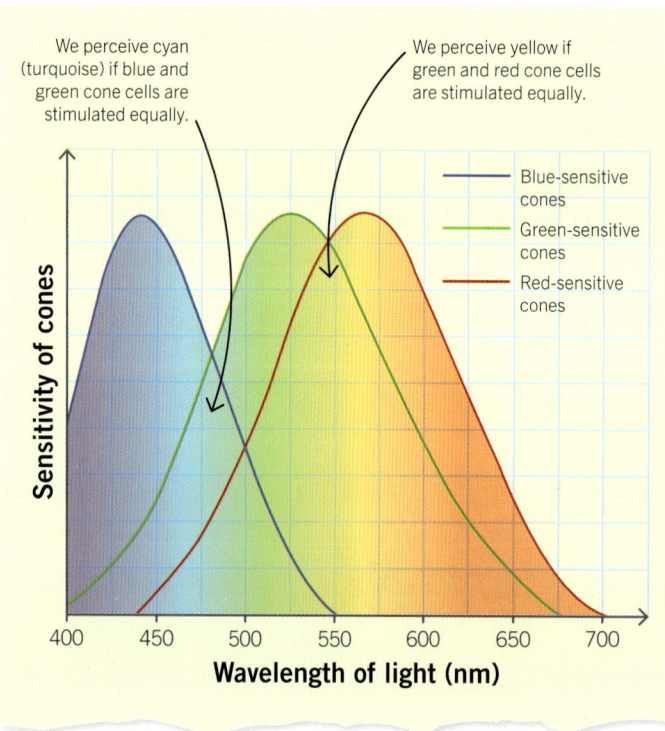

Opponent process theory

The trichromatic theory (see page 64) doesn't fully explain every aspect of colour vision. One unexplained phenomenon is the afterimage effect – the fleeting perception of reversed colours after staring persistently at a coloured pattern. In 1892, German physiologist Ewald Hering put forward the opponent process theory to explain this effect. His theory is now regarded as complementary to the trichromatic theory of colour.

Key facts

✓ The opponent process theory was put forward to explain the afterimage effect.

✓ The opponent process theory explains colour vision in terms of three sets of opponent colours: red–green, yellow–blue, and white–black.

✓ The afterimage effect occurs when reversed (negative) colours are briefly perceived after staring persistently at a coloured pattern.

Afterimage effect

If you stare closely at this image for 30 seconds, when you shift your gaze to a blank white background an image of the US flag in its true colours will appear. Hering described the opposite colours as opponent colours. According to his theory, colour vision depends on three sets of opponent colours: red–green, yellow–blue, and white–black. When we stare at a colour persistently, photoreceptors in the eye (or colour-processing neurons in the optic nerve or brain) become fatigued, allowing opponent colours to dominate the signal.

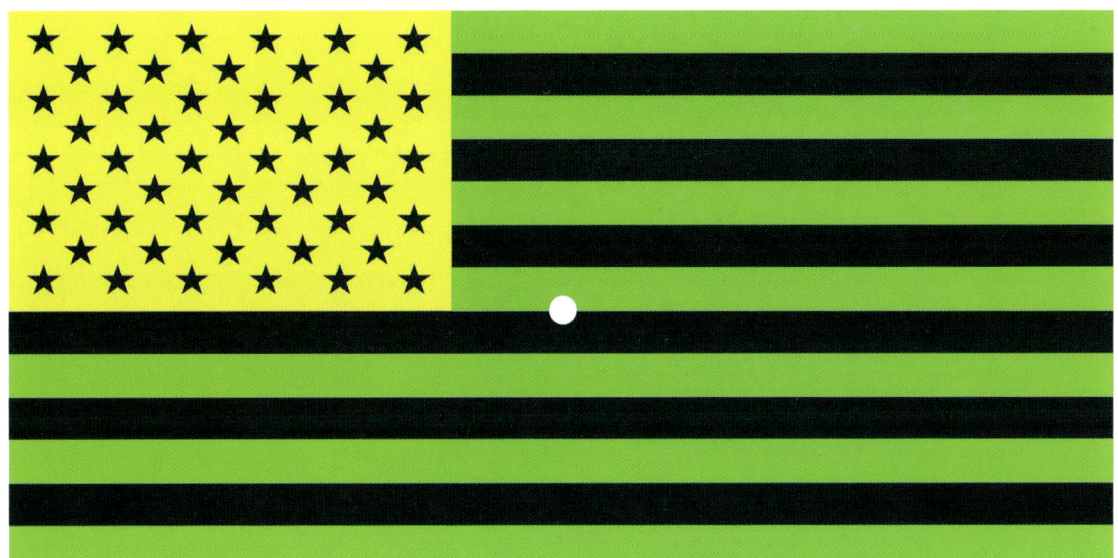

1. Stare at the white dot for 30 seconds without moving your eyes.

2. The US flag appears in its correct colours as an afterimage when looking at a white surface.

Depth perception

Our visual system provides awareness of depth, allowing us to sense the distance and size of objects in the 3D space around us. Depth perception depends partly on the integration of the sensory input from both eyes (binocular cues) and partly on information about depth that a single eye can detect (monocular cues).

Key facts

✓ Depth perception relies on binocular and monocular cues.

✓ The optic nerves cross over at the optic chiasm.

✓ The left side of the brain processes the right side of both eyes' visual fields; the right side of the brain processes the left visual fields.

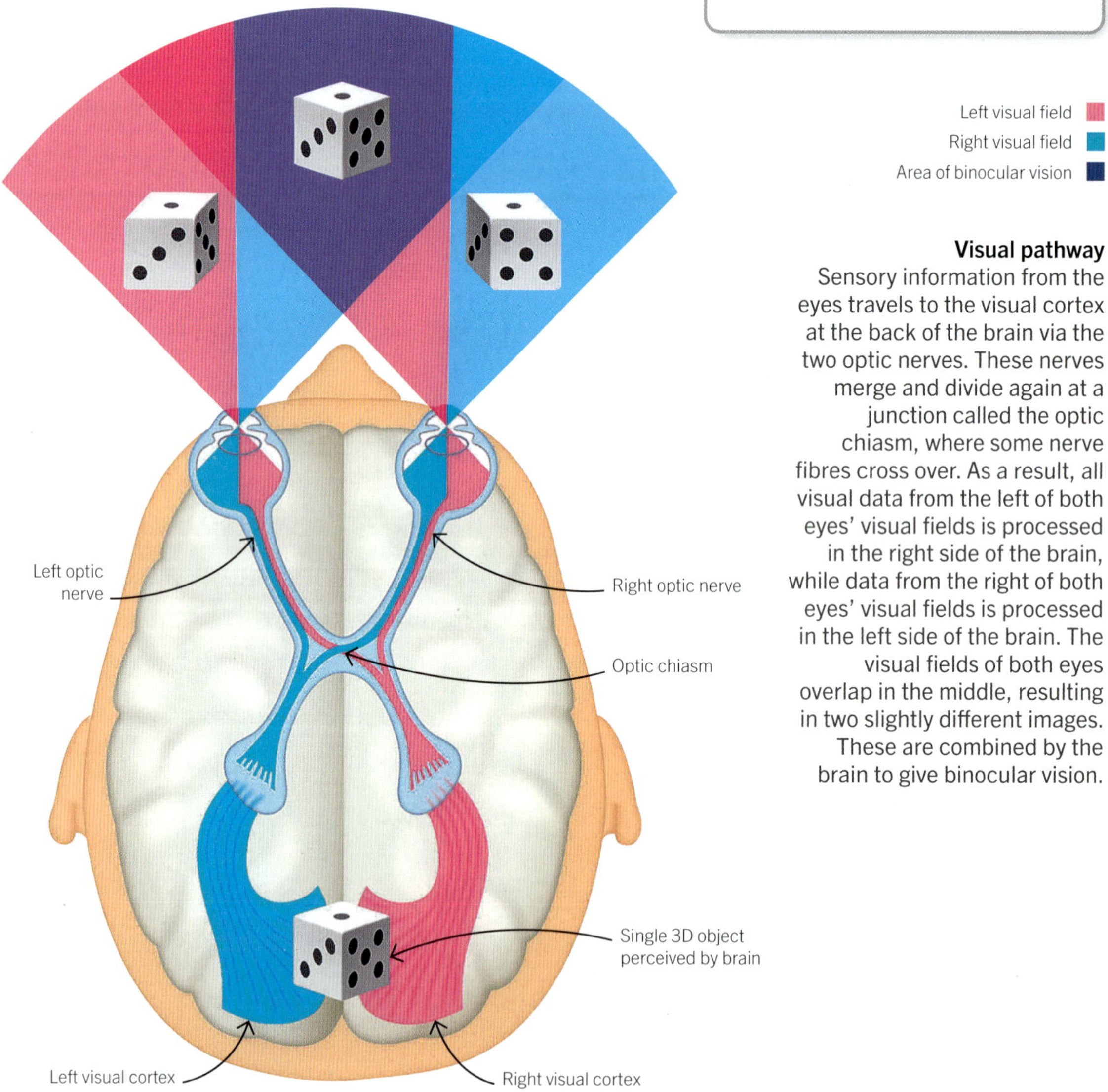

Left visual field

Right visual field

Area of binocular vision

Visual pathway

Sensory information from the eyes travels to the visual cortex at the back of the brain via the two optic nerves. These nerves merge and divide again at a junction called the optic chiasm, where some nerve fibres cross over. As a result, all visual data from the left of both eyes' visual fields is processed in the right side of the brain, while data from the right of both eyes' visual fields is processed in the left side of the brain. The visual fields of both eyes overlap in the middle, resulting in two slightly different images. These are combined by the brain to give binocular vision.

Left optic nerve

Right optic nerve

Optic chiasm

Single 3D object perceived by brain

Left visual cortex

Right visual cortex

Binocular cues

Combining the input of two eyes at once yields two sources of information about depth. One comes from the muscles that move the eyes; the other comes from the images the eyes capture.

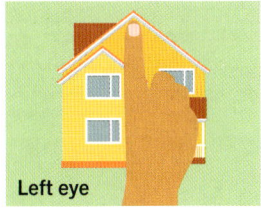 

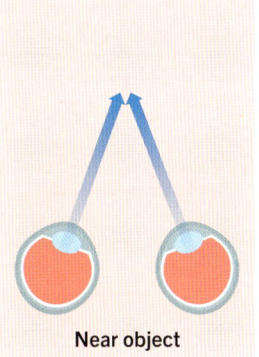 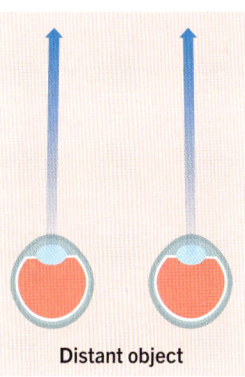

Near object   **Distant object**

Retinal disparity
The two eyes see objects from slightly different angles, resulting in different images. This is called retinal disparity.

Convergence
When focusing on a nearby object, the eyes converge. For distant objects, the eyes move towards parallel positions.

Monocular cues

Many depth cues can be seen with only one eye, such as whether or not one object is behind another. These monocular cues contribute to depth perception.

Interposition
When one object partially obscures another, the brain interprets the partially obstructed object as further away.

Relative size
Objects of the same size appear smaller as they get further away. The brain interprets this as depth.

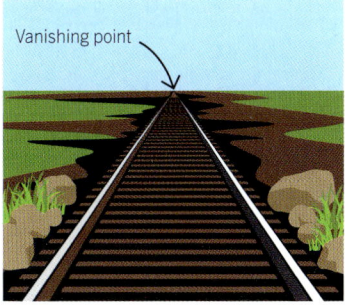

Vanishing point

Linear perspective
As parallel lines extend into the distance, they appear to converge. This aids the brain in interpreting depth.

Texture gradient
More distant objects appear less detailed. This change in texture helps the brain to determine depth.

Dimmer, darker objects are interpreted as being further away.

Light and shadow
The brightness of objects and the size and shape of shadows provide clues about how far away they are.

Long distance
Distant features in landscapes look hazier than the foreground. Distance haze is used to create illusory depth in paintings.

Anatomy of the ear

Ears detect sound, allowing people to hear and communicate. They can sense the pitch and volume of sound, and by working together two ears can tell its direction and source. Sound travels as waves of pressure in the air. These waves are funnelled by the outer ear to the eardrum, making it vibrate. The vibrations move tiny bones in the middle ear that, in turn, transmit vibrations to the fluid-filled inner ear. Here, a spiral organ called the cochlea turns sound into electrical signals that are sent to the brain.

Key facts

✓ Ears detect sound waves and convert sound information into electrical signals that are sent to the brain.

✓ The auditory cortex processes information from the ears and is essential for hearing and for understanding speech.

Cochlea
The cochlea is lined with tiny cells that detect fluid vibrations. These cells convert sound information into electrical signals (a process known as transduction).

The pinna (outer ear) acts like a funnel to direct sound into the ear canal.

The fluid-filled semicircular canals detect motion and help us balance.

Anvil bone (incus)

Hammer bone (malleus)

The vestibular nerve carries signals from the balance organs to the brain.

The auditory nerve transmits signals from the cochlea to the brain.

The stirrup bone (stapes), along with the hammer bone and anvil bone, amplifies sound vibrations.

The ear canal is a passage leading to the eardrum.

The eardrum is a thin membrane that vibrates when hit by sound waves.

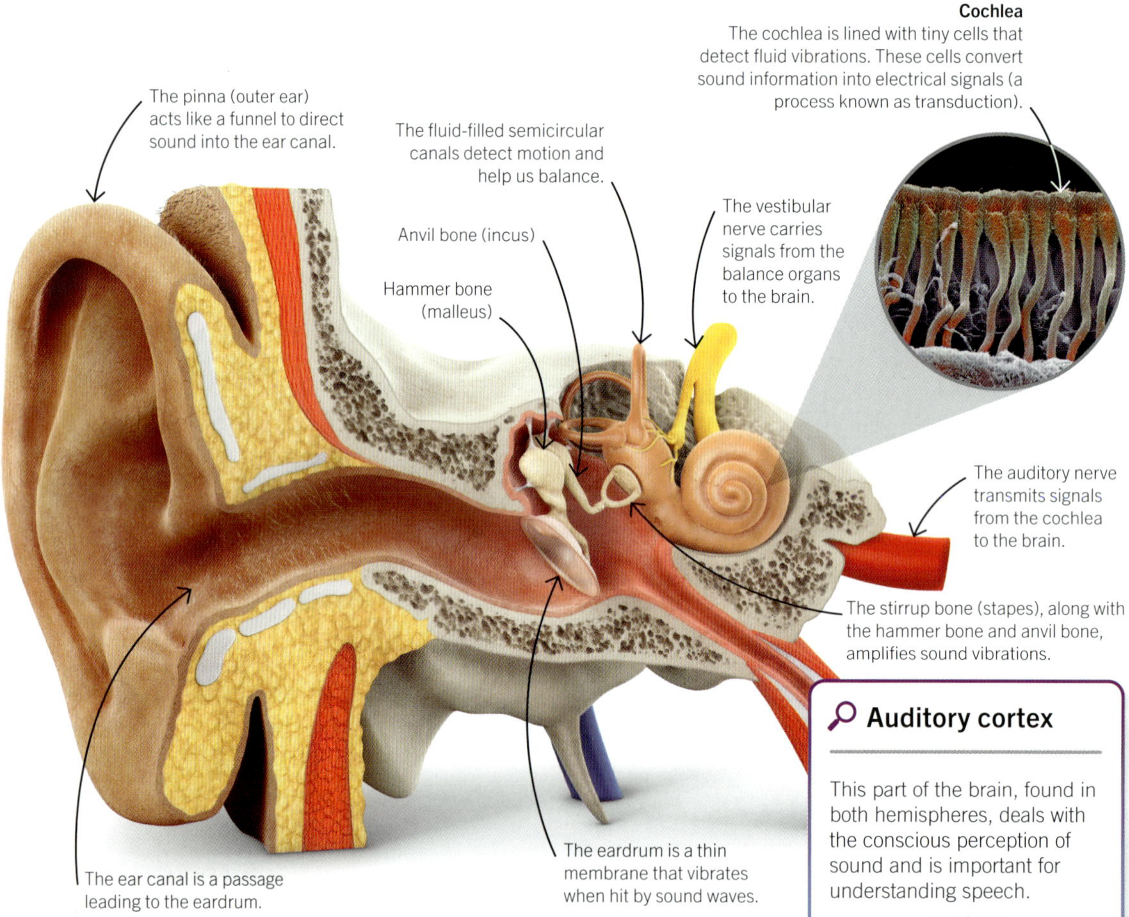

🔍 Auditory cortex

This part of the brain, found in both hemispheres, deals with the conscious perception of sound and is important for understanding speech.

Auditory cortex

Outer ear   Middle ear   Inner ear

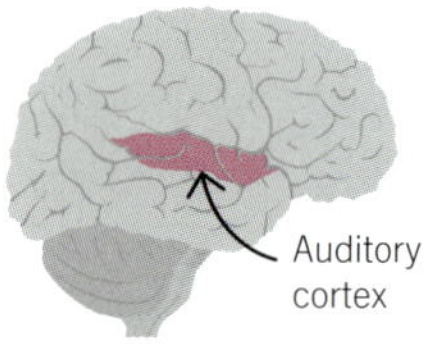

Sound

Rhythmic music, the hum of traffic, distant voices – all these sounds can tell people something about their environment. Sounds are invisible waves of pressure that race through air at 343 m (1125 ft) a second and set eardrums vibrating, giving people hearing. Sounds reveal what's happening in places humans can't see, they alert them to danger, and help them communicate through speech.

Key facts

✓ Sound travels as waves of compression.

✓ The higher the frequency, the higher the pitch.

✓ Loud sounds have greater energy than quiet sounds.

✓ The volume (intensity) of sound waves is measured in on the decibel scale, which is logarithmic.

Sound waves

Sounds travel as invisible waves of compression in the air. A bit like ripples in a pond, they spread outward from a source of sound in a concentric pattern. The number of sound waves hitting someone's ears each second is the frequency. Sounds audible to humans vary from 20 waves a second (20 Hertz) to 20,000, with higher frequencies sounding higher in pitch. The loudness of sound depends on how much energy is in each wave. In graphical representations, this is shown as the height (amplitude) of the waves.

Sound waves can be represented graphically on screen by a wavy line called a waveform.

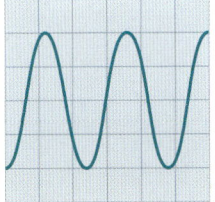

Small amplitude = quiet sound

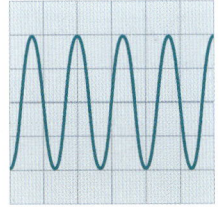

Large amplitude = loud sound

High frequency = high-pitched sound

Low frequency = low-pitched sound

Complex waveforms are typical of musical instruments

🔍 The decibel scale

The volume (intensity) of sound is measured in decibels (dB). The scale is logarithmic rather than linear, which means that an increase from 40 to 50 dB is 10 times louder, not 25 per cent louder. Exposure to sound louder than 70 dB for a prolonged period can cause hearing loss. This type of hearing loss is gradual and cumulative.

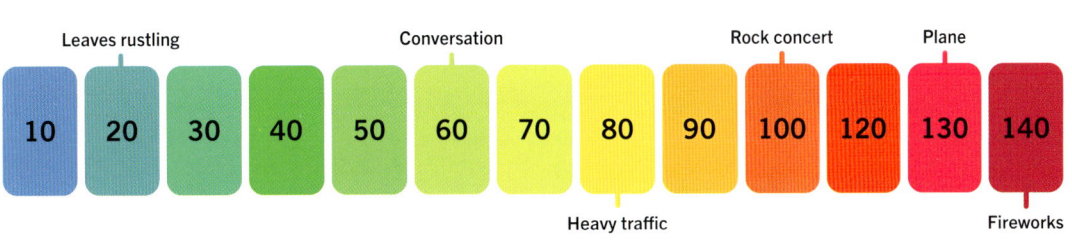

Leaves rustling · Conversation · Rock concert · Plane

10 20 30 40 50 60 70 80 90 100 120 130 140

Heavy traffic · Fireworks

Pitch and location

All the senses depend on a process called transduction: the conversion of a chemical or physical signal from the outside world into nerve impulses that the brain can interpret. In the ear, transduction takes place in a snail-shaped tube called the cochlea, which converts the information in sound waves into an electrochemical form carried by nerve cells. The brain decodes this stream of data to determine the pitch, volume, and location of sound.

Key facts

✓ Transduction (the conversion of a signal into neural impulses) takes place inside the cochlea of the inner ear.

✓ Place theory says the pitch we hear is linked to the place inside the cochlea where a sound is detected.

✓ Frequency theory says the pitch we hear is linked to the frequency of nerve impulses generated by the cochlea.

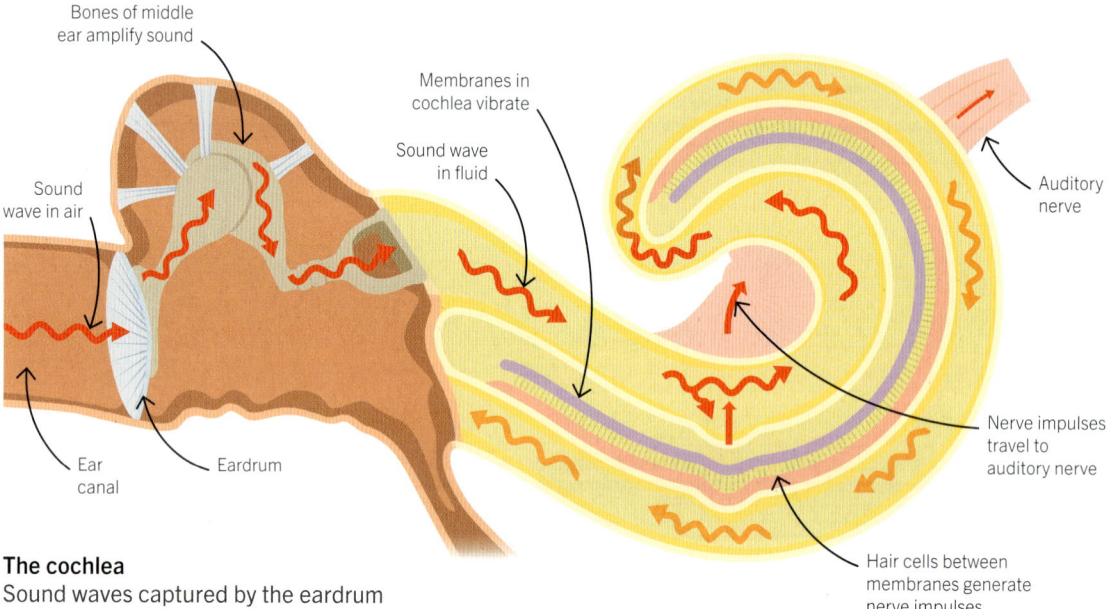

Bones of middle ear amplify sound

Membranes in cochlea vibrate

Sound wave in fluid

Sound wave in air

Auditory nerve

Ear canal

Eardrum

Nerve impulses travel to auditory nerve

Hair cells between membranes generate nerve impulses

The cochlea

Sound waves captured by the eardrum are transferred to the fluid-filled inner ear, where they travel into the cochlea. The waves cause a pair of membranes running the length of the cochlea to vibrate, deflecting microscopic hairs on sensory cells that send signals to the brain. According to "place theory", high-pitched sounds are detected at the start of the cochlea and lower sounds towards the end. According to the "frequency theory", pitch relates to the frequency of nerve impulses arriving at the brain from the cochlea.

🔍 Localizing sound

Just as two eyes give us binocular (3D) vision, two ears give us stereo hearing and allow us to pinpoint where sounds come from. Sound waves usually arrive at one ear slightly earlier and may be louder on one side too. The brain processes the lag and difference in intensity to work out where the sound came from.

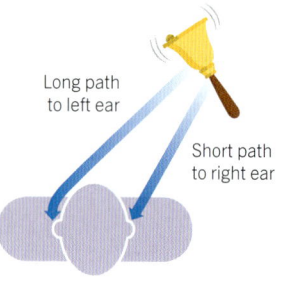

Long path to left ear

Short path to right ear

Hearing loss

Hearing loss affects most people at some point in their life, especially as they get older. There are two main categories: conductive and sensorineural. Conductive hearing loss occurs when sounds are not conducted through the delicate structures of the outer and middle ear. Sensorineural hearing loss occurs when the sensory cells of the inner ear or related nerves fail to respond to sound.

Cochlear implant
Hearing devices can support people with sensorineural hearing loss. Hearing aids amplify sound, whereas cochlear implants (right) bypass the outer and inner ear to stimulate the sound-detecting cochlea of the inner ear directly. Hearing devices are a personal choice and not the only way for people with hearing loss to communicate.

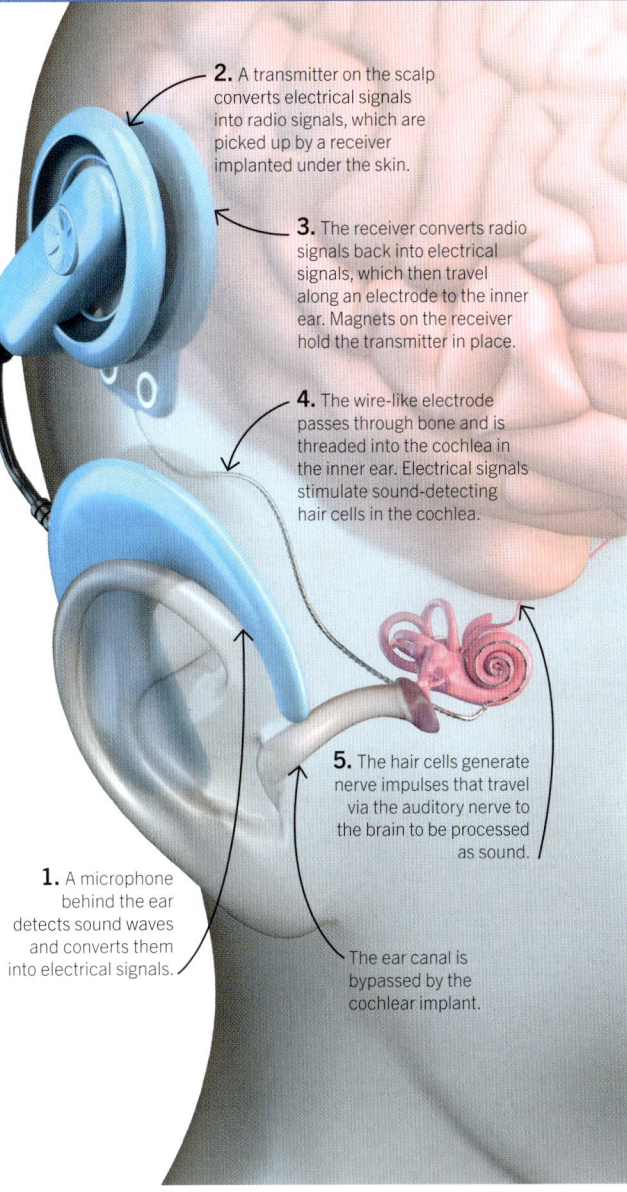

2. A transmitter on the scalp converts electrical signals into radio signals, which are picked up by a receiver implanted under the skin.

3. The receiver converts radio signals back into electrical signals, which then travel along an electrode to the inner ear. Magnets on the receiver hold the transmitter in place.

4. The wire-like electrode passes through bone and is threaded into the cochlea in the inner ear. Electrical signals stimulate sound-detecting hair cells in the cochlea.

5. The hair cells generate nerve impulses that travel via the auditory nerve to the brain to be processed as sound.

1. A microphone behind the ear detects sound waves and converts them into electrical signals.

The ear canal is bypassed by the cochlear implant.

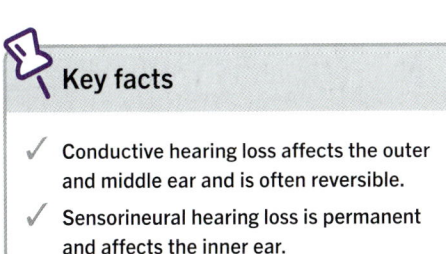

📌 Key facts

✓ Conductive hearing loss affects the outer and middle ear and is often reversible.

✓ Sensorineural hearing loss is permanent and affects the inner ear.

✓ Hearing devices can support those with sensorineural hearing loss.

🔍 Causes of hearing loss

Hearing loss has many causes, and some hearing loss is a natural consequence of ageing. Prolonged exposure to loud noise can also degrade hearing. Most hearing loss is sensorineural, which is permanent. Conductive hearing loss is often reversible.

Sensorineural
• Noise damage
• Ageing
• Drug side-effect
• Tumour
• Blast/explosion

Both
• Infection
• Genetic disorder
• Head injury

Conductive
• Ruptured eardrum
• Foreign object
• Impacted earwax
• Fluid in middle ear
• Allergies

Touch

Skin is sometimes described as the body's largest sensory organ. As well as giving us sensitivity to several different kinds of touch, skin also has receptors that detect heat, cold, and pain. Combinations of different receptors produce other sensations too, including itching, wetness, and the feeling of being tickled.

Key facts

✓ Receptors in the skin detect different types of touch, temperature, and pain.

✓ Combinations of different receptors can create sensations such as itching, wetness, and being tickled.

✓ Locations with more sensory receptors are more sensitive to touch.

✓ Touch sensations are processed in the somatosensory cortex of the brain.

Skin receptors
Touch is detected by specialized endings of sensory neurons in the skin. Also called receptors, these endings send the sensory information via the spinal cord to the somatosensory cortex in the brain.

Epidermis

Dermis

Hypodermis

Meissner endings respond to very light touch and fast vibrations.

Merkel endings sense medium levels of touch, pressure, and slow vibrations.

Ruffini endings react to being stretched and squeezed, and to changes in temperature.

Free nerve endings respond to light touch and pain.

A hair plexus at the base of each hair senses movement of the hair.

Pacinian corpuscles detect deep pressure and vibration.

🔍 Somatosensory cortex

Touch sensations are processed in the somatosensory cortex of the brain. This cortex runs across both the left and right hemispheres and is located in the parietal lobe.

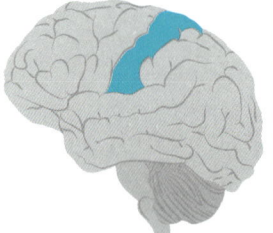

🔍 Cortical homunculus

Sensitive parts of the body, such as fingers and lips, are more densely packed with receptors. These areas map to larger areas of the somatosensory cortex than other body parts. This "cortical homunculus" shows body parts scaled in proportion to the area of cortex serving them.

Pain

Pain, though uncomfortable, is an essential function that protects us from harm. It is a warning that tells the body to avoid the stimulus that might cause injury.

Key facts

✓ Pain is an essential function that protects the body from harm.

✓ The sensation of pain is triggered by sensory receptors that detect tissue damage and send signals to the brain.

The pain pathway
Pain is detected by specialized sensory receptors (nociceptors) that detect tissue damage. They send signals via the spinal cord to the brain, which creates the conscious sensation of pain. Tissue damage also triggers a rapid reflex action that withdraws the affected part of the body from the painful stimulus, without needing input from the brain.

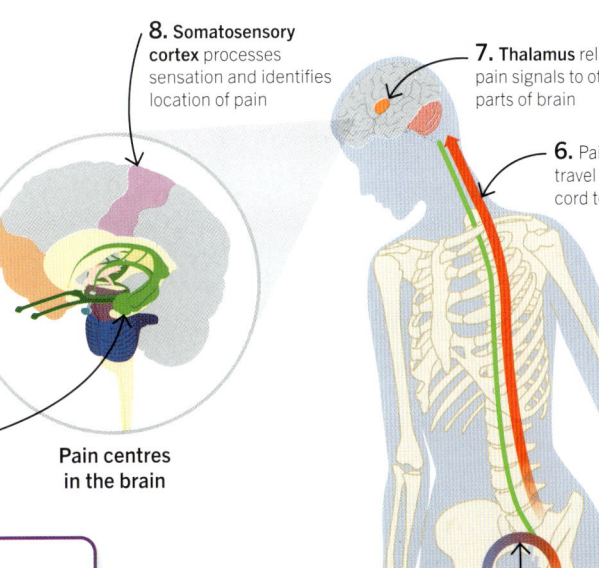

8. Somatosensory cortex processes sensation and identifies location of pain

7. Thalamus relays pain signals to other parts of brain

6. Pain signals travel along spinal cord to brain

9. Limbic system triggers threat response and emotional reaction

Pain centres in the brain

5. Leg muscles contract in reflex action to withdraw foot from stimulus

4. Spinal cord sends return motor signals to leg muscles

3. Sensory neurons carry nerve impulses to spinal cord

2. Nociceptors detect tissue damage

1. Foot stands on pin

🔍 Gate-control theory

Applying pressure, warmth, or cold, or rubbing skin at the site of an injury sometimes relieves pain. According to gate-control theory, this works because the spinal cord acts as a gate to sensory signals, blocking pain to let other competing sensory signals pass.

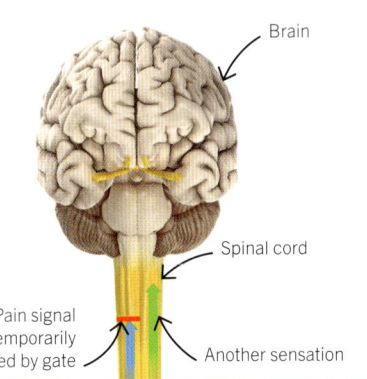

Brain

Spinal cord

Pain signal temporarily blocked by gate

Another sensation

Taste

Also called gustation, taste is a chemical sense. Sensory receptor cells in the tongue and other parts of the mouth respond to dissolved chemicals from food and transmit signals to the brain. We have only five basic chemical tastes. The complex tastes and flavours of different foods come from the senses of taste and smell working together.

Taste buds

The sense of taste comes from taste buds – clusters of sensory cells found on the sides of small bumps (papillae) on the tongue and other parts of the mouth. Microscopic hairs at the tips of the sensory cells detect certain chemicals in food and react by generating nerve impulses.

Key facts

✓ Like smell, taste is a chemical sense.

✓ Taste buds are clusters of chemical-detecting sensory cells. They are found in the mouth.

✓ Humans sense five basic tastes: salty, sweet, sour (acidic), bitter, and umami (savoury).

✓ Taste and smell combine to give food its complexity.

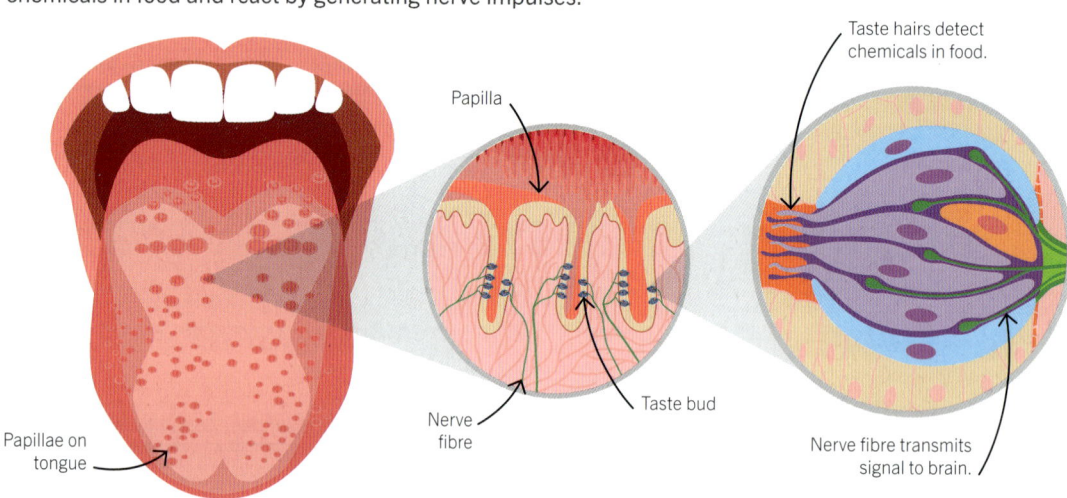

Taste hairs detect chemicals in food.

Papilla

Papillae on tongue

Nerve fibre

Taste bud

Nerve fibre transmits signal to brain.

🔍 Five tastes

Our taste buds sense five tastes, all caused by chemicals that dissolve in mucus in the mouth. Other compounds from food evaporate and travel via the back of the mouth to the nasal cavity, where they trigger smell receptors, adding complex flavours to what we eat.

Salty
Soluble minerals such as sodium chloride (table salt) are responsible for this taste.

Sweet
Foods such as fruit and honey taste sweet, which indicates that they contain sugars and are rich in energy.

Sour
This taste is caused by acids, which are found in many fruits but also in food that has soured.

Bitter
Bitterness is often a sign that food is inedible or toxic, but some edible substances are slightly bitter too.

Umami
This savoury taste indicates that a food is protein-rich. Umami foods include fish, soya, and seaweed.

Smell

Also called olfaction, smell is a chemical sense. Sensory cells in the nose detect airborne odour molecules and send nerve impulses to the brain. Smells can alert us to danger; for instance, by telling us when food is rotten and unsafe to eat. Smells are also associated with emotions and memories.

How smell works

Odour molecules pass through the nose as we breathe. Some of them stick to cilia (microscopic hairs) on sensory receptor cells in the roof of the nasal cavity, triggering nerve impulses. These impulses travel along nerve fibres that cross the skull to the olfactory bulb at the base of the brain, from where they are relayed to various parts of the brain, including the amygdala (which detects danger); the hippocampus (which processes memory); and the olfactory cortex, which relays information to other areas of the brain, including the frontal cortex.

Key facts

✓ Smell is a chemical sense, like taste.

✓ Receptor cells inside the nose detect odour molecules and transmit information about them to the brain for interpretation.

✓ Smells can warn us of danger and trigger emotions and memories.

🔎 Smell as association

How smells are perceived depends on cultural experience. One study found that the smell of wintergreen evoked a positive response in the USA, where the plant's oil is used in sweets. In the UK, however, it reminded people of medicine and was found less appealing.

The amygdala screens incoming sensory information for danger and, if appropriate, triggers the body's flight-or-fight response.

The olfactory tract carries nerve impulses from the olfactory bulb to the brain.

The olfactory bulb at the base of the brain is directly connected to odour-detecting cells in the nose.

The olfactory epithelium in the roof of the naval cavity contains sensory receptors that respond to odour molecules.

Odour molecules can enter the nasal cavity through the nostrils or from the back of the mouth.

Proprioception

Proprioception is the body's ability to sense its position, posture, and motion, using sensory cells embedded in muscles, joints, and other tissues. It is the reason we can walk, hop, skip, and stay balanced even when lifting a heavy weight. It happens mostly unconsciously.

Key facts

✓ Sensory cells called proprioceptors throughout the body provide feedback to the brain whenever the body moves.

✓ The vestibular system in the inner ear works with proprioceptors to help with balance and movement.

The vestibular system

The vestibular system in the inner ear provides the brain with information about balance and motion. Three fluid-filled semicircular canals detect rotational movements of the head, and tiny weighted organs called otoliths detect linear accelerations and gravity.

Semicircular canals detect rotation.

The cochlea detects sound.

The otoliths within vestibule detect linear movement.

Inner ear

The somatosensory area of the brain receives sensory information from the body.

The eyes send visual information about the position of the body.

The inner ear sends the brain information about motion and gravity.

Signals from proprioceptors throughout the body travel up the spinal cord.

Stretch receptors in the skin detect movement.

Sensory nerves carry information from proprioceptors to the brain.

Joints
Nerve endings within a joint detect its position and prevent overextension, which might injure the joint.

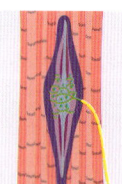

Muscles
Sensors called spindle fibres in muscles send information to the brain when muscles stretch.

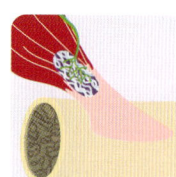

Tendons
Receptors within the tendons at the ends of muscles monitor muscle tension to prevent overstretching.

The proprioceptive system

Sensory cells called proprioceptors are located in muscles, joints, tendons, ligaments, and skin. Triggered by stretching or pressure, they send signals to the brain whenever muscles work, giving feedback about the body's movement.

Interacting senses

Senses don't work in isolation – they influence each other. This is called sensory interaction. For example, the way food tastes depends not just on taste buds on the tongue but also on scent detectors in the nose, and on touch and temperature receptors in the mouth. All these different sensory inputs combine in the brain to create a unified experience.

Thresholds and adaptation
Our bodies are continually bombarded with sensory information, and our brains must decide which signals deserve conscious attention. We only perceive stimuli above a certain threshold. A stimulus strong enough to be noticed on 50 per cent of occasions is said to be at the absolute threshold. Stimuli we notice less than this are called subliminal. A repeated or constant stimulus soon fades, which is called sensory adaptation. For instance, after we have first smelled the scent of a flower it appears to fade.

Key facts

✓ Senses interact with and influence each other.

✓ A stimulus noticed on 50 per cent of occasions is at the absolute threshold.

✓ Sensory adaptation is when a repeated stimulus fades.

✓ Synaesthesia is when one sense triggers another.

The scent of nearby flowers fades over time.

The brain combines information from multiple senses.

Our senses of taste, smell, touch, and temperature all combine as we eat ice cream.

The sight of birds makes their songs more noticeable – vision and hearing interact.

Touching the dog enhances our awareness of its sound and smell.

🔍 Synaesthesia

A small number of people experience synaesthesia, which is when one sense triggers another. For example, musical notes are perceived by some as having different colours.

Adaptation-level phenomenon

Adaptation-level phenomenon is the tendency of people to adapt to new situations or new stimuli until they become the new normal. For example, the sensation of wearing socks is strong when we first put them on but quickly fades until we don't notice them. Each stimulus is evaluated against prior experience, and repeated experience can raise the threshold for what feels new or noticeable.

Key facts

✓ Adaptation-level phenomenon is the tendency to adapt to a new situation or stimulus until it is no longer noticeable.

✓ Dishabituation is when a stimulus we have adapted (become habituated) to becomes noticeable again.

✓ According to the theory of hedonic adaptation, we quickly return to a "happiness set point" after good news or bad news.

Adapting to noise

Imagine moving from a quiet neighbourhood to a home near a busy railway line. At first the noise would seem loud and intrusive, but after a few days you would barely notice it. Repeated exposure makes the sound seem normal, reducing how much attention you pay to it. The process of becoming less responsive to a stimulus is also called habituation. The reverse – dishabituation – can also occur. For example, a visitor pointing out that the trains are loud would make them noticeable again.

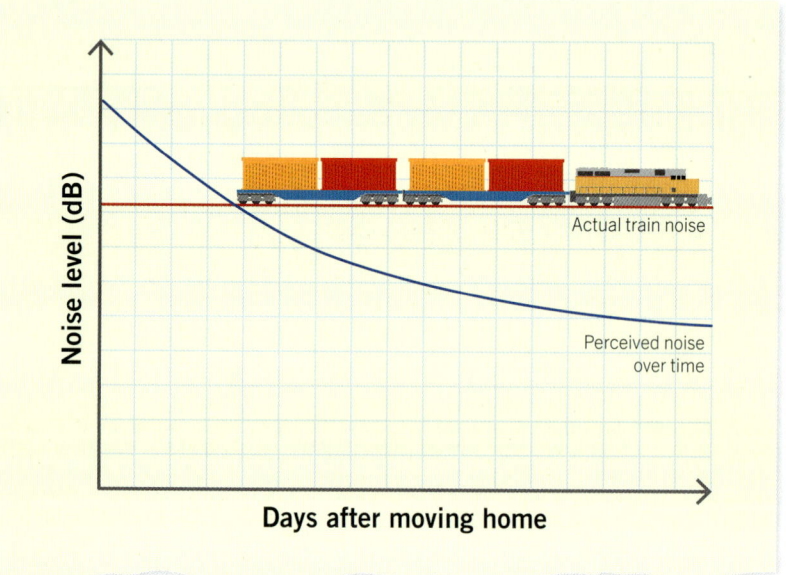

Actual train noise

Perceived noise over time

Days after moving home

🔍 Hedonic adaptation

According to the theory of hedonic adaptation, we have a tendency to quickly revert to a "happiness set point" after an emotional event, be it positive or negative. For example, on receiving a pay rise or making a major purchase, we initially feel a surge of happiness, but this subsides within days. Hedonic adaptation is often described as a treadmill, with the pursuit of wealth, status, or material goods resulting in no lasting change to how happy we are.

No matter how hard we try to be happier, we stay in the same place.

Chapter 4
Learning bases of behaviour

Stimulus-response learning

The behaviourist approach to psychology is based on stimulus-response learning. This is the idea that all behaviour can be explained as the result of the interaction between a stimulus (something in the environment) and the response it produces. Behavioural psychologists have often studied animals, arguing that they learn new behaviours in a similar way to humans.

Key facts

✓ According to stimulus-response learning theory, all behaviour is the result of interactions between stimuli (something in the environment) and the responses produced.

✓ Thorndike proposed that responses producing a satisfying effect are more likely to happen again.

Thorndike's puzzle box (1898)
US psychologist Edward L. Thorndike measured the time it took a cat to escape from a "puzzle box" he designed. By chance, the cat discovered a lever that opened an escape door when pressed. Realizing that pressing the lever resulted in a satisfying effect, the cat did it faster each time it was put inside the box.

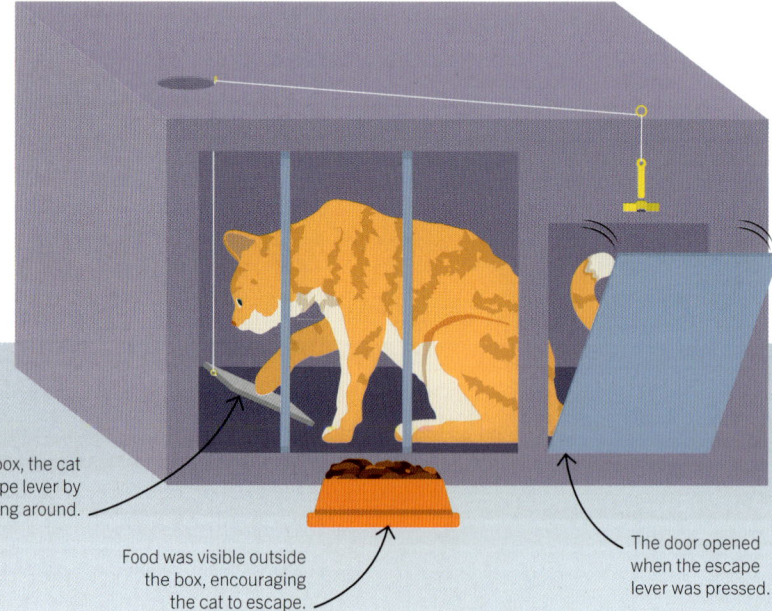

Trapped inside the box, the cat discovered the escape lever by accident, while moving around.

Food was visible outside the box, encouraging the cat to escape.

The door opened when the escape lever was pressed.

🔍 Human example

Examples of humans learning behaviours in response to stimuli are clear to see in everyday life, such as when we first learn how to respond to the stimulus of coloured lights when crossing a road. We learn at a young age that red means stop and green means go.

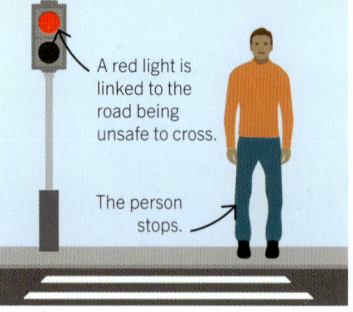

A red light is linked to the road being unsafe to cross.

The person stops.

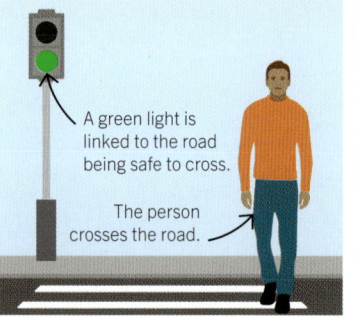

A green light is linked to the road being safe to cross.

The person crosses the road.

Classical conditioning

Classical conditioning is defined as learning by association. It describes how associations are conditioned (taught) between a neutral stimulus, to which there is no pre-existing response, and another stimulus, to which there is a pre-existing, instinctive response. Initially, the process of classical conditioning was described in dogs, but some psychologists have since used it to explain how humans learn, too.

Pavlov's dogs (1897)
Russian physiologist Ivan Pavlov studied digestion in dogs. He noticed that they often started salivating before food was placed in front of them, and sometimes just at the sight of the technician who fed them. The dogs had begun to associate the technician with food. No new behaviours were learned, but the technician had become a new reason for the dogs to display the existing reflex of salivation.

Key facts

✓ Classical conditioning is learning by association.

✓ The association is between a neutral stimulus and another stimulus, to which there is an instinctive response.

✓ After conditioning, the neutral stimulus becomes a conditioned stimulus because it produces a conditioned response.

1. Natural state
Dogs naturally salivate in response to food. Food can be described as an unconditioned stimulus (UCS). Salivation can be referred to as an unconditioned response (UCR).

Unconditioned stimulus
Food makes the dog salivate.

Unconditioned response
The dog naturally salivates when it sees food.

2. Before conditioning
A ringing bell does not naturally cause a dog to salivate. It is referred to as a neutral stimulus (NS).

Neutral stimulus
The bell does not cause the dog to salivate.

No response
The dog does not salivate.

3. During conditioning
Pavlov began to ring the bell each time the dog was presented with food. He did this repeatedly until the dog learned to associate the sound of the bell with food.

Neutral stimulus
The bell does not cause the dog to salivate.

Unconditioned response
The dog salivates when it sees food.

Unconditioned stimulus
Food makes the dog salivate.

4. After conditioning
Eventually, ringing the bell without food made the dog salivate. The bell became a conditioned stimulus (CS). Salivation became a conditioned response (CR) – a learned response to the stimulus of the bell.

Conditioned stimulus
The bell now causes the dog to salivate.

Conditioned response
The dog salivates when it hears the ringing bell.

Operant conditioning

US psychologist B.F. Skinner also studied animal behaviour. He argued that animals produce spontaneous behaviours called operants. When an operant leads to positive consequences it is reinforced (in other words, rewarded), making it more likely the behaviour will be repeated.

Key facts

✓ Operant conditioning is learning by consequence.

✓ Reinforcement makes it more likely that the behaviour will happen again.

✓ Positive reinforcement is the addition of something pleasant.

✓ Negative reinforcement is the removal of something unpleasant.

Skinner's rats

Skinner placed a rat in a purpose-built chamber, now known as a "Skinner box". The rat moved around, exploring its new environment until, by chance, it pressed a lever that triggered the release of a food pellet. It continued to explore that area, pressed the lever again, and received more food. Over time, the rat was conditioned (taught) by reinforcement (food) to reproduce the operant (lever-pressing).

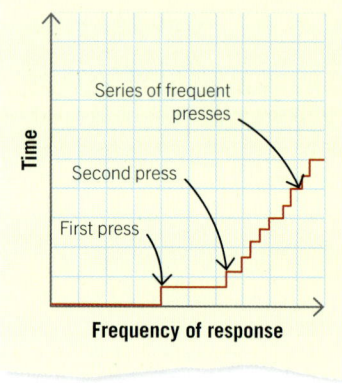

Series of frequent presses

Second press

First press

Time

Frequency of response

Response data
The lever in the Skinner box was connected to a device called a cumulative recorder, which recorded the frequency of presses. The rat's first press took a while, but after reinforcement, the behaviour was repeated with increasing frequency.

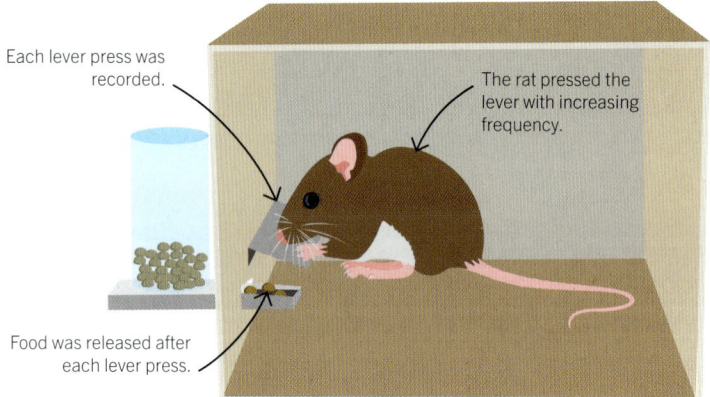

Each lever press was recorded.

The rat pressed the lever with increasing frequency.

Food was released after each lever press.

🔍 Types of reinforcement

Skinner identified two types of reinforcement – positive and negative. Positive reinforcement is the addition of something, while negative reinforcement is taking something away.

Positive reinforcement
When a behaviour is followed by the addition of something pleasant, it feels like a reward – for example, being praised for good work at school. This pleasurable outcome makes it more likely that the behaviour will be repeated.

Negative reinforcement
When a behaviour is followed by the removal of something unpleasant, it feels like a relief – for example, putting on a coat and scarf in cold weather. This pleasurable outcome makes it more likely that the behaviour will be repeated.

Contingencies of reinforcement

Basic operant conditioning involves two elements: behaviour followed by consequence. However, for some behaviours to result in reinforcement, an extra condition – known as an antecedent – must first be present. Whether reinforcement is given is contingent (dependent) on the present of the antecedent.

Key facts

✓ When a behaviour is reinforced only if a certain condition is present (an antecedent), that reinforcement is referred to as contingent (dependent).

✓ Contingencies of reinforcement help to explain how we learn to behave differently in different situations.

Skinner's rats again
To study contingencies of reinforcement, Skinner adapted his Skinner box so that pressing the lever released food for the rat only when a light was on. The rat soon learned not to press the lever if the light was off. It had realized that receiving food after pressing the lever was contingent on the light shining.

1. Antecedent
The light is on.

2. Behaviour
The rat presses the lever.

Three-term contingency
In a three-term contingency, an antecedent (A) must be in place before a behaviour (B) will produce the consequence (C) of reinforcement.

3. Consequence
A food pellet is dispensed.

Antecedent (A)	Behaviour (B)	Consequence (C)
An extra condition that prompts a behaviour (B) to occur.	The action triggered by the antecedent (A).	The outcome of the behaviour (B). It will only occur if the antecedent (A) is present.

🔍 Human example

Basic operant conditioning explains why people and animals repeat behaviours, but it does not account for how they learn to behave differently at different times. By recognizing antecedents – conditions on which reinforcement is contingent – it is possible to understand why people change their behaviour depending on the situation.

Sharing a ball in the playground
A child has learned to share a ball with other children when in the school playground. The antecedent is the playground. The sharing is reinforced by praise from the teacher.

Taking a ball on the sports field
But when playing sport, the child has learned to take the ball from their opponent, not to share it. The antecedent is the sports field. Taking the ball is reinforced by scoring points.

Schedules of reinforcement

Skinner also experimented with different ways of organizing when reinforcement was received, known as schedules of reinforcement (SOR). He wanted to find out if changing the reinforcement pattern affected behaviour. To do this, he adapted his Skinner box, originally used to experiment with rats, to test pigeons instead.

Key facts

✓ Reinforcement can be given according to different schedules.

✓ Fixed schedules are predictable; variable schedules are unpredictable.

✓ Ratio schedules base reinforcement on the number of times a behaviour is performed; interval schedules are based on the time periods between reinforcements.

Adapted Skinner box

Disc to peck for food

Food dispenser

Testing schedules of reinforcement

Like the rat, the pigeon had to perform a behaviour (pecking a disc) to receive a reinforcer (a food pellet). However, this time Skinner varied when the pigeon was given reinforcement. He tested different schedules on the pigeon to measure the effects on the response rate (how fast the behaviour appeared) and the extinction rate (how fast the behaviour died out).

SOR	Explanation	Response rate	Extinction rate	Human example
Continuous reinforcement (CR)	The reinforcer is received every time the behaviour is performed.	Fast: the pigeon quickly notices that pecking the disc results in a food pellet.	Fast: easy to notice that reinforcement has stopped.	A child receives a treat for every word they spell correctly.
Fixed-ratio schedule (FR)	The reinforcer is received after a set number of times a behaviour is performed.	Fast: the pigeon soon learns the number of pecks required to receive a food pellet.	Medium: harder to notice that reinforcement has stopped than in CR schedule.	A child receives a treat for every 10 words they spell correctly.
Variable-ratio schedule (VR)	The reinforcer is received after a random (unpredictable) number of times a behaviour is performed.	Very fast: unpredictability encourages the pigeon to peck more to avoid missing a food pellet.	Very slow: unpredictability makes it hard to notice that reinforcement has stopped.	A child receives a treat for a varying number of words they spell correctly.
Fixed-interval schedule (FI)	The reinforcer is received after a predictable time interval.	Slow just after reinforcement, but fast when next reinforcement is due.	Medium: harder to notice that reinforcement has stopped than in CR; easier than variable schedule.	A child receives a treat for every 20 minutes of spelling practice.
Variable-interval schedule (VI)	The reinforcer is received after random (unpredictable) time intervals.	Fast: unpredictability encourages the pigeon to peck frequently, but not as often as in VR schedule.	Very slow: unpredictability makes it hard to notice that reinforcement has stopped.	A child receives a treat at random points during spelling practice.

Extinction and spontaneous recovery

Animals and humans learn new behaviours by forming associations between stimuli – a process known as classical conditioning (see page 81). If the association between the stimuli is removed, the behaviour (known as the conditioned response) will gradually weaken and eventually be lost. Psychologists call this loss of the conditioned response extinction. In some cases, however, the response can reappear spontaneously for no obvious reason. This unexplained recurrence is known as spontaneous recovery.

Key facts

✓ Behaviour can be learned through acquiring an association between two separate stimuli.

✓ If the association between the two stimuli is broken, then the behaviour dies out.

✓ The original behaviour can sometimes reappear for no apparent reason – this is known as spontaneous recovery.

Conditioned stimulus

The dog associates the bell with food and begins to salivate.

Unconditioned stimulus

Conditioned stimulus

The dog does not salivate any more when the bell rings.

Conditioned stimulus

Sometimes the conditioned response spontaneously reoccurs without reason.

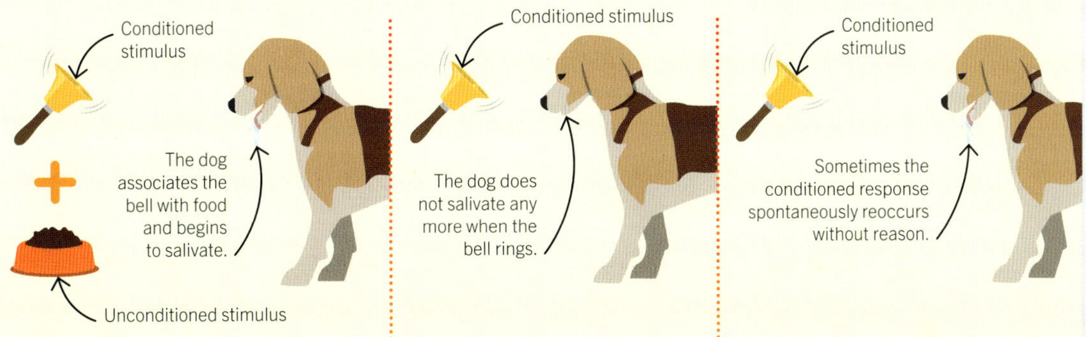

1. Acquisition
A neutral stimulus – a ringing bell – is paired with an unconditioned stimulus (UCS) – the food. The dog starts to produce a conditioned response, salivating when the bell rings. The bell is now a conditioned stimulus (CS).

2. Extinction
If food is then repeatedly presented without the bell ringing, the association between the UCS and the CS weakens and is eventually extinguished. The dog stops salivating when it hears the bell. The conditioned response is extinct.

3. Spontaneous recovery
Although it appears to have been extinguished, the conditioned response can reoccur unexpectedly – the dog salivates again. This is called spontaneous recovery. The association between the UCS and CS has not been lost completely.

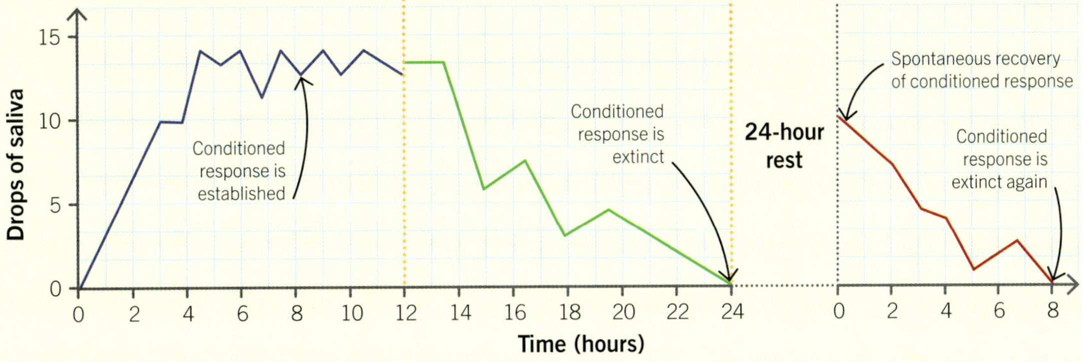

Conditioned response is established

Conditioned response is extinct

24-hour rest

Spontaneous recovery of conditioned response

Conditioned response is extinct again

Drops of saliva

Time (hours)

Social learning theory

Behaviourist theories of learning, such as classical and operant conditioning, focused on learning through direct experience. However, Canadian–American psychologist Albert Bandura's social learning theory (1961) proposed that people learn behaviours by watching others. Bandura suggested that it is possible to learn behaviour indirectly by observing and imitating other people, including those we see in the media.

The Bobo doll experiment
Bandura proposed his social learning theory after observing children interacting with a large inflatable toy, known as a Bobo doll. The clown-like doll bounced back up each time it was knocked down.

Experiment 1
1. Sitting in a playroom, a child watched as an adult, referred to in the experiment as the model, behaved in an aggressive way towards the Bobo doll, throwing, kicking, punching, and sitting on it.

2. Left alone, the child imitated the aggressive behaviours they had seen the model use towards the Bobo doll. Bandura found that children are more likely to imitate models of the same sex than of the opposite sex.

Experiment 2
1. Separately, another child observed the same adult behaving in a different way. This time, the model sat quietly and read or played with other toys, showing little interest in the Bobo doll.

2. The child who observed the non-aggressive model went on to show almost no aggression towards the Bobo doll.

> ## Key facts
>
> ✓ Social learning theory proposes that we learn through observing others and imitating their behaviour.
> ✓ People are more likely to imitate role models they identify with.
> ✓ Imitation is more likely when a person sees another person's behaviour being reinforced (known as vicarious reinforcement).

🔍 Reciprocal determinism

Bandura disagreed with behavioural psychologists who think that all behaviour is the result of environmental influence. He argued instead that personal factors (thoughts and feelings) influence behaviour as well as the environment, and that in turn behaviour influences the environment and personal factors. Each of these three factors affects and is affected by the others. Bandura's theory is known as reciprocal determinism.

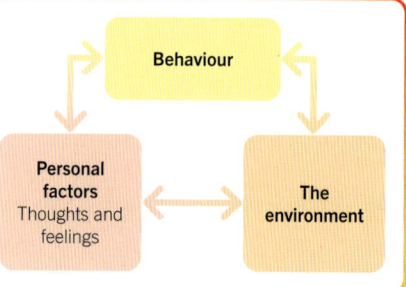

Behaviour

Personal factors
Thoughts and feelings

The environment

Mediational processes

According to social learning theory (see page 86), people do not automatically copy behaviour they have observed. Instead, four mediational processes must take place after observing a behaviour (the input). These processes influence whether or not we will imitate the behaviour (the output).

Input

We observe the behaviour of another person (the model).

1. Attention
"Look at that trick!"

We will only try to imitate a behaviour if it has caught our attention.

2. Retention
"I must remember that."

We will only imitate behaviours we remember. We forget many of the behaviours we see.

Output

The mediational processes determine whether or not we will imitate the behaviour.

4. Motivation
"I could win a competition if I did that."

We must be motivated to recreate the behaviour we have observed. If we think there is a good reward, we are more likely to imitate it.

3. Reproduction
"I think with practice I can do that, too."

We are more likely to imitate the behaviour if we think we have the ability to do it as well. If a person lacks similar skills, they are unlikely to try.

🔍 Vicarious reinforcement

If a person watches someone else being reinforced for a behaviour (vicarious reinforcement), they are more likely to imitate that behaviour themselves. For example, a child seeing another pupil receive praise for putting their hand up is more likely also to raise their hand.

Well done for putting your hand up!

One child raises their hand to answer a question.

The teacher praises the child for putting up their hand.

The other child is vicariously reinforced and also puts their hand up.

Chapter 5
Cognitive psychology: memory

Coding information

Huge amounts of information about the world come to us from our senses. Coding is the first part of the process of turning this raw data into a form that can be stored as a memory, so that it can be retrieved and made use of again at a later date. Memories can be coded and stored visually, acoustically, and semantically.

Key facts

✓ Coding is the first step in turning information taken in by our senses into memories.

✓ Information can be coded visually, acoustically, or semantically.

✓ Coding in short-term memory is mainly acoustic.

✓ Coding in long-term memory is mainly semantic.

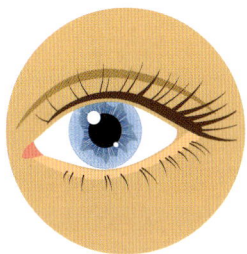

Iconic (visual) memory
The brain receives a constant stream of visual information. The iconic memory fleetingly stores these images. Information coded as iconic memories starts to decay (is lost) in less than a second.

Echoic (acoustic) memory
Auditory information (sounds) is coded and stored as echoic memories. These memories last slightly longer than iconic memories, starting to decay after 3–4 seconds.

Semantic coding
Converting raw information into meaningful memories by connecting it to existing knowledge is called semantic coding. Semantic coding forms the longest-lasting memories because we have processed them more deeply than iconic or echoic memories.

🔍 Baddeley's coding research

In 1966, British psychologist Alan Baddeley conducted research into how well participants remembered a list of words in order. Their recall was tested immediately after memorizing the list to test coding for short-term memory (STM), and after 20 minutes to test coding for long-term memory (LTM).

Recall results	Conclusion
Immediately after memorizing the list, participants found it easy to remember acoustically different words (e.g. bottle, fire, leap) in order, but hard to remember acoustically similar words (e.g. hat, cat, bat, flat).	Baddeley concluded that coding in STM is mainly acoustic (by sound) as words that sound similar conflict with each other, leading to poorer recall.
After 20 minutes, participants found it easy to remember semantically different words (e.g. bird, walk, ring) in order, but hard to remember semantically similar words (e.g. great, large, big).	Baddeley concluded that coding in LTM is mainly semantic (by meaning) as words with similar meanings conflict with each other, leading to poorer recall.

Memory models

Cognitive psychologists use theoretical models (frameworks) to describe how they believe memory and other internal processes, such as thought and perception, work. They argue that the human mind and computers process information similarly. To explain, they create computer models, a type of theoretical model, which break down mental processes into the same distinct steps a computer would use.

Information-processing models

One type of computer model is the information-processing model. According to this, making a memory is a sequence involving three stages: input, process, and output. Just like how a computer processes information, so too the human mind takes in information from the environment, processes it, then responds accordingly.

 Key facts

✓ Cognitive psychologists use theoretical models (frameworks) to explain internal processes such as memory.

✓ Computer models explain how the human mind functions by comparing it to computers.

✓ According to the information-processing model, memory comprises three basic stages: input, processing, and output.

 Brains and computers

Comparing the human brain to a computer can be misleading because, unlike computers, humans are easily influenced by emotion, and their memories can be distorted.

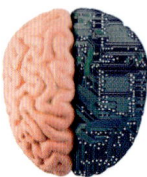

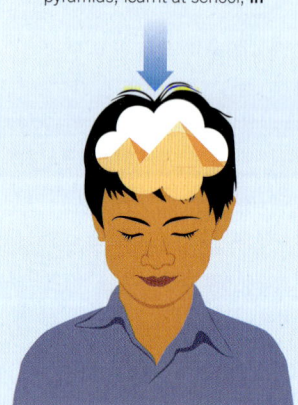

Information about the ancient pyramids, learnt at school, **in**

Input
Information must be processed in order to be retained. It is coded into a form that is easier to remember.

Information about the ancient pyramids **stored**

Processing
To remember a piece of information, we must retain it by processing, or thinking about, it. Different types of information can be stored for varying durations (lengths of time).

Information about the ancient pyramids back **out**

Output
Accessing the information again is called retrieval. Not all information is easily retrieved and sometimes we need a reminder to help us get to it.

The multi-store model of memory

In 1968, US psychologists Richard Atkinson and Richard Shiffrin proposed the multi-store model (MSM) to explain how memory works. According to the MSM, memory is formed of three storage systems: the sensory register, short-term memory (STM), and long-term memory (LTM). Each of these systems codes information differently and varies in its capacity and duration.

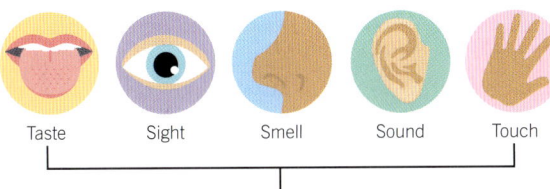

| Taste | Sight | Smell | Sound | Touch |

Sensory register
Information received from each of the senses enters the sensory register, which has separate stores for different sense inputs. A lot of uncoded information can be stored here but it decays (is lost) very quickly, in seconds or less. Information that has been paid attention to is transferred to the STM.

Attention is given to some information

Short-term memory (STM)
Information received from the sensory register is stored temporarily in the STM, where it is coded to make it easier to manage. The STM can store 7+/-2 items of information, for up to 30 seconds. After 30 seconds, the information decays unless it is rehearsed (repeated) and transferred to the LTM.

Rehearsal (mentally or vocally repeating information to extend duration)

Information can be retrieved from LTM back to STM

Effortful rehearsal (consciously try to remember information)

Long-term memory (LTM)
Information that is sufficiently rehearsed is transferred to the LTM, which can store an unlimited amount of information potentially for as long as the person lives. Coding in the LTM is primarily semantic. When information in the LTM is needed, it is transferred to the STM. Information in the LTM can decay over time.

Key facts

✓ The multi-store model proposes that memory is formed of three storage systems: the sensory register, short-term memory, and long-term memory.

✓ Each system has a different capacity (amount of information it can hold) and duration (time it can hold information for).

✓ Information is only transferred to the LTM if it is rehearsed (repeated).

The case of H.M.

Henry Molaison (known as H.M. while he was alive) had brain surgery in 1953 to treat severe epilepsy. The surgery resulted in the removal of 50 per cent of his hippocampus. Afterwards, Molaison could no longer form new memories, although his long-term memories from before the surgery remained intact. His case supports the idea that the STM and LTM are two separate stores.

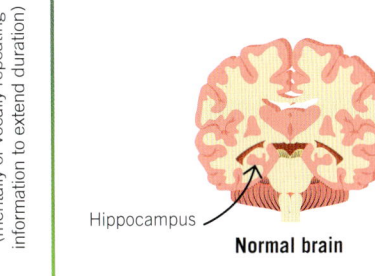

Hippocampus

Normal brain

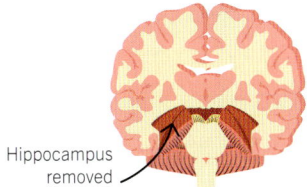

Hippocampus removed

H.M.'s brain

The serial position effect

Our memory stores information in a sequence. We tend to remember the first and last things in the sequence, such as items in a list, better than the things in the middle. This phenomenon is known as the serial position effect. The serial position effect has been used as evidence to support the multi-store model (see page 91), which suggests that there are separate stores for short- and long-term memory, each with different durations and capacities.

Testing the serial position effect
Glanzer and Cunitz (1966) tested the serial position effect by giving participants a number of words to remember and then asking them to recall them in any order. The results reliably fell into a pattern known as the serial position curve.

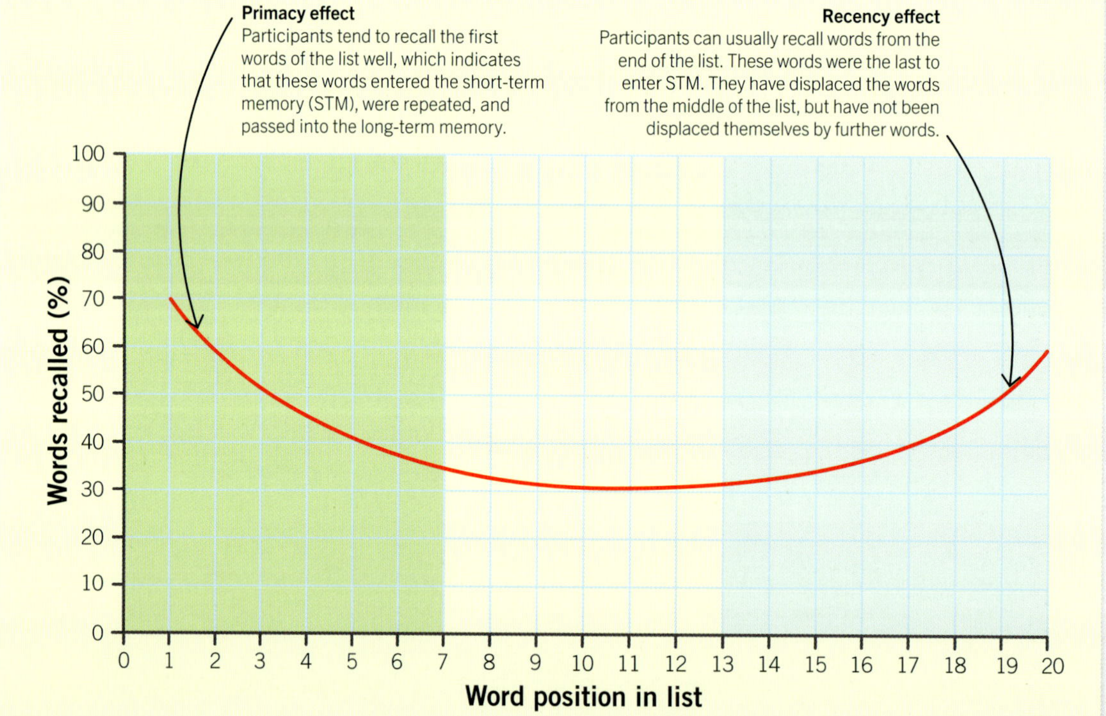

Key facts

✓ When participants memorize a list of words, recall is typically better for words at the beginning or end of the list than those in the middle.

✓ Words early in the list tend to be rehearsed, so they pass from short- to long-term memory, making them easier to recall (the primacy effect).

✓ Words towards the end of the list are still in the short-term memory when the participant is tested, so are easier to recall (the recency effect).

Primacy effect
Participants tend to recall the first words of the list well, which indicates that these words entered the short-term memory (STM), were repeated, and passed into the long-term memory.

Recency effect
Participants can usually recall words from the end of the list. These words were the last to enter STM. They have displaced the words from the middle of the list, but have not been displaced themselves by further words.

Words recalled (%) / Word position in list

The working memory model

The working memory model (WMM) was proposed by British psychologists Alan Baddeley and Graham Hitch in 1974. They disagreed with the multi-store model, arguing that short-term memory (STM) did more than just store information before it is transferred to long-term memory. They proposed instead that the STM actively processes information, hence the name "working" memory model. According to the WMM, the STM is formed of a central executive that controls two "slave" systems.

Key facts

✓ The working memory model proposes that short-term memory (STM) is an active store, formed of multiple parts.

✓ The central executive organizes the STM.

✓ The central executive controls its slave systems: the phonological loop, visuo-spatial sketchpad, and episodic buffer.

✓ The episodic buffer integrates information from the STM and sends it to the long-term memory.

Central executive
The central executive decides what sensory information should receive attention. It sends this information to its slave systems to store temporarily. The central executive has limited storage capacity.

Phonological loop
This slave system manages auditory information. It is formed of the **primary acoustic store** (the "inner ear"), which stores sounds we hear, and the **articulatory process** (the "inner voice"), which stores the words we are preparing to speak. It has limited storage capacity.

Episodic buffer
The episodic buffer pulls information from all parts of the STM and sends it to the long-term memory.

Information from the episodic buffer is passed to the LTM.

Visuo-spatial sketchpad
This slave system manages visual information. It is formed of the **visual cache** (the "inner eye"), which stores what objects look like, including their shape and form, and the **inner scribe,** which stores spatial information (the physical relationship between objects). It has limited storage capacity.

Long-term memory (LTM)

🔍 The dual-task technique

Baddeley et al. (1975) studied whether working memory can complete more than one task at a time. It was found that participants could perform a visual and verbal task at once, but they struggled to do two visual tasks at once. Baddeley proposed that the separate visual and verbal systems can manage two tasks simultaneously if different slave systems are involved, but they become overloaded if both tasks require the same system.

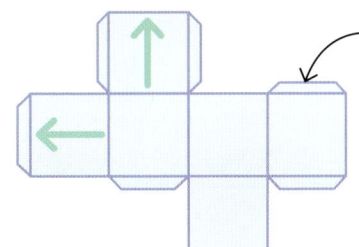

Participants had to mentally fold up cube nets to work out whether the arrows would touch (a visual task), while speaking (a verbal task).

Types of long-term memory

Like short-term memory, long-term memory (LTM) is thought to be made up of multiple stores, each with different features. LTM can be divided into two broad types: explicit and implicit. Whether memories are explicit or implicit depends on whether or not we can express them using words.

Key facts

✓ There are multiple types of LTM.

✓ Explicit memory is declarative – it can be expressed using words.

✓ Implicit memory is non-declarative – it cannot be expressed using words.

✓ Priming is when exposure to one stimulus affects the response to a later stimulus.

Explicit long-term memory
Explicit memories are declarative – we can say what they are using words. They are recalled using conscious effort. Two types of explicit memories include episodic and semantic.

Implicit long-term memory
Implicit memories are non-declarative – we cannot use words to say what they are. They do not require conscious thought to recall them. Implicit memories give us knowledge of how to do things.

Episodic memory
This memory acts as a mental autobiography or diary – it stores information about experiences, the things that happen to us. Episodic memories are linked to particular events, such as a birthday party.

Semantic memory
This memory is a mental encyclopedia of everything we have learned about the world – it is full of general knowledge, facts, figures, and meanings. Recalling semantic memories requires effort.

Procedural memory
This memory allows us to perform actions without conscious thought or effort to recall. Habits and skills such as knowing how to get dressed or pedal a bike are procedural memories.

🔎 Priming

Priming is another type of implicit long-term memory. It happens when exposure to one stimulus affects the response we give to a later stimulus. For instance, if you are given a yellow piece of paper that asks you to name a fruit, the word "banana" is likely to spring to mind because the words "yellow" and "fruit" are already linked in your memory.

Name a fruit.

"Banana"

Mnemonics

From schoolwork to shopping lists, it can be hard to remember everything we need to, but there are ways to boost memory capacity. Mnemonics are aids or techniques that can increase our ability to store and recall information.

The method of loci

This type of mnemonic involves associating information with points along a familiar journey to improve recall. It works by connecting the information with existing knowledge – a process known as elaborate rehearsal. To remember a shopping list, visualize yourself moving around your home. In each room of the house, imagine the food items you need to buy. To recall the information later, mentally walk the same route again and you'll remember all the food items.

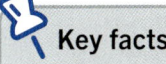

Key facts

✓ Mnemonics are aids or techniques that can help us to remember things.

✓ The method of loci technique works by connecting new information with existing knowledge.

✓ Chunking is breaking down information into manageable amounts.

Vivid images can help us remember information as the brain easily recalls mental pictures.

1. Bedroom
"I peeled a **banana** in bed."

2. Office
"I ate a **mango** while studying."

3. Bedroom
"I dropped **honey** on the bedroom floor."

4. Bathroom
"I washed **blueberries** in the shower."

5. Living room
"I drank **milk** while watching TV."

6. Hallway
"I spilled **oats** in the hallway."

7. Kitchen
"I put **strawberries** in the fridge."

Chunking

Remembering a long, unrelated string of letters or numbers is tricky, but grouping them – a technique known as chunking – can help. Short-term memory capacity is limited to 7+/-2 items (see page 91), but chunking allows this capacity to be increased because each "chunk" is made up of multiple items.

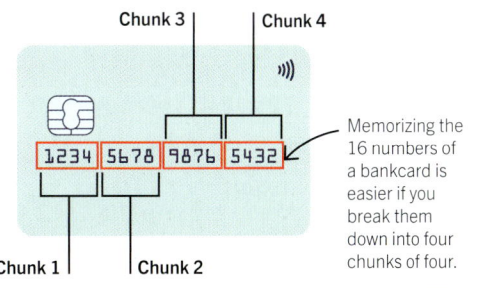

Chunk 3   Chunk 4

1234 5678 9876 5432

Chunk 1   Chunk 2

Memorizing the 16 numbers of a bankcard is easier if you break them down into four chunks of four.

Forgetting

Forgetting is the failure to retrieve memories. Psychologists have proposed different explanations for why this retrieval failure happens. It may occur because the information decays over time, or because we are unable to access the stored information.

Interference theory

According to interference theory, forgetting happens because memories are confused with or disrupted by other, often similar, information. There are two types of interference.

Key facts

✓ Forgetting is the failure to retrieve memories.

✓ Proactive interference is when old information prevents recall of new information.

✓ Retroactive information is when new information prevents recall of old information.

✓ Retrieval cues help us recall information.

Proactive interference
This is when older memories prevent recall of newer memories.

Retroactive interference
This is when newer memories prevent recall of older memories.

Proactive interference	Retroactive interference
Learn Spanish first	Learn Spanish first
↓	↓
Learn Italian second	Learn Italian second
↓	↓
Fail to recall newer language, Italian	Fail to recall older language, Spanish
↓	↓
Recall older language, Spanish, instead	Recall newer language, Italian, instead

Cue-dependent forgetting

Sometimes information is still in the LTM but it can't be located. Like a label on a file, the information needs a retrieval cue to help us find where it is stored. Without effective retrieval cues, we forget.

Context-dependent failure

When the external environment (context) changes between coding and recall, retrieval cues are missing, so forgetting is more likely. This is context-dependent failure. Godden and Baddeley (1975) asked divers to memorize words on land or underwater. Divers who memorized the words underwater had poor recall when they were on land. Those who memorized the words on land had poor recall underwater.

State-dependent failure

Forgetting is also more likely when the internal physical or emotional environment (state) changes between coding and recall. This is state-dependent failure. Overton (1972) found that participants were better at recalling information they had learned when drunk the next time they were drunk again than when they were sober, because their state was the same.

Memory distortions

Memories aren't exact reproductions of events and we can't always trust them. A vivid memory may feel incredibly real, but that doesn't mean it is accurate. Memories can be distorted in a number of ways.

Key facts

✓ Hindsight bias is when we think our previously held beliefs were consistent with what we know now.

✓ Source amnesia is remembering a piece of information but forgetting where it was learned.

✓ Confabulation is unintentionally adding false details to real memories.

✓ Information that doesn't fit with existing schema may be replaced with information that does.

Hindsight bias

Humans often forget what they knew or thought previously, instead assuming that previously held beliefs, opinions, or knowledge were the same as what they now think or know. Known as hindsight bias, this tendency can lead people to believe falsely that they had predicted something would happen.

I knew this question would come up.

Source amnesia

Misremembering or forgetting how, when, or from whom we acquired information is known as source amnesia. Once the source is forgotten, it becomes easier to think that piece of information, which might be imagined, suggested, or incorrect, is true.

From dinosaur facts to favourite songs, it is often hard to remember where and when we learned something.

Confabulation (false memories)

We may unknowingly add false details to real memories, by using them to fill memory gaps. Over time, false details merge with accurate ones, resulting in false memories that feel very real, but aren't. Unlike lying, confabulations are unintentional – the person is unaware of them.

Real memory
+
False details
↓
Inaccurate memory, recalled as true

🔍 Reconstructive memory

In 1932, British psychologist Frederic Bartlett tested participants on their recall of a story from a different culture. They left out culturally unfamiliar details, or replaced them with details consistent with their own culture, suggesting that information that doesn't fit into existing schema (see page 103) is harder to recall. Bartlett proposed that memory is not an accurate reproduction; instead, we reconstruct it ourselves, using our own schema to fill in gaps.

Easily forgotten, incompatible information

Existing schema

Easily remembered, compatible information

Eyewitness testimony

In a court of law, one of the most convincing pieces of evidence is often eyewitness testimony (EWT) — the description of events given by a person who was at the scene of the crime. However, eyewitness testimony isn't always accurate. A person's recollection of an incident, particularly an emotionally charged one, can be affected by multiple factors.

Anxiety

A witness to a crime is likely to feel anxious about being in danger. Investigating anxiety and EWT, psychologists C. Johnson and B. Scott (1976) found that people recalled well the facial features of a man they had seen with greasy hands holding a pen. However, they struggled to recall the features of a man they had seen with blood on his hands holding a knife. This is the "weapon focus effect" — the tendency to concentrate on a weapon and miss other details, reducing recall.

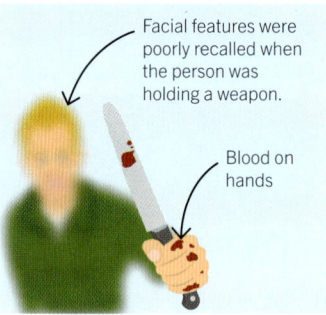

Facial features were well recalled when the person was holding a pen.

Grease on hands

Facial features were poorly recalled when the person was holding a weapon.

Blood on hands

Post-event discussion

A conversation between witnesses after an incident can influence their recollection. Gabbert et al. (2003) showed two groups a video of a girl putting a book on a table from two viewpoints. One group saw her steal money from the table, the other group didn't. After both groups conferred, 60 per cent of those who did not see the girl steal money later reported her as guilty, despite not witnessing the crime.

Group A saw the girl take money from the desk when she returned the book.

Group B didn't see a crime but — influenced by Group A — 60% still said she was guilty.

Key facts

- ✓ Eyewitness testimony can be unreliable.
- ✓ The weapon focus effect concentrates attention on the source of danger, at the expense of other details.
- ✓ Post-event discussion can alter people's recollections.
- ✓ Leading questions can influence how witnesses respond.

🔍 Leading questions

The accuracy of EWT can be affected by leading questions — these are questions that influence or guide the response. US psychologists Elizabeth Loftus and John Palmer (1976) showed participants the same videos of car accidents before asking them how fast the cars were going when they "hit" each other. Participants were given synonyms of "hit" to see whether the language used affected their answers, with the dramatic word "smashed" resulting in the highest speed estimates.

Word used in question	Average speed estimate
… contacted…	31.8 mph
… hit…	34 mph
… bumped…	38.1 mph
… collided…	39.3 mph
… smashed…	40.5 mph

Cognitive interview

There are several strategies used to improve the accuracy and detail of eyewitness testimony. US psychologists R. Fisher and R.E. Geiselman (1985) developed the cognitive interview based on research that shows that memories can be accessed via a number of different routes.

Interview techniques
The cognitive interview procedure employs four main techniques to stimulate accurate recall of events. Interviewers vary these access routes during questioning.

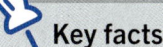

Key facts

✓ The cognitive interview process is used to improve the accuracy of eyewitness testimony.

✓ It uses four main techniques to stimulate different paths to memory retrieval.

✓ The enhanced cognitive interview adds techniques that build trust between the interviewer and eyewitness.

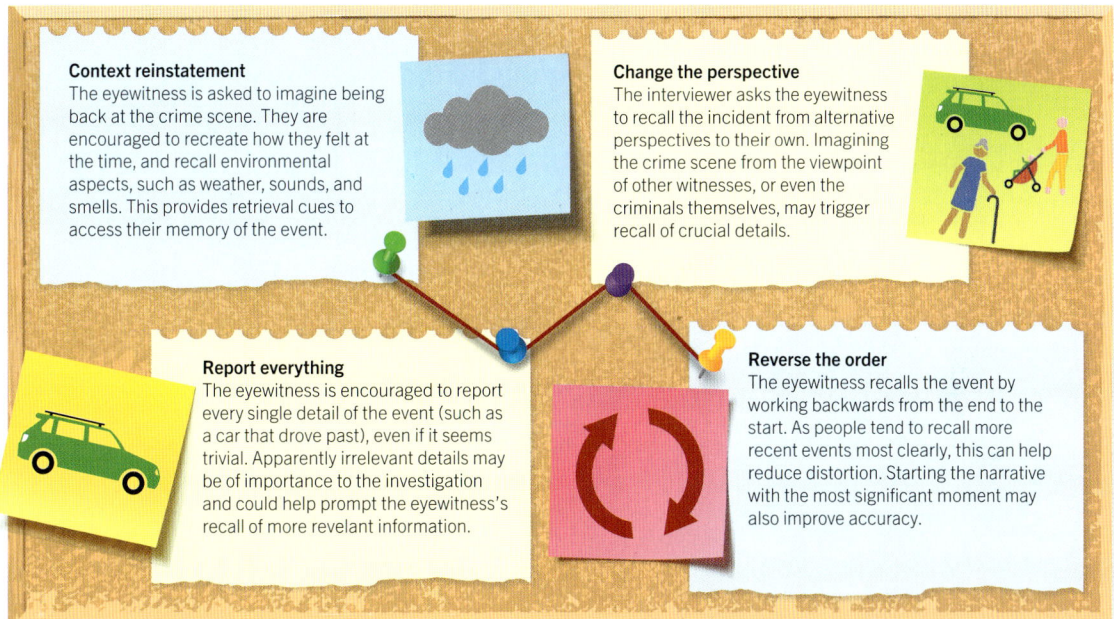

Context reinstatement
The eyewitness is asked to imagine being back at the crime scene. They are encouraged to recreate how they felt at the time, and recall environmental aspects, such as weather, sounds, and smells. This provides retrieval cues to access their memory of the event.

Change the perspective
The interviewer asks the eyewitness to recall the incident from alternative perspectives to their own. Imagining the crime scene from the viewpoint of other witnesses, or even the criminals themselves, may trigger recall of crucial details.

Report everything
The eyewitness is encouraged to report every single detail of the event (such as a car that drove past), even if it seems trivial. Apparently irrelevant details may be of importance to the investigation and could help prompt the eyewitness's recall of more revelant information.

Reverse the order
The eyewitness recalls the event by working backwards from the end to the start. As people tend to recall more recent events most clearly, this can help reduce distortion. Starting the narrative with the most significant moment may also improve accuracy.

🔍 The enhanced cognitive interview

The enhanced cognitive interview (1987) added building trust between the interviewer and eyewitness to the main techniques to enhance recall. Extra strategies include using techniques to reduce eyewitness anxiety, the use of eye contact, minimizing distractions, and asking open-ended questions. Eyewitnesses are also reminded not to guess and encouraged to speak slowly.

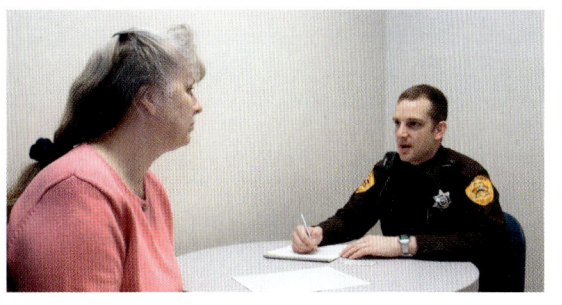

Biological basis of memory

Experiments in which rats were trained to solve mazes after removal of various parts of the brain suggest that memories are not stored in a single, specific location like folders in a filing cabinet. Instead, memories seem to be distributed across wide areas of the brain, encoded in neural networks that can be modified by changing the strength of synapses. However, certain parts of the brain play a major role in the formation of memories.

Key facts

✓ Memories are distributed across the brain.

✓ Certain brain regions play a key role in laying down new memories.

✓ Long-term potentiation is the strengthening of synapses following repeated stimulation.

Memory and the brain

Studies of people and animals with brain damage reveal that certain parts of the brain play a key role in laying down new memories. These studies also show that different kinds of memory are processed in different ways.

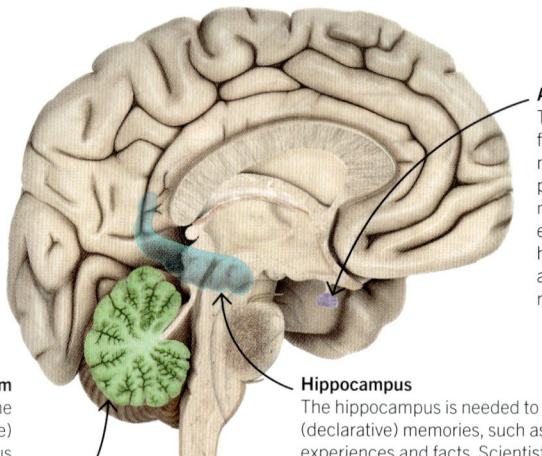

Amygdala
The amygdala is involved in the formation of the vivid "flashbulb" memories that accompany powerful emotions. For example, most people can remember exactly where they were on hearing traumatic news, such as a significant bereavement or news of a major event.

Cerebellum
The cerebellum plays a key role in the formation of implicit (non-declarative) memories, such as unconscious conditioned reflexes and motor skills. People with a damaged cerebellum cannot learn to associate a sound with a painful stimulus, such as a puff of air on the eye.

Hippocampus
The hippocampus is needed to form new explicit (declarative) memories, such as consciously remembered experiences and facts. Scientists suspect the hippocampus is a relay station, processing fresh memories before they are stored more permanently in the cortex. The hippocampus and cortex show synchronous activity during deep sleep, when memory consolidation is thought to occur.

🔍 Long-term potentiation

Search for the physical basis of memory has focused on synapses. Studies of the simple nervous systems of sea slugs have revealed that repeated stimulation strengthens synapses in a number of ways, all of which make the post-synaptic neuron more likely to fire. This increased sensitivity lasts for a long period and is called long-term potentiation (LTP). Drugs that enhance LTP improve learning, and drugs that block it interfere with learning.

Pre-synaptic neuron more likely to release neurotransmitter

More neurotransmitter molecules released

More receptor sites in post-synaptic neuron

Post-synaptic neuron fires more easily

Synapse before LTP

Synapse after LTP

Chapter 6
Cognitive psychology: thinking and language

Concepts and prototypes

A concept is a general mental category, in which we group objects that are similar. We usually have a single mental image that represents each concept, and this is called a prototype. Concepts are the starting points of cognition – the mental processes of the mind.

Concept
"Chair" is a concept for an object we sit on. There are many items that fit into this category. Some items may be used in a particular location or for a unique purpose.

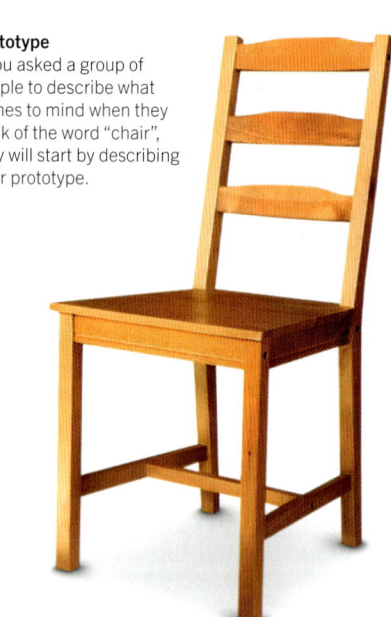

Prototype
If you asked a group of people to describe what comes to mind when they think of the word "chair", they will start by describing their prototype.

Cognitive processes

Our minds can do all sorts of tasks. We can access memories, process and produce language, solve mathematical equations, weigh up difficult choices, make judgments, analyse information, invent stories, plan for the future, and much more. These mental tasks are known as cognitive processes.

Problem-solving
Facing a challenge and determining how to work through it

Memory
Coding, storing, and recalling information

Thinking
Generating ideas, processing information

Attention
Focusing mental effort on a particular stimulus or task

Language
Communicating thoughts and ideas through words, symbols, signs, and gestures

Perception
Interpreting sensory information

Schema

Schema are mental frameworks of ideas and expectations, gained from experience, that help us to understand and interpret the world around us. It is very difficult to think without using schema. They allow us to categorize and store new information. Everybody's schema are unique to them — each person sees and experiences the world in their own way. Schema develop through assimilation (adding new information to existing ways of thinking) and accommodation (changing existing ways of thinking).

Key facts

✓ Schema are mental frameworks that help us to understand and interpret the world around us.

✓ Assimilation is when new information is incorporated easily into an existing schema.

✓ Accommodation is when an existing schema must be modified because it is challenged by new information.

Assimilation
On a trip to the zoo, a young child sees a parrot for the first time and, recognizing that it flies, she categorizes it as a bird. Although more colourful than the species she has seen before, the parrot fits easily into her existing schema of birds being animals that fly. The process of adding new information to an existing schema is assimilation.

Accommodation
Later, the child encounters a penguin for the first time. Like the pigeon and parrot, the penguin has a beak, feathers, and wings, but it is swimming, not flying. The penguin does not fit into her existing schema, which she must now change. When new information forces existing schema to be modified, it is known as accommodation.

Types of schema

There are four types of schema, which we use in different situations. Schema make understanding the world possible, but they can also cause us to dismiss new information that contradicts what we think we already know.

Self schema	Person schema	Social schema	Event schema
Ideas you have about yourself. For example, I'm sensitive and ambitious, I don't like beetroot, I want to be a doctor.	Ideas you have about another person. For example, they are funny, like animals, and are often late.	Ideas you have about how to behave in social situations. For example, how to behave at a party with friends.	Ideas you have about how to behave at certain events, such as in a business meeting or at a meal in a restaurant.

Problem-solving

Every day we encounter problems – sometimes small, sometimes big – and work out how to solve them. Problem-solving is a cognitive process that allows us to work out how to achieve a desired result. It occurs in the prefrontal cortex of the brain. People can use one or more ways to problem-solve, including trial and error, heuristics, algorithms, and insight.

Key facts

✓ To solve a problem, one or more methods can be used.

✓ The methods vary in how long they take, how easy they are, and how accurate they are.

✓ Insight has no set process – it happens spontaneously without conscious mental effort.

Method	Explanation	Advantages	Disadvantages
Trial-and-error approach	Trying out multiple different possibilities in order to find a solution. For example, trialling different combinations of ingredients in a recipe until the food tastes right to you.	• Works well when there are multiple possible solutions • Presents an opportunity to learn from mistakes • Allows for exploration and discovery	• May be time-consuming • Each trial uses up resources • Success is not guaranteed
Heuristics	Using a "rule of thumb" or general guidelines as a mental shortcut to a solution. For example, using a pinch of salt in a recipe rather than an exact measurement.	• Quick and easy • Helps to simplify the task • Reduces the mental effort it takes to solve the problem	• May not result precisely in the desired outcome • May not be suitable for all types of problems • Quick judgments are prone to cognitive bias and can lead to unsuitable solutions
Algorithms	Following a step-by-step, logical procedure that will lead to the desired solution. For example, precisely following a set recipe to make a meal.	• Produces a precise and accurate solution • The outcome is certain • Results are reliable and consistent	• May be time-consuming • May be complicated • Must be followed carefully and with the necessary resources

🔍 Insight

Insight is when a solution spontaneously occurs to you without you making any active effort. The sudden realization of a solution is often called a "eureka" or an "aha" moment. It differs from the analytical methods of the trial-and-error approach, heuristics, and algorithms because it does not require any conscious effort.

Aha!

Decision-making

We make numerous decisions over the course of a single day. Most of our moment-to-moment decisions happen so quickly, we probably do not even take time to reason them through. For this to happen, our brains use mental shortcuts known as heuristics (see page 104). These are often necessary to reduce the cognitive load of decision-making.

Key facts

✓ Heuristics are mental shortcuts that allow us to make quick decisions.

✓ Intuition is the ability to make decisions without conscious thought.

✓ The dual-process theory outlines two systems of thinking that interact to help us make decisions.

Intuition

Intuition is the ability to understand something instinctively and make decisions without the need for conscious thought. This "gut feeling" is developed through our own lived experiences. For example, if you practise a sport, you'll learn how to do certain movements instinctively without thinking about them.

Goalkeepers use their intuition to make fast decisions on the pitch.

🔍 The dual-process theory

According to dual process theory, we use two different systems of thinking to make decisions. System 1 is intuitive thinking, used to make decisions quickly. System 2 thinking is slower and more analytical, using concepts and models to weigh up the considerations. The two systems often interact, with System 2 thinking acting as a check on System 1 thinking.

System 1	System 2
Fast	Slow
Intuitive	Logical
Unconscious	Conscious
Automatic	Controlled
Requires little effort	Requires greater effort
Relies on experience	Tackles new problems
Prone to bias	May take bias into account
Gives feeling of certainty	May not provide certainty

Cognitive bias

People don't always think rationally. We sometimes make systematic thinking errors rather than weighing up matters logically and objectively. This tendency is known as cognitive bias. Such errors often result from mental shortcuts called heuristics, which are powerful problem-solving and decision-making tools that occasionally lead to poor choices. An awareness of the limitations of heuristics allows us to consider all the evidence, rather than just the evidence that supports our beliefs, and become better decision-makers.

Key facts

✓ Cognitive bias involves systematic thinking errors.

✓ Heuristics are mental shortcuts that may lead to bias.

✓ Fixation is a mental obstacle in which set ways of doing things block fresh perspectives when solving problems.

✓ There are several types of bias, including anchoring bias, confirmation bias, framing, and overconfidence.

Representativeness heuristic
Is the woman below a nursery teacher or a mechanic? If you assumed a nursery teacher, you were probably influenced by the representativeness heuristic. This mental shortcut uses judgments based on resemblances to prototypes (stereotypes).

Availability heuristic
Are you more likely to be killed by a shark or a champagne cork? The correct answer is a cork, but the vividness of a shark attack leads most people to guess wrongly. This judgment — based on what comes readily into your mind — is known as the availability heuristic. Because of its immediacy, we tend to think of it as more common.

🔍 Fixation

German psychologist Karl Duncker (1945) devised a test in which he asked participants to attach a candle to a wall. He gave them a candle, a box of pins, and some matches. Many tried to pin the candle to the wall or glue it using candle wax. Very few thought of attaching it using the box. This mental obstacle is called fixation – the inability to get a fresh perspective on a new problem. We tend to fixate on the way something worked in the past and are unable to see it afresh.

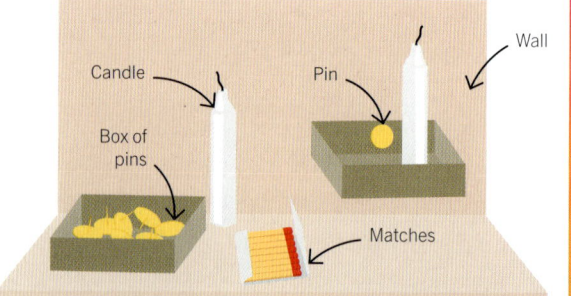

Candle   Pin   Wall

Box of pins

Matches

Problem   **Solution**

Types of cognitive bias

There are many types of cognitive bias, with new ones frequently added. These cognitive biases can affect judgment-making, problem-solving, and decision-making.

Bias	Explanation	Example
Anchoring bias	The tendency to make judgments based on the first piece of information we receive.	A person might place too much importance on the first offer they receive in a negotiation, leading them to accept a poor price.
Belief perseverance	The tendency to hold onto our beliefs, even when we are presented with evidence that disproves them.	A person continues to believe in a conspiracy theory long after it has been debunked.
Confirmation bias	The tendency to focus only on information that confirms what we already believe.	We are more likely to believe stories in the news if they support our personal views, even when the evidence is inconclusive.
False consensus effect	The tendency to overestimate the extent to which other people have the same views and behaviours as ours.	A person may assume that someone shares their political views.
Framing	The tendency for our decisions to be swayed by the way in which something is presented to us.	In a sale, a consumer chooses a product marked "25% off" over one marked at the same price with no discount, because they perceive it as better value.
Halo effect	The tendency to focus on one characteristic of someone (or something) to make positive judgments about their other characteristics.	You might assume that someone you find attractive is also a kind and caring person – solely based on their appearance.
Illusory correlations	The tendency to incorrectly identify or exaggerate a relationship between two things.	Superstitions such as a black cat crossing your path, or walking under a ladder, as omens of bad luck are illusory correlations.
Optimism bias	The tendency to take excessive risks because we think that nothing bad will ever happen to us.	Some people who smoke think they aren't at risk of serious disorders such as cancer and chronic obstructive pulmonary disease (COPD).
Overconfidence	The tendency to overestimate our skills and judgment, or think we have more control over a situation than we do.	A student underestimates the amount of time it takes to complete an essay.
Self-consistency bias	The tendency to continue to act in a certain way because we have always acted in that way.	A person does not change their job, even after a change in their interests or skills.

Creative thinking

An artist who creates a sculpture from clay, a composer who crafts a musical work, and a novelist who writes a story are all making use of a cognitive process called creativity. However, creativity is not just about producing fine art. Creativity takes place every time someone has an original idea that allows them to develop something new and valuable.

Key facts

✓ Creativity is a cognitive process involving the development of new ideas.

✓ Divergent thinking occurs when a problem has multiple possible solutions.

✓ Convergent thinking occurs when a solution is chosen from multiple options.

Creative problem-solving

Creativity is important when a person is faced with a tricky problem to solve. There are two ways of finding solutions.

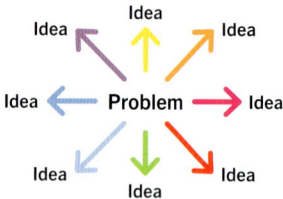

Divergent thinking
When a problem has multiple solutions, we generate these using divergent thinking. For example, if asked to think of alternative uses for a paper clip, you would use divergent thinking to come up with a number of possibilities.

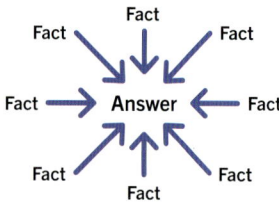

Convergent thinking
When a problem has just one solution, we use convergent thinking to narrow down the options. For example, when trying to fix a broken washing machine, you would use convergent thinking to deduce the reason for the fault from several possible options.

Components of creativity
The US cognitive psychologist Robert Sternberg identified five key characteristics of creative people.

Personality
Creative people must be willing to take risks, seek new experiences, and persevere despite obstacles.

Imagination
Seeing things in new ways and discovering new connections, patterns, or solutions are only possible with imaginative thinking.

Motivation
An innate desire to be creative and enjoyment of the process gives creative people motivation and focus to drive them forward.

Knowledge
Having greater knowledge of the world creates more opportunities to see it in new ways.

Environment
A supportive environment that encourages and nurtures gives creative people confidence and inspiration to try new things.

Stages of language development

Acquiring language is a remarkable cognitive process that develops rapidly throughout the early months and years of life. It is marked by specific milestones. Babies start to process language a few months after birth and begin to babble. By the time they are five years old, most children speak fluently with a wide vocabulary.

Key facts

✓ Speech and language develop rapidly throughout infancy and childhood.

✓ Speech is the sounds we make; language is the meaning we create with words to communicate.

✓ Development stages include babbling, one-word phrases, two-word phrases, and overgeneralization.

Age	Stage	Explanation	Example
4 months	Babbling	The baby recognizes differences between sounds, showing a preference for sounds of their native language. They babble, making consonant-vowel sounds without meaning, by opening and closing their mouth.	"ma, ma, ma"
10 months		The baby begins pairing babbles with identifiable objects in the environment. They use their body to gesture and point.	Directs the sound "mama" at their mother
12 months	One-word stage	The baby now understands that words carry meaning. They communicate in one-word phrases, using 1–5 recognizable words but understanding many more.	"mum", "no", "eat", "go", "please"
18 months		The infant now speaks at least 10 recognizable words. They begin a rapid acquisition of language, gaining 50–100 words over the next few months.	"car", "hot", "up"
24 months	Two-word stage	The toddler follows simple directions and self-identifies by name. They pair words together, often combining a noun and a verb.	"mummy eat", "go mummy"
2–4 years old	Overgeneralization	The child combines more words to create sentences. They understand and apply grammatical rules but overgeneralize, using them in ways that may be inaccurate.	"Mummy, I goed outside."
5 years old		The child now has a vocabulary of several thousand words. They use fluent speech and language, and can tell stories using a sequence of details.	"Yesterday my Daddy took me swimming."

 Components of language

Spoken languages consist of grammar, morphemes, and phonemes:

Grammar is the system of rules and structures for the formation of sentences. Without grammar, a language wouldn't make any sense.

Morphemes are the smallest units of meaning in language. For example, the word "submarines" has three:
sub = under; marine = water; s = more than one.

Phonemes are the smallest units of sound in language. For example, the word "chat" has three: ch - a - t.

Language and thought

Can language shape the way we think? US linguist Benjamin Whorf proposed that language actually determines our thought processes. This is called linguistic determinism. Whorf suggested that the way in which we see the world is bound to the words and structures of our native language. So, for example, if a language had no way to describe the past, its speakers would be unable to conceptualize it.

Key facts

✓ Language influences how we perceive and interpret the world around us.

✓ Expanding our language can expand our ability to think.

✓ Bilingual and multilingual speakers often think differently when using different languages.

Linguistic relativity

Most psychologists today think that language does not determine our thoughts but can influence them, a theory known as linguistic relativity. For example, our eyes have the ability to detect a vast array of colours but we may be limited in the ways we process them based on the vocabulary we have. Painters may think about colour in more complex ways than other people because they have a richer vocabulary of tints and hues to draw on.

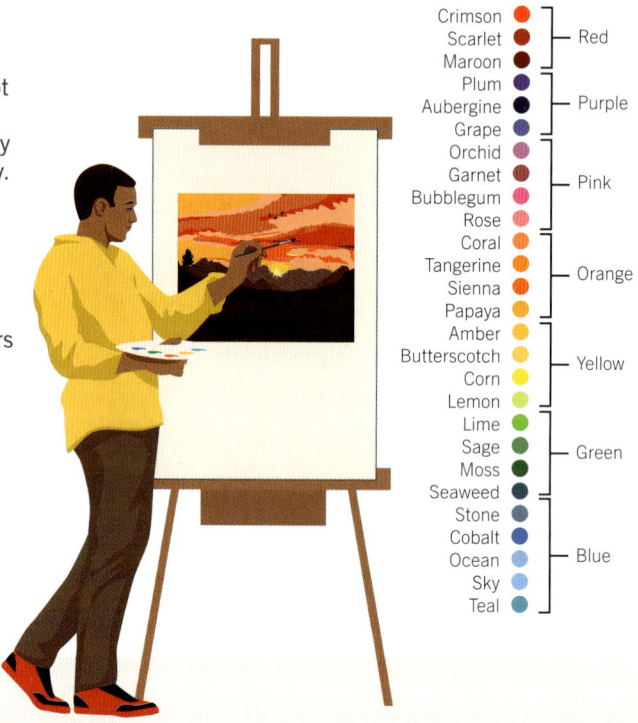

Crimson
Scarlet   } Red
Maroon
Plum
Aubergine } Purple
Grape
Orchid
Garnet
Bubblegum } Pink
Rose
Coral
Tangerine
Sienna   } Orange
Papaya
Amber
Butterscotch
Corn   } Yellow
Lemon
Lime
Sage   } Green
Moss
Seaweed
Stone
Cobalt
Ocean   } Blue
Sky
Teal

🔍 Bilingualism and multilingualism

Studies have shown that many bilingual and multilingual speakers think differently in different languages. In a study of Iranian Americans who speak Persian and English, participants demonstrated having a different self-concept (see page 162) according to the language in which they were tested (Salmani Nodoushan and García Laborda, 2014).

Cognitive processing in a technological world

Modern digital technology has made many aspects of daily life easier. It's now possible to communicate, find information, and be entertained instantly with the press of a button. The prevalence of computers and smart phones in modern society has led cognitive psychologists to ask questions about how this technology influences cognitive processes, such as memory.

Studying technology and cognition
US psychologist Betsy Sparrow et al. (2011) carried out experiments to see if modern technology has become an external type of memory for humans.

Key facts

✓ Some psychologists study how technology has influenced cognitive processes.

✓ Sparrow found that we may offload responsibility for remembering information to computers.

✓ Relying on the internet for information rather than yourself, friends, or family is called the "Google effect".

Experiment 1
Participants were asked to read and type trivia statements, pressing a key after each one. Half the participants were told pressing the key would save the statements; the other half were told this would delete them. They were then asked to recall as many statements as possible. Participants who expected the statements to be erased had better recall than those who believed they had been saved. This shows we may offload responsibility for remembering information to computers. We don't try to remember if we think the information has been stored.

Experiment 2
Participants were again asked to read and input trivia statements into a computer. After each statement, they were told the name of the folder, one of six, in which the information would be saved (for example, Facts, Data, or Names). Participants were better at recalling the folder in which statements were stored than the statements themselves. This suggests that when we believe information is stored externally, we focus more on where we can find it than on what the information is.

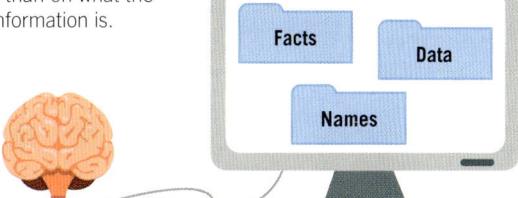

🔍 Transactive memory

The theory of transactive memory (Wegner, 1985) describes how groups of people store and recall knowledge. Over time, we learn which group member is the expert in a certain subject area. We then offload responsibility for remembering information in that area to them. This allows people access to more information than they would otherwise have. In modern times, we may offload responsibility for storing information to the internet, with different sites or apps functioning like subject-area experts. This tendency to rely on technology to store information, rather than memory, has become known as the "Google effect".

Chapter 7

Cognitive psychology: intelligence and testing

Intelligence

Intelligence is the ability to learn from experience, solve problems, and adapt to new situations. Measuring intelligence can be challenging — a person may excel in maths or be talented at sport, but struggle to read a map or understand biology. To account for individuals' varying abilities, British psychologist Charles Spearman proposed the two-factor theory of intelligence, which describes two components: general intelligence and specific intelligence.

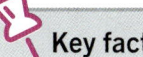

Key facts

✓ Intelligence is the ability to learn from experience, solve problems, and adapt to new situations.

✓ Spearman argued that a person's intelligence comprises their innate general intelligence (g) and specific intelligence (s), which is learned over time.

✓ A person who has high specific intelligence in one area is likely to have high overall performance (p).

The two-factor theory of intelligence (1904)
Spearman argued that intelligence comprises two factors: the general intelligence each person is born with (g factor), and specific intelligence learned over time (s factor).

A baby who goes on to be a talented musician as an adult is born with innate general intelligence (g).

The child takes music lessons, enhancing their learned specific musical intelligence (s).

Combining the adult's g factor with their s factor determines their overall performance (p).

| General intelligence (g) | + | Specific intelligence (s) | = | Overall performance (p) |

🔍 Factor analysis

Spearman was the first psychologist to use factor analysis – a way of analysing relationships between multiple variables – to study and measure intelligence. He found that if a person scored particularly highly in one test, it was likely that they had done well in all tests. Likewise, if they scored poorly in one area, they typically scored poorly in all areas. Spearman's results led him to assume that innate general intelligence was influencing their overall performance score.

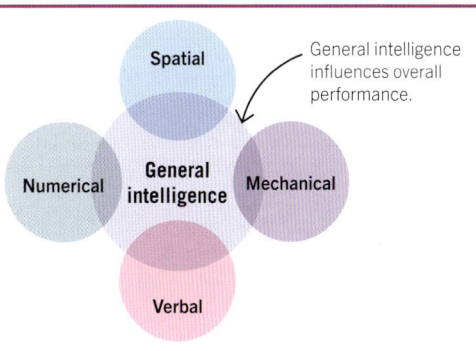

General intelligence influences overall performance.

Spatial

Numerical

General intelligence

Mechanical

Verbal

Multiple intelligences

US psychologist Howard Gardner believed that there are multiple types of intelligence. He based his theory on savant syndrome, a rare condition in which people with significant learning disabilities also display exceptional skill in a single specific area, such as mathematics, art, or music. Gardner claimed this was evidence that people can be intelligent in some ways, and less so in others. US psychologist Robert Sternberg has also theorized that multiple intelligence types exist.

Key facts

✓ According to Gardner and Sternberg, there are multiple types of intelligence.

✓ Gardner suggested eight intelligence types; Sternberg proposed three types.

✓ Savant syndrome is a condition in which a person with significant learning disabilities also has exceptional skills in a specific area.

The theory of multiple intelligence (1983)

Gardner identified eight different types of intelligence: visual-spatial, musical, body-kinaesthetic, interpersonal, linguistic-verbal, logical-mathematical, intrapersonal, and naturalistic. He suggested that most people have a mixture of these intelligence types, which make up their unique cognitive profiles. Gardner also later suggested a ninth type called existential intelligence – the ability to consider questions about life.

The triarchic theory of intelligence (1985)

Sternberg agreed with Gardner that multiple intelligences exist but he proposed just three different types: analytical intelligence (the ability to judge and analyse information), creative intelligence (the skills to come up with new ideas in different situations), and practical intelligence (the ability to operate well in the world).

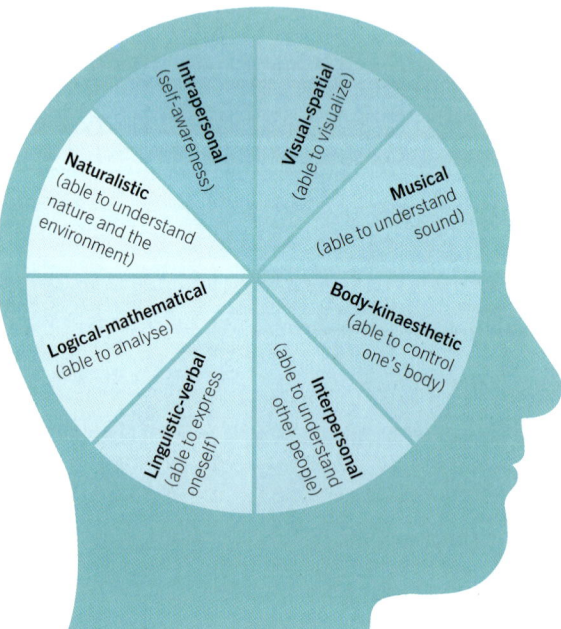

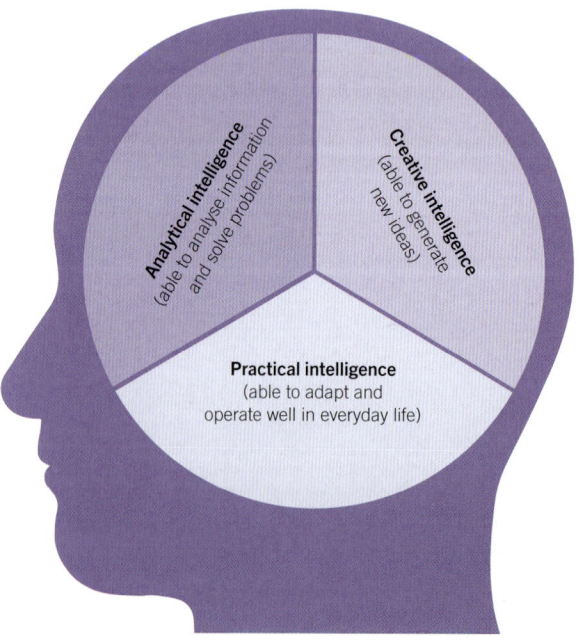

The dynamics of intelligence

Intelligence is not fixed — people get better at some things as they get older and worse at others. Crystallized intelligence refers to knowledge and skills gained over a lifetime. It increases with age. Faced with a problem, an adult may rely on crystallized intelligence, using their past experience of resolving similar issues to find a solution. Fluid intelligence refers to the ability to think logically and adapt in new situations. It decreases with age. To solve the same problem as the adult, a young teenager may rely on fluid intelligence, trying out multiple possible solutions until one works.

Key facts

✓ Crystallized intelligence is knowledge and skills gained over a lifetime.

✓ Fluid intelligence is the ability to think logically and adapt in new situations.

✓ Crystallized intelligence increases with age; fluid intelligence decreases with age.

✓ The Flynn effect describes the tendency for global mean IQ scores to rise over time.

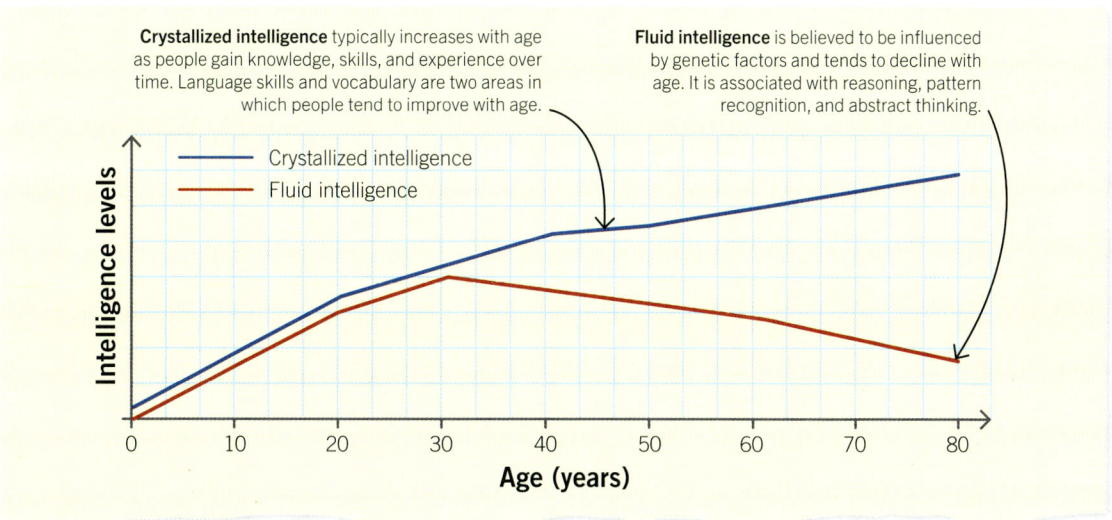

Crystallized intelligence typically increases with age as people gain knowledge, skills, and experience over time. Language skills and vocabulary are two areas in which people tend to improve with age.

Fluid intelligence is believed to be influenced by genetic factors and tends to decline with age. It is associated with reasoning, pattern recognition, and abstract thinking.

The Flynn effect

The human population has a much higher IQ than it did 100 years ago, as demonstrated by the global mean IQ level, which rose significantly throughout the 20th century. Psychologists have suggested different theories to explain this improvement, from better health and nutrition to greater education and living in a more stimulating environment.

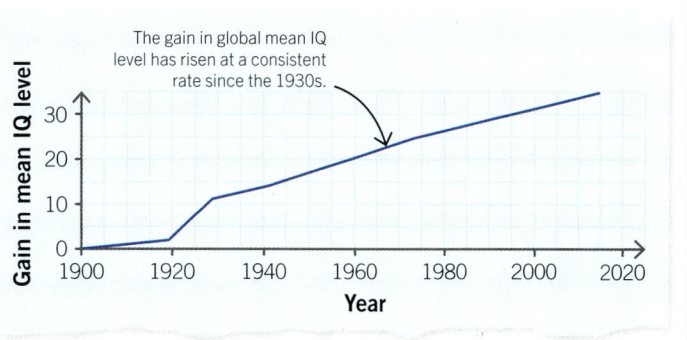

The gain in global mean IQ level has risen at a consistent rate since the 1930s.

Intelligence testing

Psychologists use intelligence tests to measure a person's general cognitive ability. Tests to measure intelligence have developed over the last 150 years, but the methods used – and ways of interpreting the results – remain hotly debated, even today.

Key facts

✓ Intelligence tests provide a numerical score that measures a person's intellect.

✓ Achievement tests are a measure of knowledge gained.

✓ Aptitude tests are a measure of potential abilities.

Desirable traits
English thinker Francis Galton is interested in whether abilities are natural or learned. He tests more than 10,000 people at his laboratory in London. He proposes that people with desirable traits should mate – an idea known as eugenics, which is considered deeply problematic today.

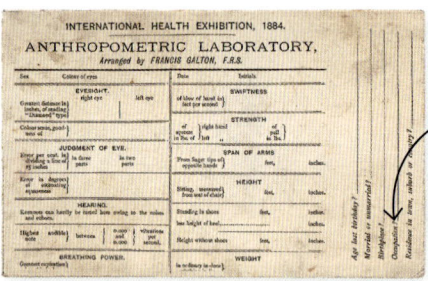

Galton recorded participants' occupations and family histories, as well as their height, weight, and strength.

The first Stanford-Binet test
US psychologist Lewis Terman of Stanford University, California, USA, recognizes that Binet's 1905 test has limitations; for example, it is only suitable for children with special educational needs. Terman revises Binet's test to create a version that works for all levels of ability.

The Stanford-Binet test featured tasks using paper dolls, toy cars, coloured cubes, and other objects.

1884   **1905**   **1912**   **1916**

Mental age
French psychologist Alfred Binet devises a test to identify children with special educational needs. Finding that some children can answer advanced questions while others struggle, he comes up with the concept of a "mental age" – a way of comparing a child's abilities to those of others in their age group.

Alfred Binet created the first modern intelligence test.

Intelligence quotient (IQ)
German psychologist William Stern coins the term *Intelligenzquotient*, based on a person's mental and chronological age. The concept of an intelligence quotient (IQ) helps psychologists to understand and compare the abilities of children while they are still growing and learning.

$$IQ = \frac{MA}{CA} \times 100$$

IQ was originally calculated by dividing a person's mental age (MA) by their chronological age (CA) and multiplying by 100.

🔍 Achievement and aptitude testing

There are two categories of intelligence test.

Achievement tests focus on what someone has already learned. They measure a person's skills or knowledge in a specific area or subject. School teachers often use achievement tests to evaluate their students' understanding of a subject.

Aptitude tests focus on the potential someone has to learn new things. They measure a person's ability to learn or perform certain tasks or skills. Employers often use aptitude tests to judge candidates' suitability for a particular job.

Army tests

US psychologist Robert Yerkes develops two IQ tests known as Army Alpha and Army Beta, and is given permission by the US government to test 1.75 million soldiers. The tests are used to assess candidates for leadership roles. Later, the government uses them to test immigrants and refuse entry to those that they characterize as "genetically inferior".

US soldiers took the Army Alpha test to measure literacy, and the pictorial Army Beta test if they could not read.

The WAIS-IV

The fourth version of the WAIS is introduced. It builds on previous versions and tests the abilities, such as vocabulary, arithmetic, and symbol recognition, of people over the age of 16. Along with the Stanford-Binet test, the WAIS-IV becomes one of the most frequently used intelligence tests.

1917   **1955**   **2003   2008**

The Wechsler Adult Intelligence Scale (WAIS)

US psychologist Alfred Wechsler develops a new approach to testing, known as the Wechsler Adult Intelligence Scale (WAIS). Multiple abilities are examined, resulting in a series of scores (unlike the Stanford-Binet test, which only gives one).

Each candidate is presented with a box of tests to complete.

The fifth Stanford-Binet test

The fifth version of the Stanford-Binet test is released. The examiner administers the test one-on-one, guiding the test-taker through increasingly difficult tasks and scoring their responses. Children as young as five years old can take the test.

Standardization

Standardization is the process of establishing consistent procedures so that the results of scientific experiments or psychological tests are reliable. For example, an IQ test only has meaning if the test has been standardized to match results given by established tests. The goal of standardization is to ensure that psychological studies produce consistent results across different researchers, settings, and time periods.

Standardizing IQ tests
IQ tests can be standardized by designing the questions and scoring system to give the same mean and standard deviation (see page 30) as existing tests. When IQ scores of the general population are plotted on a graph, they follow a bell-shaped pattern called a normal distribution. To match existing tests, a standardized test should give a mean IQ of 100, and 68 per cent of people should score within 15 points (one standard deviation) of the mean.

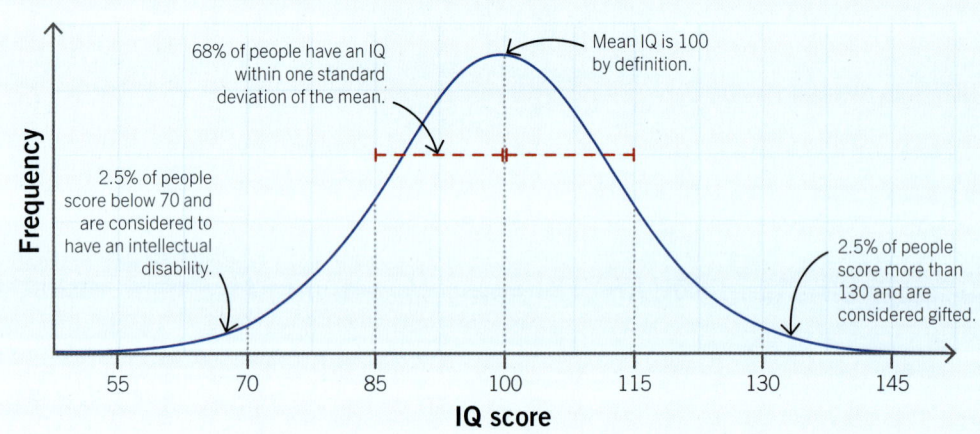

68% of people have an IQ within one standard deviation of the mean.

Mean IQ is 100 by definition.

2.5% of people score below 70 and are considered to have an intellectual disability.

2.5% of people score more than 130 and are considered gifted.

Frequency / IQ score — 55, 70, 85, 100, 115, 130, 145

Standardization in experiments

Standardization is a crucial part of the scientific process, helping to ensure that experiments are repeatable by other scientists and that results have validity. Scientists standardize conditions in experiments to prevent extraneous variables (see page 15) from affecting the outcome. For example, a group of participants taking an IQ test would all be given the same length of time to complete the test so that time was not a confounding variable.

Chapter 8

Developmental psychology:
attachment and social development

Imprinting

In the 1930s, Austrian ethologist Konrad Lorenz carried out some of the earliest work into how attachments form. He studied imprinting – the tendency for young animals to form an irreversible attachment to the first moving object they see during a critical period in the hours after being born. Lorenz tested whether newly hatched greylag goslings would imprint on him and then follow him instead of their mother when given the choice.

Key facts

✓ Imprinting is a form of attachment in which young animals follow the first moving object they see.

✓ Attachment to the "imprinted parent" is formed in the hours after being born.

✓ Lorenz studied imprinting in greylag geese.

1. Lorenz separated a large clutch of greylag goose eggs into two groups. The first group of eggs remained with their mother, so that she was the first moving object the goslings saw when they hatched out of their eggs.

The goslings' mother was the first moving object they saw.

Half of the eggs hatched in the presence of their mother.

2. The second group of eggs was placed in an incubator, where they could hatch away from their mother. Lorenz made sure that he was the first moving object the goslings saw when they hatched.

Half of the eggs hatched in the presence of Lorenz.

Lorenz was the first moving object they saw.

3. Lorenz marked the goslings, according to which group they came from. They were then mixed together before being given the choice of following their mother or Lorenz. The goslings that saw their mother when they hatched followed her, whereas the goslings that saw Lorenz followed him, as their "imprinted parent".

The goslings that saw their mother first (shown here with a red spot) followed her.

The goslings that saw Lorenz first (shown here with a blue spot) followed him.

Contact comfort

In the 1950s and 1960s, US psychologist Harry Harlow carried out a series of controversial studies on rhesus monkeys that involved separating infants from mothers. While unethical by today's standards and distressing for the monkeys, these studies revealed the importance of contact comfort (physical and emotional closeness) in creating attachment.

Key facts

✓ Harlow separated infant monkeys from their mothers to study attachment.

✓ Infants consistently chose comfort over food.

✓ Harlow demonstrated the damaging effects of being deprived of an attachment figure.

✓ In the study, attachment deprivation led to later social incompetence and distress.

Response to artificial mother
Harlow let infants choose between two artificial mothers: one gave food and the other gave contact comfort. The monkeys preferred the mother with contact comfort and visited the other only to feed.

The first mother was a wire frame with a milk bottle.

The second mother was a wire frame wrapped in soft cloth.

Response to threat
Harlow exposed the monkeys to a threat – a scary piece of apparatus. The monkeys instinctively ran to the cloth mother rather than the food mother. If no mother was present, they cowered in fear.

The apparatus made loud noises and had flashing lights.

When the cloth mother was present, the monkey felt empowered to make noises or attack the threat.

Response to a new environment
When placed in a new environment with the cloth mother, the monkeys initially clung to the mother but then explored. When with the food mother or alone, however, they were unable to explore.

The monkey felt able to explore only when the cloth mother was present.

Response to isolation
Harlow put infants in isolation chambers for periods varying from hours to months. When later exposed to other monkeys, the socially deprived monkeys showed extreme distress and poor social skills. Females reared this way had poor parenting skills.

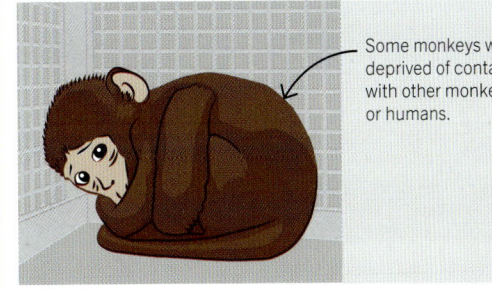

Some monkeys were deprived of contact with other monkeys or humans.

Learning theory of attachment

US psychologists John Dollard and Neal Miller's learning theory of attachment (1950) proposes that the attachments infants form with their caregivers are learned through experience, rather than being instinctive. Both classical and operant conditioning (see pages 81–82) can explain how attachments form.

Key facts

✓ The learning theory of attachment proposes that attachments are learned rather than being instinctive.

✓ Classical conditioning occurs when an infant learns to attach by association.

✓ Operant conditioning occurs when an infant forms an attachment through reinforced learning.

Classical conditioning

An infant learns to attach to a caregiver through classical conditioning. The infant associates the caregiver with the pleasure they get from being fed. Once the association is learned, the infant will feel pleasure in the presence of the caregiver, whether they provide food or not, and form an attachment

1. Before conditioning
An infant is born with a biological need to eat – the food is an unconditioned stimulus (UCS). Eating food produces an automatic feeling of pleasure, known as an unconditioned response (UCR).

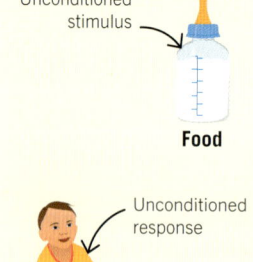

Unconditioned stimulus

Food

Unconditioned response

Pleasure

2. During conditioning
Caregivers do not naturally produce a pleasure response. They are a neutral stimulus (NS). Over time, the caregiver provides food, so the infant learns to associate them with the food and pleasure it brings.

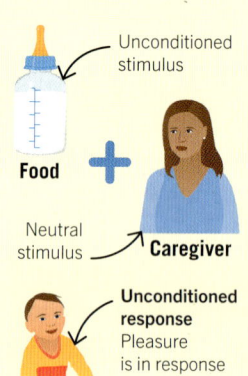

Unconditioned stimulus

Food

Neutral stimulus

Caregiver

Unconditioned response
Pleasure is in response to food.

Pleasure

3. After conditioning
The caregiver (NS) becomes a conditioned stimulus (CS), bringing the infant pleasure – now a conditioned response (CR) – with or without food. There is now an attachment between infant and caregiver.

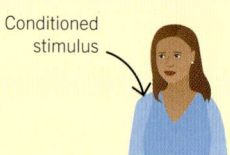

Conditioned stimulus

Caregiver

Conditioned response
Pleasure is now a learned response to the caregiver.

Pleasure

🔍 Operant conditioning

Attachment can also be explained by operant conditioning. For example, when a hungry infant cries in distress, their caregiver responds by feeding the infant to lessen their discomfort. The infant learns to repeat this behaviour in future. This is negative reinforcement – something negative (hunger) has been removed. Similarly, the infant's crying distresses the caregiver, so when feeding stops the crying, the caregiver learns to repeat this behaviour. This is also negative reinforcement – something negative (distress) has been removed.

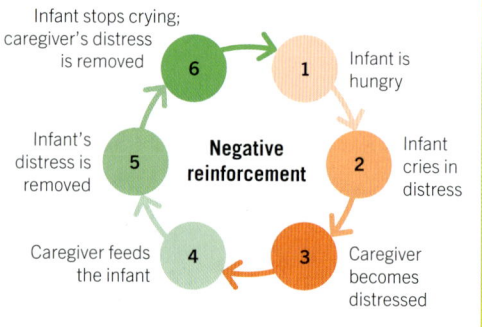

Infant stops crying; caregiver's distress is removed — 6

1 Infant is hungry

Infant's distress is removed — 5

Negative reinforcement

2 Infant cries in distress

Caregiver feeds the infant — 4

3 Caregiver becomes distressed

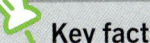

Monotropic theory

In 1969, British psychologist John Bowlby proposed his theory that humans are biologically preprogrammed to form an attachment from birth. Known as the monotropic theory, it states that an infant's inbuilt drive to attach focuses on one specific person, usually a parent or primary caregiver. This monotropic bond is formed from the age of six months to two and a half years. If it is not formed during this critical period, problems forming attachments with other people may occur later in life. The monotropic bond provides security and is adaptive (good for survival).

Key facts

✓ The monotropic theory states that infants are preprogrammed at birth to attach to one person.

✓ Infants display social releasers — behaviours that increase their chances of receiving care.

✓ The parent-child attachment provides an internal working model for all future relationships.

Social releasers

Bowlby suggested that infants are genetically programmed to perform behaviours called social releasers. These include crying and smiling, and increase an infant's chance of receiving care. Similarly, parents are genetically programmed to respond to the releasers and provide care.

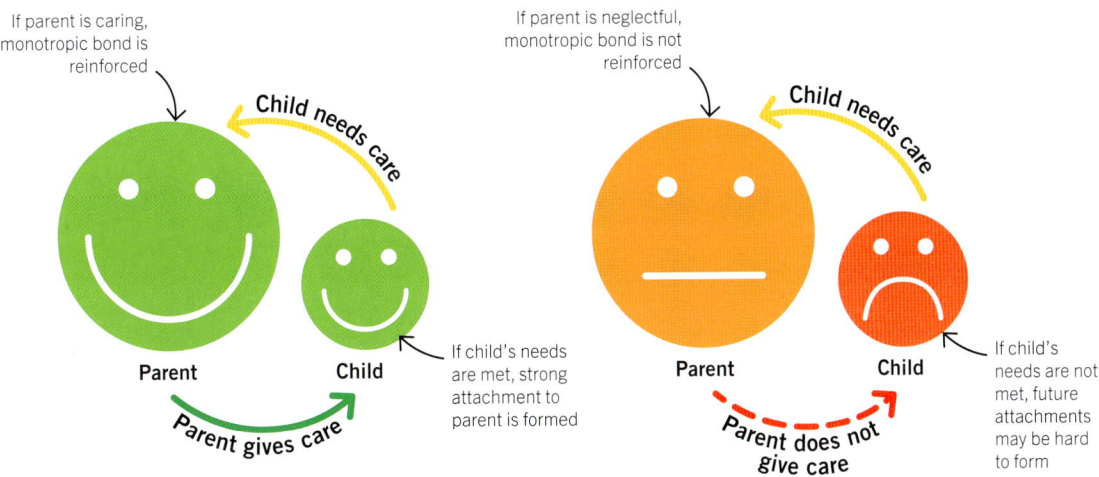

If parent is caring, monotropic bond is reinforced

Child needs care

Parent   Child

Parent gives care

If child's needs are met, strong attachment to parent is formed

If parent is neglectful, monotropic bond is not reinforced

Child needs care

Parent   Child

Parent does not give care

If child's needs are not met, future attachments may be hard to form

🔍 Internal working model

Bowlby also proposed that the type of attachment infants have with their primary caregiver creates a template for future relationships. This forms an internal working model for attachments in adulthood with romantic partners and, eventually, their own children. Adult attachment types include:

Secure attachment
Comfortable trusting and being dependent on others; also comfortable with others depending on them

Insecure-resistant attachment
Value relationships highly but anxious about rejection, making them clingy and demanding

Insecure-avoidant attachment
Uncomfortable depending on others, and with others depending on them, emotionally distant

Stages of attachment

Infants develop attachments (emotional bonds) to their caregivers and other people. Psychologists Heinz Rudolph Schaffer and Peggy Emerson (1964) assessed 60 infants in their homes at monthly intervals for the first 18 months of their life. The pair identified four stages of attachment. They also established when infants started to display separation anxiety and other behaviours.

Key facts

✓ Schaffer and Emerson identified four stages of attachment in infants.

✓ Infants around 7–9 months old experience separation anxiety when their primary caregiver leaves.

✓ From 9 months, infants form attachments with multiple figures, including grandparents, siblings, and other caregivers.

A newborn baby will respond to objects and people the same way.

Stage 1: Preattachment (0–3 months)
Babies are initially asocial, which means they respond similarly to all objects, whether these are animate (living) or inanimate (not living). At about 6 weeks, infants begin to smile at people, treating them differently from objects.

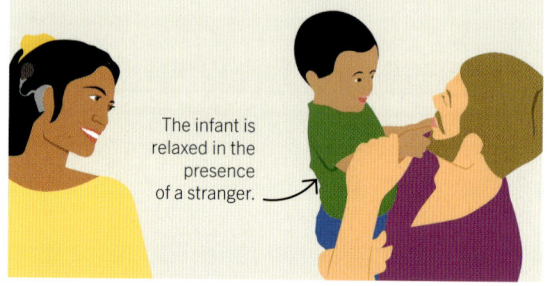

The infant is relaxed in the presence of a stranger.

Stage 2: Indiscriminate attachment (3–7 months)
From around 3 months, infants are able to recognize people who are familiar to them, especially their primary caregiver. They are not fearful of strangers but if they get upset, they are more easily calmed by the primary caregiver.

The infant becomes upset when their primary caregiver leaves.

Stage 3: Discriminate attachment (7–9 months)
By this age, infants have formed a specific attachment to their primary caregiver. They begin to show fear of strangers. They show separation anxiety and protest, usually by crying, when their primary caregiver leaves.

The infant is comfortable being left with their grandparents.

Stage 4: Multiple attachment (9 months onwards)
Infants begin to form multiple attachments. Their main attachment is usually to the primary caregiver, but there are also attachments to other contacts, such as grandparents, siblings, nursery staff, childminders, and friends. They become less afraid of strangers.

Parenting styles

How children behave may be influenced by the style of parenting they receive. Three styles — authoritarian, authoritative, and permissive — were theorized by US psychologist Diana Baumrind (1967). A fourth style — neglectful — was added by US psychologists Eleanor Maccoby and John Martin in 1983. Each parenting style involves different amounts of demandingness (control of a child's behaviour) and responsiveness (attentiveness to a child's needs).

Key facts

✓ Parenting styles can be defined as authoritarian, authoritative, permissive, and neglectful.

✓ Each parenting style differs in how the parent treats the child.

✓ Each parenting style has a different impact on the child.

Very demanding

Very unresponsive

Very responsive

Authoritarian parenting
These parents expect their children to follow strict rules, and failure to follow the rules usually results in punishment. They rarely explain why rules are set, and if a child makes a mistake, they seldom give advice on how to avoid repeating it. This parenting style can lead to children having low self-esteem.

Authoritative parenting
These parents have high expectations, but with warmth and an awareness of their children's needs. They set boundaries and rules by having open discussions. Authoritative parents punish their children less than authoritarian parents and show more forgiveness. Children raised this way tend to have high self-esteem.

Neglectful parenting
These parents may fulfil their children's basic needs, but they are generally uninvolved and detached from their children's lives. They offer little or no guidance and support, and are often indifferent, unresponsive, and dismissive. This parenting style can increase the risk of depression and behavioural issues in children.

Permissive parenting
Few demands are made on children raised this way. These parents are warm and attentive, but prioritize being their children's friends rather than parents. They have few expectations and rules (which are rarely enforced), and allow their children to make their own decisions. This parenting style can lead to low academic achievement.

Very undemanding

The strange situation

In 1969, American-Canadian psychologist Mary Ainsworth devised the "strange situation", a method used to identify the types of attachment shown by infants, based on their interactions with their mother and a stranger. The participants were observed in a laboratory that resembled a playroom over eight short scenarios, called episodes.

Types of attachment

After observing each infant's responses to the different situations, Ainsworth found that they could be categorized into one of three main attachment types. These attachment types were as follows:

Secure attachment
These infants showed moderate distress when separated from their mother. When she returned, they went to her for comfort and were easily soothed. They were wary of the stranger but explored the strange environment, looking back towards their mother for reassurance.

Percentage of Ainsworth's sample: 66%

The infant looked to the mother for comfort.

Insecure-resistant attachment
These infants were very distressed when separated from their mother. On her return, they approached but were angry and struggled to be released when picked up. They showed anxiety towards the stranger. There was limited exploration of the environment.

Percentage of Ainsworth's sample: 12%

The infant could not be comforted once the mother returned.

Insecure-avoidant attachment
These infants did not show distress when their mother left, and when she returned they did not attempt to get close to her. They showed little anxiety towards the stranger. These infants were happy to explore the environment but did not look back to the mother for reassurance.

Percentage of Ainsworth's sample: 22%

The infant was indifferent to the presence of the mother.

 Key facts

✓ The strange situation tested a infant's separation anxiety, reunion behaviour, stranger anxiety, and willingness to explore.

✓ Ainsworth proposed three attachment types: secure, insecure-avoidant, and insecure-resistant.

Stage of experiment	Description
Episode 1	The mother and infant are introduced to the room and to the observer.
Episode 2	The infant is free to explore and the mother responds if the child needs attention.
Episode 3	A stranger enters and gradually approaches the infant to interact.
Episode 4 (first separation)	The mother leaves the room. The stranger attempts to interact with the child.
Episode 5 (first reunion)	The stranger leaves and the mother re-enters, greeting the infant and settling them to play.
Episode 6 (second separation)	The mother leaves again. The infant is alone.
Episode 7	The stranger re-enters and gradually approaches the infant to interact.
Episode 8 (second reunion)	The mother re-enters and the stranger leaves. The mother settles the infant to play once more.

Cultural variations in attachment

Culture refers to the rules, customs, and morals that bind together members of a society. Different cultures raise their children in different ways. This has led to studies on whether children raised in different cultures develop different types of attachments.

📌 **Key facts**

✓ Van IJzendoorn compared attachment types across cultures.

✓ Greater difference in attachment types was found within the same culture than between different cultures.

Comparing cultures

Dutch psychologist Marinus van IJzendoorn (1988) used the "strange situation" methodology (see page 126) to compare attachment types across different cultures. The results showed that cultural differences were small. In fact, the differences within cultures (subcultural differences) were found to be 1.5 times greater than the variations between different cultures.

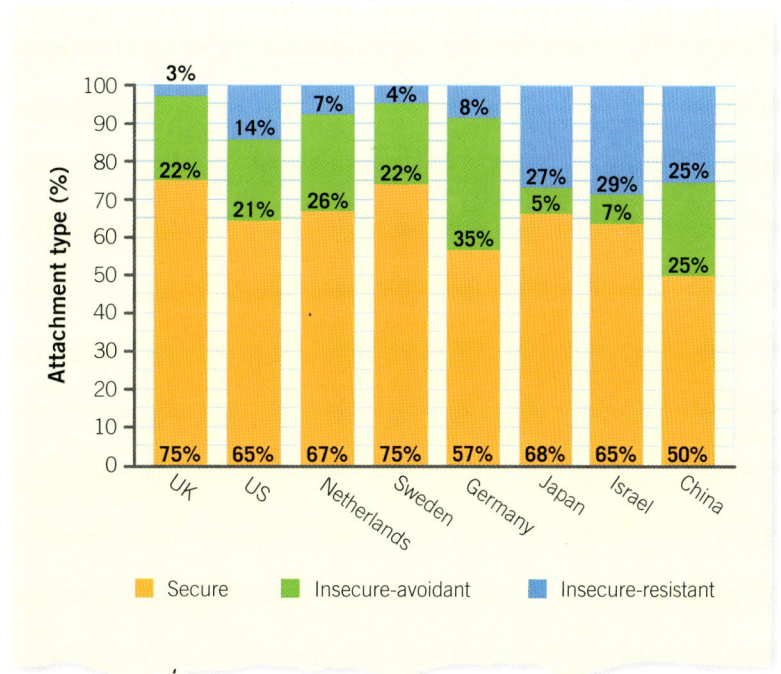

🔍 Individualism and collectivism

One broad way to group different cultures is by categorizing them as either individualistic or collectivist. Individualistic cultures, such as those in the US and northern Europe, emphasize the importance of the individual over the group. Collectivist cultures, such as in China and Japan, emphasize the importance of the group over the individual. These cultural differences can influence parenting styles.

Individualism

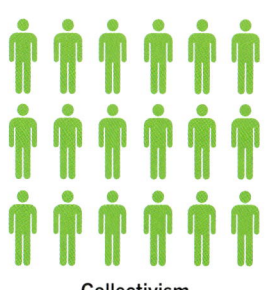

Collectivism

Maternal deprivation

British child therapist John Bowlby proposed that if a child is separated from their mother for an extended period of time in early childhood (without a suitable substitute), it will cause intellectual or psychological damage, or both. In his "juvenile thieves" study (1944), Bowlby investigated a possible link between maternal deprivation and affectionless psychopathy, a condition characterized by an inability to show affection for others and a lack of sense of responsibility. Affectionless psychopathy is also associated with criminality.

Key facts

✓ Maternal deprivation is an extended separation between a young child and their primary caregiver.

✓ Bowlby thought maternal deprivation could result in intellectual and/or psychological damage.

✓ In Bowlby's "juvenile thieves" study, 14 out of 44 children accused of stealing were categorized as affectionless psychopaths; 12 of these had experienced maternal deprivation.

Bowlby's "juvenile thieves" study

To investigate the link between maternal deprivation, affectionless psychopathy, and criminality, Bowlby studied 44 children accused of stealing (the "juvenile thieves"), alongside a control group (the "non-thieves"). He did this by conducting interviews with the children and their families.

The "juvenile thieves" group
Bowlby categorized 14 of the 44 "juvenile thieves" (32 per cent) as being affectionless psychopaths. He found that 12 of these 14 children (86 per cent) had experienced maternal deprivation, leading him to conclude that those who experience maternal deprivation may have a higher risk of affectionless psychopathy and subsequent criminality.

The control group
The control group consisted of 44 "emotionally disturbed" children who were not thieves. Of these 44, only two (less than 5 per cent) had experienced maternal deprivation. None were identified as affectionless psychopaths, suggesting that those who do not experience maternal deprivation have a lower risk of affectionless psychopathy and subsequent criminality.

Affectionless psychopaths

Not affectionless psychopaths

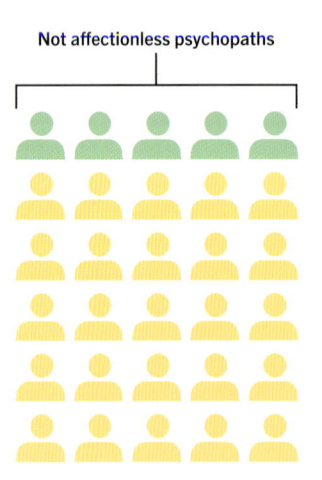

Not affectionless psychopaths

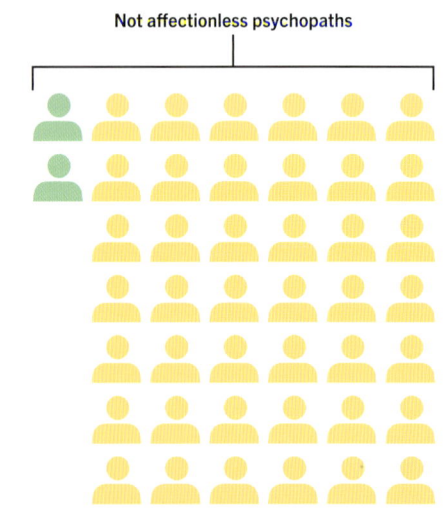

Key 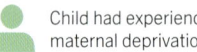 Child had experienced maternal deprivation   Child had **not** experienced maternal deprivation

Institutionalization

The negative psychological effect of spending a long period of time in an institution is called institutionalization. It is of particular concern for young children in orphanages as the lack of attachment figures and emotional care may lead to cognitive, social, and physical underdevelopment.

Key facts

✓ Institutionalization of Romanian orphans caused intellectual delay and disinhibited attachment style.

✓ Long-term effects of institutionalization can be avoided by adoption before the age of six months.

Romanian orphan studies

In the early 1990s, the world became aware of the plight of children in crowded and poorly equipped orphanages in Romania. Families from other countries offered to adopt the orphans, and many went to live in loving homes. It was unclear whether or not their early institutional life had caused lasting damage. In the early 2000s, British psychologists Michael Rutter and Edmund Sonuga-Barke began a study of the effects of institutionalization on 165 Romanian orphans adopted in the UK. The orphans were tested regularly to assess their cognitive, social, and physical development.

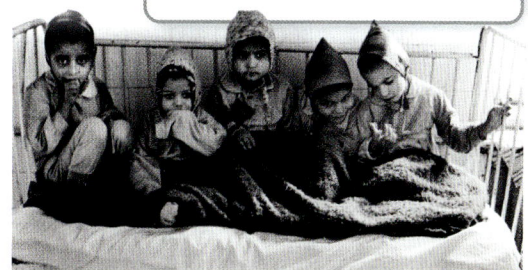

Age at adoption	Up to 6 months	Between 6 months and 2 years	Over 2 years
IQ score at age 11	102	86	77
Attachment style	Normal attachment style: severe effects of institutionalization were avoided if the child formed an attachment before 6 months.	Disinhibited attachment style: children adopted after 6 months displayed attention-seeking, clinginess, and uninhibited behaviour.	Disinhibited attachment style: children adopted after 2 years also displayed attention-seeking, clinginess, and uninhibited behaviour.

🔍 Effects of institutionalization

Intellectual delay
Institutionalization can lead to an intellectual delay. This is a problem with the cognitive abilities of a child, meaning they have not developed to the level expected for their age. This delay can affect achievements at school, career prospects, and interpersonal relationships, though there is debate over whether these effects are short- or long-term.

Disinhibited attachment
This is a style of attachment in which children are overly friendly and affectionate towards strangers. It's highly unusual behaviour for children, who are usually cautious or anxious around people they don't know. Disinhibited attachment could be viewed as an adaptation to living with multiple caregivers during the critical period in their development when attachment forms.

Physical underdevelopment
Children who have spent time in institutions are usually physically smaller than others of the same age. Research has shown that it is a lack of emotional care rather than poor nutrition that leads to this underdevelopment. The production of growth hormone is affected by the severe emotional disturbance. Research has suggested these effects may be reversible.

Chapter 9

Developmental psychology:
physical and cognitive development

Prenatal development

During pregnancy, a developing baby's brain goes through critical stages of growth and development. Adequate nutrition and the avoidance of harmful substances are important during this period to prevent physical and cognitive problems later in life.

Key facts

✓ Adequate nutrition and the avoidance of harmful substances are crucial to prenatal brain development.

✓ Teratogens are substances that can cross the placenta and harm the developing baby.

✓ Exposure of the developing baby to alcohol can cause significant cognitive impairment later in life (foetal alcohol syndrome).

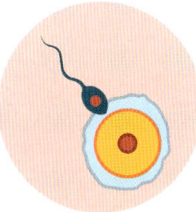

1. Conception
This occurs when a sperm (male sex cell) fertilizes an egg (female sex cell). Genes from both parents are combined in a single cell at conception. The genetic makeup and biological sex of the baby are set at this point.

2. Cell division
The fertilized egg is called a zygote at the single cell stage. Cell division begins after 24–36 hours, the number of cells doubling with each division. These cells will eventually form an embryo, placenta, and other structures.

3. Implantation
By about a week after conception, the dividing cells have formed a ball-shaped mass called a blastocyst. It travels via the fallopian tubes to the uterus, where it implants into the uterus wall.

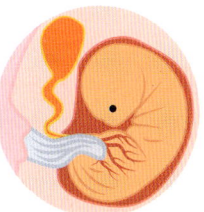

4. Embryo
The inner cells of the blastocyst form an embryo, while the outer cells form a placenta and umbilical cord. These obtain oxygen and nutrients from the mother's blood but block large molecules, cells, and harmful microorganisms.

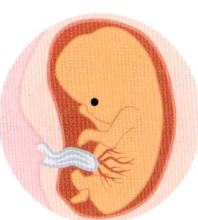

5. Foetus
After about 9 weeks, the developing baby is called a foetus and begins to look recognizably human. About the size of a kidney bean at first, the foetus has limbs, fingers and toes, a face, and most of its organs have formed.

Teratogens

Some substances a mother is exposed to during pregnancy can cross the placenta and harm the developing baby, especially in early pregnancy. Such substances are called teratogens. Alcohol, for example, can cause foetal alcohol syndrome, leading to long-term physical and cognitive problems. Other teratogens come from cigarettes, recreational drugs, medications, and infectious organisms. Exposure to ionizing radiation such as X-rays can also harm an unborn baby.

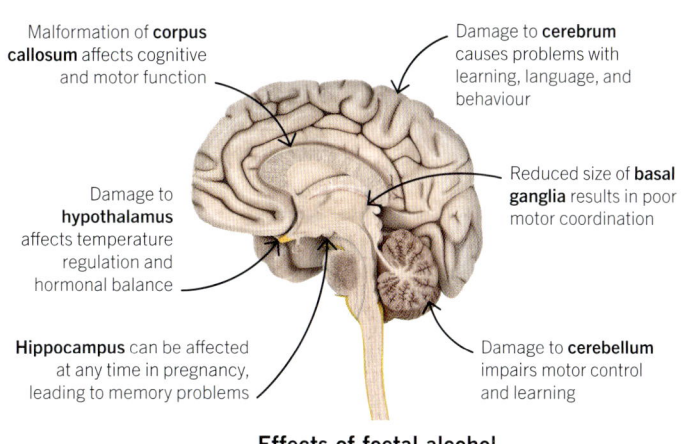

Malformation of **corpus callosum** affects cognitive and motor function

Damage to **cerebrum** causes problems with learning, language, and behaviour

Damage to **hypothalamus** affects temperature regulation and hormonal balance

Reduced size of **basal ganglia** results in poor motor coordination

Hippocampus can be affected at any time in pregnancy, leading to memory problems

Damage to **cerebellum** impairs motor control and learning

Effects of foetal alcohol syndrome on brain

The competent newborn

Babies are born with instinctive, involuntary reflexes, such as the ability to suck with the mouth and grasp with a hand. Some of these newborn reflexes disappear over the first year or two, while other reflexes (such as breathing, coughing, gagging, and blinking) last for life. Missing or unusually persistent newborn reflexes may be a sign of developmental issues.

Key facts

✓ Babies are born with involuntary reflexes.

✓ Most newborn reflexes are lost within a year or two.

✓ Missing or persistent newborn reflexes may be a sign of developmental issues.

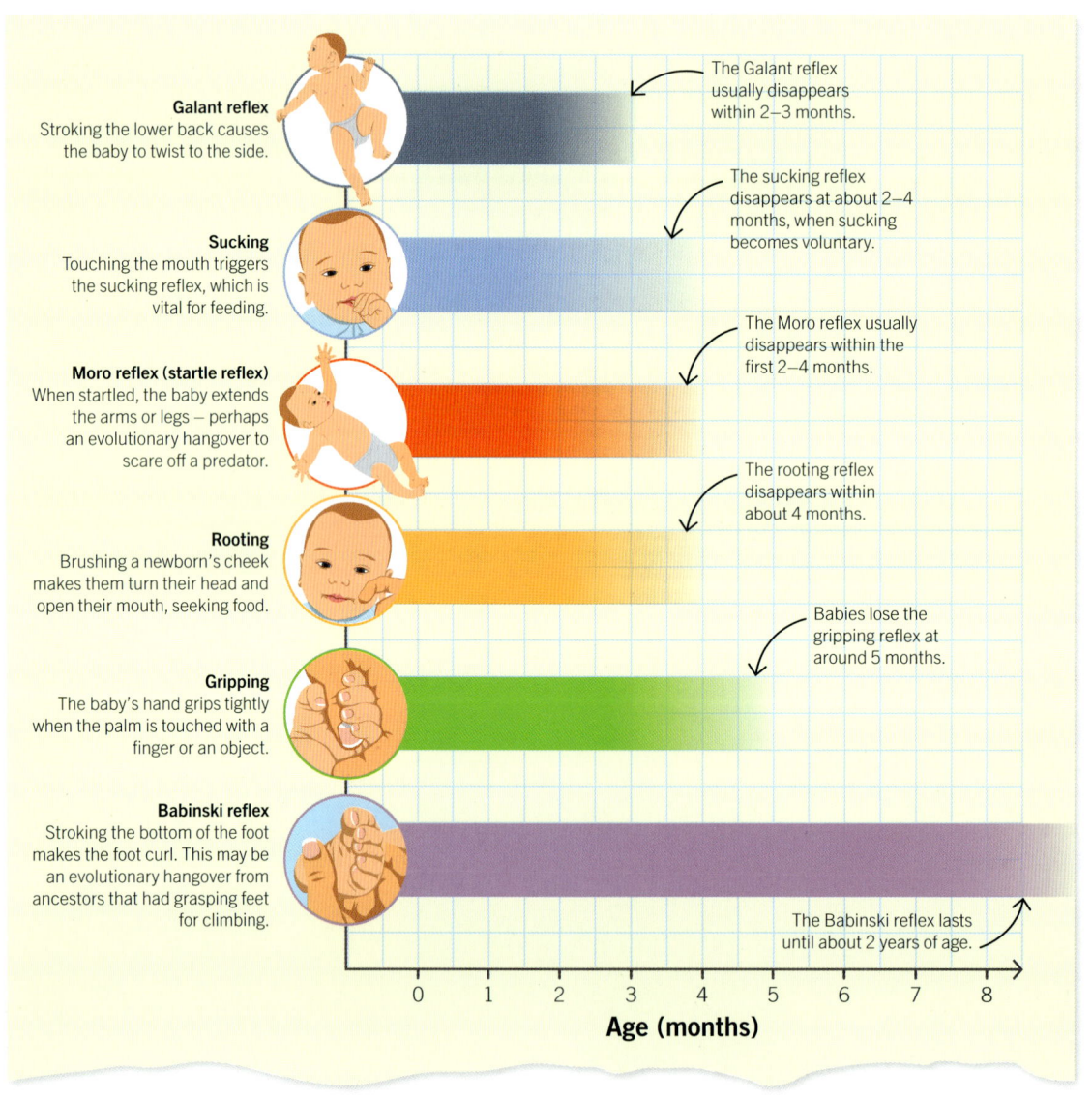

Galant reflex
Stroking the lower back causes the baby to twist to the side.

The Galant reflex usually disappears within 2–3 months.

Sucking
Touching the mouth triggers the sucking reflex, which is vital for feeding.

The sucking reflex disappears at about 2–4 months, when sucking becomes voluntary.

Moro reflex (startle reflex)
When startled, the baby extends the arms or legs – perhaps an evolutionary hangover to scare off a predator.

The Moro reflex usually disappears within the first 2–4 months.

Rooting
Brushing a newborn's cheek makes them turn their head and open their mouth, seeking food.

The rooting reflex disappears within about 4 months.

Gripping
The baby's hand grips tightly when the palm is touched with a finger or an object.

Babies lose the gripping reflex at around 5 months.

Babinski reflex
Stroking the bottom of the foot makes the foot curl. This may be an evolutionary hangover from ancestors that had grasping feet for climbing.

The Babinski reflex lasts until about 2 years of age.

0   1   2   3   4   5   6   7   8

Age (months)

Early brain development

During pregnancy, an average of 15 million new brain cells form each hour in a baby's developing brain. A newborn baby has most of the brain cells it will ever have, but the neural networks connecting them are immature. In the first 2–3 years, the number of synapses increases rapidly as an infant learns. Later, active connections are strengthened and unused ones are removed in a process called synaptic pruning.

The growing brain
The brain grows rapidly in early childhood, reaching close to adult size by the age of 6. While neuron formation (neurogenesis) mostly occurs before birth, growth of the brain after birth is driven by the formation of new synapses (synaptogenesis).

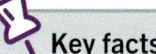

Key facts

✓ Formation of brain cells occurs mostly before birth.

✓ After birth, formation of new synapses in early childhood creates dense neural networks.

✓ Later in childhood, underused synapses are removed (synaptic pruning).

✓ Maturation occurs in an orderly sequence of steps.

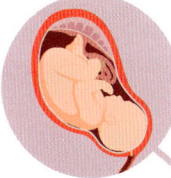

Prenatal
The brain and nervous system form. An average of 250,000 new brain cells form each minute throughout pregnancy.

Birth
Most of the neurons that will be present in the adult brain have formed, but the cells are not yet densely connected. The brain is about 25% of its adult size.

Infancy
New synapses form at a rapid rate in the first 2–3 years, creating the dense neural networks needed for learning to walk and talk. The brain reaches 75% of adult size by the age of 2.

Early childhood
Synaptic pruning begins around the age of 2. The frontal lobes grow rapidly at the age of 3–6, enabling better control of behaviour. Infant amnesia ends around the age of 4, when the earliest memories form.

Adolescence
Brain growth slows down but synaptic pruning accelerates, making existing neural pathways more efficient. Frontal lobe maturation continues into early adulthood.

🔍 **Maturation**

Although children develop at varying rates, most follow the same sequence of milestones. For example, motor skills develop in a clear sequence – infants typically learn to sit, crawl, stand, and walk, in the same order, though timings vary. This orderly process, called maturation, is controlled partly by genes (nature) but is also influenced by the environment (nurture).

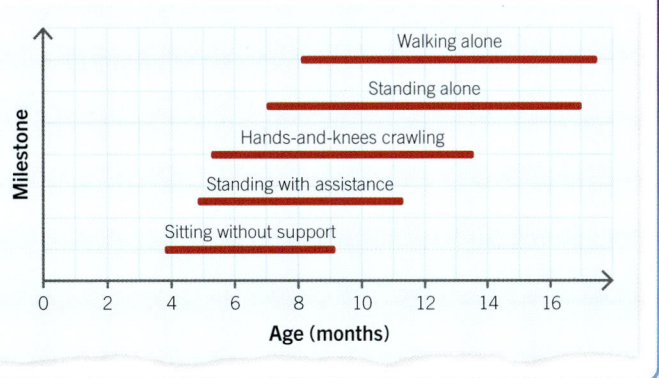

Stages of cognitive development

Swiss psychologist Jean Piaget theorized that children go through four stages of cognitive development as they grow: sensorimotor, preoperational, concrete operational, and formal operational. As they develop, children's schemas (mental frameworks that help them make sense of the world) become increasingly organized and complex.

Key facts

✓ Piaget proposed four cognitive development stages: sensorimotor, preoperational, concrete operational, and formal operational.

✓ As children move through the stages they develop object permanence, symbolic thinking, logical reasoning, and abstract thinking.

Piaget's stages (1936)

The type of thinking that children can do varies at each of Piaget's four stages, which follow a fixed sequence and build on previous stages to shape cognitive development. No stage can be skipped as earlier achievements form the foundation of later stages.

 H_2O

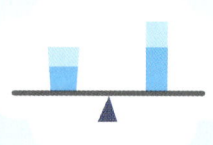

Water

Sensorimotor stage (0–2 years)
Children learn about the world through sensory and hands-on experiences with objects. They develop object permanence as they begin to understand that objects exist when out of sight. They begin to associate names and words with objects; for example, "water" with a cup of water.

Preoperational stage (2–7 years)
Children develop symbolic thinking – learning that words and images represent real objects and concepts. They know what water looks and tastes like, and that rain is water, but they don't yet understand abstract properties of water, such as its importance for survival.

Concrete operational stage (7–11 years)
Children develop logical reasoning at this stage. For example, they begin to understand the concept of conservation – they know that when water is poured from a short, wide glass into a tall, narrow glass, the amount of water doesn't change even though its shape has changed.

Formal operational stage (11+ years)
Teenagers develop abstract thinking and hypothetical reasoning, and become adept at problem-solving. With these new skills, they can increase their understanding of the world. For example, they can conceptualize unseen entities, such as the oxygen and hydrogen molecules that make up water.

More knowledgeable others

Russian psychologist Lev Vygotsky proposed that a child's mind develops by learning from more knowledgeable others (MKO). An MKO can be a parent, teacher, coach, or even a peer. Vygotsky argued that children acquire knowledge, ways of thinking, problem-solving skills, and cultural values from interactions with MKOs.

📌 **Key facts**

✓ Vygotsky proposed that children learn from more knowledgeable others (MKOs).

✓ The zone of proximal development is the space between what children are able and not yet able to do.

✓ Scaffolding describes the support structures given to a child to develop their cognitive abilities.

The zone of proximal development (1934)

Vygotsky identified a space between what a child can do alone without help and what they cannot do, even with help. He called this space the zone of proximal development (ZPD). Interaction with an MKO allows a child to cross into the ZPD, where they can acquire new skills and knowledge with support — even though the child may still be limited by their developmental stage.

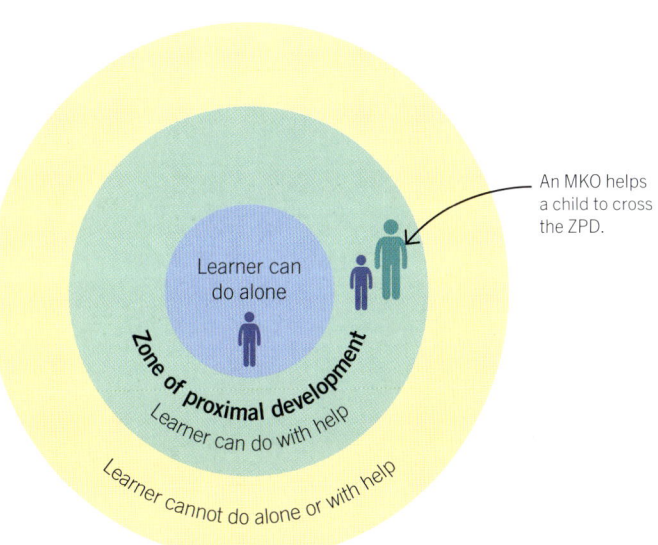

An MKO helps a child to cross the ZPD.

Learner can do alone

Zone of proximal development

Learner can do with help

Learner cannot do alone or with help

🔍 Scaffolding

Scaffolding refers to all the support structures MKOs give children to help them to cross the ZPD and develop cognitive abilities beyond their current level. These abilities may include reading, writing, or riding a bicycle.

1. When a child is learning to ride a bike, an MKO attaches stabilizers to the wheels so that the child doesn't lose their balance and fall over.

2. Once the child can cycle with stabilizers, the MKO removes them, running by the side of the child to help if they fall.

3. Eventually, after all the help from the MKO, the child can ride the bike with no stabilizers or assistance.

Autism spectrum disorder

Autism spectrum disorder (ASD) is a neurodevelopmental condition that is first noticed in early childhood. It is often characterized by impaired social skills, repetitive behavior, restricted interests, and difficulty processing sensory input. It is a lifelong condition of unknown cause and has no cure, but symptoms often become less severe with age.

Key facts

✓ Autism is characterized by impaired social skills, repetitive behaviour, and restricted interests.

✓ ASD is sometimes described as a spectrum because symptoms vary.

✓ Symptoms often become less severe with age.

ASD profiles

ASD is sometimes described as a "spectrum" because symptoms vary enormously from person to person, as the two profiles below show. Many people with ASD lead normal, independent lives and some excel in subjects that interest them, such as maths or music. However, the most severe cases are disabling and lifelong support is needed.

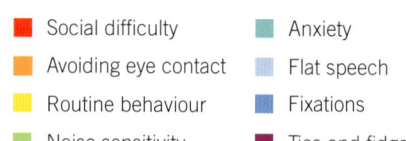

- 🟥 Social difficulty
- 🟧 Avoiding eye contact
- 🟨 Routine behaviour
- 🟩 Noise sensitivity
- 🟩 Anxiety
- 🟦 Flat speech
- 🟦 Fixations
- 🟥 Tics and fidgets

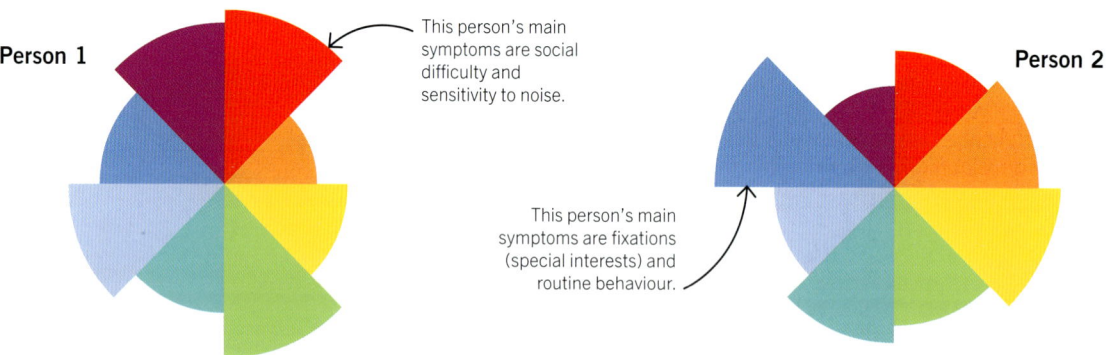

Person 1

This person's main symptoms are social difficulty and sensitivity to noise.

This person's main symptoms are fixations (special interests) and routine behaviour.

Person 2

Common symptoms of ASD			
Social symptoms	**Repetitive behaviours**	**Restricted interests**	**Sensory processing**
• Dislike of or avoidance of eye contact • Difficulty reading other people's emotions • Failure to adapt tone of voice and manner in different social settings • Difficulty forming or maintaining relationships • Demonstrate emotional responses in atypical way	• Dislike of changes to routine • Repetitive movements such as rocking or flapping hands and arms • Use of repetitive language or inability to speak for some or all of the time	• Intense enthusiasm for one or a limited range of interests • Difficulty paying attention to anything other than special interests • Unlikely to engage in the interests of others	• Over- or under-sensitive to light, touch, taste, and sound • Dislike of certain sensations, such as food textures or the feel of some clothing • Preference for a restricted, simple diet • Enhanced attention to detail

Psychology of puberty

Puberty is the developmental stage between childhood and adulthood. It typically starts between the ages of 8 and 14 for females, and the ages of 9 and 14 for males. Changing hormones transform the body, but puberty also has a significant impact on the brain. It can alter a young person's self-identity, affecting how they think and experience the world around them. Puberty can be a tricky time, packed with emotional, psychological, and social challenges to navigate.

Key facts

✓ Puberty is a period of significant change which can affect a young person's self-identity.

✓ Puberty can bring challenges such as self-consciousness, stress, and family conflict.

Physical changes
During puberty, a child's body physically matures. In biological males, the voice deepens, facial hair develops, and shoulders broaden. In biological females, the menstrual cycle begins, breasts develop, and hips widen.

Body image and self-esteem
The physical changes of puberty can affect body image and self-esteem. Self-consciousness about appearance and comparing oneself to unrealistic beauty standards may cause feelings of dissatisfaction.

Emotional changes
Hormonal changes make puberty an emotionally intense time. Teenagers can experience new emotions, mood swings, heightened sensitivity, and increased stress.

Identity formation
Exploring topics such as gender identity, sexual orientation, and personal values during the teenage years helps a young person to develop their self-identity and find their place in the world. For some, this can take a while, and might bring up challenging feelings.

Cognitive development
Abstract thinking, problem-solving skills, and empathy for others develop during the teenage years. Thoughts become more complex and individualized.

Moral reasoning
Major changes occur in the mind, emotions, and social life of a teenager. These changes shape their developing moral perspective, and can lead to questions about social norms, authority figures, and differentiating between right and wrong.

Parent-child relationships
Teenagers often start to seek greater independence while still relying on the support and guidance of their parents. Negotiating this change may lead to tension on both sides, and potentially conflict.

Peer relationships
As teens get older, the influence of parents reduces, and teens may spend more time with friends than family. They might experience peer pressure – pressure from their friends to behave in certain ways.

Sexuality and relationships
Puberty can mark the start of romantic and sexual feelings and relationships, although not for everyone. Experiencing sexual attraction can lead to intense emotions and potentially feelings of confusion.

The teenage brain

During adolescence, the brain goes through a period of developmental change that may be reflected in impulsive and rebellious behaviour and personality changes. These changes accompany a growing sense of independence and diminishing parental influence, often leading to conflict.

Key facts

✓ During adolescence, synaptic pruning removes underused synapses, causing a reduction in grey matter.

✓ Delayed maturation of the prefrontal cortex may explain the impulsive behaviour of teenagers.

✓ The sleep cycle of teenagers is delayed, causing a preference for later bedtimes and later waking times.

Pruning grey matter

The quantity of grey matter (tissue consisting of neuron cell bodies and dendrites) in the brain peaks in childhood, when neurons build many synapses. In adolescence, underused connections are removed (synaptic pruning), and frequently used pathways are strengthened by a process called myelination, making neural communication more efficient. This maturation process happens across the brain but finishes last in the prefrontal cortex, which is not fully mature until the mid-20s. As the prefrontal cortex is responsible for impulse control and planning, psychologists believe the lag may explain the impulsivity, emotional volatility, and risk-taking behaviour of many teenagers.

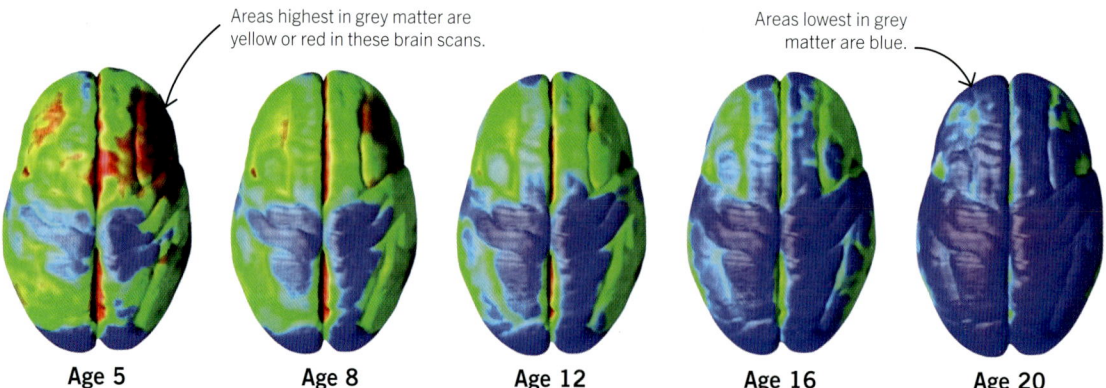

Areas highest in grey matter are yellow or red in these brain scans.

Areas lowest in grey matter are blue.

Age 5   Age 8   Age 12   Age 16   Age 20

Sleep

During adolescence, the hormone melatonin is released later in the day, causing a shift in the body's 24-hour biological clock (circadian clock) and a preference for later bedtimes and later waking times. The increasing interest in social interaction that accompanies adolescence can compound this effect, causing teenagers to stay socially active until late into the evening.

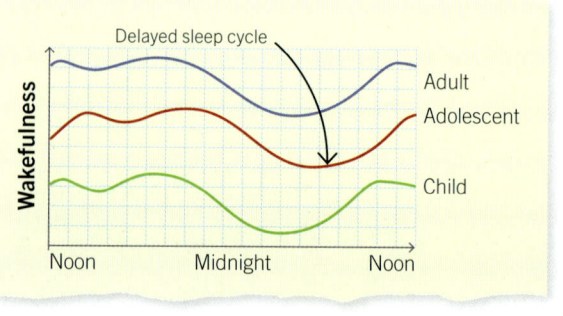

Delayed sleep cycle

Wakefulness

Adult
Adolescent
Child

Noon   Midnight   Noon

Psychosocial development

Erik Erikson proposed that people encounter eight stages in which they experience psychosocial turning points, or crises, in their relationships with others. Resolution of each crisis leads to personal growth and development, and the attainment of a virtue that helps shape their personality.

Key facts

✓ Erikson proposed eight stages of psychosocial development that people progress through during life.

✓ At each stage, a crisis needs to be resolved for personal growth and development, and the attainment of a virtue, such as purpose or love.

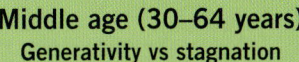

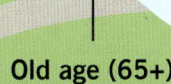

Old age (65+)
Integrity vs despair

The older adult assesses their life and the contributions they've made.

Resulting virtue: wisdom

Early adulthood (19–29 years)
Intimacy vs isolation

The young adult learns to build relationships and intimacy with others.

Resulting virtue: love

Middle age (30–64 years)
Generativity vs stagnation

The adult contributes to society and has their own family.

Resulting virtue: care

Adolescence (12–18 years)
Identity vs confusion

The adolescent tries out different identities to see which fits best.

Resulting virtue: fidelity

School age (7–11 years)
Industry vs inferiority

The child develops self-confidence in areas of competence but feels inferior when they struggle with a task or schoolwork.

Resulting virtue: competence

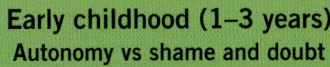

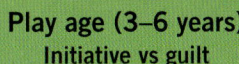

Infancy (0–1 year)
Trust vs mistrust

The infant learns to trust (or mistrust) that their carer will meet their needs.

Resulting virtue: hope

Early childhood (1–3 years)
Autonomy vs shame and doubt

The child develops independence, wanting to do things themselves.

Resulting virtue: will

Play age (3–6 years)
Initiative vs guilt

The child begins to take initiative but may feel guilt if it goes wrong.

Resulting virtue: purpose

The ageing brain

As people age, memory and other cognitive functions gradually decline. This is due to reduction in volume of parts of the brain important in memory and cognition, such as the hippocampus and cerebral cortex. For some people, a much steeper decline occurs, leading to a debilitating condition called dementia or neurocognitive disorder. Incidence of neurocognitive disorder rises with age, but it is not an inevitable consequence of ageing.

Key facts

✓ As people age, memory and other cognitive functions gradually decline.

✓ Neurocognitive disorder (dementia) is a steeper decline in mental function that affects some people.

✓ The most common cause of neurocognitive disorder in elderly people is Alzheimer's disease.

Alzheimer's disease

Neurocognitive disorder has many causes, including circulatory disease, head injury, and drug abuse, but the most common cause is Alzheimer's disease, a brain disease that becomes increasingly common with age. Alzheimer's is progressive, with early stages manifesting as memory lapses and difficulty concentrating, while later stages involve personality change, profound cognitive impairment, and problems with physical coordination and continence. The disease is thought to be caused by the accumulation of certain proteins inside and around neurons, leading to cell death and atrophy (wasting away) of brain tissue.

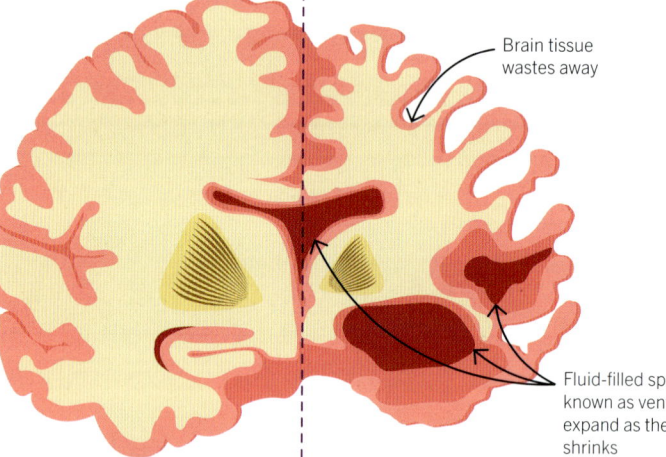

Brain tissue wastes away

Fluid-filled spaces known as ventricles expand as the brain shrinks

Normal brain

Alzheimer's brain

🔍 Lifestyle and neurocognitive disorder

We cannot change our age or genetics, but there are certain modifiable lifestyle factors that affect the risk of neurocognitive disorder. Based on existing evidence, people should refrain from smoking, get adequate sleep, eat a healthy diet, maintain healthy blood pressure, and manage their blood sugar. Numerous studies also show that regular exercise and social engagement reduce the risk of both neurocognitive disorder and the natural cognitive decline that occurs with ageing.

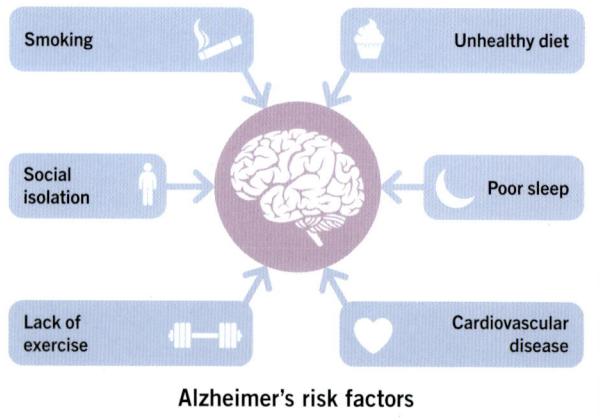

Smoking

Unhealthy diet

Social isolation

Poor sleep

Lack of exercise

Cardiovascular disease

Alzheimer's risk factors

Biological sex and gender

Biological sex and gender are closely related but distinct concepts. Biological sex is a physical characteristic determined by a person's sex chromosomes, which in turn govern levels of sex hormones (oestrogen and testosterone) and the development of sex organs. Biological sex helps to shape a person's gender – the state of being masculine or feminine in relation to prevailing cultural norms.

Key facts

✓ Biological sex and gender are closely related but distinct concepts.

✓ Biological sex is a physical characteristic determined by a person's sex chromosomes.

✓ Gender is the state of being masculine or feminine in relation to cultural norms.

Sex determination

Only two of the 46 chromosomes in human cells affect biological sex: the Y chromosome, inherited from fathers, and the X chromosome, which can be inherited from either parent. An embryo with two X chromosomes develops into a biological female, whereas an XY embryo develops into a biological male. Until about seven weeks after conception, male and female embryos are indistinguishable. After that point, a gene on the Y chromosome of males is activated, triggering a cascade of changes that include raised levels of testosterone (a hormone present in both sexes) and the development of testes. Later in pregnancy, differing levels of sex hormones also cause structural differences in the brains of boys and girls.

🔍 Klinefelter and Turner syndrome

A small percentage of people do not fit the usual chromosomal definition of male or female. In Klinefelter syndrome, boys are born with an additional X chromosome (XXY). This causes few symptoms in childhood but can cause infertility, reduced facial and body hair, and enlarged breasts in adulthood. Turner syndrome is a condition in which girls are born with only one X chromosome, leading to short stature, undeveloped ovaries, and infertility. These conditions are sometimes described as intersex, a term that also refers to people born with ambiguous genitals.

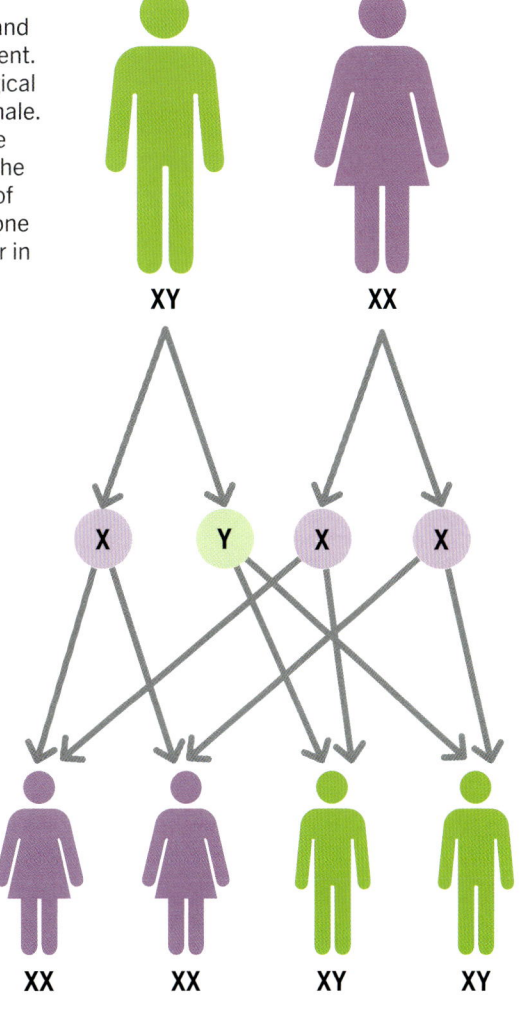

Gender development

While biological sex is set at conception, the extent to which a person conforms to stereotypical male or female roles develops during childhood and is thought to be influenced by social factors. By adulthood, most people have a gender identity that matches their biological sex, but many people do not. Psychologists have proposed various theories of gender development.

Key facts

✓ Gender identity develops during childhood and is thought to be influenced by social factors.

✓ Gender dysphoria is a mental health condition caused by a mismatch between a person's biological sex and gender identity.

Constancy theory (1966)
US psychologist Lawrence Kohlberg proposed that gender roles develop only after a child understands that their sex remains fixed and constant, which happens around the age of 5–7. Before then, Kohlberg argued that the idea of gender is more fluid and based on superficial characteristics, such as clothes or hairstyle.

Psychodynamic theories
Psychiatrists Sigmund Freud and Carl Jung theorized that small children have unconscious desires for the opposite-sex parent (the Oedipus complex in boys and the Electra complex in girls) and feelings of rivalry towards the same-sex parent. The conflict is resolved, they claimed, when children learn to identify with the same-sex parent, "internalizing" their values and taking on the same gender role.

Schema theory (1983)
According to US psychologists Carol Martin and Charles Halverson, children construct mental frameworks (schemas) about gender after learning their sex. Basic at first, the schema becomes more complex and rigid as children categorize more characteristics as male or female. The schema involves an in-group (the child's own gender, which provides cues on how to act) and an out-group (the opposite gender, which is ignored).

Social learning theory (1965)
Canadian-American psychologist Albert Bandura thought that children acquire gender roles by imitating behaviour they observe in real life or the media. Parents then reinforce these behaviours with positive or negative feedback. The social learning theory of gender sees gender as a social construct, rather than a consequence of biological sex.

🔍 Gender dysphoria

Some people suffer anxiety and depression resulting from a mismatch between their biological sex and their gender identity. This psychological distress is known as gender dysphoria and it is most common in people who identify as transgender. Treatment includes counselling to help people cope with the stigma of non-conforming gender identity and medical intervention such as surgery to change a person's gender presentation.

Sexual orientation

A person's sexual orientation describes the gender(s) of the people to whom they feel romantically or sexually attracted. It is influenced by a combination of genetic, hormonal, developmental, and social factors. The first major study of human sexuality was conducted by US sexologist Alfred Kinsey in 1948. Today, it continues to be an active area of psychological research.

Key facts

✓ Sexual orientation describes the gender(s) of the people a person wants to be romantic or sexual with.

✓ The Kinsey scale places sexuality on a continuum, from exclusively heterosexual to exclusively homosexual.

The Kinsey scale

After conducting face-to-face interviews with almost 8,000 people about their sexual experiences, Kinsey developed the Kinsey scale. The scale placed human sexuality on a spectrum from exclusively heterosexual to exclusively homosexual.

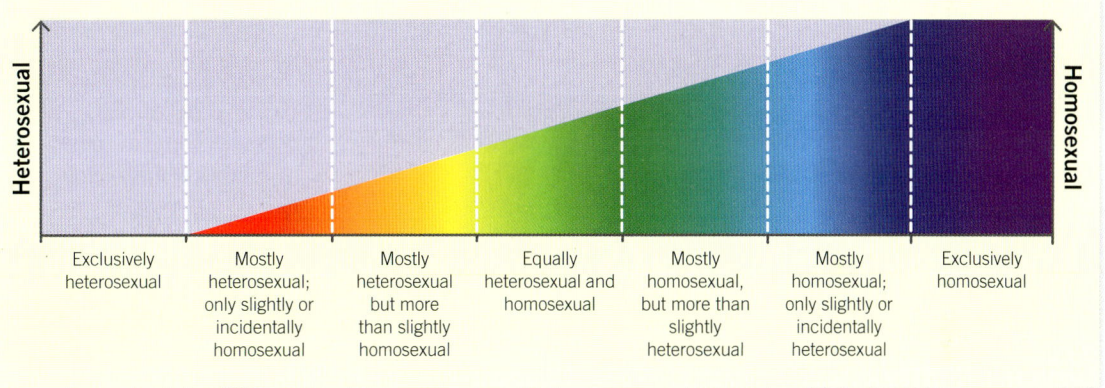

| Exclusively heterosexual | Mostly heterosexual; only slightly or incidentally homosexual | Mostly heterosexual but more than slightly homosexual | Equally heterosexual and homosexual | Mostly homosexual, but more than slightly heterosexual | Mostly homosexual; only slightly or incidentally heterosexual | Exclusively homosexual |

🔍 Criticism of the Kinsey scale

Although groundbreaking in 1948, Kinsey made assumptions that limit his scale's ability to describe all aspects of human sexuality today.

• Kinsey's sample was primarily made up of young, white, middle-class Americans. It did not represent the diversity of humanity.

• The scale assumes that if a person identifies as one thing, they will behave in the same way, however, this is not always the case; for example, a person can be romantic with one gender, but sexual with another.

• The Kinsey scale does not acknowledge asexuality.

• It also assumes that gender is binary (that there are only two genders).

🔍 Sexual and romantic orientation

This list is not comprehensive.

• **Straight (heterosexual):** romantic and/or sexual contact with the opposite gender.

• **Gay (homosexual):** romantic and/or sexual contact with the same gender.

• **Bisexual**: romantic and/or sexual contact with the same and opposite gender.

• **Pansexual:** romantic and/or sexual contact with any gender.

• **Asexual:** little or no interest in sexual contact; may or may not be interested in romantic connections.

• **Aromantic:** no interest in romantic contact; may or may not be interested in sexual connections.

Chapter 10
Motivation

The hierarchy of needs

US psychologist Abraham Maslow proposed that people are motivated by five needs, which must be met in a particular order. His 1943 theory, known as the hierarchy of needs, is often presented as a pyramid. At the bottom of the pyramid are the most basic human needs, such as food and water. At the top is self-actualization — the fulfilment of a person's true potential according to their talents and abilities.

Very few people achieve self-actualization.

Key facts

✓ Maslow's theory outlines a sequence of five needs that motivate human behaviour.

✓ Physiological needs must be satisfied first, followed by psychological needs.

✓ The theory has been criticized for assuming that human needs are universal.

Self-actualization
Achievement of full creative, intellectual, and social potential

Self-esteem
Sense of accomplishment, confidence, respect (of and from others)

Humans are motivated to reach the next level up once the needs on the previous level have been met.

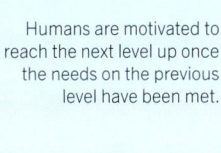

Love and belonging
Relationships with family, friends, romantic partners, and within a community

Challenges, such as bereavement, illness, or job loss, can set a person back.

Safety
Shelter, security, health, employment

Physiological needs
Food, water, sleep, warmth

🔍 Criticism of Maslow's theory

Maslow has been criticized for assuming that all humans are motivated by the same needs. While individualistic cultures (such as those of the US and northern Europe) tend to value highly the needs of the individual, collectivist cultures (such as those of China and Japan) tend to prioritize the needs of the group. In collectivist cultures, striving for strong community relationships is likely to be more important than the pursuit of self-actualization.

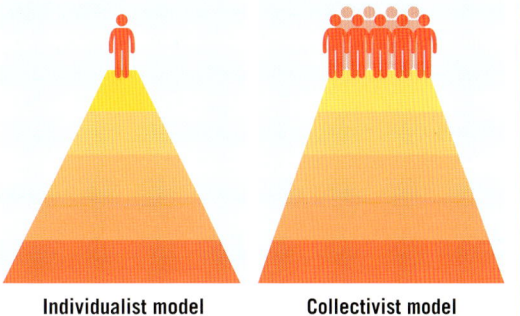

Individualist model

Collectivist model

Congruence

US psychologist Carl Rogers (1951) proposed that in order for someone to achieve personal growth, or even self-actualization (see page 145), they have to become congruent. This means that their self-image (the way they perceive themselves) is broadly equivalent to — congruent with — their ideal self (the person they want to be).

Incongruence

Congruence is difficult to achieve, and for many people a big gap exists between their image of themselves and their ideal self. This state of incongruence leads to negative feelings, such as anxiety, stress, and low self-esteem, that make it hard for that person to realize their potential.

Key facts

✓ A person achieves congruence when their self-image and their ideal self broadly overlap.

✓ A state of congruence is essential for a person to achieve self-actualization.

✓ To become congruent, a person needs to experience unconditional positive regard (love) from important people in their lives.

✓ Conditions of worth are expectations a person feels they have to meet to earn love from significant others.

Congruent
If a person's self-image and their ideal self overlap, they may be able to self-actualize.

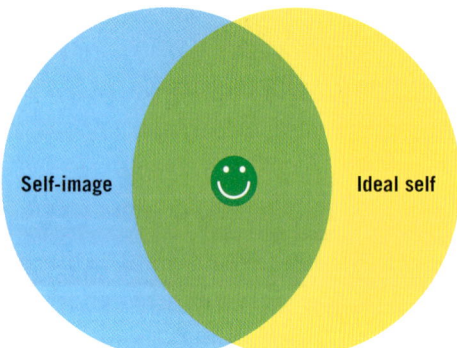

Incongruent
If a person's self-image doesn't match up to their ideal self, self-actualization is very difficult.

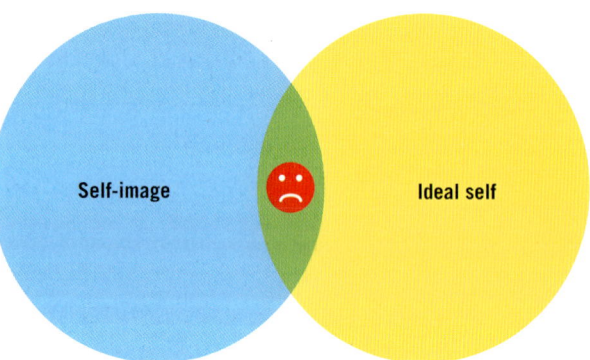

🔍 Conditions of worth

Rogers suggested that in order to fulfil their potential, a person needs to receive unconditional positive regard (unconditional love) from parents during childhood or from other important people in their lives. If the significant person sets boundaries or limits on their love, or "conditions of worth", it can lead to feelings of low self-esteem. For example, if a child feels they have to achieve something special, like winning a prize, to earn their parents' love, this may damage the child's self-image and store up problems for the future.

Drive reduction theory

According to US psychologist Clark Hull's drive reduction theory (1943), behaviour is motivated by the need to reduce unpleasant states of tension called drives. For example, the need for food creates an unpleasant feeling of hunger that we seek to reduce through eating. This behaviour reduces the drive and restores physiological balance.

Key facts

✓ Drive reduction theory proposes that behaviour is motivated by the need to reduce unpleasant states of tension (drives).

✓ Drive reduction theory is an example of homeostasis.

✓ Hull proposed that drive reduction plays a major role in learning.

Homeostasis

Drive reduction theory is based on the idea of homeostasis — the self-regulating process by which the body maintains optimum temperature, blood oxygen level, and so on. Drives are affected by stimuli. For instance, the sight of food to a hungry person is a powerful stimulus, increasing the incentive to eat. Stimuli can have a positive or negative effect. Food that looks appetizing acts as a positive incentive, increasing drive, whereas food that looks rotten acts as a negative incentive, reducing the drive to eat.

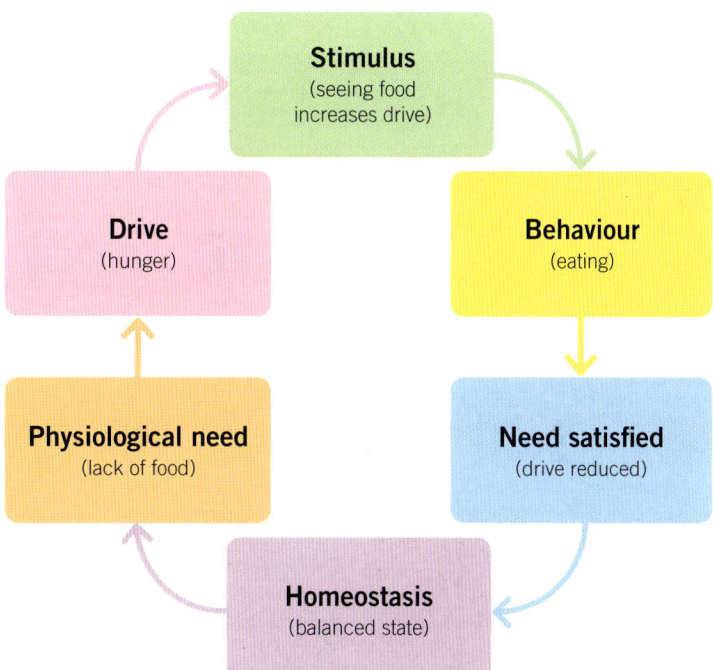

🔍 Habit formation

Hull proposed that drive reduction plays a major role in learning. Habits form as we learn which behaviours most effectively reduce drives. For example, we learn to put on more clothes when cold.

The physiology of hunger

Appetite is regulated by the complex interplay of digestive organs, the brain, and many different hormones that influence the feeling of hunger. Like body temperature control, appetite control is a homeostatic process, which means the body uses feedback systems to keep internal food stores within an optimum range. Some scientists believe that this thermostat-like system causes body weight to tend towards a stable set point.

Early theories
Early research into hunger focused on the role of the stomach. In 1912, US physiologists Walter Cannon and A.L. Washburn demonstrated that hunger pangs — sudden, sharp contractions of an empty stomach — correlate with feelings of hunger. They theorized that the contractions cause hunger, but this idea was later rejected after scientists found that surgical removal of the stomach in rats or humans did not cause hunger to disappear.

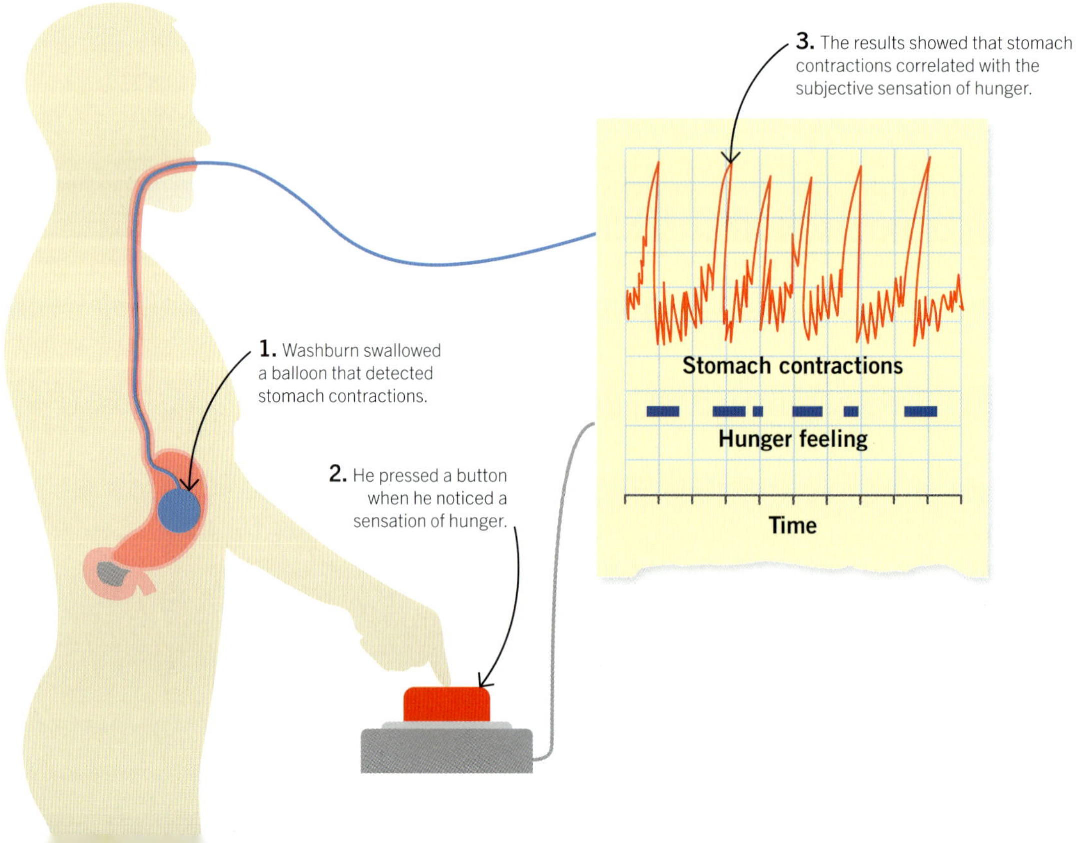

Key facts

✓ Cannon and Washburn proposed that stomach contractions cause hunger.

✓ Many hormones are involved in hunger control. Ghrelin increases hunger, and leptin reduces it.

✓ The hypothalamus in the brain plays a major role in hunger control.

✓ The set point theory of body weight proposes that a person's weight reverts to a predetermined set point after a change.

3. The results showed that stomach contractions correlated with the subjective sensation of hunger.

1. Washburn swallowed a balloon that detected stomach contractions.

2. He pressed a button when he noticed a sensation of hunger.

Stomach contractions

Hunger feeling

Time

Appetite control

Many organs are involved in appetite control. The hypothalamus in the brain plays a major role. It detects when food is needed by monitoring blood sugar and hormone levels. Two regions of the hypothalamus are involved: the lateral hypothalamus (sometimes called the hunger centre) and the ventromedial hypothalamus (the satiety centre). When the hunger centre is stimulated in animals, it causes eating; if it is damaged or removed, starvation can occur. Stimulating the satiety centre makes animals stop eating. Damage to it causes uncontrollable eating and obesity.

The hypothalamus monitors blood sugar levels. It increases hunger when blood sugar levels are low and reduces hunger when blood sugar levels are high.

The adrenal glands on top of the kidneys produce two stress hormones: adrenaline, which suppresses appetite, and cortisol, which stimulates it.

The pancreas produces the hormones insulin and glucagon, which reduce and raise blood sugar levels, indirectly affecting hunger.

When empty, the stomach secretes the hormone ghrelin, which increases hunger.

When full, the stomach secretes the hormone obestatin, suppressing hunger.

Full intestines produce the hormone peptide YY, which reduces appetite.

When fat cells are large, they secrete the hormone leptin, which reduces hunger.

🔍 Set point theory

Some people have a greater tendency to gain weight than others, and many dieters tend to regain weight quickly after losing it, leading to yo-yo dieting. According to the set point theory of body weight, a person's weight reverts to a genetically determined point or range after a change. If body weight falls, hunger increases and metabolic rate (the rate of calorie use) falls to restore normal weight; if body weight rises, the opposite happens. However, set point theory does not explain why obesity rates are rising in many countries or why obesity correlates with age and socioeconomic factors.

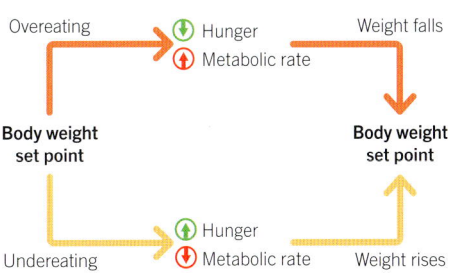

Overeating → Hunger ⬇ / Metabolic rate ⬆ → Weight falls

Body weight set point → Body weight set point

Undereating → Hunger ⬆ / Metabolic rate ⬇ → Weight rises

The psychology of hunger

The urge to eat is driven not just by physiological needs (see pages 148–149) but also by psychological factors. Our emotions, beliefs, social and cultural background, and even the way food looks can all affect how hungry we feel and how much we eat.

Key facts

✓ Hunger is affected by psychological as well as physiological factors.

✓ Psychological factors affecting hunger include emotions, social pressure, presentation of food, body image, and portion size.

Emotions
Emotional states, particularly stress, can influence our appetite. Anxiety and fear cause loss of appetite, but chronic (long-term) stress can increase appetite and lead to weight gain.

Social pressure
At social occasions where people eat together, people may eat more than they would on their own. Etiquette is also a factor – it may feel rude to refuse food or decline a second helping.

Presentation
The more appetizing food looks, the more we want to eat it. Coffee shops exploit this by arranging appealing snacks near the checkout to tempt customers waiting in the queue.

Body image
How physically attractive people believe themselves to be is shaped by cultural ideals of beauty. A negative body image can affect appetite or even lead to eating disorders (see page 194).

Portion size
Larger portion sizes often lead to increased food intake in adults and children, a phenomenon known as the portion size effect. The option to "go large" in fast-food restaurants may be an additional factor in rising obesity rates.

 ## Amnesia study

Our memory of recent meals may play a significant role in hunger. In 1998, a team of psychologists studied two male patients with amnesia so profound that they had no explicit memory of events more than a minute ago. When a second or even third full meal within 30 minutes of a previous one was offered to them, the patients consumed it enthusiastically. The authors of the study proposed that our knowledge of when and what we last ate contributes to appetite.

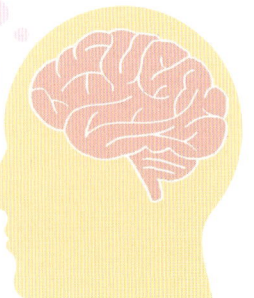

The sexual response cycle

Sexual behaviour is studied by psychologists in the same way that many human behaviours are studied – through observation and interviews. The sexual response cycle is a model that describes the physiological and psychological changes during sexual activity in both biological males and biological females.

Phases of sexual response

Masters and Johnson (1966) developed the sexual response cycle by observing volunteers and recording physiological responses. The cycle has four phases: excitement, plateau (full arousal), orgasm, and resolution. They observed three common patterns in females and found that cycles could repeat, resulting in multiple orgasms. In males, however, orgasm is followed by a refractory period in which they do not respond to stimulation.

Key facts

✓ Masters and Johnson developed the sexual response cycle model through observing sexual activity in volunteers.

✓ The cycle has four phases: excitement, plateau (full arousal), orgasm, and resolution.

✓ Differences exist between sexes in phase duration and physiological response.

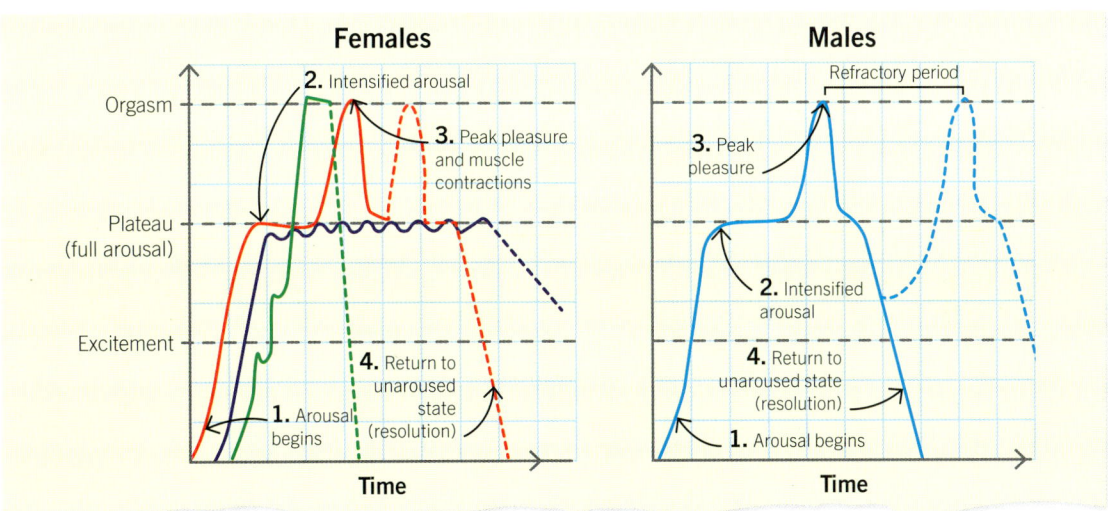

 ### Sexual motivation

Arousal and desire are influenced by a variety of biological, psychological, and social factors.

Hormones
Sex hormones affect libido (sexual drive) and desire. Testosterone occurs in both sexes but levels are higher in males. In females, oestrogen peaks at ovulation, synchronizing libido with fertility.

External stimuli
Males and females show similar levels of arousal in response to external erotic stimuli, but males show more noticeable physiological responses.

Internal stimuli
The brain has a profound role in sexual arousal. Imagination can influence desire even without physical sensation.

Social and cultural factors
Values instilled by family, society, religion, cultural expectations, and the media all affect sexual motivation and behaviour.

The need for affiliation

Humans are social beings and are innately driven to form meaningful social connections, seek acceptance, and be part of a community. Several theories of motivation describe our need for affiliation (to belong) as one of the most powerful, universal, and influential motivators. For our ancestors, the benefits of belonging to a group included their increased chances of survival and passing on their genes. It remains a motivation for us and a way of ensuring our wellbeing.

Key facts

✓ Humans naturally seek social connections.

✓ The need to belong affects behaviour and is key to happiness and self-esteem.

✓ Ostracism (social exclusion) damages mental health and is similar to physical pain.

Affiliation

Psychologists consider affiliation to be a basic human need. When it is satisfied, our happiness, wellbeing, and self-esteem are enhanced. Strong relationships contribute more to happiness than wealth. For this reason, people often put a lot of effort into making friends and joining groups.

Ostracism

When people are ostracized (deliberately excluded socially), their mental health suffers, their self-esteem is reduced, and their wellbeing is affected. They may suffer loneliness and depression. Ostracism activates the same area of the brain as physical pain, which means we feel exclusion as strongly as we feel pain.

Being left out, or ostracized, affects wellbeing and mood

🔍 Social networking online

Technological advances have led to social-networking platforms that let us connect with like-minded people, fostering a sense of belonging. They offer access to diverse communities, emotional support, and opportunities for social interaction, which can satisfy our need for belonging. However, social networking can also create superficial connections, and lead to cyberbullying and ostracism, hindering genuine belongingness and making us feel more isolated.

Ostracism may also occur with online social networking.

The need for achievement

In 1953, US psychologist D.C. McClelland et al. identified a "need for achievement" (nAch). This is a person's learned preference for tasks or activities that require effort, challenge, and skill. They are driven by a desire to excel, accomplish meaningful goals, and receive recognition for these achievements.

Key facts

✓ The need for achievement (nAch) is a desire for challenging tasks to excel at and be recognized for.

✓ People high in nAch set realistic goals, persist, and seek growth.

✓ People low in nAch fear failure, avoid challenges, and prefer easy tasks or impossibly hard ones to justify failure.

The level of n-Ach

People with a high nAch are driven to set challenging but realistic goals, seek mastery, persist through setbacks, and look for opportunities for personal growth and success. Satisfaction is obtained by striving. Conversely, those with a low nAch score tend to avoid challenging tasks, have a fear of failure, and prefer easy or familiar situations to protect their self-esteem.

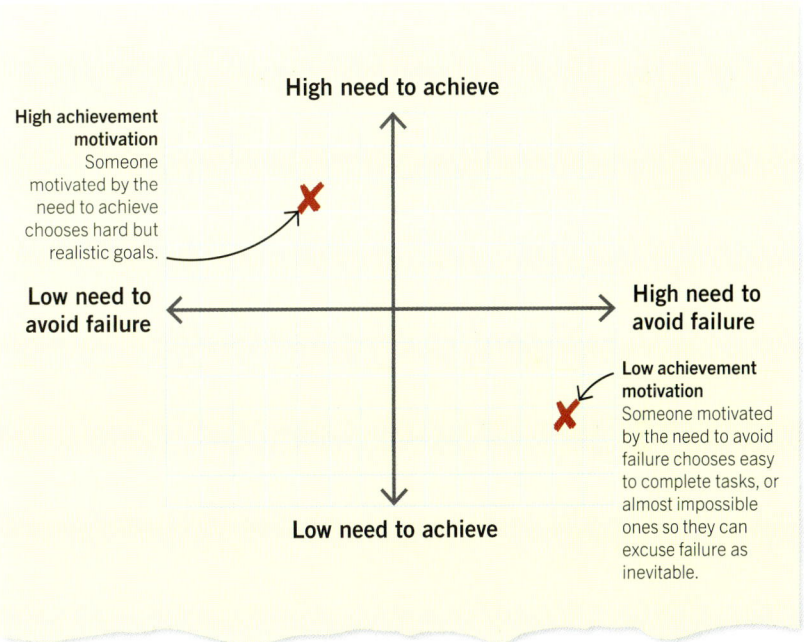

High need to achieve

High achievement motivation
Someone motivated by the need to achieve chooses hard but realistic goals.

Low need to avoid failure

High need to avoid failure

Low achievement motivation
Someone motivated by the need to avoid failure chooses easy to complete tasks, or almost impossible ones so they can excuse failure as inevitable.

Low need to achieve

🔍 Types of motivation

Intrinsic motivation is the incentive to engage in an activity out of interest and satisfaction. Extrinsic motivation is the incentive to do something because it has an external reward, such as money. Psychologists have found that intrinsic motivation decreases if a reward is offered to do the usually pleasurable activity – this is called the overjustification effect.

Intrinsic motivation

Extrinsic motivation

Arousal theory

According to arousal theory, we each have our own optimum level of arousal (alertness) at which we perform tasks best. People are motivated to engage in activities that maintain their optimum level of arousal. The theory suggests that, when under-aroused (bored or uninterested), people tend to seek exciting activities; when over-aroused (anxious or stressed), they tend to prefer calming activities.

Key facts

✓ Arousal theory proposes that each person has their own optimal level of arousal.

✓ Optimal performance requires a moderate level of arousal.

✓ Very low or very high levels of arousal decrease performance quality.

The Yerkes-Dodson Law
In 1908, US psychologists Robert Yerkes and John Dodson stated that performance quality increases with arousal level, but only up to a point, after which too much arousal causes performance quality to decrease. For example, students typically perform poorly in exams if they are either too relaxed (under-aroused) or very anxious (over-aroused).

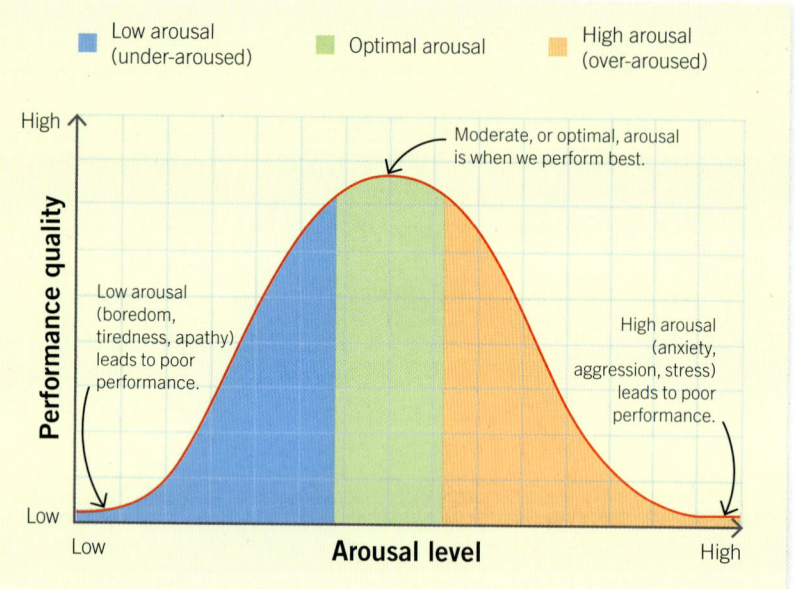

Low arousal (under-aroused)

Optimal arousal

High arousal (over-aroused)

Moderate, or optimal, arousal is when we perform best.

Low arousal (boredom, tiredness, apathy) leads to poor performance.

High arousal (anxiety, aggression, stress) leads to poor performance.

Performance quality — High / Low

Arousal level — Low / High

🔍 Task difficulty

Different tasks require different levels of arousal, depending on the amount of skill needed to perform them. Complex, difficult tasks, such as playing an instrument in front of an audience, are generally best done at lower levels of arousal (high arousal can impair performance). Easier tasks, such as brushing your teeth, are best done at higher levels of arousal to provide motivation.

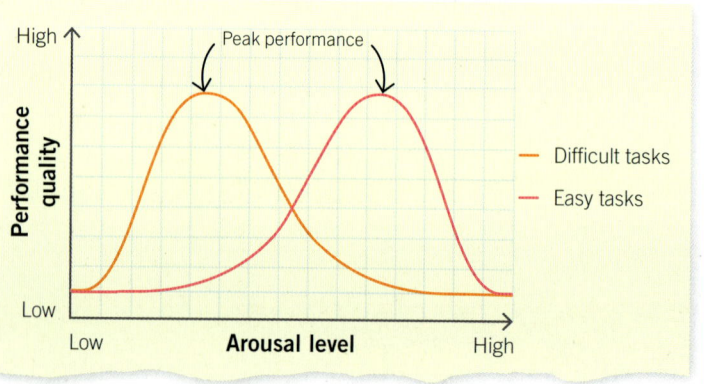

Peak performance

Performance quality — High / Low

Arousal level — Low / High

— Difficult tasks
— Easy tasks

Chapter 11

Personality

The psychodynamic approach

Based on the work of Austrian neurologist Sigmund Freud, the psychodynamic approach divides the mind into three levels of consciousness. It suggests that we are only aware of a tiny fraction of our thoughts and memories, as most of them are out of reach in parts of our minds not readily available to us. Our thoughts and behaviours are influenced by these unconscious drives and memories, even though we are not aware of them.

Key facts

✓ According to the psychodynamic approach, the mind is divided into three levels of consciousness: conscious, preconscious, and unconscious.

✓ Although we aren't aware of thoughts in the unconscious mind, they still affect our behaviour.

✓ Personality has three aspects: the ego, superego, and id. In healthy individuals, the ego balances the demands of the id and superego.

Levels of consciousness

In 1915, Freud proposed that the mind has three levels of consciousness — conscious, preconscious, and unconscious.

Conscious mind
This is the part of the mind that a person is aware of – the ideas, memories, and emotions that a person is able to access freely.

Preconscious mind
This part of the mind stores memories that a person can retrieve with a little effort.

Dreams are thought to reveal the unconscious mind. They may include things that are too disturbing for the conscious mind to process.

Unconscious mind
This part of the mind is hard to access. It hides a person's impulses and desires, which still affect their behaviour and feelings.

The structure of the personality

According to Freud, there are three aspects to an individual's personality: the superego (which wants to do the right thing), the ego (seat of reason), and the id (pure instinct). He descibed the relationship between them using the analogy of an iceberg. Parts of the ego and superego make up the conscious mind — the tip of the iceberg above the water. The rest of the ego and superego, and all of the id, make up the unconscious mind and are hidden underwater.

Conscious mind

Unconscious mind

Ego
The ego balances the demands of the irresponsible id and the strict superego. It is the moderate voice of reason.

Superego
The superego is the moral conscience: it considers whether something is morally right or wrong. It acts like a strict parent.

Id
The id is like a demanding young child. It is selfish, impulsive and unaware of rules. It seeks instant gratification.

Defence mechanisms

Freud believed that the conscious mind is vulnerable to being overwhelmed by difficult or traumatic thoughts or memories. To protect the conscious mind, the unconscious mind uses various strategies, known as defence mechanisms. Defence mechanisms are not necessarily unhealthy but can be problematic if used too often, or for too long.

Mind mechanisms

In her book *The Ego and Mechanisms of Defence* (1936), Anna Freud (the daughter of Sigmund Freud), described 10 mechanisms that protect the conscious mind. Today, psychologists think there may be more than 30, but here are just a few:

Key facts

✓ Freud believed that the conscious mind protects itself from unpleasant thoughts or memories using defence mechanisms.

✓ Studies show that the mind may use up to 30 types of defence mechanism.

Ignoring real-world problems can make them worse.

Denial
When a person unconsciously refuses to accept the reality of a situation because it causes difficult thoughts or feelings, it is called denial.

Repressed traumatic memories can still affect a person's behaviour.

Repression
Unpleasant thoughts or memories are sometimes locked, or repressed, in the unconscious mind to avoid having to face them.

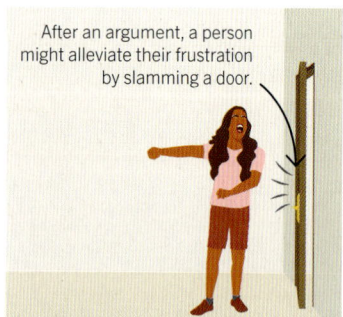

After an argument, a person might alleviate their frustration by slamming a door.

Displacement
Redirecting a strong emotional response from the original source to another person or object is called displacement.

Reverting to childlike behaviour might be a way of getting help.

Regression
When facing challenges, a person may regress to acting as if they were younger, and behave in a childish way.

🔍 Freudian slips

Freud thought that information stored in the unconscious mind could occasionally bubble up and surface in the conscious mind. One way in which this occurs is parapraxis, known commonly as a "Freudian slip". This is a verbal mistake that is thought to reveal private feelings. For example, accidentally calling a teacher "Mum" suggests that you like them.

Mum!

Psychosexual stages

Freud thought that children go through five phases in their development of sexual awareness, known as the psychosexual stages. He argued that how these stages are experienced has a significant effect on the rest of a person's life.

Timeline of psychosexual stages
Each of the five stages focuses on the way in which a child experiences pleasure and expresses libido (life energy) through a specific body part (erogenous zone).

Key facts

✓ According to Freud, children go through five phases of sexual development, known as the psychosexual stages.

✓ How children move through each psychosexual stage may affect their adult behaviour.

🔍 Fixation

Freud claimed that if children were over gratified (found too much pleasure) or under gratified (did not find enough pleasure) at an early stage, they could become fixated, or "stuck" there. This can be seen in adult behaviour; for example, fixation in the oral stage may lead to chewing gum or nail biting – the mouth is still the source of pleasure.

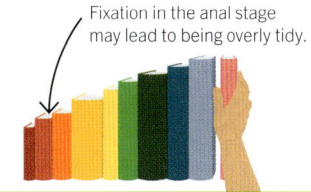

Fixation in the anal stage may lead to being overly tidy.

1. Oral stage (Ages 0–2)
The main source of pleasure is the mouth. Babies explore the world by putting things in their mouths, sucking, and crying.

2. Anal stage (Ages 2–3)
Toilet training occurs. This is the first time parents place demands on the child to control their own behaviour, and fail to praise if they do not meet expectations.

3. Phallic stage (Ages 3–6)
Pleasure is derived from the genitals. Boys wish to possess their mother and view their father as a rival. They fear harm so learn to identify with the father to reduce this risk.

4. Latent stage (Ages 6–12)
No particular body part is associated with sexual pleasure at this time. Sexual pleasure is repressed. Children typically spend time with other children of the same gender.

5. Genital stage (Ages 12 to death)
The genitals are now the primary source of a person's sexual pleasure. This can be indulged through adult relationships.

Projective tests

A projective test is a type of personality test in which a person gives immediate responses to ambiguous stimuli, usually in the form of images or words. These tests are so named because the participant is thought to be projecting aspects of their unconscious through their answers. Psychotherapists analyse the responses to help explain the causes of psychological disorders such as anxiety, depression, and phobias.

Key facts

✓ Projective tests are used to reveal our subconscious.

✓ The Rorschach test involves interpreting inkblot images.

✓ The thematic apperception test involves making a story up based on picture cards.

The Rorschach inkblot test

This widely used projective test was created by Swiss psychiatrist Hermann Rorschach in 1921. It involves showing a participant a series of inkblots and asking them to describe what they see and why. The participant's responses can reveal a lot to the psychotherapist; for example, repressed memories of a traumatic event, which could explain a current disorder. Rorschach tests are unreliable, as psychotherapists may differ in how they interpret participants' responses.

🔍 The thematic apperception test

The thematic apperception test (TAT) was developed in the 1930s. In the test, a participant is shown ambiguous picture cards and asked to describe what is happening in each card, and how the characters depicted are feeling. The stories are thought to reveal something about the participant's subconscious, such as an explanation for a phobia they may have.

Trait theory

Trait theory describes personality in terms of traits. Traits are the individual characteristics that motivate our behaviours, and are consistent over time. Each person has a different combination of traits, and they can be assessed by personality inventories or tests.

Key facts

✓ Traits are the characteristics that make up our personalities.

✓ The five-factor personality model organizes traits into five categories.

✓ Traits are assessed using personality inventories.

Describing traits

In 1936, US psychologist Gordon Allport compiled a list of 4,504 words that describe personality traits. He grouped them into three categories, which he argued define who we are:

| **Cardinal**
Traits dominant in a personality | **Central**
Major traits that form a personality | **Secondary**
Traits only evident in certain situations |

Five-factor personality model (The Big Five)

US psychologists Paul Costa and Robert McCrae (2011) categorized traits into five factors that make up personality. They form the mnemonic OCEAN. People can score highly in some traits and low in others.

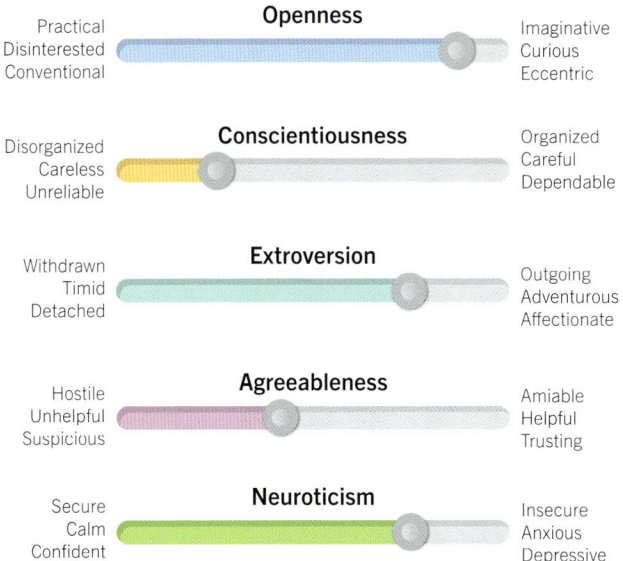

Openness
Practical / Disinterested / Conventional — Imaginative / Curious / Eccentric

Conscientiousness
Disorganized / Careless / Unreliable — Organized / Careful / Dependable

Extroversion
Withdrawn / Timid / Detached — Outgoing / Adventurous / Affectionate

Agreeableness
Hostile / Unhelpful / Suspicious — Amiable / Helpful / Trusting

Neuroticism
Secure / Calm / Confident — Insecure / Anxious / Depressive

Assessing personality

Personality inventories are used to assess traits.

Eysenck Personality Inventory

German-British psychologist Hans Eysenck developed an inventory that measures people on two scales of traits. Eysenck argued that highly neurotic, extrovert personalities are more likely to exhibit psychotic (antisocial, aggressive) behaviour, and commit crimes.

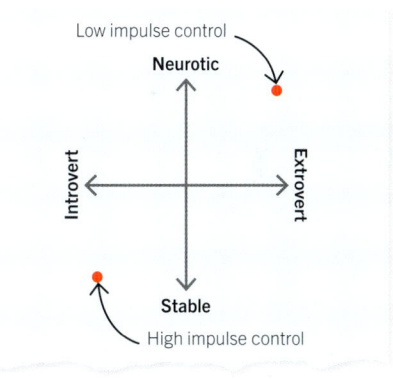

Minnesota Multiphasic Personality Inventory (MMPI-2-RF)

In the MMPI, often used to diagnose disorders, participants respond to more than 500 statements with true or false answers. Participants who do not answer truthfully score highly on the test's "lie scale", designed to improve its validity.

Exploring the self

The self encompasses the things that make you a unique and distinct entity, including your thoughts, feelings, perceptions, and personal identity. It represents your subjective experience of being an individual able to live life and make things happen. A person's sense of self is usually stable throughout life, but it can be influenced by social or environmental factors.

Key facts

✓ The self is all the things, including your thoughts and personality, that make you who you are.

✓ Self-esteem, self-efficacy, and self-concept are aspects of how people see themselves.

✓ Self-serving bias is the tendency to think of yourself favourably.

✓ Narcissistic people tend to be self-important and self-absorbed.

Self-concept

In general terms, self-concept is a person's perceptions of their own behaviours, abilities, interests, and unique characteristics. For example, you may have beliefs such as "I am a good friend", "I like dogs", or "I am terrible at sport". These beliefs and countless others are all part of your self-concept.

You may see yourself as a keen reader.

Self-esteem and self-efficacy

How you feel about your worth as a person is known as self-esteem. People with high self-esteem usually feel confident and have a healthy sense of self-worth. Those with low self-esteem may struggle with self-doubt and lack confidence. Self-efficacy is a person's belief in their ability to accomplish specific tasks or handle challenging situations. High self-efficacy is associated with greater motivation and resilience, while low self-efficacy can lead to decreased motivation and feelings of inadequacy.

Self-serving bias

The tendency for a person to attribute their successes to internal factors, such as their abilities, while attributing failures to external factors, such as luck, is called self-serving bias. It protects self-esteem by helping to maintain self-image (personal view of oneself).

Positive results   Negative results

The spotlight effect

Sometimes people feel that they are being noticed and judged much more than they actually are. This sensation is known as the spotlight effect, making a person feel self-conscious. Studies have shown, however, that people are noticed much less than they think they are.

Narcissism

This personality trait is characterized by a grandiose sense of self-importance, a need for excessive admiration, and a lack of empathy for others. A narcissist may have an extreme focus on their own achievements, talents, and appearance, while disregarding the needs and feelings of others. Narcissism exists on a spectrum, ranging from disproportionate self-confidence to extreme self-absorption.

Narcissistic people have an inflated self-image, often seeking validation and admiration from others.

Social comparison

Social comparison can be healthy if a person is motivated by the idea that people in similar situations have achieved lofty goals (observational learning – learning by watching others). It can be unhealthy, however, if the person compares themselves with those who have more resources and advantages.

Chapter 12

Emotion

Emotion

Emotion is a complex human experience. An emotion is a combination of three components: consciously experienced feelings and thoughts; physical changes in the body; and expressive behaviours, such as facial expressions and body postures. For example, when you're angry, your thoughts focus on the source of your frustration, your heart rate increases, and your brow furrows.

Key facts

✓ Emotions have three components: consciously experienced feelings and thoughts; physical changes; and expressive behaviours.

✓ According to evolutionary theory, emotions are evolved adaptations that promote survival and reproduction.

Conscious experience
These are the feelings and thoughts that make up our experience of an emotion.

Physical changes
These can include a change in breathing, heart rate, perspiration, and trembling.

Hairs may stand on end, causing goosebumps.

Expressive behaviours
Our emotional state is revealed by expressive behaviours, such as facial expressions and body language.

🔍 Evolutionary theory of emotion

Charles Darwin and other evolutionary biologists have proposed that primary emotions such as fear are evolved adaptations that promote survival and reproductive success. According to this theory, primary emotions are innate and universal, which means they are shared across cultures. Darwin also noticed that many animals show similar emotional reactions to humans, which reflects a common evolutionary history.

A cat's hairs stand on end when it is threatened. This involuntary reaction makes it look larger, helping intimidate an aggressor. In humans, the same physiological response produces goosebumps.

The physiology of emotion

Emotions don't just happen in the mind — they have powerful effects on the body. Suppose you're walking in the woods when a bear steps into your path. Your heart beats faster, you gasp for breath, your eyes widen, and your skin prickles with sweat. These reactions, which are common to many strong emotions, involve activation of the autonomic nervous system, which increases arousal (alertness) levels and prepares the body for action.

> 📌 **Key facts**
>
> ✓ The autonomic nervous system has two divisions: sympathetic and parasympathetic.
>
> ✓ Strong emotions involve activation of the sympathetic nervous system.
>
> ✓ Although the subjective experience of each emotion is different, many share the same physiological response.

Emotion and arousal

The autonomic (involuntary) nervous system has two divisions: the sympathetic nervous system, which prepares the body for action (the fight-or-flight response); and the parasympathetic nervous system, which calms the body down (the rest-and-digest response). Powerful emotions such as fear, surprise, and anger all activate the sympathetic nervous system, with the effects shown here. The subjective experience or feeling of these emotions is very different, but the physiological response is the same.

🔍 Emotions in the brain

Brain scans reveal that some emotional reactions are localized in the brain. Positive moods involve greater activation of the left frontal lobe than the right, while disgust and sadness involve more right frontal lobe activity. Certain parts of the brain play a role in multiple emotions. The amygdala is involved in fear, anxiety, and aggression. The insular cortex is active when we feel anger, fear, disgust, happiness, or sadness. It is also important in social emotions, including empathy, moral disgust, disbelief, and romantic love.

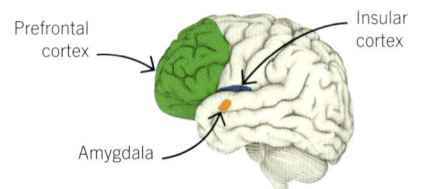

Prefrontal cortex

Insular cortex

Amygdala

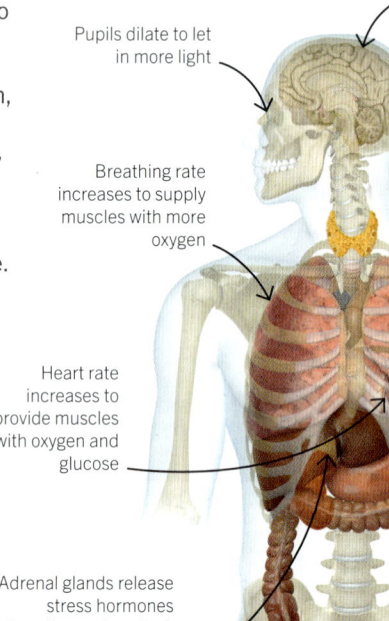

Mental alertness improves

Pupils dilate to let in more light

Skin perspires, ready to cool the body during physical exertion

Breathing rate increases to supply muscles with more oxygen

Heart rate increases to provide muscles with oxygen and glucose

Adrenal glands release stress hormones adrenaline and cortisol, both of which raise blood glucose levels

Universal facial expressions

Though emotion is felt in our bodies and processed in our minds, it is also displayed on our faces. The mind feels the emotions but the body shows them, particularly the face. In the 1970s, US psychologist Paul Ekman began a study to discover if different cultures displayed the same facial expressions for the same emotions.

Key facts

✓ Emotion is processed in the mind and displayed by the body.

✓ Ekman identified cross-cultural (universal) facial expressions.

✓ He proposed that there are seven basic emotions, although other psychologists disagree.

Primary emotions

Ekman decided to visit an isolated community in Papua New Guinea in Oceania. At the time, the community had not encountered people outside their own tribe. Ekman identified six emotional expressions that were also displayed by other cultures around the world. He concluded that regardless of language or culture, facial expressions for the basic human emotions are universal. Later, he added contempt to make seven universal expressions. Other psychologists have agreed with Ekman's theory of universal emotions but argued there may be more or fewer in number.

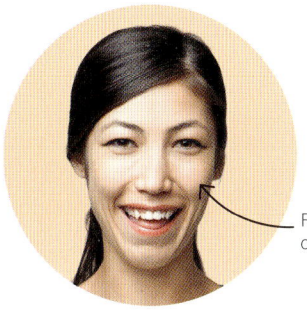

Raised cheeks

Happiness

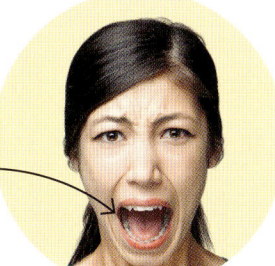

Downturned mouth

Sadness

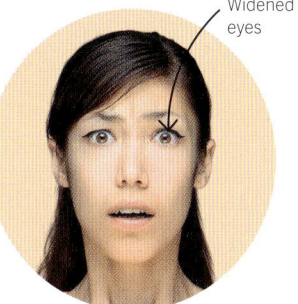

Open mouth

Widened eyes

Fear

Surprise

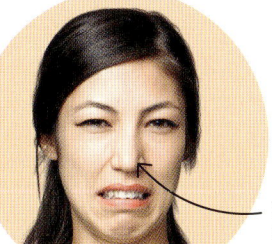

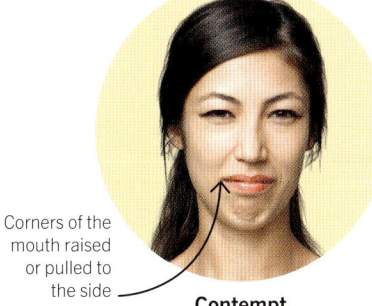

Corners of the mouth raised or pulled to the side

Contempt

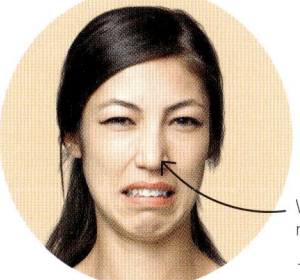

Wrinkled nose

Disgust

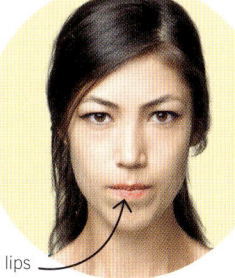

Tightened lips

Anger

Theories of emotion

Emotions involve physiological changes in the body, conscious thought processes, and behavioural reactions such as facial expressions. Over the years, psychologists have proposed various conflicting theories that attempt to explain how these different processes interact.

> 📌 **Key facts**
>
> ✓ Over the years, psychologists have proposed six main theories of emotion.
> ✓ Some theories of emotion separate physiological arousal from subjective experience.
> ✓ Some theories involve moderation of emotion by cognitive appraisal.
> ✓ Some theories see emotions are automatic, subconscious reactions that do not require conscious awareness.

James-Lange theory (1885)
Early psychologists William James and Carl Lange proposed that a stimulus triggers a physiological change first, which we then recognize as a emotion. For example, the sight of a shark causes physiological arousal, which leads to the emotion of fear.

Stimulus: sight of shark → **Physiological arousal** → Emotional response: fear

Cannon-Bard theory (1927)
A problem with the James-Lange theory is that different emotions involve the same physiological changes, such as a racing heart. Walter Cannon and Philip Bard proposed a rival theory, arguing that the stimulus independently triggers physiological changes and the subjective experience of an emotion.

Stimulus: sight of shark → **Physiological arousal** / Emotional response: fear

Two-factor theory (1962)
Stanley Schachter and Jerome Singer proposed the two-factor theory of emotion, which includes a cognitive appraisal of the situation. For example, a shark seen while swimming might trigger fear, but a shark seen in an aquarium would trigger curiosity instead.

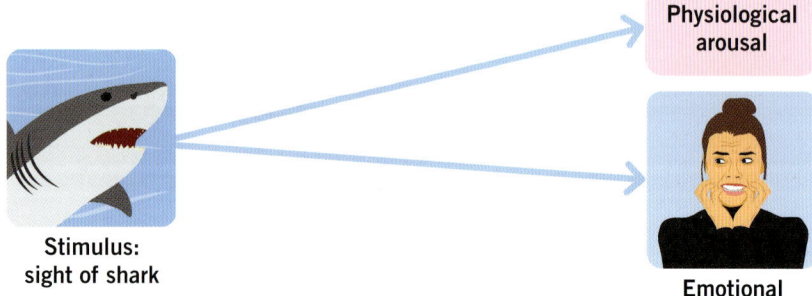

Stimulus: sight of shark → **Physiological arousal** → **Cognitive appraisal** → Emotional response: fear

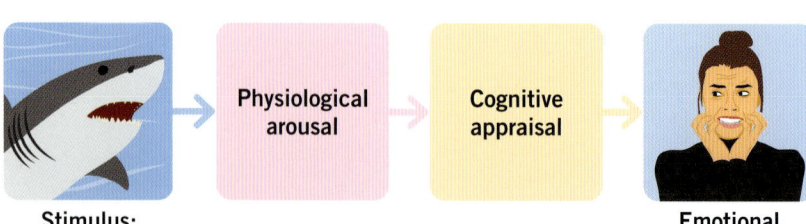

Lazarus's theory (1991)

Richard Lazarus argued that cognitive appraisal comes first. A stimulus is evaluated and, if appropriate, the physiological response and subjective feeling of an emotion follow. This is also called the cognitive appraisal theory of emotion.

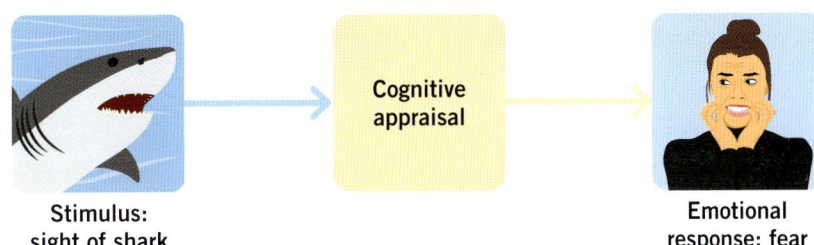

Stimulus: sight of shark

Cognitive appraisal

Emotional response: fear

Zajonc's theory (1998)

Dangerous situations require rapid reactions. Robert Zajonc argued that emotions can occur without or before cognitive appraisal of a situation, triggering responses that are rapid and automatic. For example, a noise might startle us before we figure out what it is.

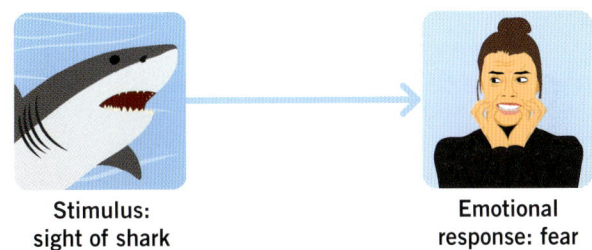

Stimulus: sight of shark

Emotional response: fear

LeDoux's theory (2002)

Joseph LeDoux proposed that fear involves two neural pathways: a rapid one (the "low road"), which is subconscious, and a slower one (the "high road"), which involves the cerebral cortex and gives us conscious awareness.

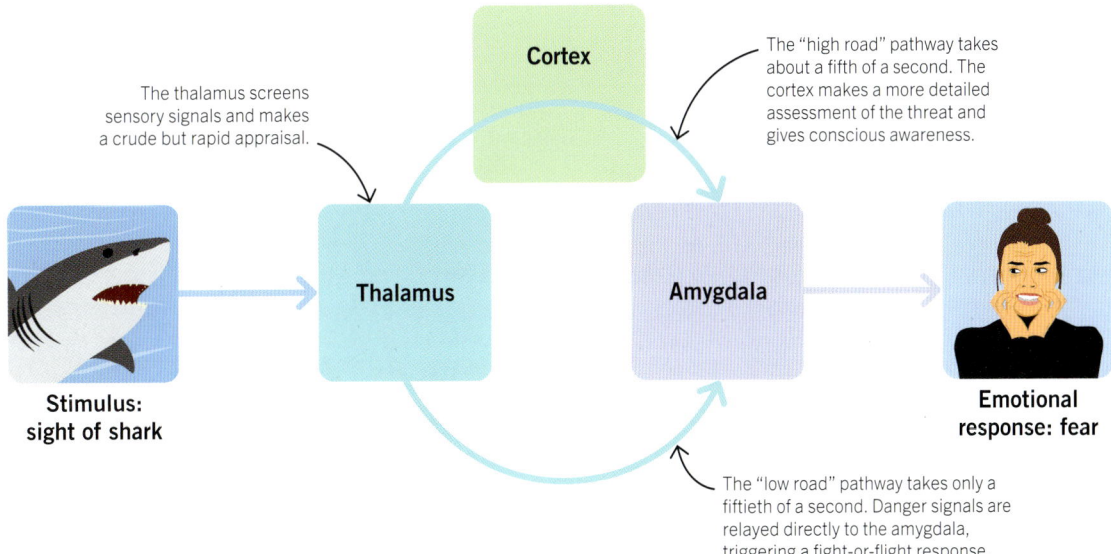

Cortex

The thalamus screens sensory signals and makes a crude but rapid appraisal.

The "high road" pathway takes about a fifth of a second. The cortex makes a more detailed assessment of the threat and gives conscious awareness.

Stimulus: sight of shark

Thalamus

Amygdala

Emotional response: fear

The "low road" pathway takes only a fiftieth of a second. Danger signals are relayed directly to the amygdala, triggering a fight-or-flight response.

The stress response

Stress occurs when we don't have the resources to cope with environmental pressures. It is a physical response to feeling threatened or challenged. The body's reaction would have been useful in the past when confronting predators, but it is less helpful in modern society when stressors (stressful events or situations) are typically psychological and long-term.

The general adaptation syndrome
Hungarian-Canadian scientist Hans Selye (1936) described the effect of stress on the body over time. The longer the stressor lasts, the greater the physical impact and risk of illness.

Key facts

✓ Stress is a physical response to feeling threatened or challenged.

✓ Stressful events or situations are called stressors.

✓ The general adaptation syndrome describes how stress affects the body over time.

✓ People respond to stress in different ways.

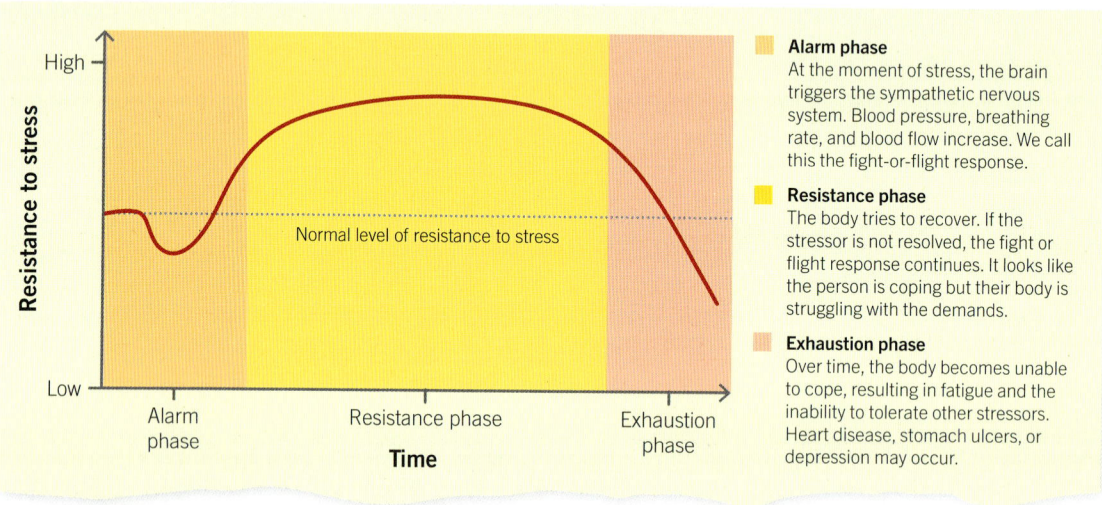

Alarm phase
At the moment of stress, the brain triggers the sympathetic nervous system. Blood pressure, breathing rate, and blood flow increase. We call this the fight-or-flight response.

Resistance phase
The body tries to recover. If the stressor is not resolved, the fight or flight response continues. It looks like the person is coping but their body is struggling with the demands.

Exhaustion phase
Over time, the body becomes unable to cope, resulting in fatigue and the inability to tolerate other stressors. Heart disease, stomach ulcers, or depression may occur.

🔍 Responses to stress

There are many well-known physiological responses to stressful situations, in addition to the fight-and-flight response. Studies show that women may also exhibit "tend and befriend" responses, which are stimulated by oxytocin – a hormone that can aid recovery, reduce feelings of fear, and potentially encourage protection of others.

Fight
React with aggression and fight your way out of the situation.

Flight
React by getting away from the situation.

Freeze
Do not respond to the situation in any way. Remain still.

Tend
React by caring for and saving the people around you.

Befriend
Make friends and form alliances to deal with the situation.

Polygraph tests

A polygraph is a device used to monitor common bodily responses to stress. Some people argue that a polygraph test can reveal if someone is lying. This idea is based on the assumption that lying is stressful and results in physical changes, such as high heart rate and blood pressure, fast breathing, pupil dilation, voice change, and increased sweating. Because polygraphs are only able to detect stress, not deception, they are not a reliable or accurate method of lie detection.

Key facts

✓ A polygraph monitors a person's bodily responses to stress.

✓ High heart rate and blood pressure, fast breathing, and increased sweating may all indicate the person is feeling stressed.

✓ Polygraphs are not a reliable method of lie detection.

Sensors on the chest and abdomen monitor the participant's breathing rate.

A cuff on the participant's arm measures heart rate and blood pressure.

The computer screen displays the participant's bodily responses.

Sensors placed on the fingertips detect how much sweat the skin produces.

The interview starts with neutral questions, such as "What day is it?", to establish the participant's baseline measurements for truthful answers.

Once the test is underway, responses higher than the baseline measurements could indicate that the participant is stressed.

Stress and the immune system

Acute (short-term) stress caused by transient (temporary) stressors can boost the immune system, as the body activates its defences ahead of a potential threat. However, chronic (long-term) stress causes the body to release a hormone known as cortisol. Cortisol limits production of lymphocytes (white blood cells that attack viruses and bacteria), reducing the body's ability to fight infection.

Chronic stress and colds

In 1991, US psychologist Sheldon Cohen interviewed participants on the stressors they were experiencing. He then exposed them to a common cold virus. Cohen found that participants experiencing chronic stressors were more likely to become ill than less stressed participants, suggesting a link between high stress and poor functioning of the immune system.

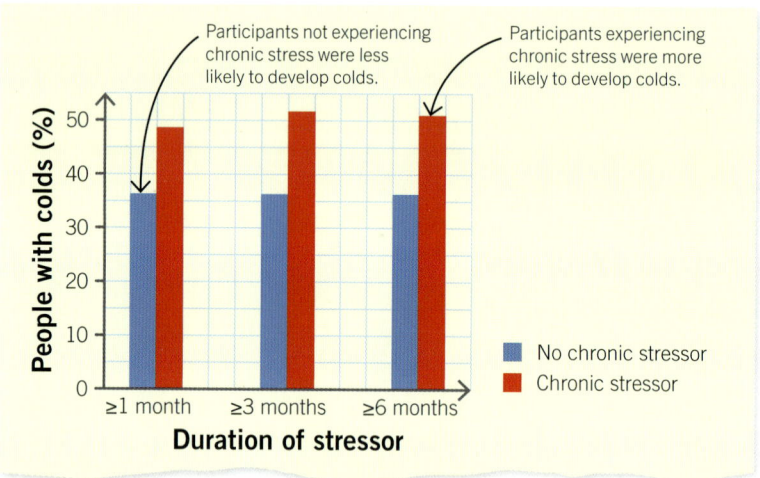

Participants not experiencing chronic stress were less likely to develop colds.

Participants experiencing chronic stress were more likely to develop colds.

People with colds (%)

Duration of stressor

■ No chronic stressor
■ Chronic stressor

The social readjustment rating scale

In 1967, US psychiatrists Thomas Holmes and Richard Rahe created a scale of 43 stressful life events. A person's score is calculated by adding up the "life change unit" of events they have experienced in a year. Scoring highly indicates high stress levels and a greater risk of ill health in the next two years.

Rank	Life event	Life change unit
1	Death of a spouse	100
2	Divorce	73
3	Marital separation	65
4	Jail term	63
5	Death of a close family member	63
6	Personal injury or illness	53
7	Marriage	50
8	Fired from work	47

The higher the number, the more stressful the event is.

Stress and heart disease

Chronic stress can increase the risk of heart disease – when the cardiovascular system is damaged and stops functioning properly. The damage happens in one of two ways. It can occur directly as a result of the body's stress response. When stressed, the body produces the hormone cortisol. If stress is ongoing, cortisol starts to damage the body. It can also result from unhealthy behaviours, such as poor diet and smoking, triggered by stress.

Key facts

✓ The risk of heart disease is increased by chronic stress.

✓ People who are more reactive to stress (personality types A and C) are more likely to experience heart disease.

✓ Heart-damaging behaviours are made more likely by stress.

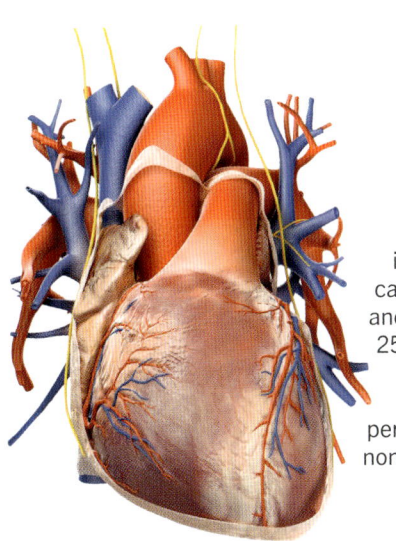

Personality types

An individual's personality traits can influence the likelihood of heart disease. In 1976, 8.5 years after interviewing 3,154 men, US cardiologists Meyer Friedman and Ray Rosenman found that 257 of them had experienced heart attacks. Of the 257 patients, 69 per cent were personality type A. In contrast, none of the personality type Bs experienced a heart attack.

Type	Description
Type A	Type As are motivated, impatient, competitive, and easily angered. They have a higher risk of heart disease.
Type B	Type Bs are easy-going and relaxed. They have a lower risk of heart disease.
Type C	Type Cs are precise, logical, and conscientious. They thrive in stable environments, so when these change, the stress caused may increase their risk of heart disease.

🔍 The impact of stress

The hormone cortisol increases blood pressure and raises the levels of blood sugar and fatty substances such as cholesterol in the blood. The fatty materials build up on arterial walls and can cause blockages. When this happens in the heart's coronary artery, it can cause a heart attack.

Healthy artery

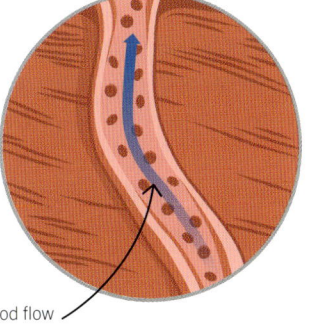

Normal blood flow

Blocked artery

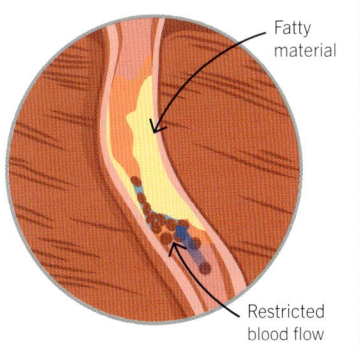

Fatty material

Restricted blood flow

Positive psychology

Psychologists have traditionally studied mental states that harm quality of life, such as mental illness. More recently, attention has turned to positive psychology — the study of what makes us happy. Evidence suggests that happiness does more than just make us feel good. It is strongly correlated with career success, higher lifetime earnings, greater life expectancy, and more stable personal relationships.

Subjective wellbeing

Researchers rely on self-report questionnaires to measure happiness. US psychologist Ed Diener (1984) devised a measure called subjective wellbeing, which combines scores for three separate components: life satisfaction, frequency of positive feelings (positive affect), and frequency of negative feelings (negative affect).

Key facts

✓ Happiness correlates with career success, earnings, life expectancy, and stable relationships.

✓ Subjective wellbeing is a measure of happiness based on three components: life satisfaction, positive affect, and negative affect.

✓ Relative deprivation is an unpleasant feeling caused by comparing ourselves to people who are better off.

Life satisfaction
Do you feel successful in your career and fulfilled by work? Are you satisfied with your health, relationships, and prospects?

Positive affect
How frequently do you feel active, excited, enthusiastic, inspired, proud, or strong?

Negative affect
How frequently do you feel angry, afraid, anxious, guilty, ashamed, or upset?

🔍 Happiness factors

Studies of subjective wellbeing are correlational, making it difficult to draw conclusions about exactly what causes happiness. However, the following factors are known to be associated with greater subjective wellbeing:
• Close relationships with family and friends
• Regular physical exercise
• Adequate sleep
• A sense of control over life
• Personality traits such as optimism, extroversion, and agreeableness
• An active religious faith or community
• Work or pastimes that engage a person's skills
Factors that show little or no correlation with happiness include age, gender, and physical attractiveness.

🔍 Relative deprivation

How happy we are depends partly on social comparison. When we sense we are worse off than our peers, we experience an unpleasant, envious feeling known to psychologists as relative deprivation. Conversely, comparing ourselves to people who are worse off gives us a feeling of contentment.

The facial feedback theory

Can the simple act of smiling or frowning change how we feel? To test this idea – known as the facial feedback theory – German psychologist F. Strack et al. (1988) forced a group of participants to smile, by asking them to hold a pencil horizontally between their teeth. They made a second group frown, by holding a pencil vertically between the lips. Told to watch and rate a cartoon, the smiling group reported finding it funnier than those who were frowning, suggesting emotional experience is influenced by facial expression.

Key facts

✓ Facial expressions can influence emotions – this is known as the facial feedback theory.

✓ Smiling with increasing intensity can increase positive feelings.

✓ Body language, including posture, gestures, and movement, can affect emotions.

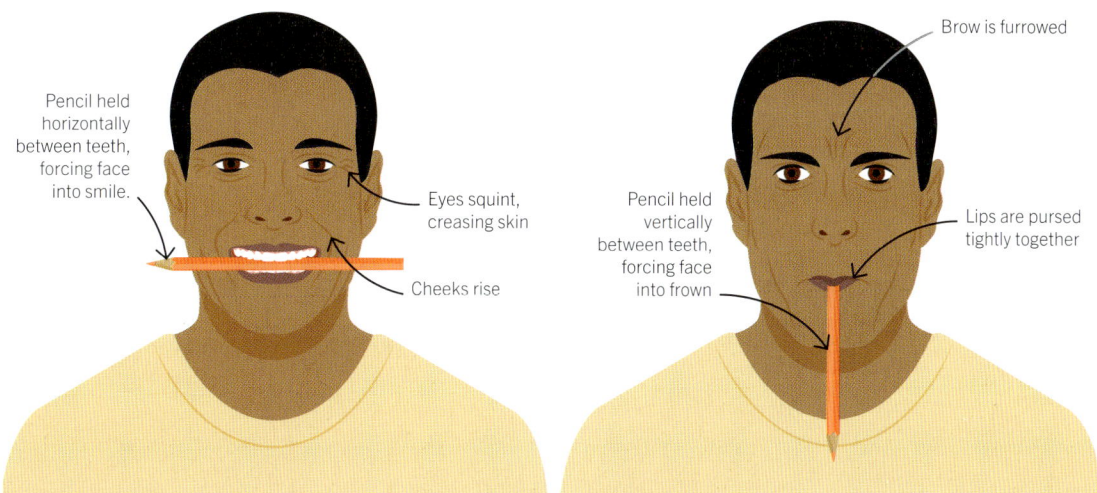

Pencil held horizontally between teeth, forcing face into smile.

Eyes squint, creasing skin

Cheeks rise

Brow is furrowed

Pencil held vertically between teeth, forcing face into frown

Lips are pursed tightly together

🔍 Behaviour and emotion

Not only can facial expressions influence mood, body language, including posture and movements, can too. A 2014 study led by German psychologist J. Michalak tested 39 participants, who were instructed to walk either in a fast, upbeat way or in a slow, downbeat way. At the same time, they were given positive or negative words to remember. When tested later, those who walked in an upbeat way recalled more positive words, while those who walked in a downbeat way recalled more negative words.

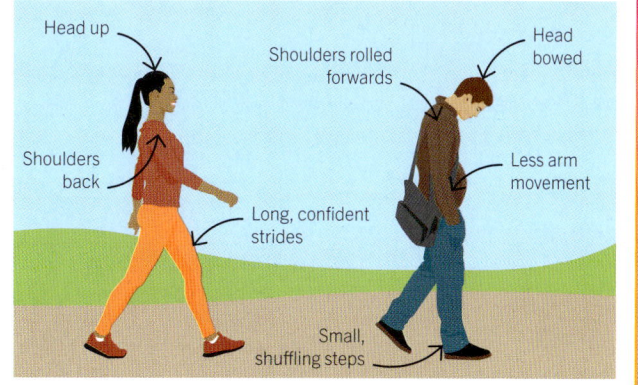

Head up

Shoulders back

Long, confident strides

Shoulders rolled forwards

Head bowed

Less arm movement

Small, shuffling steps

Chapter 13

Clinical psychology: psychological disorders

Classifying psychological disorders

When diagnosing psychological disorders, psychologists use their training and expertise. They may also refer to either the World Health Organization's *International Classification of Diseases* (ICD) or the American Psychiatric Association's *Diagnostic and Statistical Manual of Mental Disorders* (DSM). These two manuals describe and categorize psychological disorders, but differences in the way they do this can make it difficult to identify disorders consistently.

Key facts

✓ Psychiatrists and psychologists may diagnose patients using the ICD or DSM.

✓ These manuals describe and classify psychological disorders but not always in the same way.

✓ Attitudes towards mental health have changed over time – the ICD and DSM are updated to reflect social developments.

The International Classification of Diseases (ICD)

The ICD is produced by the World Health Organization (WHO), and is used worldwide. It originated in 1900 as a way of classifying diseases. The latest version, the ICD–11, was published in 2022.

It includes psychological and physical disorders.

The ICD–11 classifies disorders into 21 general categories, and then into increasingly smaller subcategories, with each disorder having its own code. Categorizing like this can make it hard to differentiate disorders with overlapping symptoms or to diagnose patients with multiple disorders.

The Diagnostic and Statistical Manual of Mental Disorders (DSM)

The DSM is produced by the American Psychiatric Association (APA), and is predominantly used in the USA. The first edition, the DSM–I, was published in 1952. The latest version, the DSM–5, was published in 2013.

The scope of the DSM is narrower than that of the ICD, as it only includes psychological disorders.

The DSM–5 contains 297 different disorders, split across 22 categories. It describes the symptoms of each disorder, which are used as criteria to diagnose patients. It also contains a section for potential new disorders that need further research.

🔍 Changing ideas of mental health

Over time, the views of society change about what constitutes a psychological disorder. Both the ICD and DSM are updated following new research and changes in social attitudes, although it can take time. In 1973, homosexuality was removed from the DSM as a psychological disorder, following protests starting in 1969 by LGBTQ+ campaigners in the USA against its inclusion.

DSM-5 categories of disorders

Key facts

✓ Psychological disorders involve atypical patterns of thoughts, feelings, or behaviours.

✓ The DSM-5 categorizes psychological disorders according to symptoms, etiology, or diagnostic criteria.

Psychological disorders are conditions characterized by abnormal patterns of thoughts, feelings, or behaviours that cause distress or impaired functioning. The DSM-5 classifies psychological disorders into categories based on symptoms, etiology (set of causes), or diagnostic criteria.

Categories of disorders	Examples
Neurodevelopmental disorders: symptoms typically appear in childhood and may cause impairment in cognitive, social, or emotional functioning.	Attention deficit hyperactivity disorder (ADHD); autism spectrum disorder (ASD); learning disabilities
Psychotic disorders: cause abnormal thinking, hallucinations, or delusions and unusual behaviour.	Schizophrenia; schizoaffective disorder; brief psychotic disorder
Bipolar and related disorders: extreme mood disturbance, with periods of mania and depression.	Bipolar I disorder; bipolar II disorder; cyclothymic disorder
Depressive disorders: involve disturbances in mood, which primarily affect a person's emotional state.	Major depressive disorder, persistent depressive disorder, premenstrual dysphoric disorder
Anxiety disorders: involve excessive fear, worry, or anxiety, leading to significant distress or inability to function.	Generalized anxiety disorder; panic disorder; social anxiety disorder; phobias
Obsessive-compulsive disorders: involve obsessive thoughts and behaviours due to underlying, severe anxiety.	Body dysmorphic disorder; hoarding disorder; trichotillomania (hair-pulling disorder)
Trauma- and stress-related disorders: occur as a result of exposure to traumatic or stressful events.	Post-traumatic stress disorder (PTSD); adjustment disorder; reactive attachment disorder
Dissociative disorders: involve disruptions or perceived changes to a person's identity, consciousness, memory, or perception of reality.	Dissociative identity disorder (DID); dissociative amnesia
Eating disorders: characterized by abnormal eating behaviours, distorted body image, and an intense preoccupation with body weight and shape.	Anorexia nervosa; bulimia nervosa; binge-eating disorder; pica (eating non-food substances)
Sleep-wake disorders: characterized by disturbances in sleep patterns.	Insomnia; narcolepsy; sleep apnea
Substance-related and addictive disorders: involve the misuse of, or dependence on, substances, which results in distress and inability to function.	Abuse of or dependence on substances such as alcohol or drugs; addictive behaviours such as gambling or compulsive sexual activity
Personality disorders: unstable, enduring patterns of thoughts and behaviours that cause distress and interfere with the ability to function in society.	Paranoid personality disorder; borderline personality disorder; antisocial personality disorder (APD); narcissistic personality disorder

ICD-11 categories of disorders

Published in 2019, the latest version of the World Health Organization's *International Classification of Disorders* — ICD-11 — has 19 categories of psychological disorders, some of which are shown below.

> **Key facts**
>
> ✓ The ICD-11 divides psychological disorders into 19 categories, including mood disorders and obsessive compulsive or related disorders.

Categories of disorders	Examples
Neurodevelopmental disorders: cognitive and behavioural disorders that occur in early life	Disorders of intellectual development; autism spectrum disorder; attention deficit hyperactivity disorder (ADHD)
Schizophrenia or other primary psychotic disorders: loss of touch with reality, with changes in behaviour	Schizophrenia; acute and transient psychotic disorder; delusional disorder
Mood disorders: changes in mood to depression or elation, often related to stress	Bipolar disorder; depression; substance-induced mood disorder
Anxiety or fear-related disorders: excessive anxiety or fear that causes significant distress	Agoraphobia; specific phobia; panic disorder; generalized anxiety disorder
Obsessive compulsive or related disorders: thoughts and fears that lead to repetitive behaviours	Obsessive compulsive disorder; body dysmorphic disorder; hoarding disorder
Disorders specifically associated with stress: trauma that results from stressful events	Post-traumatic stress disorder; prolonged grief disorder; adjustment disorder
Dissociative disorders: a loss of connection with one's memory, emotions, and sense of identity	Dissociative amnesia; trance disorder; dissociative identity disorder
Feeding or eating disorders: abnormal feeding or eating habits, often with a preoccupation with weight	Anorexia nervosa; bulima nervosa; binge-eating disorder; pica
Disorders due to substance use or addictive behaviours: addiction to mind-altering substances or rewarding behaviours	Disorders due to the use of alcohol and other drugs; gambling disorder; gaming disorder
Personality disorders and related traits: difficulty in managing emotions, leading to impulsive and irresponsible behaviour	Antisocial personality disorder; borderline personality disorder

The history of clinical psychology

Clinical psychology is the branch of psychology that studies, assesses, and provides therapies for people with psychological disorders. Over time, the treatment of patients with psychological disorders has shifted dramatically, as clinical psychologists have increased their understanding of the disorders and found new ways of treating them.

Many soldiers were traumatized by their experiences of trench warfare in World War I.

Asylums
Early hospitals for mentally ill patients, commonly known as lunatic asylums, become widespread in the 1700s. Psychological disorders are poorly understood and treatments such as bloodletting are common. Patients are often restrained with chains or straitjackets.

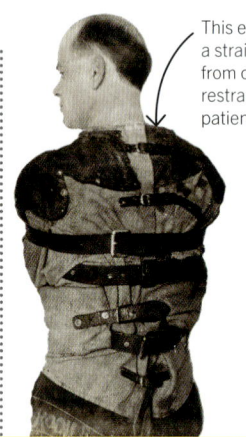

This example of a straitjacket is from c.1890 – it restrained the patient's arms.

Responding to crisis
Clinical psychology gains momentum as a distinct medical field, largely due to the psychological issues of soldiers with shell shock (a type of post-traumatic stress disorder), returning from the battlefields of World War I and later World War II.

18th century   18th–19th century   1883   1918 onwards

Humane treatment
Campaigners instigate changes for the better understanding and treatment of people with psychological disorders. They include English philanthropist William Tuke, French physician Philippe Pinel, US psychiatrist Eli Todd, and US advocate Dorothea Dix.

Classifying mental health
German psychiatrist Emil Kraeplin publishes what is often thought to be the first classification system of psychological disorders. He argues that psychiatry is a branch of medical science and that it should be studied scientifically.

This painting shows Pinel unchaining inmates at Salpêtrière asylum in Paris in 1795.

Key facts

✓ People with severe psychological disorders were often physically restrained and kept in asylums. Campaigners fought to improve patient conditions.

✓ The biomedical model uses drugs to treat psychological disorders.

✓ The biopsychosocial model integrates biological, psychological, and social factors to treat disorders.

The first edition of the DSM described 106 different psychological disorders.

Publication of DSM
The *Diagnostic and Statistical Manual of Mental Disorders* (DSM) is published in the USA. Regularly updated, it is used to diagnose and treat psychological disorders.

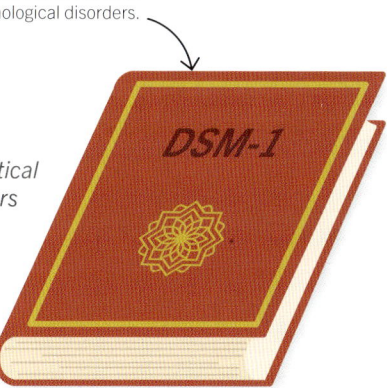

Mental health disorders
First published in 1893, the *International Classification of Diseases* (ICD) has descriptions of all known medical disorders. In 1949, it includes mental health disorders for the first time.

The biopsychosocial model
US psychiatrist George L. Engel introduces an approach to treatment that recognizes the interaction between biological, psychological, and social factors. It emphasizes seeing the person as a whole and heavily influences the treatment of psychological disorders.

| 1948 | 1949 | 1952 | 1960s–1980s | 1977 |

The biomedical model
Drugs are first used to treat psychological disorders — an approach known as the biomedical model, in which mental illnesses are viewed as having biological causes, such as a chemical imbalance in the brain. Lithium is used to treat mania in 1948 and chlorpromazine to treat psychosis in 1952.

Ward of a psychiatric hospital

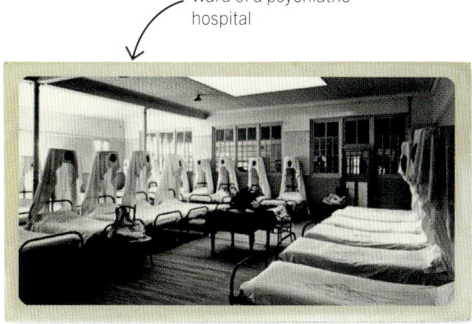

This corked lithium bottle is from the mid-1900s.

Deinstitutionalization
Awareness of the prevalence of psychological disorders increases. The number of people in institutions drops dramatically, and the length of inpatient stays shortens. More people are now treated in their communities.

Defining abnormality

Clinical psychology is the area of psychology concerned with understanding, diagnosing, and treating mental illness. This branch of psychology is also known as psychopathology or abnormal psychology. Defining what is abnormal in a clinical sense is difficult as people's ideas vary about what is normal. Four approaches to defining abnormality are shown here.

Key facts

✓ The deviation from social norms definition of abnormality sees abnormal behaviour as behaviour that violates social rules or standards.

✓ The deviation from ideal mental health definition sees abnormality as any failure to meet criteria for ideal mental health.

✓ The failure to function adequately definition is based on inability to cope with everyday life.

✓ The statistical infrequency definition sees abnormality as statistically rare.

Deviation from social norms
Every society has norms (standards or rules) that people conform to. Some norms are explicitly written in law, but others are implicit, such as when physical contact is appropriate. According to the deviation from social norms definition, behaviour that violates social norms is abnormal. By this definition, people who are merely eccentric, flamboyant, or nonconformist might be classed as abnormal. Another problem is that social norms vary between different cultures.

Deviation from ideal mental health
Austrian–British psychologist Marie Jahoda (1958) proposed that a person only has ideal mental health if they exhibit the six characteristics shown here. According to the deviation from ideal mental health definition of abnormality, failure to meet any of these criteria indicates that a person has a psychological abnormality.

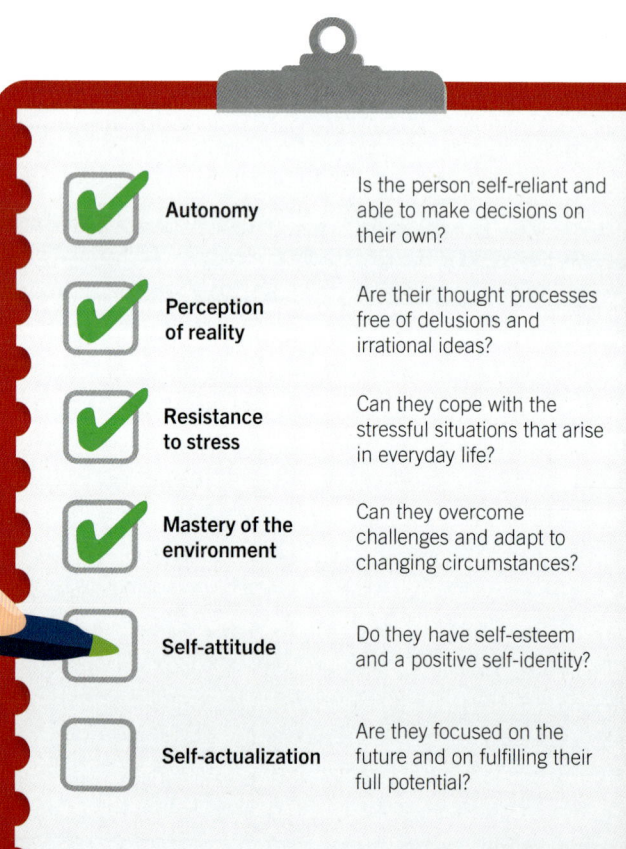

Autonomy — Is the person self-reliant and able to make decisions on their own?

Perception of reality — Are their thought processes free of delusions and irrational ideas?

Resistance to stress — Can they cope with the stressful situations that arise in everyday life?

Mastery of the environment — Can they overcome challenges and adapt to changing circumstances?

Self-attitude — Do they have self-esteem and a positive self-identity?

Self-actualization — Are they focused on the future and on fulfilling their full potential?

Failure to function adequately

If a person's psychological problems make them unable to cope with everyday life, they fit the failure to function adequately definition of abnormal. This definition focuses on individual suffering and allows clinicians to rate how dysfunctional a person is using the Global Assessment of Functioning (GAF) scale. However, some people with dangerous personality disorders don't fit the definition as they function normally in everyday life. US psychologists David Rosenhan and Martin Seligman (1989) proposed using seven criteria to assess whether a person's behaviour is dysfunctional.

Personal distress	Is the person experiencing distress, such as anxiety or depression?
Maladaptive behaviour	Does their behaviour stop them from attaining life goals?
Unpredictable behaviour	Is their behaviour unpredictable or out of control?
Irrational behaviour	Are they thinking or behaving in ways that are not rational?
Observer discomfort	Does their behaviour make people around them uncomfortable?
Violation of norms	Does their behaviour violate society's moral standards?
Unconventional	Is their behaviour unconventional?

Statistical infrequency

According to the statistical infrequency definition, abnormal means statistically rare. Measurable characteristics such as IQ follow a bell-shaped pattern called a normal distribution (see page 32), with most people clustered near the central mean. People in the tails of the graph are abnormal. By this definition, positive traits such as high IQ are classed as abnormal. Another problem is that very common mental disorders, such as depression, don't fit the definition.

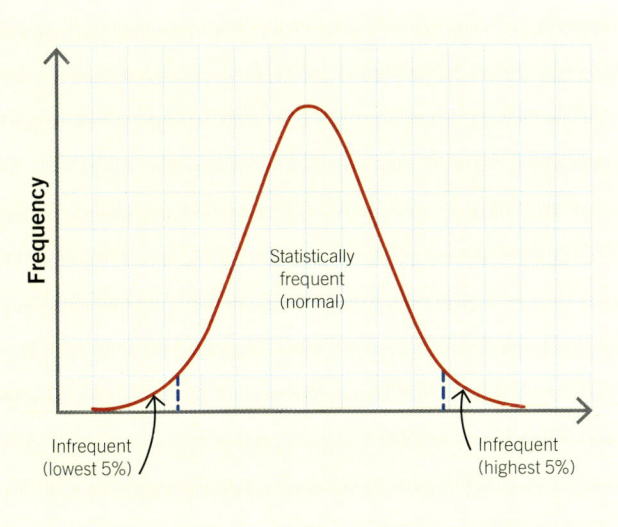

🔍 The Rosenhan experiment

In 1973, Rosenhan conducted a famous experiment to demonstrate how difficult diagnosing psychiatric illness can be. Rosenhan and eight other sane people faked hallucinations in order to gain admittance to psychiatric hospitals, acting normally thereafter. All were diagnosed with schizophrenia and prescribed medication, even after saying their hallucinations had stopped. Some genuine patients were able to spot the pseudo-patients, but the staff could not.

Phobias

A phobia is a persistent, irrational, and extreme fear that is out of proportion to any actual threat or risk. People with phobias are typically aware that their fears are irrational but they are unable to control them.

Symptoms

Phobias are common, but how much they affect a person's daily life can vary widely depending on severity and the source of their fear. A person who is unable to manage their symptoms should seek help.

Key facts

✓ Phobias are characterized by an intense fear of a stimulus, such as an object, feeling, or situation.

✓ Severity of symptoms can vary.

✓ Behavioural psychologists believe they are created by classical conditioning and maintained by operant conditioning.

Uncontrollable, persistent fear
An extreme, ongoing fear of a stimulus, typically starting in childhood. It may improve or worsen with age.

Physical responses
Involuntary physical changes such as increased heart rate, sweating, nausea, trembling, shortness of breath, and dizziness.

Inability to function
Overwhelmed by fear and unable to continue with normal, everyday tasks.

Behavioural characteristics
Avoiding situations in an attempt to avoid the feared stimulus, thereby restricting day-to-day life. Panicking in the presence of the stimulus, and screaming, crying, or trying to escape.

Cognitive characteristics
Irrational thinking and inability to focus on anything else (known as selective attention), despite understanding that their fear is excessive.

Emotional characteristics
Experiencing extreme and unpleasant fear and anxiety. May also have feelings of guilt, shame, or embarrassment.

🔍 Types of phobia

Simple (specific) phobias	Complex phobias	
	Social phobias	**Agoraphobia**
Fear of a specific thing or environment; for example, arachnophobia (fear of spiders), hydrophobia (fear of water), or claustrophobia (fear of small spaces). The effect on a person's life may be limited if they do not often come into contact with their feared stimulus.	Fear of social interaction or performing in public (meeting new people or speaking on the phone, for example). This type of phobia can be much harder to manage, as social situations cannot be avoided without restricting everyday life.	Fear of being trapped or unable to escape public places or situations where help will not be available. Agoraphobia can make people afraid to leave their houses and be in crowded places. It can have a severe impact on daily life.

The two-process model

According to behavioural psychologists, phobias are acquired and then maintained through a two-process model. The phobia is learned initially through classical conditioning (learning by association), and then maintained through operant conditioning (learning by reward).

Process 1: classical conditioning

Behavioural psychologists think phobias are first learned by association. In 1920, US psychologists John B. Watson and Rosalie Rayner carried out a deeply unethical experiment on an 11-month-old child referred to as Little Albert. They wanted to see whether Albert could be conditioned to fear a white rat (neutral stimulus) by pairing it with an unpleasant, loud noise (unconditioned stimulus).

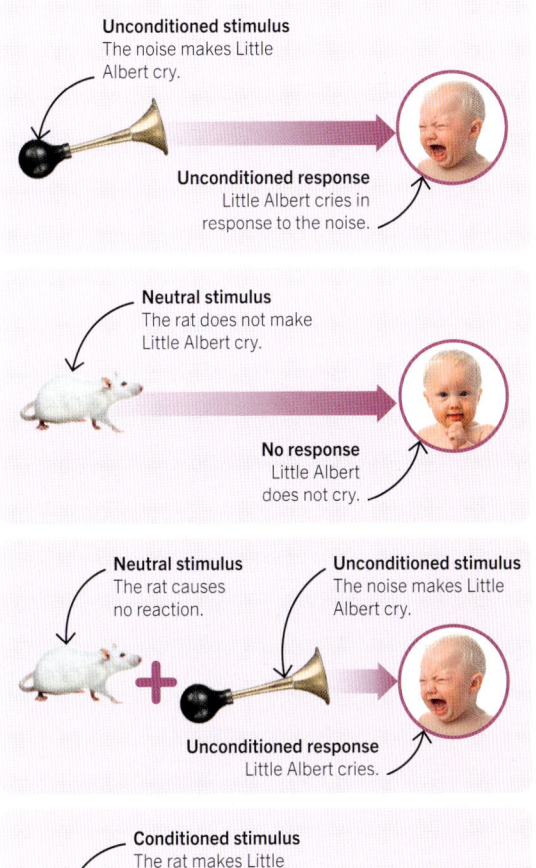

Unconditioned stimulus
The noise makes Little Albert cry.

Unconditioned response
Little Albert cries in response to the noise.

Neutral stimulus
The rat does not make Little Albert cry.

No response
Little Albert does not cry.

Neutral stimulus
The rat causes no reaction.

Unconditioned stimulus
The noise makes Little Albert cry.

Unconditioned response
Little Albert cries.

Conditioned stimulus
The rat makes Little Albert cry.

Conditioned response
Little Albert cries at the rat, even without the noise.

Process 2: operant conditioning

Once a phobia has been acquired, it is maintained by operant conditioning (see page 82). Avoiding or escaping the feared stimulus gives the person a feeling of relief, which acts as negative reinforcement (the removal of an unpleasant stimulus). It makes it more likely that the person will avoid the stimulus again, so the phobia continues.

Avoiding a situation brings relief from fear, making this behaviour likely to occur again in the future.

Anxiety disorders

Feelings of fear and dread disproportionate to their situations are known as anxiety disorders. There are different types, and they may be accompanied by physical symptoms, such as heart palpitations, "butterflies in the stomach", and sweating. Everyone experiences short-lived anxiety in response to a clear threat. However, anxiety disorders are long-lasting and may not have an identifiable trigger.

 Key facts

✓ Anxiety is a normal experience for everyone; anxiety disorders are prolonged and may not have a specific trigger.

✓ There are several types of anxiety disorder, each with different symptoms.

✓ Anxiety disorders can have a negative effect on someone's wellbeing.

General anxiety disorder (GAD)
This disorder isn't linked to a specific event or stimulus, and people with GAD may feel anxious and fearful for prolonged periods of time (days, weeks, or months). People with GAD usually function well but have trouble relaxing and often feel unsettled.

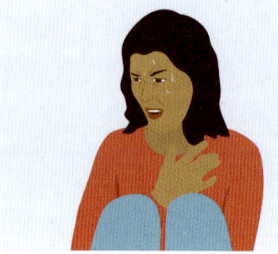

Panic disorder
People who have panic disorder experience frequent, unexpected panic attacks, which in turn lead to anxiety about suffering further panic attacks. This fear can interfere with their normal social activities and result in prolonged anxiety.

Social anxiety disorder
This disorder is triggered by a disproportionate fear of being judged, embarrassed, criticized, or humiliated in social situations. This can lead to an avoidance of social situations, have an impact on relationships, and often result in depression.

 Everyday emotions versus anxiety disorders

Anxiety and stress are normal human emotions that everyone experiences in certain situations. However, when these feelings become more extreme, take over someone's life, and prevent them from functioning normally, they may need to get help. Both medical and psychological treatments for anxiety disorders can be effective and improve quality of life.

Everyday anxiety
- **is triggered** by an external stimulus (such as work, a break-up, or financial concerns)
- resolves **when the stimulus ends**
- **is proportionate** to the stimulus
- **includes feelings** of self-consciousness in social situations

Both may include
- excessive worry
- loss of sleep
- headaches

Anxiety disorder
- **is internal**, with no specific trigger
- **is a persistent feeling that** affects daily life
- **doesn't go away** regardless of the situation changing
- **is disproportionate** and excessive
- **leads to feeling unable** to participate in social situations

Obsessive compulsive disorder

Obsessive compulsive disorder (OCD) is an anxiety disorder characterized by recurrent, intrusive thoughts (obsessions) and repetitive behaviours (compulsions). People with OCD alleviate their anxiety by performing compulsive actions, such as ritualized hand-washing, checking and rechecking doors are locked, or ordering and rearranging possessions.

Key facts

✓ OCD is an anxiety disorder characterized by recurrent, intrusive thoughts and compulsive behaviours.

✓ Biological explanations include possible genetic and neural causes, but these are unproven.

The OCD cycle

OCD tends to follow a repeating cycle, with compulsive behaviours providing a self-reinforcing reward by giving temporary relief from anxiety.

Obsessions are recurrent, often intrusive thoughts. For example, touching an object with clean hands might trigger thoughts about contamination with germs.

The obsessive thoughts cause anxiety, making the person feel agitated and compelled to take action.

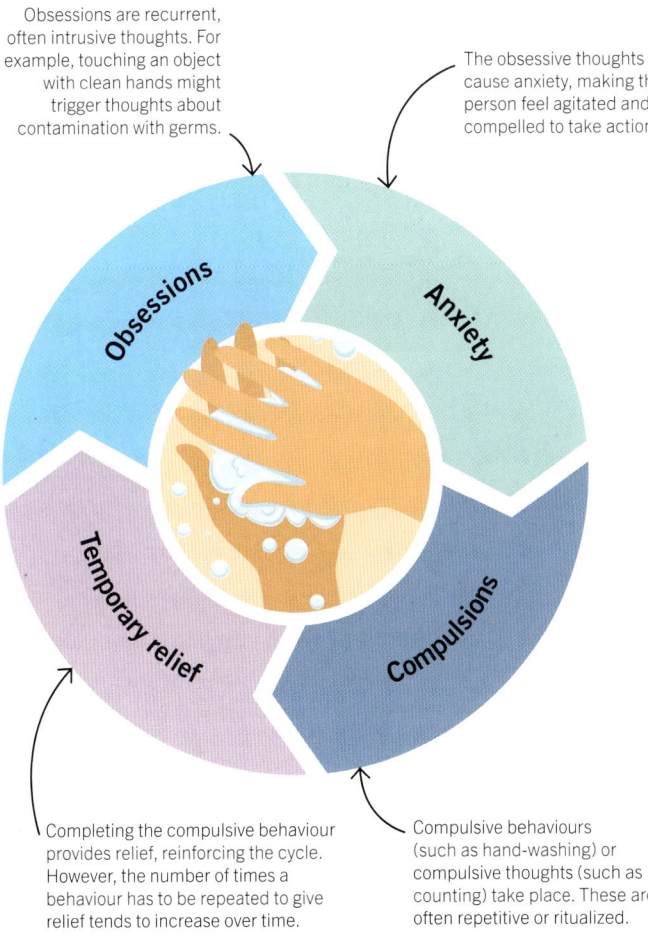

Obsessions

Anxiety

Temporary relief

Compulsions

Completing the compulsive behaviour provides relief, reinforcing the cycle. However, the number of times a behaviour has to be repeated to give relief tends to increase over time.

Compulsive behaviours (such as hand-washing) or compulsive thoughts (such as counting) take place. These are often repetitive or ritualized.

Biological explanations

OCD may have biological causes, but these remain unproven. At least one gene is implicated, as are problems with the frontal cortex – the part of the brain involved in impulse control.

Neural explanations

Functional brain scans (see pages 46–47) have revealed unusual activity in a part of the brain called the orbitofrontal cortex in some people with OCD.

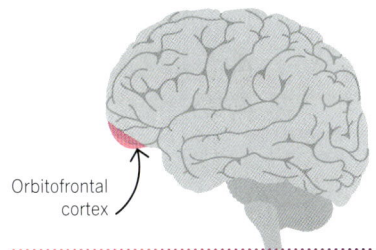

Orbitofrontal cortex

Genetic explanations

The COMT gene produces an enzyme that breaks down the neurotransmitter dopamine. A variant of this gene has been associated with OCD, but many other genes may play a role, too.

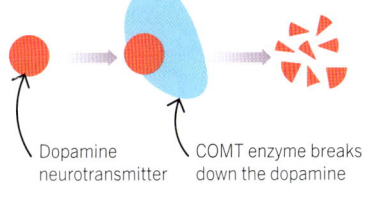

Dopamine neurotransmitter

COMT enzyme breaks down the dopamine

Depression

Depression, also known as major depressive disorder, is characterized by extreme low mood and/or feeling numb, and a loss of interest in previously enjoyed activities. A person is considered to have depression if their low mood does not reflect their life circumstances, and if it interferes with their daily life for a prolonged period of time.

Characteristics of depression

The symptoms of depression can be emotional, behavioural, and cognitive – it affects how people feel, behave, and think. For a diagnosis, five or more symptoms must be present every day during a two-week period. These must include either low mood or loss of interest in activities.

Key facts

✓ Depression, also known as major depressive disorder, is a type of mood disorder.

✓ For a diagnosis of depression, a person must have at least five symptoms lasting for at least a two-week period.

✓ Cognitive psychologists argue that depression is caused by faulty thought patterns.

✓ Ellis' ABC model says that the beliefs we have about a negative event determine how the event affects us.

Emotional characteristics	Behavioural characteristics	Cognitive characteristics
Depressed, low mood	Changes in activity level	Negative view of the self
Low energy, feeling tired	Changes in appetite	Negative view of the world
Loss of interest in activities	Speaking and moving slowly	Negative view of the future
Feeling numb	Aggression	Problems thinking or concentrating
Feeling irritable or angry	Self-harm	Difficulty making decisions
Low self-worth and self-esteem	Sleep disturbance, including sleeping too much or too little	Recurrent thoughts of death
Loss of hope	Agitated behaviours, such as fiddling or pacing	
Feeling guilty		

🔍 Biological and environmental factors

Genetic factors
Evidence suggests that people who have a close family member with depression are more likely to experience depression themselves, suggesting a genetic link.

Neural factors
People with depression sometimes have low levels of serotonin, a neurotransmitter that causes feelings of wellbeing. Extreme changes in hormone levels may also trigger depression.

Environmental factors
Evidence suggests that certain life experiences may increase the risk of depression – for example, living in poverty or experiencing trauma.

Beck's negative triad

Cognitive psychologists believe depression is caused by faulty or systematically biased ways of thinking. US cognitive psychologist Aaron T. Beck proposed three types of negative thinking that occur automatically in people with depression, regardless of the reality of their life circumstances at the time. These are negative views about the self, the world, and the future. Such self-critical views can exacerbate negative emotions.

Negative views about the self
"I am worthless."

Negative views about the future
"Nothing will ever change."

Negative views about the world
"Everyone thinks I am worthless."

Ellis's ABC model

According to US psychologist Albert Ellis's ABC model, it is not an activating difficult event (A) but the belief (B) we have about it that leads to the consequence (C) of depression.

Activating event (A)
Failing a test

Belief (B)
Faulty way of thinking
"I can't do this; what is the point of trying?"

Consequence (C)
Feeling demotivated and not working

Activating event (A)
Failing a test

Belief (B)
Rational way of thinking
"I didn't study enough. I'll try harder next time."

Consequence (C)
Feeling motivated and working harder

🔍 Explanatory styles

Abramson et al. (1978) proposed that the way people explain negative events to themselves determines whether or not they will experience depression. A person who self-blames is more likely to experience depression. A person who attributes negative events to external causes is less likely to experience depression.

- **Internal**: cause is personal failings ("I failed because I'm stupid.")
- **Stable**: cause is permanent ("I'll never get any better.")
- **Global**: cause is related to all aspects of the person ("I fail at everything I try.")

- **External**: cause is out of their personal control ("That test was really hard.")
- **Unstable**: cause is temporary ("I'll do better next time.")
- **Specific**: cause is only related to one aspect of the person ("There are other things I'm good at.")

Post-traumatic stress disorder

When people experience an extremely stressful event — often referred to as a trauma — it can have a long-lasting impact on their mental health. In some cases, experiencing one, or possibly multiple, traumatic events can lead to post-traumatic stress disorder (PTSD). Some people recover naturally, but for others PTSD is a chronic (long-term) condition that needs treatment.

Key facts

✓ Experiencing a single or multiple extremely stressful event(s) may — although not always — cause a person to develop post-traumatic stress disorder (**PTSD**).

✓ Symptoms of PTSD may include flashbacks, negative emotions, anxiety, sleep disturbance, substance abuse, hypervigilance, and avoiding triggering situations.

Symptoms
PTSD is characterized by multiple symptoms, although not everybody with PTSD will experience them all.

Avoidance
Avoiding situations that might provoke memories of the traumatic incident(s); for example, busy or noisy places. Withdrawing from social situations.

Flashbacks
Experiencing vivid, intrusive memories of the traumatic event(s). Feeling a strong sense that the trauma is happening again.

Negative emotions
Feeling low, irritable, or guilty. Experiencing a sense of isolation and disconnection from loved ones. Loss of interest and pleasure in previously enjoyable activities.

Sleep disturbance
Experiencing disturbed sleep caused by nightmares related to the trauma. Difficulty falling or staying asleep (insomnia).

Substance abuse
Facing an increased risk of drug or alcohol abuse, often used as a way to cope with or numb other symptoms. This may lead to addiction issues.

Anxiety
Experiencing feelings of fear or worry that are not connected to, or are out of proportion with, the present situation.

Hypervigilance
Being overly aware of the environment in anticipation of further danger. Increased sensitivity to sensations such as unexpected noises or smells.

Possible causes

- Being bullied and/or abused
- Being physically and/or sexually assaulted
- Experiencing life-threatening illness
- Being in a car crash
- Experiencing a traumatic childbirth
- Witnessing or experiencing violence or war
- Experiencing a natural disaster

Bipolar disorder

Bipolar disorder involves swinging between two different states or "poles" — mania (characterized by extremely high energy and mood, and chaotic thought processes) and depression (characterized by extremely low energy levels and mood). Between mania and depression there are periods of stability. Symptoms of bipolar disorder and the length, frequency, and intensity of manic and depressive periods varies between people.

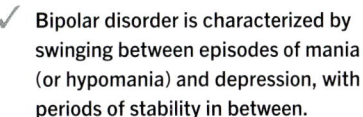

Key facts

✓ Bipolar disorder is characterized by swinging between episodes of mania (or hypomania) and depression, with periods of stability in between.

✓ It can be caused by a combination of biological, social, and environmental factors.

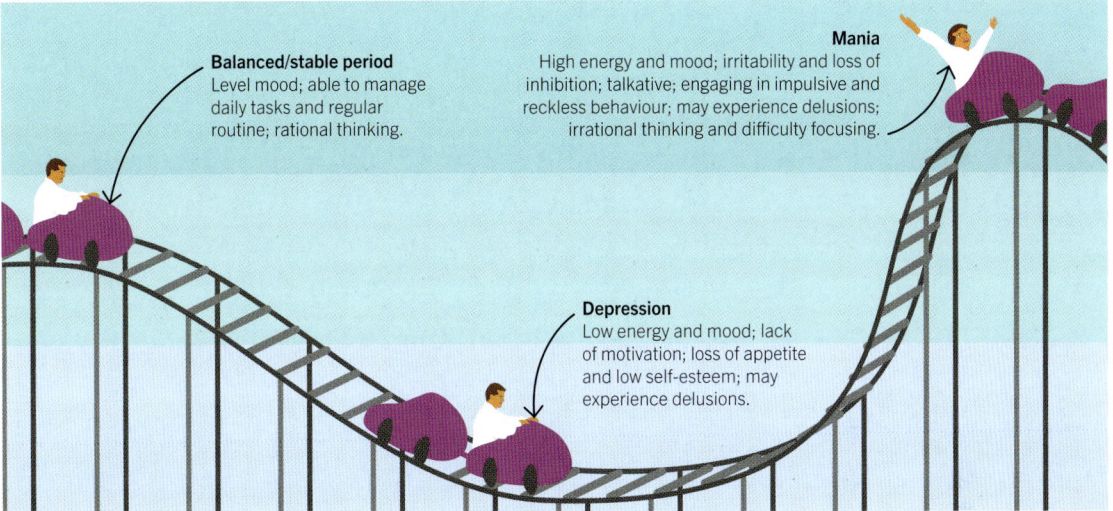

Balanced/stable period
Level mood; able to manage daily tasks and regular routine; rational thinking.

Mania
High energy and mood; irritability and loss of inhibition; talkative; engaging in impulsive and reckless behaviour; may experience delusions; irrational thinking and difficulty focusing.

Depression
Low energy and mood; lack of motivation; loss of appetite and low self-esteem; may experience delusions.

Types of bipolar disorder

Bipolar I disorder	Mania lasts 1 week or more. Depression lasts 2 weeks or more.
Bipolar II disorder	Hypomania (milder than mania) lasts 4 days or more, and depression lasts 2 weeks or more.
Cyclothymic disorder (Cyclothymia)	Less extreme and more frequent cycles of mild depression and hypomania over at least 2 years.

Possible causes

Psychologists think a mix of biological, social, and environmental factors may increase the risk of bipolar disorder:

- Reduced grey matter has been observed in the prefrontal cortex of people with the disorder, although it is unclear whether this is a cause or a consequence.

- Similarly, unbalanced levels in the brain of the neurotransmitters dopamine and serotonin may be linked to the disorder, but it's not known if this is a consequence or a cause.

- Bipolar disorder often runs in families, suggesting a possible genetic and/or social link.

- Stressful life events such as illness, bereavement, or financial worries can trigger episodes of (but not cause) bipolar disorder.

Somatic symptom disorder and related disorders

Some people seek medical help for pain or other bodily (somatic) symptoms for which no physical explanation can be found. In most cases the symptoms are not being faked — they are just as real and distressing as in people suffering from an organic disease or injury. Such disorders are common and are thought to have psychological roots, so treatments include counselling, cognitive behavioural therapy, and psychiatric drugs.

Key facts

✓ Somatic symptom disorder and related disorders cause distressing symptoms for which no physical cause can be found.

✓ Treatments include counselling, cognitive behavioural therapy, and psychiatric drugs.

Psychosomatic medicine

Medical practitioners have long known that a person's frame of mind can influence the onset, severity, and course of a disease. For example, people with no mental disorders often recover faster from illness after taking dummy pills (placebos) they believe to be effective. Psychosomatic medicine acknowledges that the mind and body are linked and that recovery is promoted if psychological factors such as stress are managed.

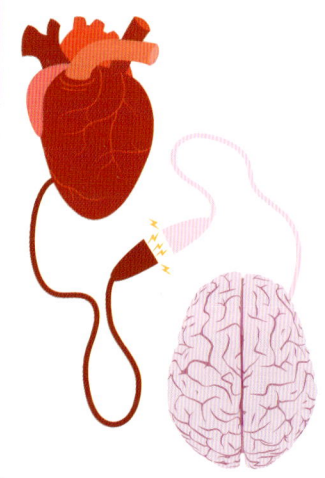

Disorder	Symptoms	Causes	Treatments
Somatic symptom disorder	Pain, weakness, fatigue, shortness of breath	Associated with anxiety, depression, childhood trauma, and negative thinking	Antidepressants and cognitive behavioural therapy
Conversion disorder	Poor movement, trouble walking, and blindness	May be triggered by stress in people with other psychiatric disorders, such as depression	Counselling, cognitive behavioural therapy, psychotherapy
Illness anxiety disorder	Excessive anxiety about serious illness but no physical symptoms	Associated with other anxiety disorders and often follows illness or the death of a close family member	Antidepressants such as selective serotonin reuptake inhibitors (SSRIs)
Factitious disorder	Symptoms of serious illness deliberately faked in order to obtain medical attention and care	Associated with an abusive or turbulent childhood and low self-esteem	Psychotherapy and cognitive behaviour therapy to help develop coping skills

Dissociative identity disorder

Dissociative identity disorder (DID) is when an individual has multiple personalities, each with its own distinct identity. DID typically appears as a result of severe, recurring trauma in childhood. In extreme distress, the brain forms separate personalities, helping the person to cope.

Key facts

✓ DID is when one person (the host) has multiple personalities.

✓ Each additional personality is known as an alter.

✓ Alters may not be aware of one another's existence.

✓ DID usually results from severe, recurring childhood trauma.

Hosts and alters
The identity that feels like the core self is known as the host. The other personalities, which can be of varying genders and ages, are known as alters. The alters take turns to control the host's body. The host may not be aware of an alter, leaving memory gaps, which can cause distress.

Each alter can have different likes and dislikes, hobbies, and tastes.

The main personality is referred to as the host.

An alter could be older than the host.

Alters don't have to be human; they may be a mythical creature such as a fairy, or even objects.

An alter can behave like a young child.

Alter 1 · Alter 2 · Host · Alter 3 · Alter 4

The Three Faces of Eve

A case study in the 1950s by US psychiatrists C.H. Thigpen and H.M. Cleckley followed a married mother, Eve White (a given name), who sought help following blackouts. During therapy, Eve was replaced by two alters, of whom she was unaware. Eve Black, who was single and did not have children, was confident and loud, in contrast to Eve White, who was shy and quiet. A second alter, Jane, seemed more stable than either of the Eves. After years of therapy, Eve integrated the alters into one personality.

Eve Black · Eve White · Jane

Eating disorders

People with eating disorders use certain food-related behaviours to help them cope with difficult feelings and experience a sense of control. Disordered eating behaviours can include restricting foods, extreme over- or under-eating, and getting rid of food in unhealthy ways, such as by vomiting or extreme exercise. Eating disorders can damage the body and may become life-threatening if left untreated.

Types of eating disorder

Anorexia nervosa, bulimia nervosa, and binge eating disorder are distinct types of eating disorder. There are some similarities in their symptoms.

Key facts

✓ Eating disorders are characterized by unhealthy food-related behaviours.

✓ These behaviours may be a way of managing emotions or gaining a sense of autonomy.

✓ Anorexia nervosa, bulimia nervosa, and binge eating disorder are examples of eating disorders.

✓ There are different explanations for why eating disorders develop.

Anorexia nervosa
This disorder involves fear of, and efforts to avoid, weight gain. People with anorexia nervosa eat less food than the body requires to be healthy, and are at least 15 per cent below their expected body weight.

Bulimia nervosa
This disorder involves cycles of eating large amounts of food (bingeing), followed by emptying behaviours such as vomiting (purging) or intense exercise. People with bulimia nervosa may not be over- or underweight.

Binge-eating disorder
This disorder involves eating large amounts in a short period of time (bingeing), despite feelings of distress, shame, or disgust. People with binge-eating disorder are not necessarily overweight.

Possible explanations

Psychologists have proposed a range of biological, cognitive, environmental, and social explanations for why eating disorders may develop.

- **Genetic explanation** There is some evidence that eating disorders run in families, suggesting a genetic link.

- **Neural explanation** People with increased levels of the neurotransmitters dopamine or serotonin, involved in feelings of reward, are potentially at higher risk of developing an eating disorder.

- **Cognitive explanation** Irrational beliefs about food and body image can lead a person to develop maladaptive (inappropriate) behaviours to do with eating.

- **Family systems theory** Disordered eating may result from certain family dynamics, particularly those where family members are heavily involved in one another's lives. In families where members have little autonomy, an individual may restrict food intake to create a sense of control.

- **Social learning theory** The role models and social expectations people are exposed to in everyday life and the media are thought to affect their risk of developing an eating disorder. Feeling pressure to look a certain way, and seeing celebrities or models praised for losing weight or excessive exercise, may lead people to imitate their behaviours.

Addiction

Addiction is a psychological disorder in which a person compulsively takes a substance or engages in a behaviour that feels rewarding in the short term but leads to serious harm in the long term. A person with an addiction becomes dependent on the substance or behaviour and suffers discomfort or even physical illness (withdrawal syndrome) when they stop.

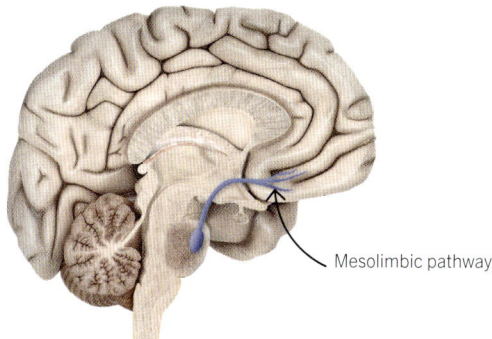

Mesolimbic pathway

Drug addiction
Drugs that cause addiction include depressants (such as alcohol and heroin) and stimulants (such as nicotine and cocaine). Drug addiction can be explained by operant conditioning: the pleasurable sensation acts as a reward, reinforcing drug-taking behaviour. Some drugs act directly on the neural pathways that reinforce behaviour, leading to rapid addiction. Nicotine, for instance, triggers the release of the neurotransmitter dopamine in the mesolimbic pathway, a part of the brain involved in motivation and reward. As a result, nicotine is highly addictive despite giving little pleasure besides relief from craving.

Gambling addiction
Gambling addiction can also be explained by operant conditioning, with the excitement of a win reinforcing behaviour. Gambling wins follow an unpredictable schedule (see page 84), which makes the reinforcement especially powerful. Addiction to gambling can also be explained by cognitive biases. An example is the gambler's fallacy: the mistaken belief that a run of heads when tossing a coin makes tails more probable on the next toss. This fallacy makes gamblers continue to bet during a losing streak.

Slot machines are designed to reward gamblers intermittently, reinforcing the desire to bet.

📌 Key facts

✓ Addictions involve operant conditioning, with addictive behaviour reinforced by rewards.

✓ Some addictive substances act directly on the neural pathways that reinforce behaviour, leading to rapid addiction.

✓ Gambling addiction is reinforced by intermittent rewards and cognitive biases.

✓ Risk factors for addiction include genetics, stress, personality, family influences, and peer pressure.

🔎 Risk factors

The causes of addiction are complex, but evidence suggests that there are five main risk factors.

- Twin studies show higher rates of concordance for addiction in identical twins, indicating a genetic susceptibility. However, the concordance occurs only for specific kinds of addiction – there is no evidence for an "addictive personality".

- Stress and mental illness may lead people to self-medicate with drugs to feel better, leading to addiction. Stress in early childhood is also associated with increased risk of drug addiction later in life.

- Children in families that use addictive substances or have positive attitudes towards them are more likely to become addicted.

- Adolescents are at greater risk of addiction if they believe parents are not monitoring their behaviour.

- Adolescents are at greater risk of addiction if their peers use addictive substances or have positive attitudes towards them.

Antisocial personality disorder

Antisocial personality disorder (APD) is a mental health disorder in which an individual persistently disregards and violates the rights of other people and engages in manipulative and dangerous behaviours, without any sense of remorse. Genetics, parents with a history of alcohol abuse, and environmental factors, such as childhood neglect and abuse, poverty, and poor relationships, may increase the risk of developing APD.

Key facts

✓ APD is characterized by disregard for and violation of other people's rights, and engagement in manipulative and dangerous behaviours, with no remorse.

✓ Traits of APD can be observed and diagnosed as conduct disorder in children by the age of eight. Left untreated, symptoms may lead to a diagnosis of APD by the age of 18.

Diagnosing APD

APD is diagnosed by a qualified mental health professional after an assessment of symptoms. A diagnosis can only be given to adults, but APD traits are often identified in childhood as conduct disorder by the time a child is eight years old. Left untreated, an individual has a higher risk of being diagnosed with APD by the age of 18. APD is the most common mental health diagnosis given to people convicted of repeated violent crimes and serial murder.

Symptoms	Behaviours
Disregard for other people	Displays indifference towards and repeatedly violates the rights of other people; shows no regard for their wellbeing.
Lack of empathy	Shows an inability to consider the feelings or emotional states of other people.
Disregard for societal norms	Shows a persistent lack of respect for the law and societal values; engages in antisocial and illegal activities.
Impulsive, dangerous actions	Regularly engages in reckless behaviour (such as excessive drinking, substance abuse, gambling, and unsafe sex).
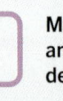 **Manipulation and deceitfulness**	Frequently manipulates, lies to, and deceives other people for personal gain or to avoid punishment.
Lack of remorse	Shows no regret or guilt for actions that cause pain or upset to others; blames others to justify behaviour.

Schizophrenia

Schizophrenia is the most commonly diagnosed psychotic disorder and affects around 24 million people worldwide. Onset usually occurs in early adulthood, with males typically diagnosed at 18–25 years and females at 25–35 years.

Symptoms of schizophrenia

The most common symptoms of schizophrenia are delusions and hallucinations. Symptoms that are abnormal additions to a person's behaviour are described as "positive". In contrast, "negative" symptoms involve a loss or decline of a normal behaviour. Schizophrenia may be acute (sudden and severe), episodic, or chronic (long-lasting). Recovery is less likely in chronic cases.

Key facts

✓ Schizophrenia is a psychotic disorder that begins in early adulthood.

✓ The most common symptoms are delusions and hallucinations.

✓ Positive symptoms are additions; negative symptoms are losses.

Positive symptoms

Delusions
These are false, often paranoid beliefs that vary from plausible to impossible.

Hallucinations
For example, seeing things or hearing voices that aren't there.

Disorganized speech
Speech may be rapid, uncontrolled, and incoherent.

Psychomotor
Restless movement and excessive fidgeting often occur.

Negative symptoms

Speech poverty
Speaking may be minimal, with long pauses between words.

Flat emotion
Expression of emotion through facial expressions or voice may be limited.

Avolition
Loss of motivation reduces ability to complete tasks.

Social withdrawal
Lack of social interest and engagement may occur.

 ## Diagnosing schizophrenia

Diagnosing schizophrenia can be difficult as there may be co-morbid (simultaneous) conditions, such as anxiety or depression. To ensure that diagnoses are both reliable and valid (see pages 18–19), health practitioners base their assessment on symptoms in official guidelines such as the DSM-5 (see page 178). Two or more symptoms, at least one of which is positive, must be present for at least a month. In some countries, rates of diagnosis are higher in certain ethnic groups and genders, but whether this reflects higher incidence, a bias in diagnosis, or both factors is controversial.

Schizophrenia

Depression

Anxiety

Schizophrenia: brain differences

Researchers have discovered numerous anatomical and chemical differences between the brains of people with and without schizophrenia. These features are called "neural correlates" as they coincide with the disease, but it is not clear whether they represent causes or effects.

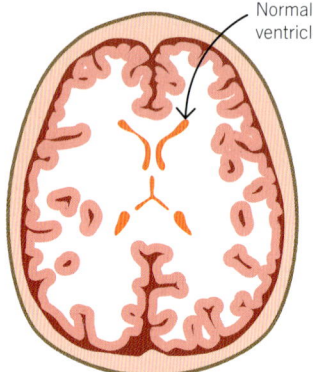

Key facts

✓ Brain anatomy is different in some patients with schizophrenia.

✓ Higher dopamine levels are seen in some patients with schizophrenia.

✓ The dopamine hypothesis does not fully explain schizophrenia.

Anatomical differences

Brain scans and post-mortems of people with schizophrenia have sometimes (but not always) found enlargement of the brain's fluid-filled ventricles (cavities) and shrinkage of other parts of the brain, including the frontal and temporal lobes, hippocampus, corpus callosum, and thalamus. These changes are most often associated with negative symptoms. Functional brain scans have also found changes in activity in the frontal lobes, thalamus, amygdala, and Wernicke's area (a part of the temporal lobe involved in speech).

Normal ventricle

Enlarged ventricle

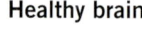
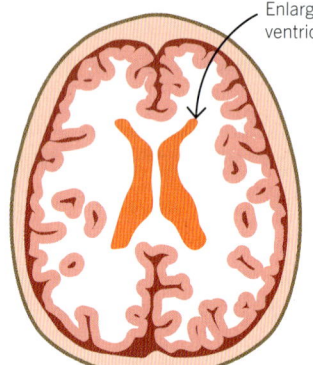

Healthy brain

Schizophrenia

The dopamine hypothesis

Postmortems of people with schizophrenia have found raised levels of the neurotransmitter dopamine and its receptors. Drugs that block dopamine can relieve symptoms, and drugs that increase dopamine can cause schizophrenia-like effects. These findings led to the theory that a fault in dopamine processing causes the disease. Some scientists regard this theory as simplistic because dopamine blocker drugs do not always work, not all patients have raised dopamine levels, and other neurotransmitters, including serotonin and glutamate, are implicated too.

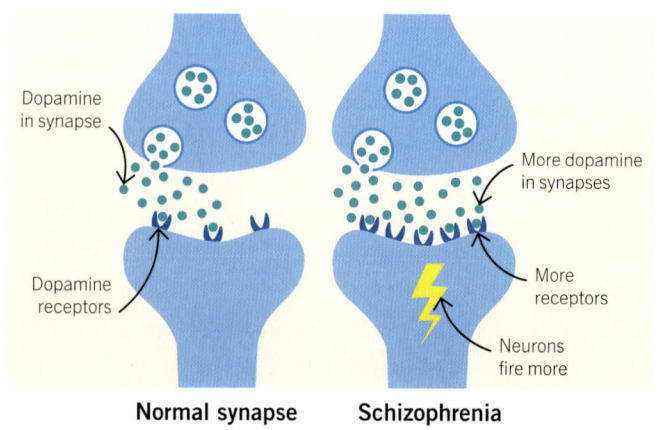

Dopamine in synapse

More dopamine in synapses

Dopamine receptors

More receptors

Neurons fire more

Normal synapse   **Schizophrenia**

Schizophrenia: genetic factors

Although the causes of schizophrenia are not fully understood, studies of heritability (see page 56) show that genes play a major role. However, schizophrenia is not caused by a single gene, and genes alone do not trigger the disease. Instead, vulnerability is polygenic (involving multiple genes), and onset is thought to be triggered by gene–environment interactions.

Key facts

✓ Many genes affect the risk of developing schizophrenia.

✓ Onset is caused by gene–environment interactions.

✓ According to the diathesis-stress model, stress or trauma triggers disease in people with a predisposition.

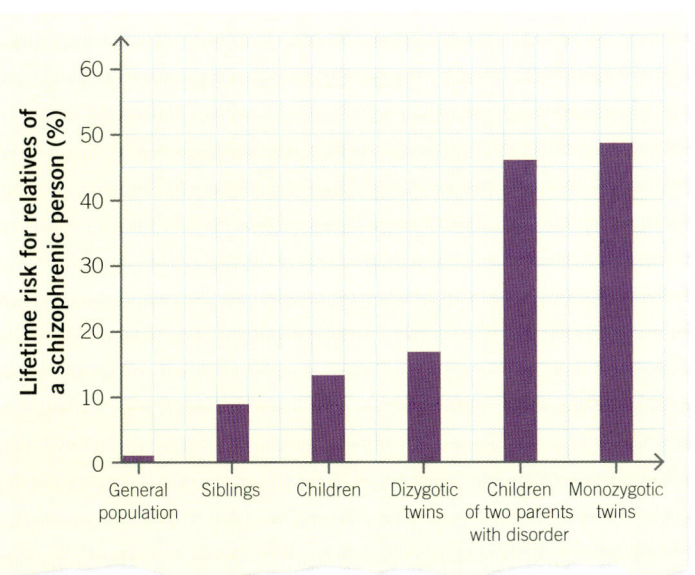

Twin and family studies
Evidence that genes affect the risk of schizophrenia comes in part from twin and family studies, which show higher rates of concordance for the disease with higher levels of genetic relatedness. For example, this chart is from a 1991 study that found an identical twin had a 48 per cent chance of developing schizophrenia if their twin had it, whereas the equivalent risk for a fraternal twin was 17 per cent. Such studies show that vulnerability is inherited, but environmental factors must also be involved as the disease is not inevitable.

Diathesis-stress model

The diathesis-stress model is a theory that attempts to explain how psychological disorders arise by interaction between an underlying vulnerability (the diathesis) and stress. For example, schizophrenia (or an episode of schizophrenia) is thought to be caused by interaction between an underlying genetic predisposition and a psychological trigger, such as family conflict or drug misuse. The interactionist approach to treatment addresses both causes, combining antipsychotic medication to treat the biological cause with cognitive behavioural therapy to treat the psychological cause.

| Diathesis (vulnerability, which may be genetic) | + | Stress (such as prenatal trauma, abuse, family conflict, drug misuse, significant life change) | → | Disorder |

Schizophrenia: prenatal risk factors

Schizophrenia has both environmental and genetic causes. Scientific evidence suggests that some of the environmental factors that raise the risk of schizophrenia in adulthood occur before birth. These "prenatal risk factors" are thought to disrupt foetal development, but exactly how this leads to the disorder is unknown.

Key facts

✓ Prenatal risk factors may increase the risk of schizophrenia later in life.

✓ These include certain infections, complications, malnutrition, and stress.

✓ Prenatal risk factors are thought to affect foetal brain development.

In the womb
Factors found to be associated with schizophrenia include maternal infection, complications during pregnancy or birth, malnutrition, and stress. None of these is directly responsible for causing the disease, but each seems to increase the risk.

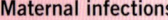

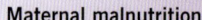

Maternal infections
Certain infections during pregnancy, such as influenza or rubella, have been linked to an increased rate of schizophrenia. Scientists suspect that the mother's immune response to these infections may affect foetal brain development.

Maternal malnutrition
Healthy nutrition is essential for foetal brain development. Scientists think that poor diet and a lack of key nutrients during pregnancy may increase the risk of developing schizophrenia in adulthood.

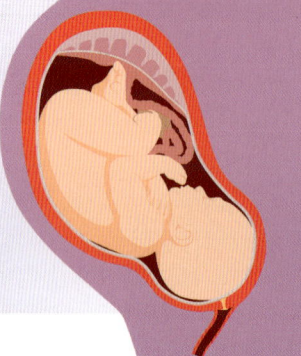

Complications
Complications that occur during pregnancy and birth – such as maternal diabetes, pre-eclampsia, or premature birth – are associated with a higher risk of developing schizophrenia.

Maternal stress
Stress hormones in the mother's body can cross the placenta and pass to a baby. High levels of these hormones may affect foetal brain development, potentially increasing the likelihood of schizophrenia later in life.

Schizophrenia: psychological explanations

Psychological explanations for schizophrenia attempt to explain why the disorder develops or why schizophrenic episodes are triggered. These theories fall into two classes: family dysfunction explanations and cognitive explanations.

Key facts

✓ The double-bind theory proposes that conflicting emotional signals from carers increases the risk of schizophrenia.

✓ High levels of expressed emotion are linked to increased risk of relapse in schizophrenia.

✓ Egocentric bias is the tendency to over-interpret external events as having personal relevance, leading to delusions.

✓ People with schizophrenia have poor central control, leading to disorganized thinking.

Family dysfunction

According to family dysfunction explanations, abnormal patterns of communication within a family increase the risk of schizophrenia. Two examples of family dysfunction theories are the double-bind theory and expressed emotion.

Double-bind theory
This theory proposes that children who receive conflicting messages from carers are more likely to develop schizophrenia. For example, if a father tells his son he loves him but his body language is hostile, the mixed messages cause confusion and fear, which may evolve into paranoid delusions.

Expressed emotion
High levels of expressed emotion by a carer – including hostility, criticism, and emotional over-involvement – have been linked to an increased risk of relapse in people with schizophrenia, though this is not seen as a cause.

Cognitive explanations

According to cognitive explanations, dysfunctional thinking can cause or intensify the symptoms of schizophrenia. Cognitive behavioural therapy aims to reduce symptoms by addressing dysfunctional thinking.

Egocentric bias
According to this explanation, delusions are related to a tendency to over-interpret external events as having personal significance. For example, a person with schizophrenia who hears strangers laughing may think the laughter is directed at them.

Central control
Central control is the ability to suppress a knee-jerk reaction while performing a task – such as stating the colour in which a word is printed rather than reading the word when the two conflict (the Stroop test). People with schizophrenia have poor central control, leading to disorganized thinking.

Chapter 14

Clinical psychology:
treating psychological disorders

Evidence-based practice

Before making decisions about a patient's treatment, the therapist gathers evidence about their condition. They consider their patient's preferences, study the latest clinical research about the condition, and use their own professional experience to make a treatment plan that is backed by evidence and as effective as possible.

Key facts

✓ Evidence-based practice involves input from the patient, therapist, and research evidence.

✓ A therapeutic alliance is the bond between the patient and therapist.

✓ Meta-analysis assesses previous research studies.

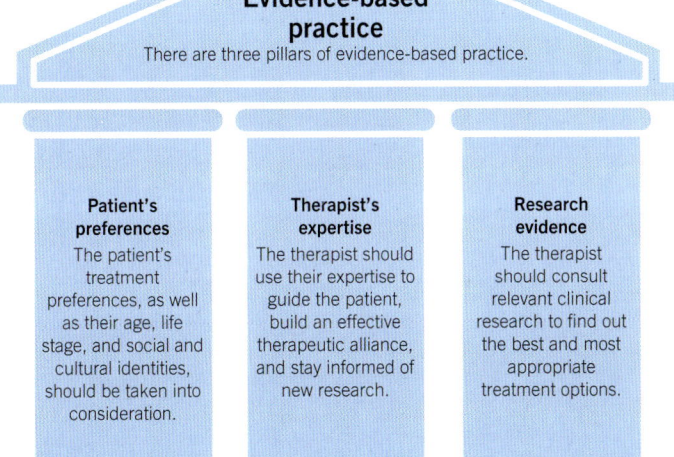

Evidence-based practice
There are three pillars of evidence-based practice.

Patient's preferences
The patient's treatment preferences, as well as their age, life stage, and social and cultural identities, should be taken into consideration.

Therapist's expertise
The therapist should use their expertise to guide the patient, build an effective therapeutic alliance, and stay informed of new research.

Research evidence
The therapist should consult relevant clinical research to find out the best and most appropriate treatment options.

🔍 Therapeutic alliance

The collaborative and trusting relationship between a therapist and a patient is known as a therapeutic alliance. This bond can be crucial for the success of therapy. The alliance should include mutual respect, understanding, care, empathy, and a shared commitment to the goals of the therapy.

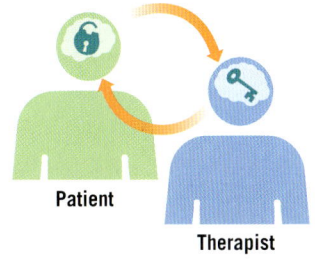

Patient

Therapist

🔍 Meta-analysis

A meta-analysis combines the data from multiple studies to reach an overall conclusion. Meta-analysis is helpful when deciding on the most effective treatment for a psychological disorder. To show which treatments work best, a meta-analysis gathers data from many clinical trials, potentially making it more reliable than just using results from a single study.

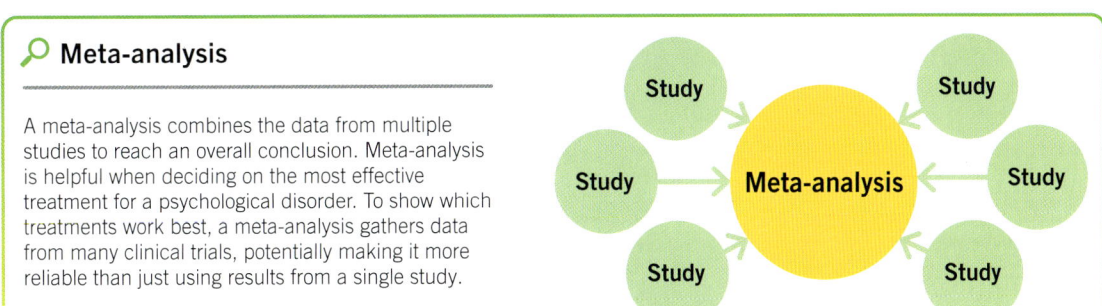

Study
Study
Study
Meta-analysis
Study
Study
Study

Psychodynamic therapy

Psychodynamic therapy explores the unconscious processes that drive a person's thoughts, feelings, and behaviours. It is based on Austrian neurologist Sigmund Freud's theory that life experiences, particularly in childhood, influence adult behaviour (see pages 156–157). Psychodynamic therapists use different techniques to help clients reduce their psychological distress by learning more about themselves.

Key facts

✓ Psychodynamic therapy involves exploring the client's unconscious processes to understand why they behave the way they do.

✓ Transference is when the client unconsciously projects their feelings onto the therapist.

✓ Countertransference is when the therapist projects their unconscious responses onto the client.

Interpretation
The therapist analyses and interprets their client's thoughts, emotions, and dreams (even if these appear aimless). They identify patterns to help the client understand reasons for their behaviour.

Transference
Clients may project emotions (such as love or hatred), conflict, or desires from childhood or past relationships onto the therapist – this is known as transference. By pointing this out, the therapist helps the client to become aware of their relationship patterns.

Resistance
Clients may resist exploring painful emotions or memories with defence mechanisms. These could include changing the subject, forgetting things, or making jokes. Clients may be unaware they are using these mechanisms, so it is the therapist's job to inform them.

Insight
When the therapist helps the client to gain awareness of why they behave the way they do, it is referred to as insight. Clients must make the breakthrough themselves, rather than be told directly.

🔍 Countertransference

Countertransference refers to any unconscious responses that the therapist may have towards their client. The responses can be positive or negative but in either case they can affect the behaviour of the therapist and how well they understand and work with their client. The therapist must carefully manage their personal responses (such as having awareness of their own prejudices) to avoid them interfering with the process of therapy.

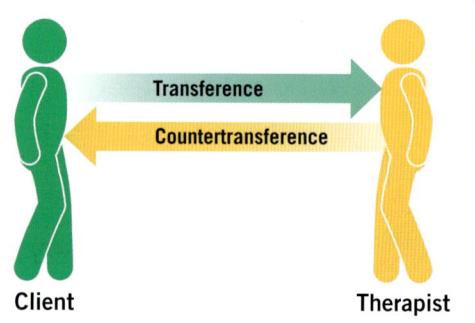

Client Therapist

Transference

Countertransference

Counterconditioning

Based on the principles of classical conditioning
(see page 81), counterconditioning aims to change an
unwanted emotional or behavioural response triggered by
a particular stimulus. It involves replacing the unwanted
response with an alternative, preferred response.
Types of counterconditioning include systematic
desensitization, flooding, and aversion therapy.

Key facts

✓ Counterconditioning aims to
change unwanted responses.

✓ Systematic desensitization and
flooding are used to treat phobias.

✓ Aversion therapy is used to treat
undesirable behaviours.

Systematic desensitization
This therapy is used to overcome fears or phobias. It involves
teaching the person relaxation techniques to use while they
are gradually exposed to something they fear, such as a
spider. The person works through an anxiety hierarchy –
from least to most scary encounter. They learn by exposure
that the catastrophic result they expect does not occur.

Flooding
This therapy is based on the idea that an anxious response
lasts for a limited period of time. So, when a person is
exposed to a feared situation or object at its worst (rather
than gradually) for a prolonged period, they will eventually
start to calm down. Flooding works much faster than
systematic desensitization but it can be traumatic.

Aversion therapy

Also known as aversive conditioning,
this treatment aims to associate an
undesirable behaviour (such as
excessive alcohol drinking) with
an unpleasant response (such as
nausea) to discourage the behaviour.
The goal of this therapy is for the
person to develop an aversion to the
behaviour, leading to its reduction.

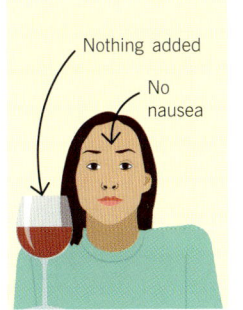

Wine

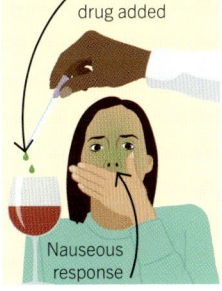

Wine with drug

Wine without drug

Cognitive behavioural therapy

Cognitive behavioural therapy (CBT) aims to help people identify and change problematic patterns of thinking and behaviour. US psychologist Aaron Beck first developed CBT in the 1960s. Today it is a broad field, with therapists using a wide range of techniques. CBT can be used to treat many psychological disorders, including OCD, anxiety, and depression.

Key facts

✓ CBT focuses on the connection between thoughts, feelings, and behaviours.

✓ It can treat a variety of psychological disorders.

✓ The therapist helps the client to challenge unhelpful thoughts.

✓ CBT also involves making behavioural changes to improve mood.

Principles of CBT

Beck developed CBT based on the idea that our thoughts, feelings, and behaviours are connected and influence one another. He believed that negative thoughts lead to problematic feelings and behaviours, and vice versa. According to Beck, changing one of these factors can affect the others.

Thoughts
How we think affects how we feel and behave.

Our thoughts may not always reflect the reality of a situation.

Feelings
How we feel affects how we think and behave.

Behaviour
How we behave affects how we think and feel.

🔍 Disputing irrational thoughts

In CBT, the therapist works with the client to identify negative, irrational thoughts and find ways to challenge them. The therapist can approach this task in three ways:

1. Empirical disputing
Challenging the client on whether there is evidence to support their negative belief.

2. Logical disputing
Challenging whether the client's negative belief is reasonable or rational.

3. Pragmatic disputing
Challenging whether the negative belief is actually helpful in solving their problems.

🔍 CBT for depression

CBT for depression can help reduce feelings of hopelessness and lack of pleasure in everyday life. The person is helped to understand the connection between the thoughts, feelings, and behaviours that perpetuate their low mood. CBT strategies are then used to create more helpful ways of thinking, thereby improving the person's state of mind.

New skills

Unlike psychodynamic therapy, which typically reflects on past experiences to gain insight, CBT focuses on the current challenges that the person is experiencing. A CBT therapist will try to improve their client's emotional wellbeing and everyday functioning by suggesting behavioural changes and new skills. The exact techniques that a therapist suggests will depend on the psychological disorder being treated, but they could include a combination of some or all of the following strategies:

Cognitive restructuring

The main skill taught in CBT is to re-evaluate and manage negative, irrational thoughts. Noticing problematic patterns of thinking allows people to replace them with more effective ones. It does not mean always thinking positively, but instead learning to think in a balanced, objective way.

Meditation can be an effective way to relieve stress.

Stress management

CBT therapists may suggest techniques to reduce stress, such as meditation, deep breathing, muscle relaxation, visualizing calming scenes, and mindfulness (focusing on the present moment and bodily sensations). By calming the body, it is possible to help calm the mind.

Enjoyable activities such as cycling can trigger positive emotions.

Behavioural activation

The activities we engage in often influence our moods, for better or worse. CBT encourages behavioural activation – purposefully choosing behaviours that make us feel better. The therapist works with their client to remove any barriers to participating in activities, such as low motivation.

CBT can help people navigate daily challenges.

Problem-solving

In CBT, clients are encouraged to work on their problem-solving skills to help them manage the challenges in their everyday lives. CBT teaches people to identify the solvable problems they face and start to take small, practical steps towards resolving them.

Self-monitoring

CBT only works if the client is an active and willing participant in the process. Between sessions, they should practise self-reflection by writing a journal of their thoughts, feelings, and behaviours. They should also attempt to apply the skills learned from CBT to real-life situations.

Rational emotive behaviour therapy

Rational emotive behaviour therapy (REBT) was developed by US psychologist Albert Ellis in the 1950s. Ellis argued that depression can be caused by irrational beliefs and unhealthy ways of thinking (see page 189). He proposed that by reevaluating and managing dysfunctional thought patterns, it is possible to reduce emotional distress.

Key facts

✓ Rational emotive behaviour therapy (**REBT**) involves identifying irrational beliefs and dysfunctional thought patterns, and replacing them with more helpful ways of thinking.

✓ REBT is based on Ellis's ABC model of depression, but extends it to include additional components: **D** (dispute) and **E** (effect).

Challenging perceptions of reality

REBT is based on Ellis's ABC model of depression. According to Ellis, it is a person's belief (B) about an activating event (A) – not the activating event itself – that causes a potentially distressing emotional consequence (C). He proposed that we can influence our emotional response to events by changing the way we think about them. To explain the process of REBT, Ellis added two additional stages to his ABC model – D for dispute and E for effect.

Activating event (A)
The event that triggers irrational thoughts.
For example, a student not being selected for a school athletics team.

⬇

Belief (B)
An automatic, self-defeating response to the external situation.
"I am a terrible athlete, I should give up, I'll never get better."

⬇

Emotional consequence (C)
Experiencing unhealthy emotions, such as depression, anger, blame, self-loathing, and low self-esteem.
The student might give up on training.

⬇

ABC model

Disputing irrational thoughts can be hard to do, so during REBT the therapist will actively question a client on why they believe what they do (see page 206).

Dispute (D)
Challenging the belief that is making them sad.
"If I keep practising, I will get better. I can deal with this disappointment and try again."

⬇

Replacing irrational beliefs with more positive ones can have a dramatic impact on a person's emotional wellbeing.

Effect (E)
New beliefs are practised until they become automatic.
"I would have loved to be on the team, but I am a capable person and I will continue to try."

REBT

Client-centred therapy

Client-centred therapy, also known as the person-centred approach to counselling, was developed in the early 1950s by US psychologist Carl Rogers. Rogers used the term "client" instead of "patient" to indicate that the therapist works in partnership with an individual to develop their self-awareness and personal growth, rather than trying to "fix" or "cure" them.

Key facts

✓ Rogers developed client-centred therapy in the 1950s.

✓ His approach emphasizes the importance of the therapist creating a non-judgmental, supportive environment for the client.

✓ Client-centred therapy aims to develop self-awareness in the client.

Safe space
By creating a non-judgmental, supportive environment using several different techniques, the therapist allows the client — considered the expert on their own life — to safely explore their thoughts, feelings, and experiences.

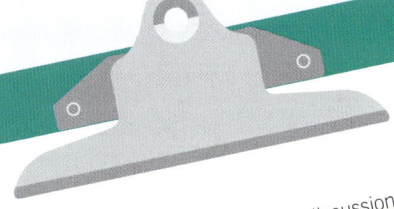

Letting the client lead
The therapist does not try to control the discussion. The client sets the agenda.

Showing empathy
The therapist demonstrates understanding, care, and respect, allowing the client to express themselves without fear of criticism or rejection.

Active listening
The therapist echoes and confirms what the client says. They acknowledge the client's responses, with phrases such as "that must have been hard for you" if they can see the client is upset.

Focusing on the present and future
The therapist tries to understand how the client is feeling now, rather than dwelling on the past.

Unconditional positive regard
The therapist accepts what the client says without judgment. That does not necessarily mean always agreeing with the client. Allowing the client to feel accepted improves their self-worth.

Theory of planned behaviour

Why is it that some people succeed in quitting addictive drugs or gambling while others fail or relapse? The theory of planned behaviour (TPB) is used to predict the success of treatment for addiction by assessing the strength of a person's intention.

 Key facts

✓ The TPB is used to predict the success of treatment for addiction.

✓ Three factors contribute to intention to quit: attitude, subjective norms, and perceived control.

✓ According to Prochaska's six-stage model of behaviour change, overcoming addiction involves a series of six stages.

Four-part model

Polish psychologist Icek Ajzen's theory of planned behaviour (1991) assesses the strength of a person's resolve to end an addiction by examining three key factors that contribute to intention: attitude, subjective norms, and perceived control. The stronger the intention to quit is, the greater the chance of success. The theory grew out of an earlier, simpler one (the theory of reasoned action, 1975) that failed to take into account perceived control.

Attitude
What is the person's personal attitude to their addiction? Do they acknowledge that they have a problem and are they eager to be helped?

Subjective norms
How does the person perceive the social consequences of quitting? Do they have supportive friends and family who will approve of quitting? Or will peer pressure from other addicts make quitting difficult?

Perceived control
Does the addict have faith in their ability to quit, or do they suffer from a defeatist belief that they can't control their behaviour?

Intention
Attitude, subjective norms, and perceived control all contribute to the strength of an addicted person's motivation to quit.

Behaviour

🔍 Prochaska's six-stage model

US psychologist James Prochaska proposed a six-stage model of behaviour change (1977) after studying people trying to quit smoking. He observed that they don't transition directly from addicted to healthy but instead pass through a series of transitional stages in which thinking and behaviour change. None of the stages is constant, and relapse can occur at any point before termination, which most people fail to reach.

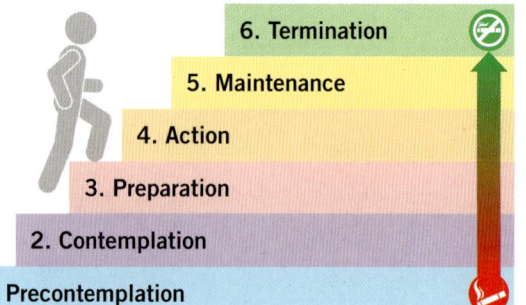

6. Termination
5. Maintenance
4. Action
3. Preparation
2. Contemplation
1. Precontemplation

Token economies

In a token economy, people engaging in desirable behaviours earn tokens, which can be exchanged for rewards. This behavioural therapy technique is based on operant conditioning (see page 82), in which desirable behaviours are encouraged through reinforcement with rewards. Positive reinforcement makes it more likely that the desirable behaviour will happen again. Token economies may be used with schizophrenia patients to help reduce symptoms such as avolition (low motivation) and social withdrawal.

Key facts

✓ Token economies are a behavioural therapy technique that can be used with schizophrenic patients in hospitals to encourage desirable behaviours, such as taking medication.

✓ Desirable behaviours are recognized with tokens that can be exchanged for rewards.

✓ The reward is known as the primary reinforcer; the token is known as the secondary reinforcer.

The token economy in a hospital situation

1. The patient has no tokens. They are aware that if they carry out a desirable behaviour they will be given tokens that can be exchanged for a reward. The reward is selected to motivate the patient.

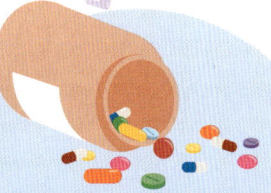
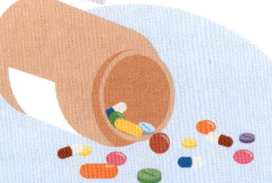

2. The patient carries out a desirable behaviour, such as taking their medication on time or interacting socially. They choose to engage in this behaviour knowing that they will receive tokens as a consequence.

3. The patient receives their tokens, marking progress towards reaching their reward. Delayed reinforcement, where the reward is earned after collecting a set number of tokens, increases the likelihood of appropriate behaviour. The prospect of not acquiring tokens reduces instances of inappropriate behaviour.

The tokens are called secondary reinforcers as they do not have any value to the patients until they are associated with primary reinforcers.

4. The patient exchanges their tokens for their preferred reward; for example, playing video games. This positive reinforcement motivates the patient to engage in the desirable behaviour again in the future.

The rewards are called primary reinforcers as they have value and are desirable outside the token economy.

Virtual reality exposure therapy

Virtual reality exposure therapy (VRET) uses VR technology to create lifelike simulations of feared situations. It can be used to treat phobias, such as fear of heights, flying, or public speaking, with real-time support from a therapist. The person is gradually exposed to their feared stimulus in a 3D virtual environment, starting with less anxiety-provoking situations, then progressing to more challenging ones. The goal of treatment is to reduce the person's anxious responses to the feared stimulus both virtually and in the real world.

Key facts

✓ VR technology can be used to treat phobias, in a type of treatment known as virtual reality exposure therapy (VRET).

✓ The virtual environment can be customized to the person's particular phobia.

✓ A therapist can provide support throughout the session.

The therapist can customize the virtual environment to match the person's specific phobia.

Wearing a VR headset immerses the person in a virtual environment where they can face the source of their fear in a safe, controlled way.

Medication

The most common treatment for psychological disorders is medication. Psychiatric drugs can significantly improve mental wellbeing, but like all drugs they can cause side-effects, and finding the right drug and the right dose is not always easy. Most psychiatric drugs work by changing the activity of neurotransmitters in synapses (junctions between neurons), but some work in unknown ways.

Key facts

✓ Medication is the most common treatment for psychological disorders.

✓ Psychiatric drugs cause side-effects.

✓ Most psychiatric drugs work by changing the activity of neurotransmitters in synapses.

Drug type	Example	Used for	Symptoms treated	How it works	Problems
Typical antipsychotic	Chlorpromazine	Schizophrenia, bipolar disorder	Hallucinations, delusions, paranoia	Blocks dopamine receptor sites	Sluggishness, tremors, involuntary movements
Atypical antipsychotic	Clozapine	Schizophrenia, bipolar disorder, OCD	Hallucinations, delusions, paranoia, depressive symptoms	Blocks dopamine and serotonin receptor sites	Weight gain, diabetes
Antianxiety	Diazepam	Anxiety disorders	Tension, stress, agitation, panic attacks	Enhances effects of GABA, an inhibitory neurotransmitter	Addiction
Antidepressant	Fluoxetine	Depression, PTSD, OCD, and anxiety	Sadness, fatigue, loss of appetite	SSRIs raise levels of the neurotransmitter serotonin in synapses	Weight gain, insomnia, dizziness, raised blood pressure
Mood stabilizer	Lithium	Bipolar disorder	Extreme high and low moods	Unknown	Weight gain, kidney and thyroid problems

Antidepressant SSRIs

Selective serotonin reuptake inhibitors (SSRIs) are a class of drugs used to treat depression and anxiety disorders such as OCD. They are the most widely prescribed psychiatric drugs in the world and have fewer side-effects and lower risk of dependence or overdose than other antidepressant and antianxiety drugs. Even so, SSRIs cause various adverse effects, including dizziness, weight gain, insomnia, and sexual dysfunction.

Key facts

✓ SSRIs are antidepressant drugs used to treat depression and anxiety disorders.

✓ They work by preventing the reuptake of serotonin by pre-synaptic neurons, increasing the amount of serotonin in synapses.

✓ Side-effects include dizziness, weight gain, insomnia, and sexual dysfunction.

How SSRIs work

SSRIs act on synapses (junctions between neurons) that use serotonin, a neurotransmitter involved in mood, sleep, and appetite. Normally, after serotonin has diffused across a synapse and transmitted its message to the next neuron, it is reabsorbed to be used again. SSRIs prevent this by binding to reuptake channels and blocking them, raising the level of serotonin in the synapse. As serotonin is an inhibitory neurotransmitter, this makes the post-synaptic neuron less likely to fire.

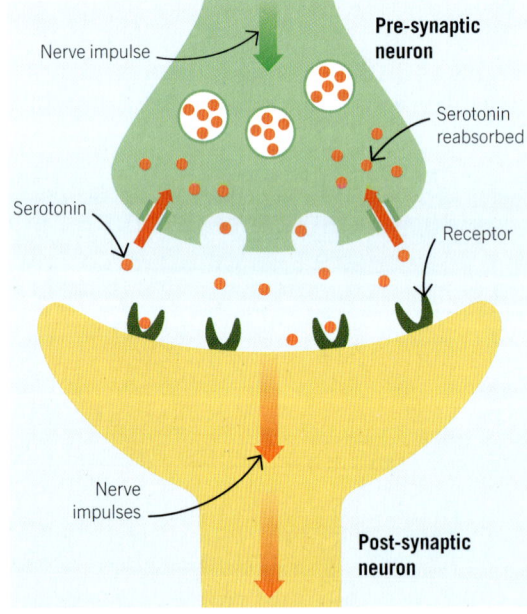

Before treatment
Serotonin molecules (orange) are quickly reabsorbed by the pre-synaptic neuron in a process called reuptake.

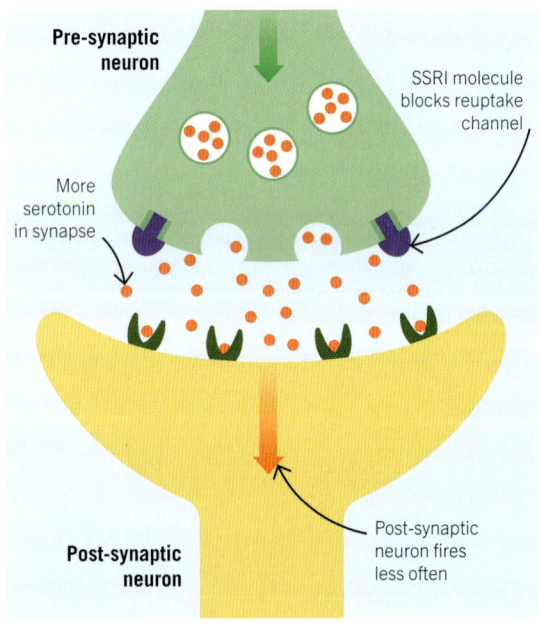

After treatment
SSRI molecules block reuptake channels, raising levels of serotonin in the synapse and so causing reduced excitation of the post-synaptic cell.

Brain stimulation therapy

Electrical or magnetic stimulation of the brain may be used to treat patients with conditions such as severe depression, OCD, or Parkinson's disease, who have not responded to medication. There are four main types of brain stimulation therapy, which work by applying electric currents or magnetic pulses to the brain. This treatment comes with benefits and risks, and may require long-term monitoring of the patient.

Key facts

✓ Severe or medication-resistant conditions can be treated by stimulating the brain with an electric current or magnetic pulses.

✓ Types of brain stimulation include electroconvulsive therapy (ECT), transcranial electrical stimulation (TES), repetitive transcranial magnetic stimulation (rTMS), and deep brain stimulation (DBS).

Electroconvulsive therapy (ECT)

An electric current is briefly passed through the brain of the anaesthetized patient, causing a controlled, short seizure. ECT is used to treat severe depression, but may result in short-term memory loss. Widely used in the 1950s, ECT was often carried out on conscious patients, but this is no longer the case.

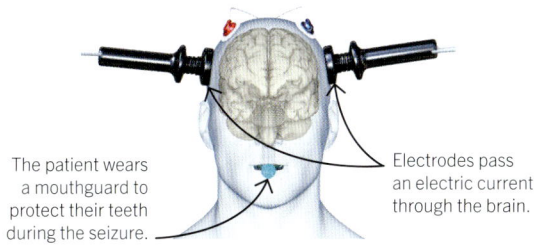

The patient wears a mouthguard to protect their teeth during the seizure.

Electrodes pass an electric current through the brain.

Transcranial electrical stimulation (TES)

A series of weak electric currents is applied to the cerebral cortex via electrodes on the scalp and forehead. TES is a potential new treatment for conditions such as depression and anxiety, but more research is required to establish how well it works.

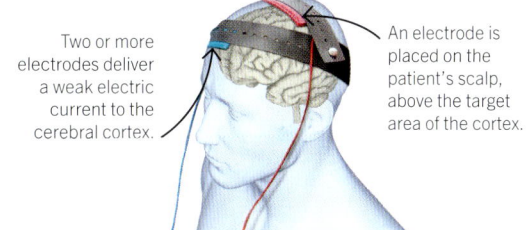

Two or more electrodes deliver a weak electric current to the cerebral cortex.

An electrode is placed on the patient's scalp, above the target area of the cortex.

Repetitive transcranial magnetic stimulation (rTMS)

Magnetic pulses are sent into the brain to disrupt activity in specific areas. Repeated disruptions cause long-term changes in brain functioning. rTMS can increase neuronal activity in areas underactive in patients with depression, and decrease activity in areas overactive in patients with OCD. It is generally considered safe but may cause headaches.

The wand produces a magnetic field, which activates neurons in the target area.

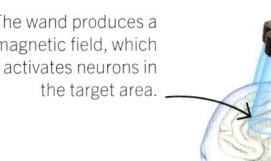
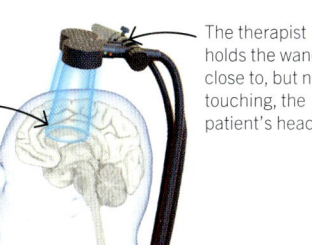

The therapist holds the wand close to, but not touching, the patient's head.

Deep brain stimulation (DBS)

Electrodes are surgically implanted deep into the brain, and connected to a pulse generator inside the chest, which controls when the electrodes produce electric currents. DBS can regulate abnormal brain activity in people with OCD and Parkinson's disease. Patients must be regularly monitored due to the risk of surgical complications.

Each electrode emits an electric current.

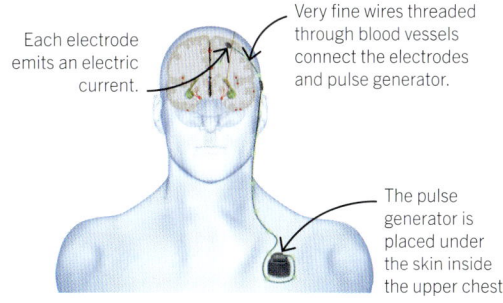

Very fine wires threaded through blood vessels connect the electrodes and pulse generator.

The pulse generator is placed under the skin inside the upper chest.

Psychosurgery

At the extreme end of the spectrum of biomedical treatments is psychosurgery – surgery on the brain. It can be used to treat severe cases of conditions such as OCD, schizophrenia, depression, and chronic pain disorder. Psychosurgery is irreversible. It involves burning away tissue in specific parts of the brain to remove connections that may be contributing to a condition. Due to ethical concerns and the availability of more effective options, psychosurgery is rarely used, and only when other treatments have not worked.

Key facts

✓ In psychosurgery, the brain is operated on to alleviate severe mental illnesses that have not responded to other treatments.

✓ No longer practised, lobotomy is an extreme form of psychosurgery that involves the removal or disconnection of certain brain regions.

Under the knife

At the University of California, USA, surgeons operated on a conscious patient to insert a brain pacemaker. This device helps to treat Parkinson's disease. The patient was a musician, and during surgery, he played his guitar to help the surgical team locate (by monitoring brain activity) where the device's electrodes needed to be placed inside his brain.

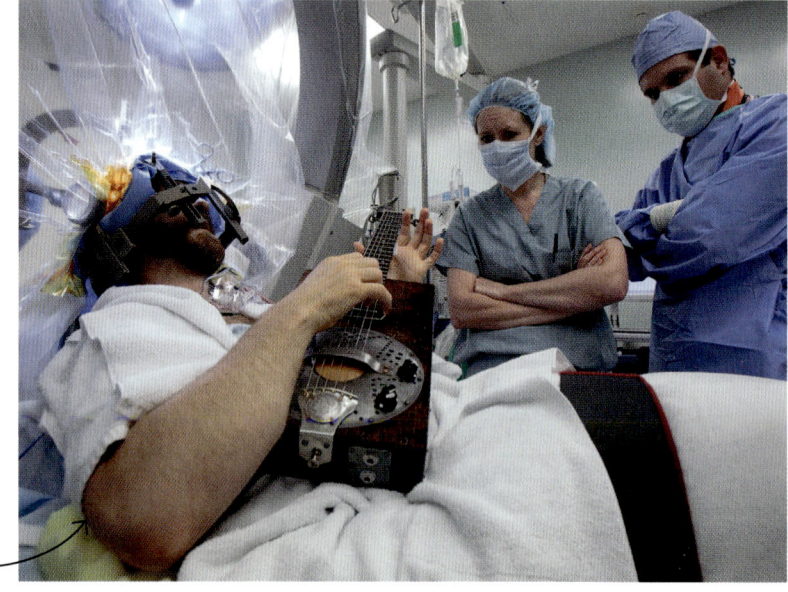

Prior to surgery, the patient had suffered hand tremors which affected his guitar playing. The surgery resolved the tremors so he was able to perform again.

🔍 Lobotomy

Lobotomy, also known as prefrontal leukotomy, is an extreme form of psychosurgery. It involves the removal or disconnection of certain brain regions (known as lobes, which give lobotomy its name) – particularly the prefrontal cortex. The procedure has significant side effects, including personality changes, cognitive impairment, and emotional blunting. It was developed as a treatment for severe schizophrenia, but was used extensively in the mid-20th century for a wide range of other conditions, many of which did not require such extreme intervention. Today, advances in medication and other therapies mean that lobotomy is no longer used.

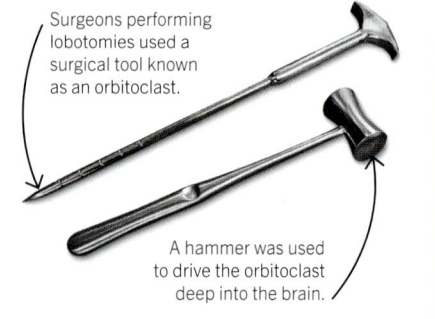

Surgeons performing lobotomies used a surgical tool known as an orbitoclast.

A hammer was used to drive the orbitoclast deep into the brain.

Chapter 15
Social psychology

Conformity

Also called majority influence, conformity is the tendency to change views or behaviours in response to the influence of a larger group. Whether the social pressure we feel from the majority group is real or imagined, it can lead to deep changes in attitudes and behaviour. A well-known study of conformity was conducted by US psychologist Solomon Asch in 1951.

Key facts

✓ Conformity is the tendency to change our views or behaviours to match those of a larger group.

✓ Asch's tests on conformity revealed that people were willing to give an obviously wrong answer to avoid standing out from the crowd.

✓ Asch changed different variables to see how these affected conformity rates, including unanimity (agreement), group size, and the difficulty of the task.

Asch's lines study

To test whether people conform to group pressure — even if it means giving a wrong answer in a simple task — Asch showed students four lines and asked them to judge which two were the same length. All but one of the small group of participants were confederates (actors) who deliberately gave the wrong answer.

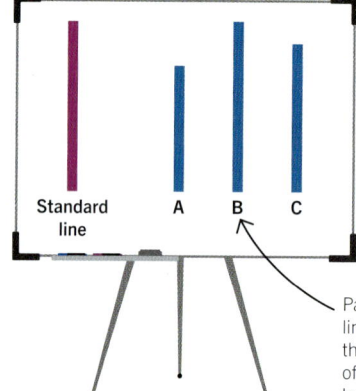

Participants were shown a series of lines, comprising a standard line and three comparison lines (A, B, C). One of the comparison lines was the same length as the standard line.

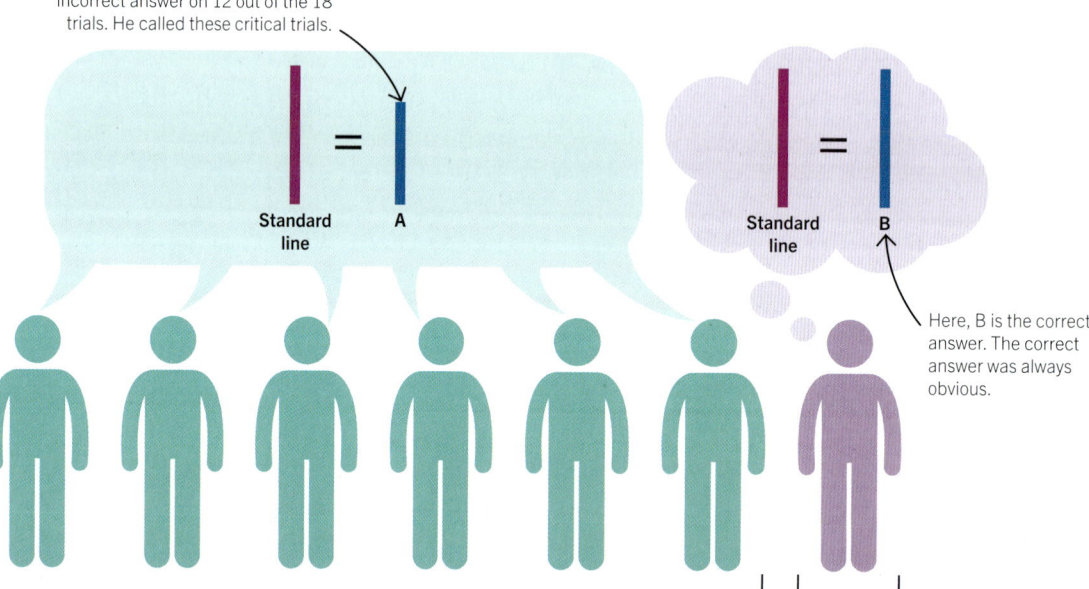

Asch instructed the confederates to unanimously give the same incorrect answer on 12 out of the 18 trials. He called these critical trials.

Here, B is the correct answer. The correct answer was always obvious.

Confederates
All but one of the participants were confederates working for Asch. All confederates gave the same incorrect answer.

True participant
Only one true participant was tested each time. The true participant was always the second to last to answer.

Variables affecting conformity

Asch found an average (mean) rate of conformity of 37 per cent in the trials with confederates, meaning that true participants agreed with the incorrect majority answer in just over one-third of the critical trials. Asch then conducted variations of this study to investigate how manipulating variables affected the conformity rate.

The true participant was more likely to give the correct answer if one of the confederates also gave it.

1. Unanimity

Asch instructed one of the confederates to dissent (disagree) and give a different answer from the other confederates. The presence of a dissenting ally for the true participant meant that the conformity rate dropped to 5.5 per cent. Asch concluded that when a group's unanimity is broken, the pressure to conform is greatly reduced.

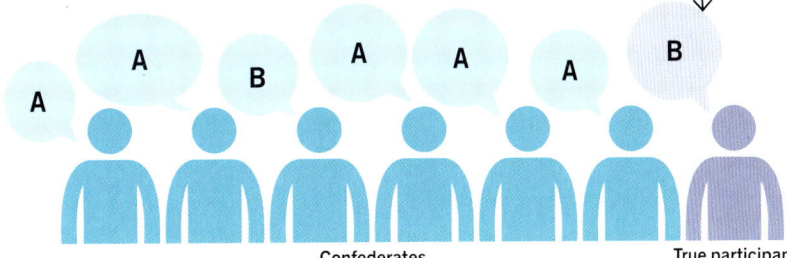

Confederates   True participant

2. Group size

Asch changed group sizes to see how this affected the pressure to conform. In a small group with one or two confederates, conformity rates were low. In groups containing three confederates, conformity rates increased to 32 per cent. However, in large groups with seven confederates or more, conformity began to decrease. Asch concluded that the size of the majority is important but only up to a point.

3. Task difficulty

Asch manipulated the difficulty of the task, to test whether a harder task makes people more likely to conform because they are less confident of their own judgment and so look to others for guidance. Asch tested this by making the lines study task more difficult. When he made the standard and comparison lines more similar, he found the conformity rate increased.

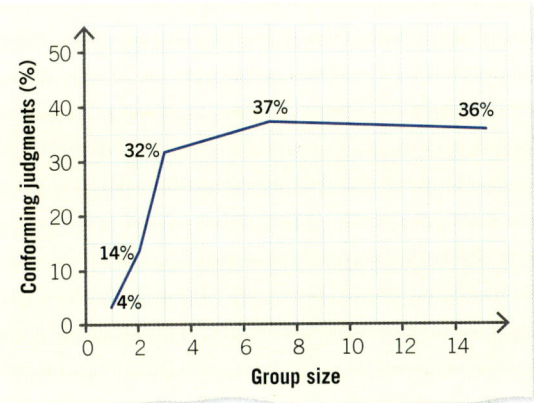

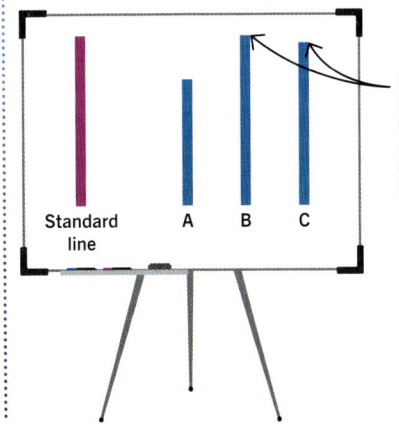

Conformity rates increased when the task was made harder by increasing the similarity of the comparison lines.

Strengths of the study	Weaknesses of the study
The study was highly controlled and easy to replicate, allowing other psychologists to confirm Asch's findings.	The task was unrealistic. Judging the length of lines with a group of strangers is meaningless and unimportant. Asch's findings about line lengths may not tell us much about conformity in real-life situations.
Asch could repeat the research, adjusting variables (such as unanimity, group size, or task difficulty) to understand their specific influence on conformity.	Asch's study was unethical as it involved deceiving participants, who were told that the study was testing their perception of line length and that the other participants were genuine.

Types of conformity

Also known as majority influence, conformity is the act of adapting our behaviour or beliefs due to pressure or influence from a larger, dominant group. Conformity is generally positive (for example, when it helps us get along better), but may be negative (for example, when it occurs because of fear of persecution). Psychologists have identifed three types of conformity.

Key facts

✓ Conformity is adapting behaviour or beliefs to fit in with a dominant group.

✓ There are three types of conformity: compliance, identification, and internalization.

✓ Compliance is the most superficial type of conformity, whereas internalization is the deepest.

Type	Description	Duration	Example
Compliance	Compliance is behaving in the way that's appropriate to fit in and be accepted. It is the person's public but not private acceptance of the dominant group's beliefs and behaviours.	Short term	Telling your friends you like a particular singer or band to gain their approval or avoid their disapproval, when you secretly prefer a completely different type of music.
Identification	Identification involves changing behaviour and opinions due to a desire to be part of the dominant group. The person publicly and privately accepts their beliefs and norms, but it's not permanent.	Medium term	Eating a vegetarian diet with your housemates because everyone else in the house is vegetarian; however, still eating meat when away from the house and housemates.
Internalization	Internalization means thoroughly accepting the dominant group's behaviours and opinions publicly, privately, and usually permanently.	Long term	Agreeing to attend a protest march with some friends and then signing up for the next march despite none of those friends being able to make it.

Most superficial type of conformity

Deepest type of conformity

Explanations for conformity

Psychologists have offered different explanations for why people conform, as reasons may vary depending on the situations people find themselves in. These explanations, which include informational social influence and normative social influence, also help explain the different types of conformity (see page 220).

Key facts

✓ There are different reasons why people conform.

✓ Informational social influence (ISI) describes how people look to others for help when they are feeling unsure.

✓ Normative social influence (NSI) describes how the desire to be liked and accepted leads to conformity.

Informational social influence

If you're asked an ambiguous question – with no obvious right or wrong answer – you'll probably look to others for help. This desire to be right by following the guidance of others is called informational social influence (ISI). It helps explain internalization, in which people change their opinions and behaviours to conform with those they feel have more knowledge.

In Jenness's 1932 study, people revised down estimates of how many jelly beans were in a jar after hearing the guesses of others – an example of ISI.

Normative social influence

The desire to be liked and accepted by a group is called normative social influence (NSI). This need helps explain compliance – in which people go along with the behaviour and attitudes of others without truly believing or accepting them. Some people care much more than others about being liked. Psychologists McGhee and Teevan (1967) called these people "nAffiliators", as they have a greater need for affiliation and relationships with others. They suggested that affiliators may be strongly influenced by NSI and found that students who were nAffiliators were more likely to conform than others.

I don't get the joke but I'll laugh anyway.

Conformity to social roles

Social roles are the behaviours expected of someone who holds a particular social position, such as a teacher, student, or police officer. Conformity to a social role occurs when a person changes the way they act to fit in with the expected behaviours associated with that role. A police officer, for example, might conform to the role of being confident and showing authority.

The Stanford prison experiment
In 1973, US psychologist Philip Zimbardo set up a mock prison to investigate whether the pressure to conform to social roles changes people. He selected 24 male students and randomly assigned them to be prison guards or prisoners. Within hours, the guards began to harass the prisoners, becoming increasingly aggressive. After a rebellion was dealt with harshly, the prisoners became increasingly passive. All participants appeared to lose their sense of personal identity, identifying instead with their new social role.

Key facts

✓ Zimbardo set up a mock prison to study conformity to social roles.

✓ 24 male student volunteers were randomly allocated to the role of either prison guard or prisoner.

✓ The prison guards became increasingly aggressive and the prisoners became increasingly passive, conforming to the social roles they had been given.

✓ The study was due to last for two weeks but was terminated after just six days due to the psychological harm it was causing.

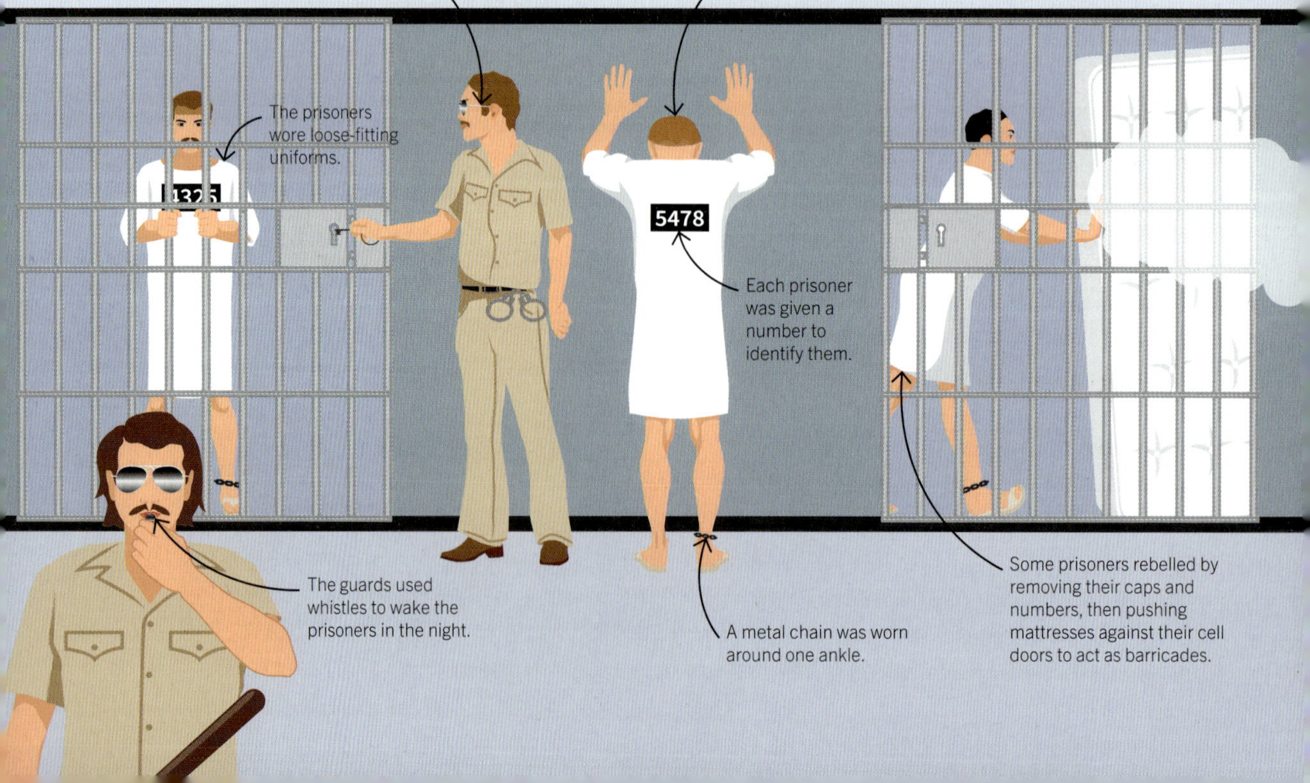

The guards wore reflective sunglasses to prevent them from making eye contact with the prisoners.

The prisoners wore caps made from nylon stockings to make it look as though their hair had been shaved off.

The prisoners wore loose-fitting uniforms.

Each prisoner was given a number to identify them.

The guards used whistles to wake the prisoners in the night.

A metal chain was worn around one ankle.

Some prisoners rebelled by removing their caps and numbers, then pushing mattresses against their cell doors to act as barricades.

Termination of the study

As the study went on, Zimbardo came under pressure from other psychologists and worried parents. Prisoners were behaving in concerning ways and some of the guards were behaving sadistically. Zimbardo was also criticized for poor behaviour in his role of superintendent. Originally planned to last two weeks, the study was terminated after just six days.

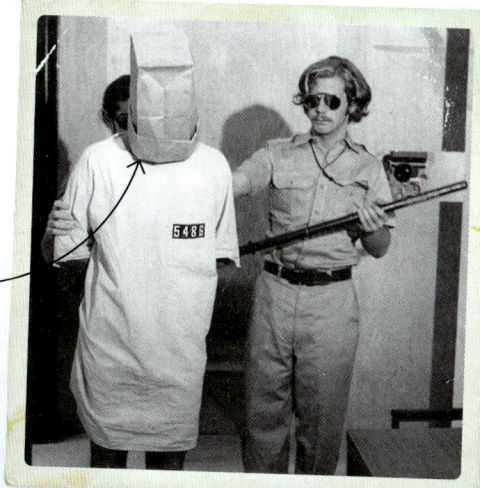

At times, prisoners were forced to wear paper bags over their heads.

🔍 Ethical concerns

The study has been called one of the most unethical psychology studies in history. The harm the "prisoners" experienced led to stricter ethical guidelines for psychologists. Zimbardo was criticized for bias and even fraud, with reports that the guards were coached to be aggressive. The study, however, prompted discussion about the way prisons and similar settings are run.

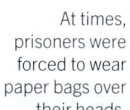

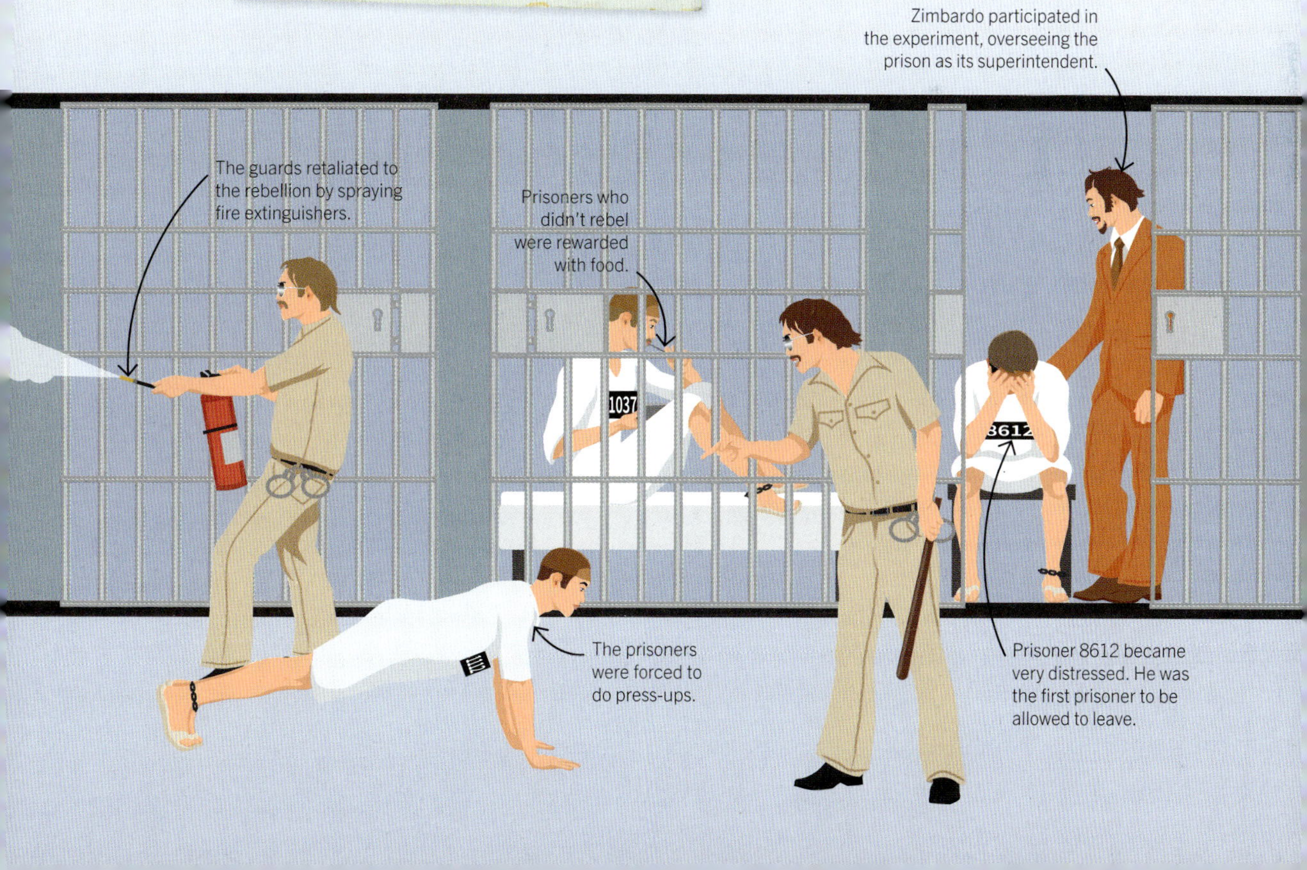

Zimbardo participated in the experiment, overseeing the prison as its superintendent.

The guards retaliated to the rebellion by spraying fire extinguishers.

Prisoners who didn't rebel were rewarded with food.

The prisoners were forced to do press-ups.

Prisoner 8612 became very distressed. He was the first prisoner to be allowed to leave.

Obedience to authority

In 1963, US psychologist Stanley Milgram tested whether people would obey a figure of authority, even if doing so would cause someone else harm (destructive obedience). Milgram investigated what happened when participants were ordered to give increasingly intense electric shocks to people they couldn't see. He found that more than 60 per cent of participants were willing to give the maximum electric shock allowed, despite hearing cries of pain.

Milgram's obedience study

Milgram assigned a true participant to act as a "teacher", and paired them with a "learner" who was a confederate (actor). The teacher was instructed by a researcher to punish the learner for incorrect responses in a word-pairing test, by administering electric shocks of increasing intensity. The teacher could hear the learner shout in pain, but could not see them. The electric shocks were not real, but the teacher did not know this until the experiment was over.

Experiment set-up
The experiment was carried out in two rooms at Yale University, Connecticut, USA. The teacher and researcher were in the same room. The learner (a confederate) sat in a separate room, connected to the fake electric shock machine.

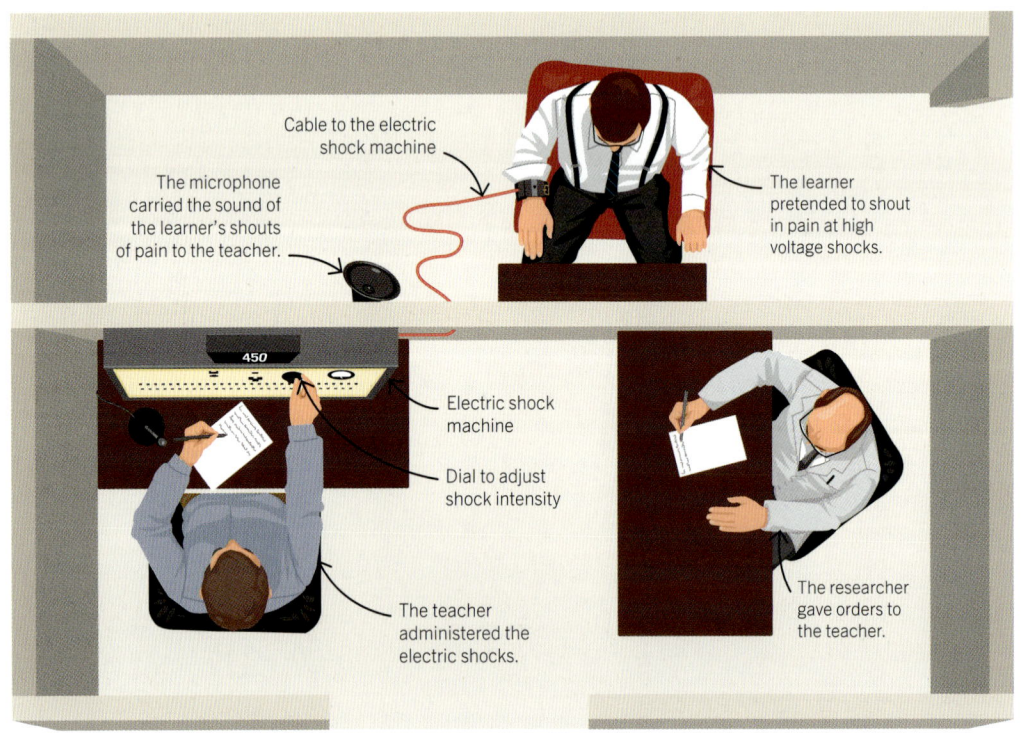

Cable to the electric shock machine

The microphone carried the sound of the learner's shouts of pain to the teacher.

The learner pretended to shout in pain at high voltage shocks.

450

Electric shock machine

Dial to adjust shock intensity

The teacher administered the electric shocks.

The researcher gave orders to the teacher.

Shock intensity
The shocks began at 15 volts and increased in 15-volt increments, up to the maximum shock of 450 volts. About 65 per cent of teachers applied the maximum shock. Many showed signs of extreme stress – they shook, sweated, and argued with the researcher, but still obeyed.

All of the teachers applied shocks up to 300 volts, when the learner started shouting in pain.

At 315 volts, the learner became silent.

Strengths of the study	Weaknesses of the study
Milgram reproduced similar results with 40 different participants. It was a reliable experiment.	The task's extreme nature may have meant that participants did not believe the shocks were real. They may have acted as they thought they were meant to.
The experiment was conducted in laboratory conditions. It was easy to replicate, and Milgram was able to test multiple variables to see their effects.	The task was unrealistic, so it may not tell us much about real instances of obedience, such as orders to harm others during a war.
Milgram could compare the behaviour of different participants using a numerical scale. The level of volts applied could be used as a measure of obedience.	Participants were deliberately deceived, causing them a great amount of anxiety.

🔍 Variables affecting obedience

Proximity: when the researcher gave orders over the telephone instead of in person, the obedience rate dropped from 65 per cent to 21 per cent.

Location: when the experiment took place in a run-down office instead of a prestigious university, the obedience rate dropped from 65 per cent to 48 per cent.

Uniform: when the researcher in a white lab coat was replaced by a person dressed in everyday clothes, the obedience rate dropped from 65 per cent to 20 per cent.

Explanations for obedience

Psychologists have offered a number of explanations for why people obey. Some of these explanations are situational (to do with the environment that people are in when they receive orders) and some are dispositional (to do with the state of mind of those receiving orders). It may be that multiple explanations are needed to understand why people obey a particular order.

Key facts

✓ The reasons why people obey are related to their environment and their mental state.

✓ Some people are more likely to obey individuals who are seen to have legitimate power.

✓ Some people will obey if they believe they are acting as an agent for someone else.

Agentic state
One explanation of obedience focuses on how our state of mind changes when we obey. We shift from an autonomous state, in which we have control over our thoughts and actions, to an agentic state, in which we have less free will and see ourselves as agents for an authority figure. The process frees us from responsibility and our conscience, allowing us to obey orders even when they are destructive.

Legitimacy of authority
This explanation for obedience suggests that we take orders from people we perceive to have legitimate (real) authority. If they wear a uniform, for example, they carry social power, and we're more likely to obey as we trust them to be worthy of the power invested in them. Alternatively, we may obey because they have the power to punish us. Either way, the perception is that their authority should not be questioned.

🔍 Authoritarian personality

The type of personality that's highly susceptible to obeying people in authority is called an authoritarian personality. People with this kind of personality are very conscious of their own and others' status. They are hostile to people of inferior status but show excessive respect and obedience to those of higher status. Rigid in their beliefs and opinions, they uphold traditions and conventions. It's argued that this personality type results from strict parenting.

The authoritarian personality type will obey someone they believe to be of high status.

Cognitive dissonance

Attitudes are feelings partly formed by our beliefs. When our attitudes and our actions don't match, the result is an inner tension called cognitive dissonance. Proposed in the 1950s, US psychologist Leon Festinger's cognitive dissonance theory explains how we resolve this inner tension.

Key facts

✓ Attitudes are feelings partly formed by our beliefs.

✓ When our attitudes don't match our actions, the resulting inner tension is called cognitive dissonance.

✓ Cognitive dissonance theory explains how we resolve this inner tension.

Cognitive dissonance theory

A person has an exam. They judge themselves to be a dedicated student (belief), but rather than study, they play video games (action). To solve the inner tension, the person can justify their existing belief, change their existing belief, or reduce the importance of the problem.

Change existing belief
"I'm obviously not that clever so studying won't help."

Justify existing belief
"I'm clever enough to pass without studying."

Reduce importance of problem
"It doesn't matter if I fail."

Dissonant state

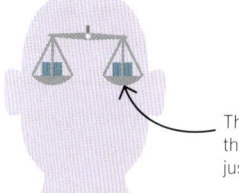

The person resolves the inner tension by justifying their action.

Conflict resolved

🔍 Festinger's chore

In 1959, Festinger gave volunteers boring tasks to do. However, they were asked to tell the next participants that the tasks were fun. Half were paid $1 and the other half $20. Would forcing them to experience cognitive dissonance by lying about the tasks they didn't enjoy change their attitude towards them?

$1 group
Festinger found that $1 was not enough to justify lying. To reduce the cognitive dissonance, many members of this group changed their existing belief, convincing themselves that the experiment was fun.

$20 group
Members of this group knew the tasks were dull, but also knew they had enough justification to say that the tasks were fun because they were paid $20. They freely admitted later that the tasks were boring.

Attribution theory

We explain the behaviour of other people in one of two ways: dispositional attribution is the act of explaining behaviour using their internal disposition (personal traits); situational attribution is the act of explaining behaviour using external factors (circumstances and constraints such as time or money). Only by considering both dispositional and situational factors is it possible to understand why people behave the way they do.

Key facts

✓ Humans tend to attribute other people's behaviour to internal dispositional factors (personal traits) or situational factors (circumstances and constraints).

✓ Fundamental attribution error is when a person overestimates dispositional factors, and underestimates situational factors, when explaining another person's behaviour.

Fundamental attribution error

Have you ever judged a classmate as irresponsible or impolite for being late, despite the fact they were stuck in terrible traffic? The fundamental attribution error is the tendency to overestimate the role of dispositional factors (such as being irresponsible) when explaining another person's behaviour (such as being late), while underestimating situational factors (such as a traffic jam). We typically judge others more harshly than we judge ourselves.

🔍 Causes of fundamental attribution error

- **Cognitive bias**: sometimes our brains take shortcuts, or commit "cognitive biases", to process information quickly, as it requires less mental effort.

- **Cultural differences**: these can lead to misunderstandings and unfair judgements of others.

- **Actor-observer bias**: people tend to attribute the actions of others to dispositional factors but attribute their own actions to situational factors.

- **Perceptual salience**: people assign importance to things that capture their attention. They tend to be highly aware of the actions of

others and see them as important, while missing the bigger picture.

- **Outgroup homogeneity bias**: people assume members of their own group (the ingroup) are diverse, while outgroup members (those from a different group) lack diversity.

Resistance to social influence

Most of the research on social influence has focused on what makes people change their views and behaviour in response to perceived social pressure. However, US psychologists Julian B. Rotter and Solomon Asch have sought to explain the factors involved in withstanding this pressure to change.

Key facts

✓ Resistance to social influence is the ability to withstand pressure to conform to other people's views and behaviours.

✓ The locus of control is the amount of control a person believes they have over their own life and behaviour.

✓ Social support is the amount of solidarity that someone feels they have with others.

Locus of control

Rotter developed the concept of the "locus of control", which is the degree of control a person thinks they have over their life and behaviour. It's usually measured using questionnaires in which participants are scored from high internal to high external, with levels in between.

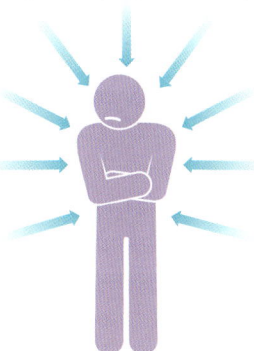

Internal locus of control
People with a high internal locus of control believe they are in control of their life and own actions. This sense of personal responsibility makes them more likely to resist social influence.

External locus of control
People with a high external locus of control believe outside influences like other people or luck determine the course of their life. Lacking a sense of personal responsibility may make them less likely to resist social influence.

Social support

Resistance to social influence may be affected by social support – perceived solidarity with others. People are more likely to resist if others do, too. Pressure to conform or obey is strongest when a group is unanimous (every group member agrees to act in the same way) and everyone obeys a figure of authority. Asch's research into conformity (see pages 218–219) demonstrated the importance of social support.

Well, if everyone else agrees...

We don't agree with this decision.

Group 1

Group 2

Minority influence

Minority influence is the ability of a smaller group (the minority) to change the beliefs and actions of a larger group (the majority). It differs from conformity, in which the majority does the influencing. Minority influence is more likely to lead to internalization – when both public behaviour and private beliefs change.

Key facts

✓ Minority groups can influence and change the actions of the majority.

✓ Consistency in the minority view is effective in influencing the majority.

✓ Flexibility and commitment are also factors that make the minority view more influential on the majority.

Factors affecting minority influence

Whether a minority group is successful in persuading the majority of their viewpoint depends on them being consistent, showing willingness to compromise, and displaying self-sacrifice to make their point heard.

Consistency

In 1969, French psychologist Serge Moscovici devised a test to see whether a minority could influence a majority to give an incorrect answer. He divided participants into groups of six (which included two confederates and four true participants). Each participant had to state the colour of 36 slides, which were all clearly shades of blue. The confederates (the minority) tried to influence the true participants (the majority) to give the incorrect answer green. The minority was sometimes able to influence the majority, although not always, and they were more influential if they were consistent.

	Confederate response	True participant response
Consistent condition	The two confederates said 36 of 36 slides were green (incorrect).	They said green in 8.42% of trials. The true participants were more likely to agree with the incorrect answer when the confederates gave consistent answers.
Inconsistent condition	The two confederates said 24 slides were blue (correct) and 12 slides were green (incorrect).	They said green in 1.25% of trials. The true participants were less likely to agree with the incorrect answer when the confederates gave inconsistent answers.

Flexibility

US psychologists Charlan Nemeth and A.G. Brilmayer (1987) proposed that flexibility may be more important than consistency in minority influence. They asked a group, which included one confederate, to discuss the amount of compensation paid to someone in a ski-lift accident. When the confederate argued for a very low amount, they failed to influence the group if they refused to compromise. However, when the confederate showed flexibility, they successfully altered the group's view.

Commitment

When a minority group shows great commitment to its cause, it is more likely to be influential. In 1955, Rosa Parks refused to give up her seat on a bus to a white passenger. At the time, US society was deeply racially divided, and this courageous act resulted in her arrest. By demonstrating her commitment to her beliefs through personal sacrifice, Parks successfully influenced large numbers of people to support the US civil rights movement.

Prejudice and discrimination

Humans often form judgments about individuals or groups based on unfair assumptions – this is called prejudice. Prejudice can be directed against people because of their gender, sexuality, age, race, nationality, social class, or physical abilities. Acting on prejudice, by treating people differently due to characteristics they have or are perceived as having, is discrimination. Psychologists study prejudice to understand why social issues such as discrimination and conflict exist.

Key facts

✓ Prejudice occurs when fixed, preconceived judgments are made about individuals or groups, based on characteristics such as gender, sexuality, age, race, nationality, social class, or physical abilities.

✓ Stereotyping categorizes people according to oversimplified ideas.

✓ Discrimination is the act of treating people unfairly due to their characteristics.

Stereotyping

This is a way of categorizing individuals or groups using fixed and oversimplified ideas. Categorizing people in this way allows the brain to simplify incoming information, but it can lead to prejudice and discrimination.

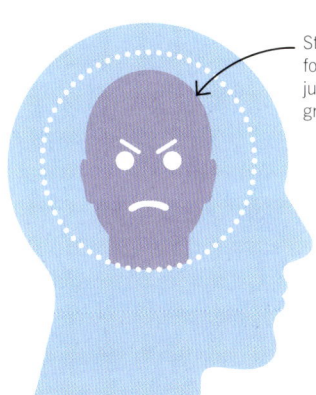
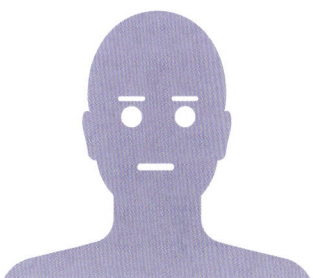

Stereotypes can cause people to form hostile opinions of others just because they belong to a group that is perceived negatively.

Discrimination

This is the biased treatment of individuals or groups based on their perceived differences. It may include exclusion, unfair treatment, or denial of resources and opportunities. Studying discrimination reveals the damaging effects it has on individuals and societies, and helps psychologists to find ways to reduce harm by building more inclusive communities.

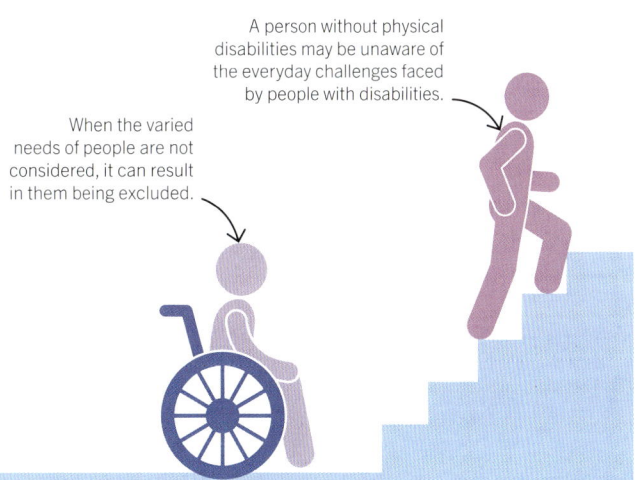

A person without physical disabilities may be unaware of the everyday challenges faced by people with disabilities.

When the varied needs of people are not considered, it can result in them being excluded.

Roots of prejudice

Prejudice is often linked to race, with people often favouring those from their own race over people from other races. People can form prejudices if they have little or no exposure to individuals or communities from outside their own limited social circle. Lack of contact with people from other backgrounds can lead to stereotypes and negative attitudes, which may result in discrimination — treating people from those groups unfairly.

Key facts

✓ People belong to groups with like-minded people — the in-group; everyone else is in an out-group.

✓ Belonging to an in-group can lead to prejudice such as bias and victim-blaming of people in the out-group.

✓ People tend to be better at recognizing faces from their own race.

In-group and out-group

Polish psychologist Henry Tajfel and British psychologist John Turner's social identity theory, formulated in the 1970s, explains prejudice using the idea of in-groups and out-groups. The in-group is the social group to which a person belongs. Like-minded, they tend to share an identity. The out-group is everyone else — they are seen as different or "other". In-group members view their group positively, while out-group members are perceived negatively. The out-group is viewed and treated poorly to boost the in-group's sense of self-identity and enhance their social status.

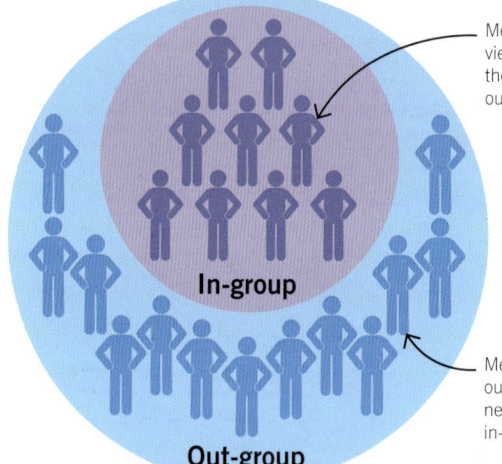

Members of the in-group view themselves favourably; they feel superior to out-group members.

In-group

Members of the out-group are viewed negatively by the in-group.

Out-group

Out-group homogeneity bias

People often think of members of an out-group as homogeneous (very similar), with less diversity than the members of their own in-group. This bias may be due to limited exposure to out-group members and a reliance on stereotypes, as well as not paying attention to individual differences in the out-group.

Members of the out-group are perceived as lacking individuality.

In-group

Out-group

Scapegoating

Sometimes individuals or groups are unfairly blamed for the problems or tensions within a larger group. Known as scapegoating, this happens when people avoid taking responsibility for issues and instead blame a vulnerable out-group, often selected based on stereotypes or prejudices. Scapegoating usually arises from anxiety or frustration in times of uncertainty or social unrest.

Victim-blaming theory

Prejudiced attitudes can lead to people assuming that victims of misfortune are responsible for their own adversity. This bias creates a sense of control. It helps people to maintain the illusion that bad things won't happen to them. Victim-blaming theory is based on the just-world hypothesis, which is the false assumption that the world is a fair place in which people get what they deserve.

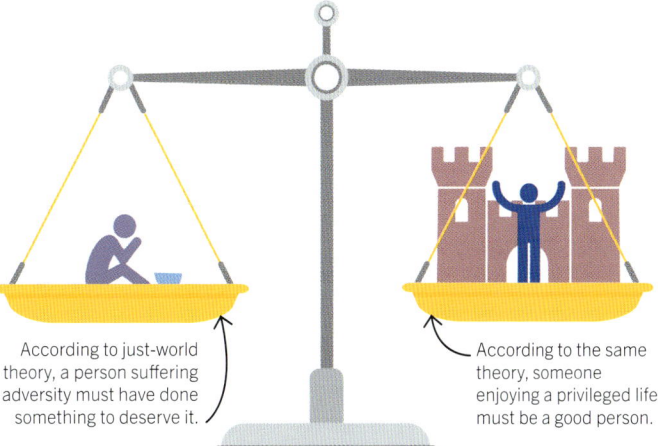

According to just-world theory, a person suffering adversity must have done something to deserve it.

According to the same theory, someone enjoying a privileged life must be a good person.

Vivid cases

Emotionally charged incidents reported in the media can leave strong impressions. These vivid cases tend to be more influential than factual information in shaping people's attitudes. Extreme events showing negative behaviour by someone from an out-group can lead to generalizations about that whole group.

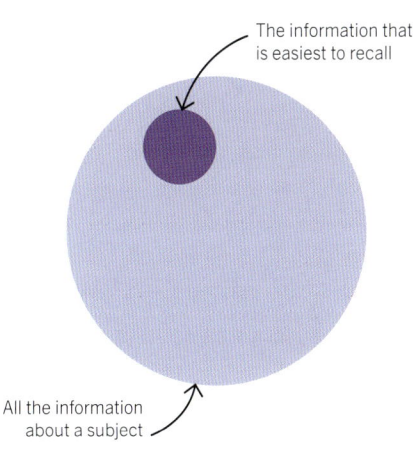

The information that is easiest to recall

All the information about a subject

The other-race effect

Research has shown that humans are better at recognizing faces from their own race than from other races. This could mean that they may favour people from their own race, preferring to trust and form friendships with people who look "familiar".

Group influence

People in groups tend to make decisions differently from how they would alone. Group influence can drive members to more extreme viewpoints (known as group polarization), or to prioritize harmonious relations at the expense of evaluating all the options properly (known as groupthink). Knowing how groups make decisions is important – group polarization and groupthink have resulted in governments and businesses making catastrophic decisions in the past.

> 📌 **Key facts**
>
> ✓ Group polarization occurs when, following discussion, the opinions of a group become more extreme than the individual members' initial points of view.
>
> ✓ Groupthink is a phenomenon in which maintaining group cohesion is valued over critical thinking, leading to poor decision-making.

Group polarization

When like-minded people come together, their discussions tend to strengthen rather than cause them to question their existing beliefs, resulting in a more extreme viewpoint. This tendency is known as group polarization. It can lead a group to make decisions that are more extreme than individual group members might otherwise have made.

Before group discussion

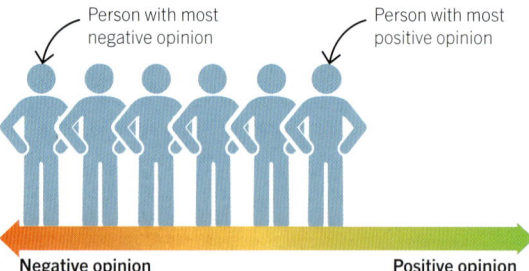

Person with most negative opinion

Person with most positive opinion

Negative opinion   Positive opinion

After group discussion

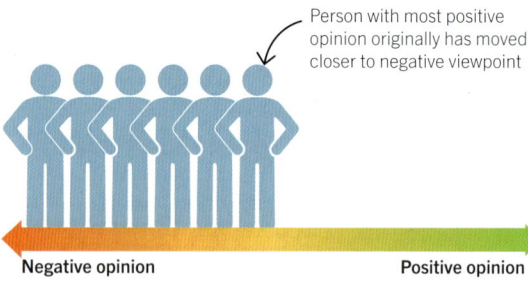

Person with most positive opinion originally has moved closer to negative viewpoint

Negative opinion   Positive opinion

Groupthink

People in groups typically desire cohesion and harmony, which can lead them to set aside their private opinions and agree with the majority. It can cause groups to make poor or irrational decisions because dissenting views are not voiced or heard. US psychologist Irving Janis called this phenomenon "groupthink". Groupthink often emerges in high-stress situations where there is pressure to conform, or commanding leadership, or when the group is isolated from other viewpoints.

It's a bad idea but I trust them – maybe it will be all right.

I disagree but everyone else has their hand up – I must be wrong.

They seem sure it will work. I don't know but I suppose we could try.

Terrible idea but I don't want to be awkward.

Although some group members disagree privately, all raise their hand in agreement.

Group dynamics

Social psychologists are interested in how people behave when they are in groups. Being among other people often leads individuals to behave differently from how they would when alone – this phenomenon is known as group dynamics.

Social loafing and social facilitation

When given a group task, people tend to put less effort in than they would if they were working alone – this is known as social loafing. However, if group members feel that they are being observed they will increase the effort they make – this is called social facilitation. Social facilitation can lead to two effects: if someone is good at something, they typically perform better when observed, but if they are poor at the task, they typically perform worse when observed.

Key facts

✓ People can behave in uncharacteristic ways when they are part of a crowd.

✓ Social loafing is the tendency to make less effort when in a group than when alone.

✓ Social facilitation is the tendency to make more effort when we think we are being observed.

✓ The diffusion of responsibility means that a person in a crowd feels less individual accountability.

The bigger the group, the less effort people put in.

Social loafing
When in a group, people put less effort in than they would if they were working alone.

The red coach is monitoring the red team, making them all work harder.

Social facilitation
People put in more effort when they are being watched and assessed.

🔍 Deindividuation

Being part of a large crowd can give people a sense of anonymity (referred to as deindividuation). This makes them more likely to behave in uncharacteristic ways. For example, violence at sporting events often involves people who do not usually behave aggressively. Individuals in a crowd are unlikely to be identified, meaning that personal accountability for poor behaviour is transferred to the crowd in a "diffusion of responsibility".

The bystander effect

Whether a person offers help to someone in need is determined by the number of other people who also witness the situation. A person alone spotting someone needing assistance is likely to help, yet if there are other people present, they are less likely to respond. This failure to act is known as the "bystander effect". It occurs because everyone present assumes somebody else will help.

Subway study

US psychologists Jane Piliavin, Judith Rodin, and Irving Piliavin (1969) set up an experiment on a New York subway train, in which a confederate played the role of a victim needing help. Appearing to be either blind or drunk, the confederate collapsed. Observers watched the reactions of genuine train passengers. In this context, they found that the blind victim received help faster and more often than the drunk one. Men helped more often than women.

Help is less likely to be offered if there is a perceived risk of harm to the bystander.

Help is more likely to be offered if the person in need is similar to the bystander.

A person is more likely to help if they are the only one present. When others are around, responsibility is diffused.

I don't know first aid. I could make it worse.

Last time I offered help, I was rejected.

There are other people around who know what to do.

Could I get injured if I get involved?

He's about my age, maybe I should help too...

People are more likely to assist if they feel confident in their ability to help.

Altruism

Some social psychologists study what motivates people to help others. When we show unselfish concern for and kind behaviour towards other people, it is called altruism. There are different theories that attempt to explain prosocial (voluntary, kind) behaviour.

 Key facts

✓ Altruism is the unselfish concern for others.

✓ Social exchange theory states that people will help when it is in their own interest.

✓ Helping may be part of a reciprocity norm: you help others because you have been helped.

✓ A social responsibility norm suggests that we should help people who can't help themselves.

Social exchange theory

This theory states that people are motivated to be altruistic when it's in their own interest. If someone feels that the personal benefits outweigh the costs, they will help. If the costs of helping are higher than the personal benefits, they won't help.

Reciprocity norm

Altruism may be due to the reciprocity norm. This is the idea that helping is cyclical — you help others because you've been helped yourself. It's the same as "returning the favour" or "paying it forward".

Social responsibility norm

The expectation that people should help those who cannot help themselves is called the social responsibility norm. For example, if you see a child who has fallen over and injured their leg, you are likely to feel obliged to help them even though they won't be able to return the favour, because they are young and potentially vulnerable.

🔍 **Deviating from the norm**

Social norms provide a framework for expected behaviour in society. When someone deviates from the norm, by being excessively helpful, for example, people may feel uncomfortable. Similarly, when expected help is withheld, others may be disappointed or confused.

Some people may avoid helping someone in trouble.

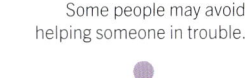

Aggression: biological causes

Aggression is behaviour intended to harm or intimidate others. Aggression is widespread in the animal world and has multiple causes. Some of the factors that influence aggression most directly, both in humans and animals, are biological. These include neural processes in the brain and the effects of genes and hormones.

> ## Key facts
>
> ✓ Biological factors that can explain aggression include the functioning of the limbic system, genetics, and hormones.
>
> ✓ A defective MAOA gene may lead to more aggressive behaviour.
>
> ✓ High levels of testosterone are correlated with greater aggression.

Neural causes of aggression

The limbic system in the base of the brain plays a primary role in aggression. It triggers the fight-or-flight response, which primes the body for action when we are angry or afraid. Animal studies show that removing the amygdala in the limbic system prevents fearful or aggressive behaviour. The frontal lobes are also involved in aggression. Damage to these areas can increase impulsive or aggressive behaviour.

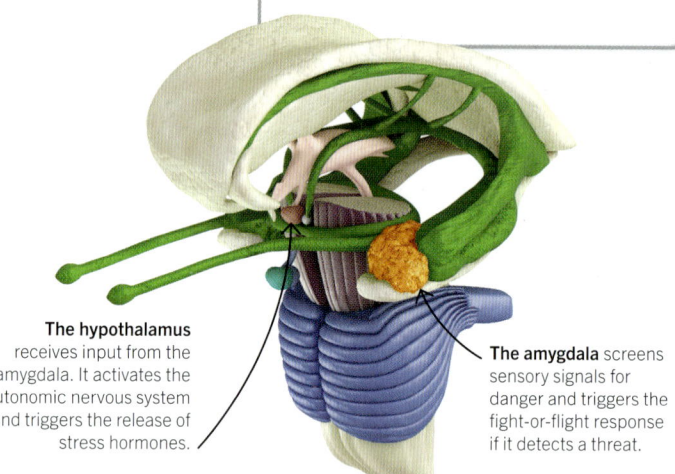

The hypothalamus receives input from the amygdala. It activates the autonomic nervous system and triggers the release of stress hormones.

The amygdala screens sensory signals for danger and triggers the fight-or-flight response if it detects a threat.

Genetic causes of aggression

Some genes influence how aggressive a person is. The MAOA (monoamine oxidase A) gene helps regulate levels of the neurotransmitters serotonin and dopamine. People with a defective copy of the gene are likely to have an overactive amygdala and reduced activity of the frontal lobe. If children with the defective gene experience trauma, they are more likely to become aggressive adults.

Hormonal causes of aggression

Animal studies show that raised levels of the male sex hormone testosterone are associated with increased aggression between males. In humans, testosterone levels correlate with aggression, dominance, and criminality, but the causal relationship is unclear as testosterone levels rise as a result of competitive behaviour. Testosterone may may explain why there are more men than women in prison.

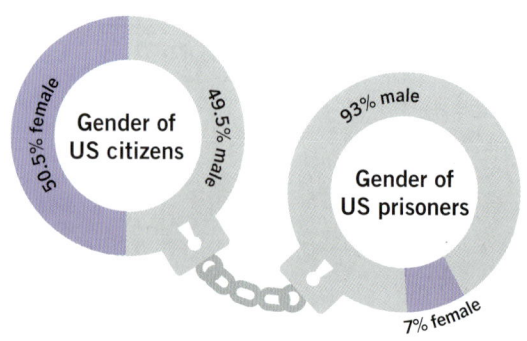

Abuser

As an adult, they are more likely to abuse others.

Child with defective MAOA gene

50.5% female
49.5% male
Gender of US citizens

93% male
7% female
Gender of US prisoners

Aggression: social and psychological causes

According to social and psychological theories of aggression, aggressive behaviour often has a social or psychological explanation.

Key facts

✓ Aggression can have social and psychological causes.

✓ Social and psychological theories of aggression include frustration–aggression, de-individuation, and social learning.

✓ Some psychologists believe that violent films and computer games might cause increased aggression.

> Not a red light! Now I'm going to be late on top of everything else that's gone wrong today!

> I'm going to push in – these people don't know me, so I'll get away with it!

> I've been waiting for ages and this car is pushing in. I should do the same!

Frustration–aggression theory
According to this theory, aggression is triggered when a goal is thwarted. The closer the goal, or the greater the effort invested, the greater the frustration and resulting aggression.

De-individuation theory
This theory says that people are more likely to act aggressively when they feel anonymous or when they are part of a larger group, with a diminished sense of individual identity.

Social learning theory
This theory proposes that people become more aggressive by imitating the aggressive behaviour of others. Observing a positive outcome reinforces the behaviour.

🔍 Media violence

Whether viewing violent films or playing violent computer games leads to violence is unclear. Some psychologists argue that watching media violence is harmless or "cathartic". Others claim that exposure to fictional violence increases a person's tendency to be aggressive or violent in the real world.

Potential impact	Explanation
Desensitization	Repeated exposure to violence leads to a reduced emotional response, increasing the risk of aggression.
Disinhibition	A change in the perception of what constitutes appropriate behaviour leads to a diminished sense of responsibility and greater aggression.
Cognitive priming	Exposure to media violence leads to thoughts or ideas about violence, increasing readiness to respond aggressively.

Aggression and ethology

Ethologists (scientists who study animal behaviour) view aggression in animals as an adaptive trait that can be explained by evolution. In other words, if aggressive behaviour helps animals survive conflict or improves their chance of reproducing, any genes underlying such behaviour are likely to pass from parent to offspring and spread through the population.

Key facts

✓ According to evolutionary theories of aggression, aggressive behaviour in animals can be adaptive.

✓ A fixed action pattern is a stereotypical sequence of actions performed by an animal in response to a specific stimulus.

✓ The territorial aggression of male sticklebacks is an example of a fixed action pattern.

Fixed action patterns

Aggression in some animals sometimes takes the form of a fixed action pattern – a stereotypical sequence of actions performed in response to a specific stimulus. Fixed action patterns are thought to be largely innate and therefore hard-wired into an animal's genes. A famous example is the territorial aggression seen in male sticklebacks in the mating season.

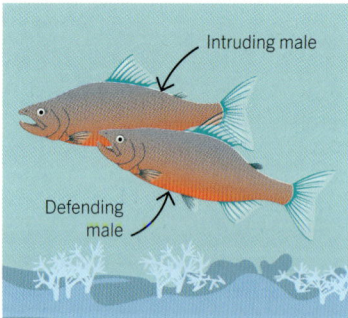

Intruding male

Defending male

When ready to mate, male sticklebacks develop red bellies and become territorial. The sight of an intruding male triggers a fixed action pattern: the defending male's spines rise, and he charges and bites the intruder.

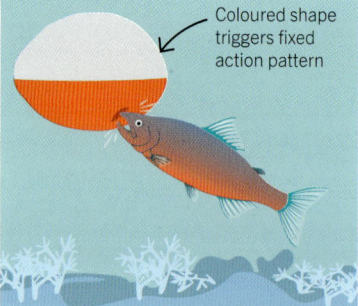

Coloured shape triggers fixed action pattern

Dutch ethologist Niko Tinbergen presented various coloured shapes to male sticklebacks and discovered that the fixed action pattern is triggered by a specific stimulus: red coloration on the underside of the shape.

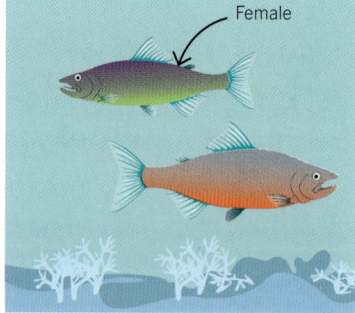

Female

Males who successfully defend their territory are more likely to mate and therefore pass on the genes responsible for the fixed action pattern. The aggressive behaviour is favoured by natural selection.

🔍 Sexual competition

Aggression between rival males is widespread in the animal world. For example, stags fight for dominance, and the victor wins access to females and fathers the most offspring. Human behaviour has been shaped by the same evolutionary forces as animal behaviour. Some psychologists argue that sexual jealousy in humans might be an adaptive trait with an evolutionary origin.

Origins of conflict

Conflicts arise when two parties have incompatible goals. In some situations, the pursuit of self-interest by conflicting parties leads to a worse outcome for everyone than cooperation. This is known as a social trap.

Prisoner's dilemma
The prisoner's dilemma is a theoretical example of a social trap in which acting rationally leads to the worst overall outcome. Two partners in crime are interrogated separately and can choose to stay silent or betray their partner. From a self-interested point of view, it always pays to betray the other partner, but paradoxically the best outcome is if neither partner betrays.

Key facts

✓ Conflicts happen when two parties have incompatible goals.

✓ A social trap is a conflict in which acting out of self-interest leads to a worse outcome than cooperating.

✓ The prisoner's dilemma is a theoretical scenario in which acting rationally leads to the worst outcome.

✓ Mirror-image perceptions are mutually hostile views held by two parties.

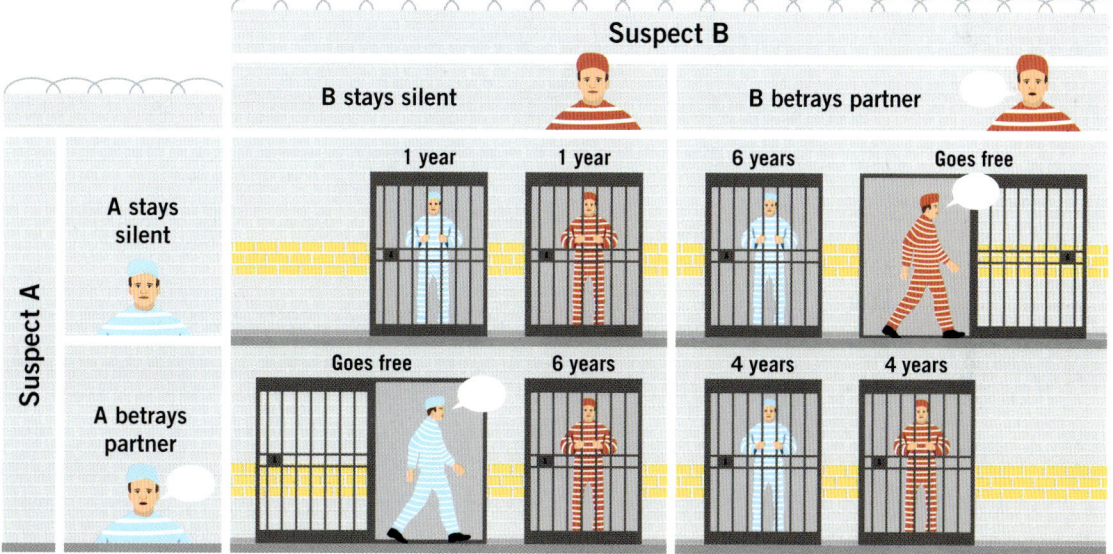

Mirror-image perceptions

A mirror-image perception forms when two individuals or groups see each other in a way that reflects their own negative views. This dynamic creates a cycle of hostility, with each side perceiving the other as untrustworthy and intent on harm. The conflict then intensifies, making it harder to find common ground or achieve a resolution. To break the cycle, communication and empathy between the conflicting parties are essential.

The other person is seen as hostile.

The other person is seen as hostile.

The social clock

The social clock is a timeline of milestones (major life events) that society expects people to achieve or pass through at an appropriate age. Depending on the culture in which a person lives, important milestones could include finishing school, getting married, starting a career, having children, or retiring. These norms (social expectations) are sometimes viewed as unspoken pressures that society puts on people. Keeping up with the social clock, or not, can affect self-esteem and overall mental health.

Key facts

✓ The social clock outlines society's preferred timings for major life events.

✓ Milestones are culturally dependent.

✓ They may include finishing school, getting married, starting a career, having children, or retiring.

✓ Social expectations are also known as norms.

✓ Norms can put pressure on people if they diverge from them.

Keeping up with the social clock can boost a person's self-esteem.

People who do not follow the social clock, whether by choice or not, may feel judged by society.

Attraction

Interpersonal attraction is the positive feelings and behaviours that draw people towards one another. It plays a key role in forming social relationships, including friendships, romantic partnerships, and even professional connections. Attraction is a complex concept, influenced by a combination of factors, including individual preferences and cultural norms.

Filter theory

US psychologists Alan Kerckhoff and Keith Davis (1962) proposed filter theory to explain how people find and select relationship partners. It states that the number of possible partners (field of availables) is narrowed down by factors (filters) in three consecutive stages to those most realistically suitable (field of desirables).

Field of availables

Social demography
Available partners are generally limited to those a person is likely to meet in day-to-day life.

Similarity of attitudes
Sharing common views and interests increases the likelihood of attraction.

Complementarity
Meeting one another's needs increases the chance of long-term compatibility.

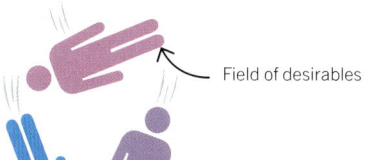

Field of desirables

Key facts

✓ Attraction involves feelings and behaviours that draw people to one another.

✓ Filter theory states that there are factors that limit the number of available romantic partners.

🔍 How attraction develops

Attraction may arise in many different ways. Psychologists have suggested the following:

- **Physical attraction** is an instinctive reaction to another person based on their appearance. People may assume that individuals they find physically attractive also possess other desirable qualities, such as kindness (the halo effect).

- **Mere-exposure effect** suggests that people develop a preference for individuals they encounter repeatedly, even if the exposure is minimal. People may be drawn to others simply because they are familiar.

- **Proximity** (nearness) often fosters familiarity, which may develop into attraction. People who live or work near each other are likely to have frequent encounters, leading to opportunities for interaction.

- **Sharing similar values**, interests, attitudes, and backgrounds can encourage attraction between people, as they perceive each other as compatible.

- **Complementarity** is the idea that people are attracted to those who have qualities that complement or enhance their own, such as the need to be caring and the need to be cared for.

- **The matching hypothesis** suggests that people look for romantic partners with what they believe to be equal attractiveness. This balance reduces the fear that their partner will leave them for someone more attractive.

Romantic relationships

Love is the intense emotional attraction and affection between two people. It is often characterized by an overwhelming desire to be with the other person. Passion is a central aspect of early-stage romantic relationships. For such relationships to endure, other factors such as intimacy and commitment are important.

Key facts

✓ Sternberg's triangular theory of love states that love has three components: passion, intimacy, and commitment.

✓ Rusbult's investment model of commitment looks at the factors that result in a stable relationship.

✓ Relationships endure due to factors such as equity and self-disclosure.

Triangular theory of love
US psychologist Robert Sternberg's triangular theory of love (1986) proposes that love is made up of three components: passion, intimacy, and commitment. Different combinations of these components produce eight types of love, including non-love (the absence of all three components). Compassionate love, which includes a balance of passion, intimacy, and commitment, is considered to be the ideal type of love.

Intimacy

Companionate love is a deep and affectionate attachment between two people, characterized by intimacy and commitment. This type of love is more stable and enduring than romantic love. It develops as a relationship matures.

Romantic love
Passion + Intimacy

Companionate love
Intimacy + Commitment

Romantic love is associated with strong physical and emotional attraction and a heightened focus on a partner. It occurs at the start of a relationship.

Compassionate love
Passion + Intimacy + Commitment

Passion

Commitment

Fatuous love
Passion + Commitment

Fatuous love is a passionate but emotionally shallow relationship that lacks depth or genuine intimacy. It involves immediate infatuation, followed by rapid commitment without a strong emotional connection.

Investment model of commitment

Proposed by US psychologist Caryl Rusbult in 2011, the investment model of commitment explains why people stay together in relationships. It suggests commitment is influenced by three factors: satisfaction level, investment size, and comparison with alternatives (whether there are any better potential partners). A strong commitment in turn increases the likelihood of a stable, long-term relationship.

Satisfaction level
Does your partner meet your needs?

Investment size
How much have you invested in the relationship? Would ending it be costly?

Comparison with alternatives
Is there anyone else available who meets your needs better?

Commitment
High satisfaction and investment size – and no alternative partners – leads to commitment.

Relationship stability
With a strong commitment, a relationship can endure ups and downs and remain stable.

🔍 Social exchange theory

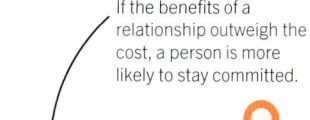

Social exchange theory views all relationships as an exchange of benefits and costs. According to the theory, one person's willingness to commit to another is based on whether the benefits of the relationship (for example, the company and support of a partner) outweigh the costs (for example, the effort required to make the relationship work).

If the benefits of a relationship outweigh the cost, a person is more likely to stay committed.

🔍 Enduring relationships

Multiple factors are thought to influence happy, long-lasting relationships; for example:

Equity
If both partners perceive their inputs (efforts) and outputs (benefits) as balanced, they see the relationship as equal, leading to satisfaction. The perception of unbalanced inputs and outputs can cause resentment.

Self-disclosure
Sharing personal thoughts, feelings, and experiences with a partner creates intimacy. Not opening up to a partner can prevent the relationship from evolving over time.

Positive support
Being kind and supportive to one another, and avoiding hurtful comments or scorn that can create tension in a relationship, help it to endure. These actions create a positive environment and also build trust.

Social support
If friends and family approve of a relationship, their help, care, and support can help it to endure through difficult periods. Couples without this support may find it harder to navigate challenging times.

Relationship breakdown

As well as studying the way romantic relationships between people begin, psychologists have also investigated how relationships break down and end. While every relationship is different, it's been proposed that there are common stages that most relationships go through. In 1982, British psychologist Steven Duck outlined the four phases people go through during the end of a relationship. Later, in 2001, he added reasons for these phases, in his phase model of relationship breakdown.

Key facts

✓ There are common phases that mark the end of a relationship.

✓ Duck identified four phases of breakdown: intrapsychic, dyadic, social, and grave-dressing.

✓ Phases are reached by one or both partners, beginning with private doubts, then discussions, and finally preparing for the next relationship.

✓ Duck also described three reasons why breakdowns occur: pre-existing doom, mechanical failure, and sudden death.

I can't stand this any more.

Phase 1: intrapsychic phase
When a person recognizes that they are unhappy in their relationship, the intrapsychic phase begins. This person considers why they are dissatisfied and decides they can no longer cope. The focus of this stage is the dissatisfied person's thought processes.

I'm unhappy

Me too

Phase 2: dyadic phase
The dyadic phase begins when the person decides they are justified in leaving the relationship. They confront their partner to discuss their dissatisfaction and the future. The focus of this phase is the interpersonal processes between the two partners.

Phase 3: social phase
In the social phase, the dissatisfaction felt by one or both of the partners becomes public. The breakdown now involves the couple's friends and families mediating or taking sides. The focus of this phase is the wider processes involving the couple's social network.

We weren't right for each other...

Phase 4: grave-dressing phase
The grave-dressing phase is reached when the relationship is over. The former partners attempt to justify their actions to others and present themselves in a good light to attract a new partner. The focus of this phase is the relationship's aftermath and looking to the future.

🔍 Duck's reasons for relationship breakdown

Pre-existing doom
If two people are not well suited from the outset, then eventually this incompatibility will be the reason their relationship ends.

Mechanical failure
Breakdown occurs most often when couples grow apart and become emotionally distant, despite having once been compatible.

Sudden death
A traumatic event such as a major argument or the discovery of a partner's infidelity may trigger the end of a relationship.

Chapter 16
Criminal psychology

Offender profiling

Building a picture of an unidentified offender by investigating the crime and the crime scene is called offender profiling. There are different ways of putting together an offender profile. They include the top-down approach, which was developed in the USA, and the bottom-up approach, which emerged in the UK.

Top-down approach

This approch to profiling categorizes people who kill as either organized or disorganized, based on crime-scene analysis. The offenders' methods for each category are thought to correlate to certain social and psychological characteristics.

Key facts

✓ Offender profiling attempts to identify criminals by studying the characteristics of their crimes and the crime scenes.

✓ The top-down approach categorizes offenders uses crime scene analysis to determine a criminal's characteristics.

✓ The bottom-up approach uses statistical analysis of similar crimes to build a profile of the offender.

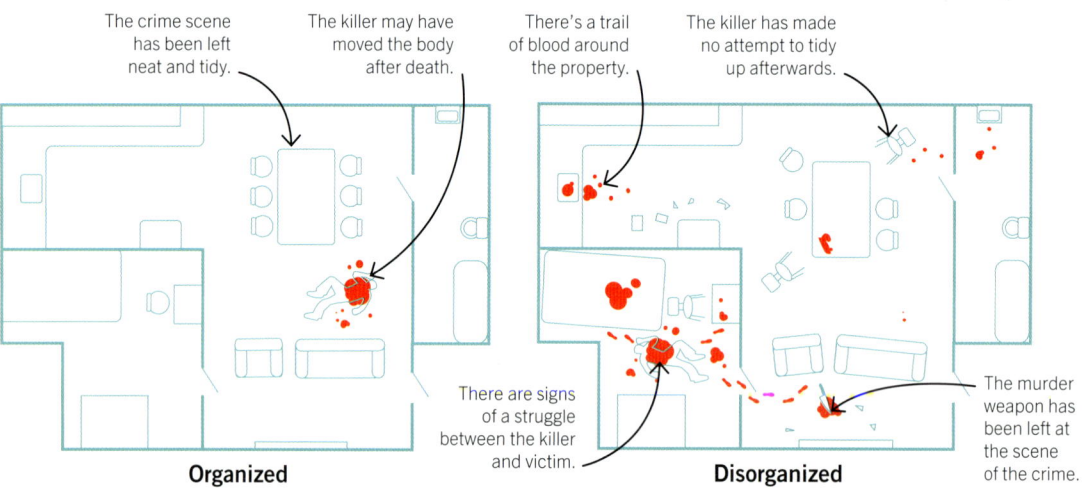

The crime scene has been left neat and tidy.

The killer may have moved the body after death.

There's a trail of blood around the property.

The killer has made no attempt to tidy up afterwards.

There are signs of a struggle between the killer and victim.

The murder weapon has been left at the scene of the crime.

Organized

Disorganized

Type of offender	Offender characteristics	Crime characteristics
Organized offender	• Highly intelligent and good at planning • Skilled, professional occupation • Socially and sexually competent • Usually lives with a partner, often far from the crime scene	• Carefully planned • Control of the victim, often with a weapon • Few clues left at the scene
Disorganized offender	• Lower intelligence • Unskilled job or unemployed • Socially and sexually incompetent • Usually lives alone near the crime scene	• Little planning or preparation • Minimum use of constraint on the victim, often with evidence of a struggle • Little attempt to hide evidence

The bottom-up approach
This approach to profiling is data-driven, emerging through a thorough statistical analysis of the crime scene and the evidence. A number of techniques are used in this approach.

Smallest space analysis
This bottom-up technique involves inputting data about crime scenes and offender characteristics into a statistical database to identify patterns. This can indicate links between crimes and help build offender profiles.

Geographical profiling
The locations of a connected series of crimes are analysed in this bottom-up technique. It focuses on the spatial relationship between the crime scenes, which can provide clues as to where the offender lives, works, and socializes.

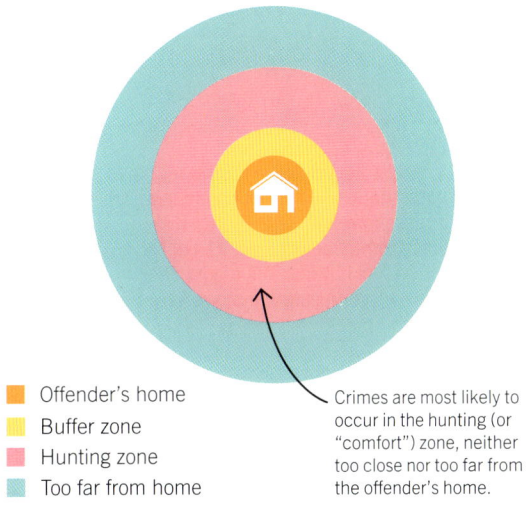

- ■ Offender's home
- ■ Buffer zone
- ■ Hunting zone
- ■ Too far from home

Crimes are most likely to occur in the hunting (or "comfort") zone, neither too close nor too far from the offender's home.

🔍 Top-down approach evaluation

Strengths	Weaknesses
The top-down approach is simple and easy to use.	The top-down approach is based on interviews with just 36 serial sex offenders, which may be unrepresentative of other types of criminal.
Copson (1995) found that 82 per cent of US police officers surveyed reported that the approach was useful.	Not all crime scenes fit neatly into one of two categories (organized and disorganized) and the distinction may be an oversimplification.

🔍 Bottom-up approach evaluation

Strengths	Weaknesses
The use of objective statistical analysis removes the risk of bias from the profiler when interpreting crimes as being organized or disorganized.	The data can only be derived from offenders who have been caught. It tells us little about criminals who evade capture.
The bottom-up approach can be used to investigate a wider range of crimes. The top-down approach is generally limited to more serious crimes like rape and murder.	Copson (1995) found that more than 75 per cent of police officers said that the approach was useful. However, only 3 per cent said it had helped to identify the offender.

Genetic explanations for criminal behaviour

It has been suggested that genetics may be a cause of criminal behaviour, which often runs in families. Studies investigating delinquency in twins and adoptees have supported this theory. Additionally, two genes have so far been identified that may predispose people with faulty copies of these genes to criminality.

Key facts

✓ Research suggests that genetics plays a role in criminal behaviour.

✓ Twin and adoption studies can demonstrate the influence of genetics on criminality.

✓ Two genes have been linked to criminal behaviour.

Twin research

British psychologist Adrian Raine (1993) reviewed research into delinquency in twins and found a 52 per cent concordance rate (see page 57) for monozygotic (identical) twins compared with just 21 per cent for dizygotic (nonidentical) twins. The higher concordance rate for monozygotic twins show that genes are a significant factor in delinquency.

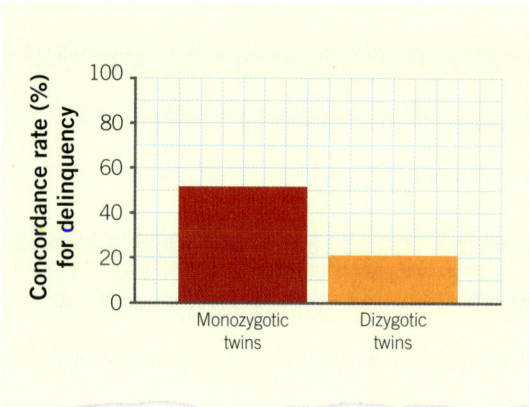

Adoption research

US psychologist S. Mednick et al. (1984) studied more than 14,000 adoptees and looked at the concordance rates of criminal convictions between the adoptees and their adopted and biological parents. They found the rate higher between adoptees and biological parents than between adoptees and adoptive parents. It was highest when both sets of parents had convictions. These results suggest that genetics plays a bigger role than environment in criminal behaviour.

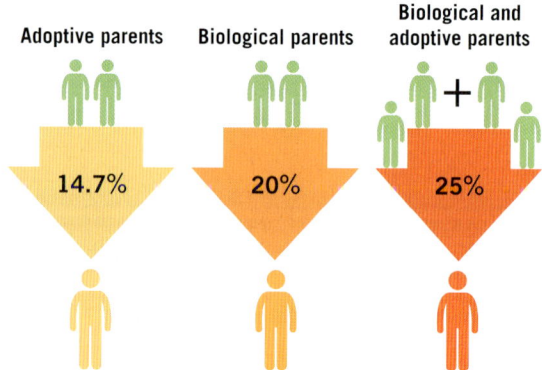

🔍 Genes and criminal behaviour

Two genes have been identified that may predispose people to criminal behaviour if they have faulty copies of the genes. Low activity of the MAOA gene, on the X chromosome, may cause uninhibited and aggressive behaviour, and low activity of the CDH13 gene, on chromosome 16, has been linked to substance abuse and attention deficit disorder. Tiihonen et al. (2015) found that people with faulty copies of both genes are much more likely to have a history of aggressive behaviour, increasing the risk of criminality.

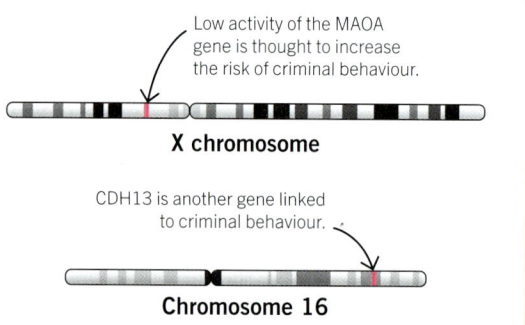

Low activity of the MAOA gene is thought to increase the risk of criminal behaviour.

X chromosome

CDH13 is another gene linked to criminal behaviour.

Chromosome 16

Neural explanations for criminal behaviour

The structure and function of the brain may be slightly different in people who commit crimes. The areas thought to be involved in offending behaviour include the prefrontal cortex and the amygdala. The neurotransmitter serotonin has also been linked to criminal behaviour.

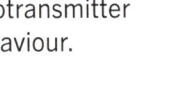

Key facts

✓ Criminality may be caused by abnormalities in brain structure and function.

✓ Low activity in the prefrontal cortex has been linked to criminal behaviour.

✓ Low levels of serotonin may cause aggressive behaviour.

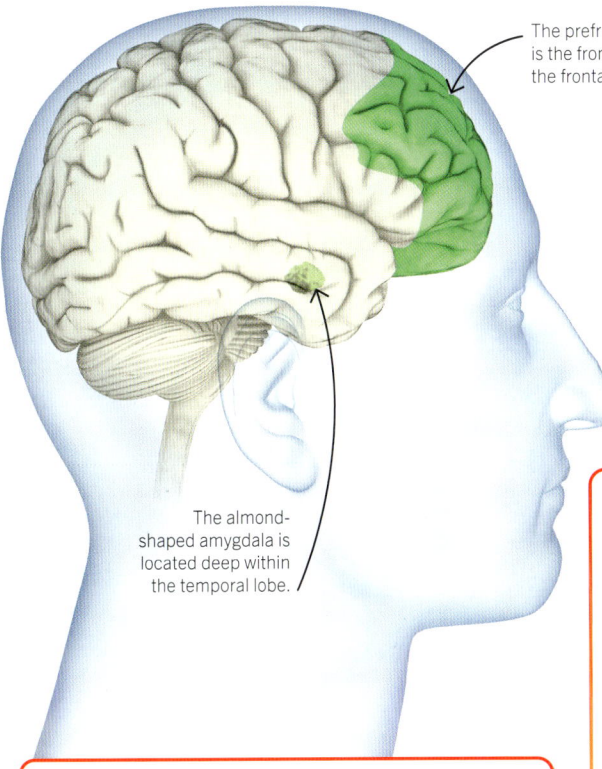

The prefrontal cortex is the front part of the frontal lobe.

The almond-shaped amygdala is located deep within the temporal lobe.

Brain areas involved in criminal behaviour
The prefrontal cortex has many functions, including the regulation and control of emotions. Reduced activity in this area (for example, due to brain damage) can cause a loss of control over behaviour, increasing the risk of criminality. The amygdala plays a key role in how we respond to challenges such as danger. When alerted, the amygdala can trigger aggressive behaviour.

PET scan research

Raine (1994) carried out PET scans of the brains of 41 people convicted of murder, pairing them with a "normal" control group of 41 people of similar age and profile. The colour scans, which show metabolic activity in the brain (in red), revealed that the brains of people who had been convicted of murder showed significantly reduced activity in their prefrontal cortex, which is responsible for self-control.

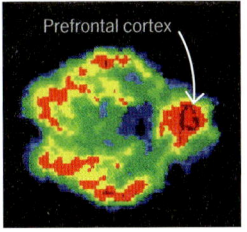

Prefrontal cortex

Control-group brain

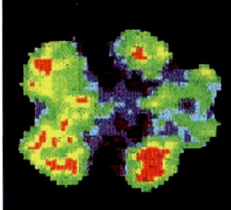

Convicted murderer's brain

Serotonin

Low activity of the neurotransmitter serotonin is associated with aggression and offending behaviour, partly because it has an inhibitory role in the body. If a person cannot produce sufficient serotonin, they may have difficulty dampening emotional responses generated by the amygdala, leading to an increased risk of impulsive, aggressive, and often criminal behaviour.

Cognitive explanations for criminal behaviour

Our beliefs and thought processes affect the likelihood of committing criminal acts. Research in this area has focused on cognitive distortions — irrational ways of thinking about ourselves, other people, and the world. Two examples of cognitive distortion that can explain criminal behaviour are hostile attribution bias and minimalization.

Key facts

✓ Cognitive distortions (irrational ways of thinking) can lead to criminal behaviour.

✓ Hostile attribution bias is a tendency to interpret situations as threatening.

✓ Minimalization downplays the significance of events, such as criminal acts.

Hostile attribution bias

The tendency to judge ambiguous situations, or the actions of others, as threatening when they aren't is called hostile attribution bias. For example, if someone looks at you, it could mean a number of things. People with hostile attribution bias are more likely to interpret expressions negatively, which may lead to an aggressive response.

People with a hostile attribution bias are likely to see hostility in a neutral expression.

🔍 Minimalization

The tendency to downplay the significance of events is known as minimalization. In the context of criminal behaviour, minimalization occurs when an offender reduces any negative interpretation of their behaviour before or after they have committed a crime. In doing so, the offender feels less guilt about their behaviour. For example, a shoplifter might think that stealing a few items from a supermarket doesn't hurt anybody, just a company, and that they are doing it to support their family.

Differential association theory

US sociologist Edwin Sutherland's differential association theory (1939) proposes that crime is a behaviour learned from interactions with small but influential social groups. If a person associates with a group that values and practises criminal behaviour, it is likely that they will adopt these values and practices themself.

Key facts

✓ Sutherland's differential association theory states that crime is a learned behaviour.

✓ Crime is learned from interactions with social groups, especially groups that value criminal behaviour.

✓ The theory can explain a wide range of crimes, regardless of sex, age, or background.

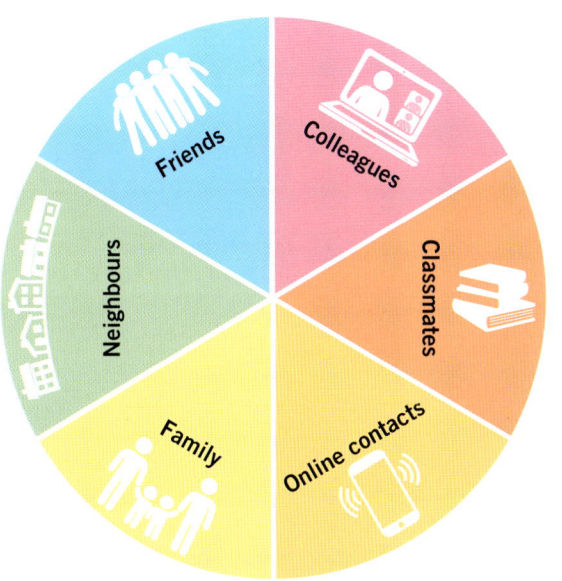

Learning crime

People interact with a variety of social groups, including colleagues, friends, and online contacts. How much time is spent with particular groups varies, as does the amount of influence each group has. Different groups will have different attitudes towards the law. If one or more social groups have favourable attitudes towards crime and a strong influence on a person, the person may then be likely to adopt these pro-criminal attitudes and go on to offend.

Evaluation of the differential association theory

Strengths	Weaknesses
The theory can explain a wider range of crimes than many other theories, which have tended to focus on violent crime.	The theory cannot explain all crimes – for example, why people who aren't exposed to any criminal influences go on to commit crime themselves.
It explains why some types of crime cluster in certain areas, and why some areas (such as urban areas) have higher rates of crime than others.	It's also less successful in explaining more impulsive, violent crimes, such as assault and murder.

The psychology of custodial sentencing

A custodial sentence is a punishment in which a court requires a person convicted of a crime to be held for a period of time in a prison or other closed institution, such as a young offender's institute or a psychiatric hospital. Psychologists investigate the effectiveness of custodial sentencing for dealing with criminal behaviour and the psychological effects it has on people who are imprisoned.

Aims of custodial sentencing

Custodial sentencing has four main aims, but there is debate over which aims are more important than others. Whether or not these aims are achieved depends on both the prison and the person who is imprisoned.

Key facts

✓ A custodial sentence is a prison sentence or confinement in a similar institute, such as a psychiatric hospital.

✓ Custodial sentencing has four key aims: rehabilitation, deterrence, retribution, and incapacitation.

✓ The psychological effects of imprisonment may include anxiety, depression, institutionalization, and prisonization.

Rehabilitation

Prison should rehabilitate (reform) the person to prevent recidivism (a relapse into crime). Those who have been convicted should be offered opportunities to reflect on their crimes and given access to education and treatment (such as anger management), so they leave prison ready to return to society.

Deterrence

The unpleasant prison experience is designed to deter people from committing crimes. General deterrence aims to send a message to society that crime will not be tolerated. Individual deterrence aims to reduce the likelihood of recidivism among people who have experienced prison.

Retribution

Society enacts retribution (revenge for the crime) by making the person who has committed an offence suffer, with the degree of suffering proportionate to the seriousness of the crime. This aim can be particularly important for the victim and their friends and family, making them feel that justice has been done.

Incapacitation

The person accused of the offence is incapacitated – taken out of society to protect the public and prevent recidivism. The need for incapacitation depends on the severity of the offence. For example, society requires more protection from a person convicted of murder than from someone refusing to pay their taxes.

🔍 Psychological effects of custodial sentencing

Anxiety and depression appear to increase in prison. Self-harm and suicide are higher in prisons than among the general population.

Institutionalization is the process of becoming so accustomed to the norms and routines of prison life that it becomes hard to return to normal society.

Prisonization is a process in which an imprisoned person assimilates into inmate culture, usually with its own "inmate code". This code may encourage and reward behaviour inside the prison that's considered unacceptable in general society.

Anger management

A cognitive behavioural therapy, anger management teaches people to recognize the signs that trigger anger, so they can then control their feelings with a range of cognitive, behavioural, and physiological strategies. Anger management programmes are one of the most common rehabilitation strategies in prisons. The programmes tend to follow three phases.

1. Cognitive preparation
In prison, people are asked to reflect on situations that provoke anger in them and consider whether or not their thoughts are rational. The therapist then helps them to redefine these situations as nonthreatening.

2. Skill acquisition
They learn skills to help them deal with anger-provoking situations. Techniques may be cognitive (such as self-talk to encourage calmness) and behavioural (such as communication skills to resolve conflict peacefully).

3. Application training
Finally, they apply their new skills in safe situations; for example, in role-plays of scenarios that previously made them angry. They receive feedback from the therapist and others in the anger management programme.

Evaluation of anger management

Strengths	Weaknesses
Anger management has been praised for its varied approach, which uses cognitive, behavioural, and physiological strategies.	Anger management programmes are expensive to run, and many prisons don't have the resources to fund them.
By addressing thought processes, rather than behaviour, this may lead to deeper and longer-lasting change.	Success depends on a willingness to change by people who may be uncooperative.
Taylor and Novaco (2006) found it was effective. They reported 75 per cent improvement rates.	Not all crimes are motivated by anger. Anger management is less suitable for people convicted of non-violent crimes.

Moral development

Moral reasoning is making judgments about what's right and wrong. US psychologist Lawrence Kohlberg (1968) developed a theory of moral development, describing different levels of moral reasoning. He argued that criminals are more likely to be classed at the lowest level of moral reasoning, while non-criminals have generally progressed to the upper levels. The pre-conventional (lowest) level is characterized by the need to avoid punishment and gain rewards. So, people at this level may commit a crime if they can get away with it.

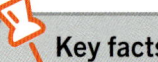

Key facts

✓ Kohlberg described three levels of moral development – pre-conventional, conventional, and post-conventional – each with two stages.

✓ Kohlberg's theory linked moral growth with age and experience.

✓ Kohlberg suggested that criminals may not have progressed beyond the pre-conventional level.

Kohlberg's theory of moral reasoning

Kohlberg proposed six stages of moral reasoning, from infancy to adulthood, and grouped them into three levels. People progress through these stages based on their ability to reason and exposure to moral dilemmas. Kohlberg suggested that criminals do not progress beyond level 1.

Principled orientation
People follow universal ethics. They believe laws should be just, and unjust laws should be opposed or changed.

Social contract
People have an awareness of the rules benefiting the majority, yet sometimes may question these rules.

Level 3
Post-conventional
14 years upwards

Law and order
Children have an awareness of the wider rules of society. Their judgments are concerned with upholding the law and maintaining social order.

Pleasing others
Actions are driven by conforming to the expectations of social groups or roles in order to be seen as a good person by others.

Level 2
Conventional
8–13 years

Self-interest
Choices are based on personal gain and rewards. For example, a child will do chores in return for a reward such as playing with a toy.

Avoiding punishment
Children focus on the consequences of their actions. They will obey the rules to avoid being punished.

Level 1
Pre-conventional
3–7 years

Chapter 17
Issues and debates

Universality

A finding in psychology has universality if it can be generalized to all people, irrespective of sex, gender identity, age, culture, era, and other differences. For instance, US psychologist Paul Ekman proposed that basic emotions and the related facial expressions are common to all cultures (see page 167). Psychologists often aspire to reach universal conclusions, but biased sampling and biased attitudes can undermine their claims.

Establishing universality
Universality is difficult to demonstrate without basing research on a representative sample of people from all over the world. Many studies in psychology use students at Western universities as participants, but this introduces several sources of bias: participants may be similar in age, socioeconomic background, nationality, and culture.

Using an equal mix of male and female students in a study avoids gender bias but not cultural bias or age bias.

⚲ **Key facts**

✓ Universality means a finding in psychology can be generalized to all people.

✓ Biased sampling in psychological studies makes universality difficult to establish.

✓ An example of a study that does not show universality is Ainsworth's "strange situation" experiment.

🔍 **The "strange situation"**

Ainsworth's "strange situation" experiment (see page 126) was affected by cultural bias and gender bias. Ainsworth studied the reactions of US babies briefly separated from their mothers and found that most had a "secure attachment" style. Similar studies in Germany and Japan found more children with "insecure attachment" styles, leading to unflattering conclusions about their mothers. However, the studies failed to account for cultural differences. In Japan, for example, babies are rarely separated from their mothers.

Ainsworth's study involved only mothers and not fathers – an example of gender bias.

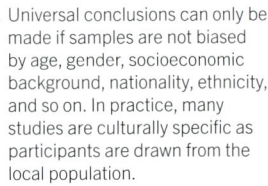

Universal conclusions can only be made if samples are not biased by age, gender, socioeconomic background, nationality, ethnicity, and so on. In practice, many studies are culturally specific as participants are drawn from the local population.

Gender bias

Gender bias occurs when differences between males and females are either exaggerated or ignored. Most 20th-century psychologists were male, and key research studies sometimes used male-only samples. This led to a male-centred perspective known as androcentrism, with male behaviour regarded as the norm and female differences as deviations from the norm. More recently, psychologists have tried to reduce gender bias. US psychologists Rachel Hare-Mustin and Jeanne Marecek (1988) proposed that gender bias has two forms: alpha bias and beta bias.

Key facts

✓ Gender bias is the misrepresentation of the differences or similarities between males and females.

✓ Androcentrism is the view that male behaviour is the norm.

✓ Alpha bias is the exaggeration of gender differences.

✓ Beta bias is the minimization of gender differences.

Alpha bias

This type of gender bias exaggerates differences between the sexes. For example, autism spectrum disorder is sometimes characterized as an extreme manifestation of the male brain. The condition is diagnosed far more frequently in males, but recent research suggests autism is underdiagnosed in females partly because of alpha bias and partly because it presents differently.

Beta bias

Beta bias is the tendency to disregard sex differences and assume that what is true for males is also true for females. An example is the fight-or-flight stress response that occurs when people feel threatened. Some studies suggest the stress response is different for females during a social conflict, with greater release of pacifying hormones such as oxytocin favouring conflict resolution over aggression.

🔍 Reducing gender bias

Equal opportunity legislation in Western countries and the feminist movement have contributed to a change in culture within psychology, reversing more than a century of gender bias. Nevertheless, major points of contention remain.

• Some academics argue that gender differences are social constructs and that males and females are not fundamentally different, whereas others believe there are genuine differences rooted in biology.

• The historical emphasis on quantitative rather than qualitative research in psychology has been criticized as reflecting a male bias towards systematizing rather than empathizing. Some have argued that women are better suited to qualitative research requiring social skills, though this argument implies a gender-biased assumption that men are better at maths.

• Modern definitions of gender have evolved, with gender identity now seen as distinct from biological sex.

Cultural bias

Cultural bias occurs when researchers in psychology or other social sciences fail to take into account differences between cultures or nationalities. A common cause of cultural bias is biased sampling – most research takes place in Western countries, using participants drawn from the local culture. Findings from such studies cannot necessarily be generalized to other cultures. Another source of cultural bias is ethnocentrism: the tendency to judge the beliefs and behaviour of others relative to one's own cultural norms. Ethnocentrism can lead to misunderstandings or prejudiced ideas about foreign cultures, which may be perceived as abnormal or inferior.

Key facts

✓ Cultural bias occurs when researchers fail to take cultural differences into account.

✓ Causes of cultural bias include sampling bias and ethnocentrism.

✓ Ethnocentrism is viewing one's own culture as the norm by which other cultures can be judged.

✓ Cultural relativism is the view that there are no universal values and that behaviour can only be understood within the context of a particular culture.

Studying different cultures
In the 1950s, anthropologists coined the terms etic and emic for two different ways of studying foreign cultures. Both approaches aim to avoid cultural bias, and each has different strengths and weaknesses.

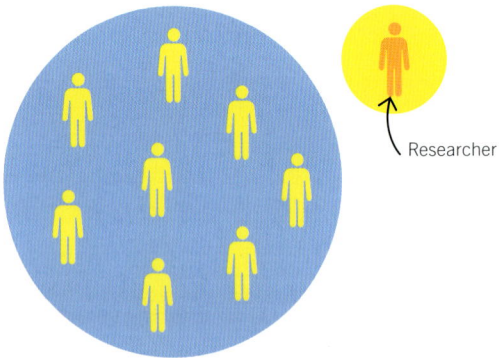

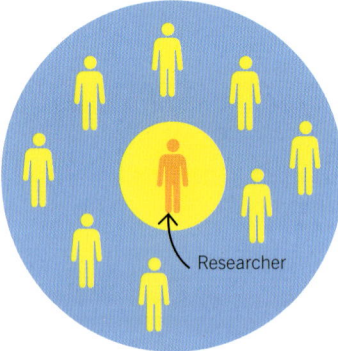

Etic approach
This approach takes an outsider's perspective, aiming to study behaviour within a culture from an objective, scientific point of view. The etic approach has been used to explain the functional or evolutionary significance of behaviour. For example, a food taboo might be explained as a way of avoiding parasites or diseases spread by certain foods.

Emic approach
This approach takes an insider's point of view, explaining behaviour in terms of the beliefs and values of a specific culture. The emic approach avoids cultural bias but is highly specific to the culture in question. For example, a food taboo might be explained in terms of compliance with religious rules and customs.

🔍 Cultural relativism

Cultural relativism is the belief that there are no universal values by which people can be judged. Instead, each person's beliefs and behaviour can only be understood within the context of their particular culture. Some strict relativists extend this idea to all aspects of psychology, arguing, for example, that psychiatric diseases are culturally specific. However, many psychologists believe that core mental attributes are universal.

The nature versus nurture debate

The nature versus nurture debate is a long-standing controversy over whether people's personalities and abilities are shaped primarily by their genes (nature) or by their upbringing and environment (nurture). Many psychologists believe that the two are closely intertwined.

Key facts

✓ Nativists argue that personality and ability are largely genetic (nature).

✓ Empiricists argue that personality and ability are largely environmental (nurture).

✓ Interactionists believe that nature and nurture are both important and are intertwined.

Scientists on the nature side of the debate (nativists) believe that most aspects of human nature are genetic and therefore inherited and shaped by evolutionary forces.

Scientists on the nurture side of the debate (empiricists) argue that the mind is a blank slate at birth and that personality and abilities are formed by processes such as conditioning and social learning.

Nature **Interactionism** **Nurture**

Most psychologists believe that nature and nurture both play a significant role and can influence each other. Studies of heritability (see page 56) can reveal the relative importance of heredity and environment.

Interactionism

Nature influencing nurture
Our genes can influence our environment. For example, a child with a natural aptitude for sport might seek out friends who love sport, too, leading to more exposure to sport and ever greater skill. In this way, a genetically determined personality has led the child to select a particular environment.

Nurture influencing nature
Research in genetics shows that genes can be turned on or off by environmental triggers. Chronic stress, for example, changes the expression of genes in the brains of mice. The study of environmental changes to genes is known as epigenetics. Experience can even change the structure of the brain. Brain scans of taxi drivers who had memorized a map of London revealed enlargement of the hippocampus – a part of the brain that helps store memories.

Three identical strangers

The 2018 film *Three Identical Strangers* tells the true story of identical triplets who were adopted at birth and raised in different families, only to discover each other by accident at age 19. Controversially, the boys were deliberately separated by scientists investigating the effects of nature and nurture. They were placed into families with different socioeconomic backgrounds and secretly studied without the parents' consent. The study's results were never published.

Free will versus determinism

Free will is the notional ability to make conscious choices about what we do — a powerful, intuitive sense that we can think and make decisions. However, determinists reason that since all our thoughts and choices have underlying causes, the sensation of conscious control is an illusion. Opinions about free will range across a continuum. While some scientists and philosophers reject it, others take a softer stance, arguing that some aspects of behaviour are determined and others involve an element of free will.

 Key facts

✓ Free will is the notional ability to consciously control behaviour.

✓ Determinism is the idea that behaviour is determined by forces other than free will.

✓ There are three main types of determinism: biological, environmental, and psychic.

Hard determinism

Our intentions are the result of internal or external forces that we do not choose. For example, the decision to eat snacks depends on hormones that affect hunger and on social pressure that makes us conscious of our weight.

Soft determinism

Internal and external forces affect our behaviour, but we can still make conscious choices. Hunger might compel us to eat, but we can also exert free will and resist the temptation to eat snacks.

Free will

We have the power to consciously control everything we think or do, without restraint.

🔍 Types of determinism

Biological determinism
Biological determinism explains behaviour as resulting from biological processes. For example, competitive or aggressive behaviour between males could be explained as resulting from their biological sex or from the presence of the sex hormone testosterone.

Environmental determinism
Behavioural psychologists (see page 80) think behaviour is the result of learning processes such as classical and operant conditioning, which in turn depend on environmental stimuli. Stimulus-response learning has been used to explain everything from attachment to phobias.

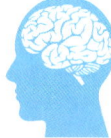

Psychic determinism
Psychotherapists such as Freud argue that our actions stem from unconscious causes that are beyond our control. According to Freud, adult behaviour is powerfully influenced by innate drives and early childhood experiences.

Holism versus reductionism

Psychologists debate whether behaviour is best explained in reductionist or holistic terms. Holism considers behaviour and its context as a whole, asserting that the sum of the parts does not equal the whole. In contrast, reductionism explains behaviour in terms of simple, separate components that can be studied scientifically, such as genes and neurons.

Key facts

✓ Holism considers behaviour and its context as a whole.

✓ Reductionism explains behaviour by breaking it down into simple parts.

✓ Biological reductionism focuses on genes, hormones, and the brain.

✓ Environmental reductionism focuses on stimulus-response learning.

Levels of explanation

Many aspects of human psychology can be studied or explained at a variety of different levels, from purely holistic to purely reductionist. Holistic explanations consider the wider social and cultural context. Learning and memory, for example, are influenced by the culture we live in. Psychological explanations focus on cognitive processes, such as the way different kinds of memory (facts, skills, events) are processed. Biological explanations are often reductionist, explaining functions such as memory in terms of brain structure, brain cells, and chemicals such as neurotransmitters.

Social and cultural
The culture we live in affects what we remember and learn as we grow up.

Psychological
Memories can be categorized into different cognitive types, such as procedural (skills) and semantic (facts).

Biological
Memory can be explained in terms of cells and neurotransmitters.

🔍 Types of reductionism

Biological reductionism	Environmental (stimulus-response) reductionism
This type of reductionism explains behaviour at the lowest level, focusing on genes, hormones, brain cells, and brain regions. For example, the dopamine theory of schizophrenia explains the disease as resulting from high levels of the neurotransmitter dopamine.	This type of reductionism explains behaviour in terms of learned associations between stimuli and responses. For example, attachment in childhood is explained as forming as the child learns to associate a caregiver with feeding.

Idiographic versus nomothetic

Is it better for a psychologist to study one individual at a time to find out their unique personal story, or large groups of people to discover general (universal) laws of human behaviour? These two contrasting techniques are known respectively as the idiographic and nomothetic approaches to psychological investigation.

Key facts

✓ The idiographic approach focuses on the individual and typically produces qualitative data.

✓ The nomothetic approach involves large numbers of people and uses quantitative data to formulate laws.

✓ The two approaches often complement each other.

Idiographic approach
The idiographic approach focuses on the person's unique subjective experience, motivations, and values. This approach is associated with research methods that produce qualitative data, such as interviews, case studies, and observations. An experimental method (see page 14) is not possible, so conclusions about cause and effect cannot be made.

Nomothetic approach
This approach aims to formulate general theories about human nature and typically uses quantitative data collected from many people in experiments. For example, brain scan studies allow generalizations about where mental functions are localized in the brain. Nomothetic studies often involve statistical analysis and may offer conclusions about cause and effect.

🔍 Complementary approaches

The idiographic and nomothetic approaches often complement each other. For example, our modern understanding of memory comes partly from tests carried out on thousands of healthy volunteers and partly from case studies, such as the famous study of Henry Molaison (see page 91), who became unable to form memories after the surgical removal of his hippocampus. The goal of modern psychology is to provide a rich, detailed description of human behaviour as well as explaining this behaviour within a framework of general laws.

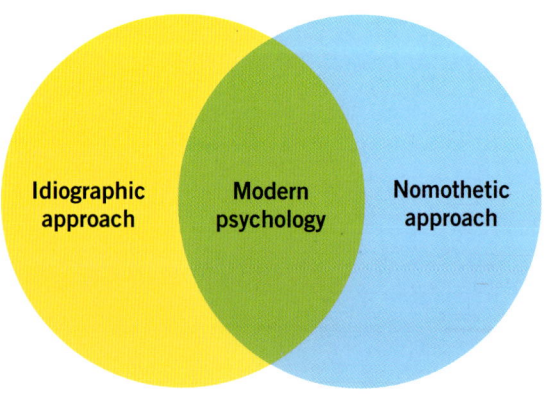

Socially sensitive research

Some research studies have the potential to cause offence or even harm to participants, their families, or wider communities. Sensitive issues can make participants or their families feel to blame, and media attention can stigmatize people and cause prejudice. Should such research take place? Many psychologists argue that it is their duty as scientists to carry out research into all aspects of human nature, however controversial the topic.

Key facts

✓ Socially sensitive research may have consequences for participants, their families, and society.

✓ Psychologists should consider the ethical risks of socially sensitive research.

The ripple effect
The effects of socially sensitive research can spread like ripples in a pond, first affecting participants, then their families, and finally the wider society. For example, research exploring the idea that schizophrenia is caused by family dysfunction can make the families of schizophrenics feel they are at fault. Publishing the findings may lead to media coverage, stigmatizing families affected by schizophrenia.

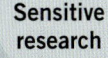

Sensitive research

Participants

Participants' families

Wider society

🔍 Ethical risks

Sieber and Stanley (1988) developed guidelines that highlight some of the pitfalls of socially sensitive research.

Research aims	Public policy	Institutional context	False beliefs
The research aim itself may be sensitive. For example, asking whether there are racial differences in IQ could be inflammatory, leading to media coverage that causes prejudice.	The way findings might inform public policy should be considered. For example, past studies of the heritability of IQ led to selective schooling based on intelligence tests in some countries.	Private institutions might misuse, misrepresent, or withhold data. For example, drug companies might decide not to publish findings that they think could harm sales.	Findings may lead people to form harmful false beliefs. Bowlby's theory of maternal deprivation, for example, might cause people deprived of maternal care in childhood to form self-fulfilling ideas about their inability to form relationships.

Glossary

Abnormality Thinking or behaviour that deviates from ideal mental health; body structures or processes that are unusual or defective.

Abstract thinking The ability to think about and understand concepts such as happiness, jealousy, and intelligence that are not attached to concrete objects. It is important in problem-solving and creative thinking.

Acetylcholine A neurotransmitter that plays an important role both in learning and memory, and in sending messages from motor nerves to visceral muscles.

Action potential A brief pulse of electrical current, generated by a neuron, which may be transmitted to neighbouring cells. Also called a nerve impulse.

Active listening Attentive listening in which the listener restates and reflects on what the speaker says. It is a key part of client-centred therapy.

Adaptation A change in behaviour to suit new circumstances; an inherited characteristic that spreads because it provides an advantage to survival.

Adaptation-level phenomenon The tendency to adapt to new situations or new stimuli until they become the new normal and less attention is paid to them.

Addiction Dependency upon a substance such as a drug or an activity such as gambling.

Adrenaline Also called epinephrine, a hormone that prepares the body for action during times of danger or excitement.

Adversity A distressing or difficult situation.

Affiliation need The basic human desire to belong to a group or community.

Afterimage effect The short-lived perception of reversed colours after staring at a coloured pattern.

Agentic state A state of being in which an individual obeys an authority figure, even if they are uncomfortable with the orders. The individual regards themselves as an agent for the authority figure to avoid responsibility.

Agonist A molecule that binds to a receptor and stimulates the cell to fire; see also antagonist. An agonist is often a chemical that mimics the effect of a naturally occurring neurotransmitter.

Algorithm A step-by-step logical procedure used in problem-solving.

Altruism Unselfish concern for the wellbeing of other people.

Alzheimer's disease A progressive brain disease thought to be caused by the accumulation of certain proteins inside and around neurons that causes memory lapses, difficulty concentrating, profound cognitive impairment, and problems with physical coordination.

Amnesia A general term for memory deficit.

Amygdala A small region in the brain that is important for feeling emotions, especially fear.

Androcentrism A male-centred perspective that regards male behaviour as the norm and female differences as deviations from the norm.

Androgens The sex steroid hormones (including testosterone), responsible for male sexual maturation and associated with stereotypically masculine behavioural traits.

Anger management A form of cognitive behavioural therapy that helps people avoid or control angry behaviour.

Antagonist A molecule that blocks or prevents activation of a receptor.

Antisocial behaviour Behaviour that is unfriendly or hostile, or that violates social norms.

Arousal A state of alertness or excitement that results from emotions such as surprise, fear, and anger, or from sexual stimulation.

Association A link between two psychological processes, formed as a result of their pairing in past experience.

Asylum Also called a lunatic asylum, an early hospital for mentally ill patients.

Attachment An important emotional bond between a child and an adult caregiver, formed in the early years of the child's life.

Attention The process of focusing our perception on one element in our environment and ignoring others.

Attention deficit hyperactivity disorder (ADHD) A syndrome of learning and behavioural problems characterized by a short attention span and often by inappropriately energetic or frenzied activity. It usually occurs first in early childhood.

Authoritarian A term used to describe people who are controlling and do not allow others to think and act for themselves.

Authoritarian personality A personality type that is submissive to authority and unfriendly to those perceived as lower status.

Autism The informal term for autistic spectrum disorder (ASD) – a cluster of symptoms that include impaired social skills, repetitive behaviour, and challenges with sensory processing.

Autonomic nervous system
A component of the peripheral nervous system, responsible for regulating the activity of internal organs. It includes both the sympathetic and parasympathetic nervous systems.

Autonomous state A state of being in which an individual has control over their thoughts and actions.

Availability heuristic A mental shortcut in which something that comes readily to mind is given more importance when making decisions or evaluating a topic.

Aversion therapy Also known as aversive conditioning, a treatment that aims to associate an undesirable behaviour (such as excessive alcohol drinking) with an unpleasant response (such as nausea) to discourage the behaviour.

Axon The fibre-like extension of a neuron that carries electrical signals to other cells. Most neurons have only one axon.

Basal ganglia A bundle of nuclei in the base of the forebrain, including the striatum and globus pallidus. It is mainly concerned with selecting and mediating movements.

Behaviourist A psychologist who studies observable behaviour, rather than internal processes such as thinking or emotion.

Binocular vision Sight that combines the visual fields of two eyes to create 3D images.

Biological reductionism A way of understanding behaviour by reducing it to the simplest components, such as genes, hormones, brain cells, and brain regions.

Bipolar disorder An illness that is characterized by dramatic mood swings.

Bloodletting An outdated, harmful medical practice in which blood is withdrawn from a patient to treat disease.

Body image A person's mental image of their own body.

Bottom-up approach An approach to offender profiling that uses statistical analyses of similar crimes to build a profile of the offender.

Brainstem The region at the base of the brain that controls essential functions, such as heart rate and breathing.

Brainwaves Rhythmic patterns of electrical activity in the brain caused by nerve impulses and detected by an EEG machine. Different mental states have distinctive brainwaves.

Broca's area A frontal-lobe brain region, concerned with understanding and articulating speech.

Bystander effect A phenomenon in which the more people present, the less likely one of them is to help a person in distress.

Case study An in-depth investigation of an individual, group, institution, or event.

Caudate nucleus A C-shaped, subcortical structure of the brain involved in motor processes, learning, and inhibition of impulses.

Cell The smallest living part of the body; every person is made up of millions of cells.

Cell body The central structure of a neuron; also referred to as the soma.

Central nervous system (CNS)
The brain and spinal cord.

Central traits In Gordon Allport's theory, the main personality traits that are used to describe a person, such as "shy" or "good-natured".

Cerebellum The part of the brain at the back of the skull, below the cerebrum; important for coordinating movement and balance.

Cerebral cortex The deeply folded outer surface of the cerebrum (the main part of the brain).

Cerebral hemispheres The two nearly symmetrical halves into which the cerebrum is divided.

Cerebrum The major part of the brain, excluding the cerebellum and brainstem.

Chromosome A microscopic, threadlike structure made of protein and DNA, which carries genetic information. Human cell nuclei have 46 chromosomes each.

Circadian rhythm A cycle of behaviour or physiological change lasting about 24 hours.

Classical conditioning A type of learning in which a neutral stimulus acquires the capacity to trigger a particular response by becoming paired with an unconditioned stimulus.

Client-centred therapy Also known as the person-centred approach to counselling, a humanistic therapy developed by US psychologist Carl Rogers in which the therapist works in partnership with an individual to develop their self-awareness and personal growth.

Clinical psychology The branch of psychology that studies, assesses, and provides therapies for people with psychological disorders.

Clinical trial A research study on human participants to test new ways of diagnosing, treating, or preventing disorders.

Cochlea The spiral-shaped bony canal in the inner ear, containing the hair cells that convert sound into electrical impulses.

Coding The processing of sensory information into memory.

Cognition Conscious and unconscious brain processes, such as perceiving, thinking, learning, and remembering information.

Cognitive To do with mental processes, such as perception, memory, or thinking.

Cognitive behavioural therapy (CBT) A type of therapy that encourages patients to manage their problems by changing the way that they think and behave.

Cognitive bias An illogical assumption that influences decision-making, often leading to bad judgments.

Cognitive dissonance A feeling of unease that arises when a belief or attitude that we hold is not consistent with how we act.

Cognitive distortion Irrational thinking about ourselves, other people, or the world around us.

Cognitive interview A process that aims to improve the accuracy of eyewitness testimony by using techniques to stimulate as many different paths to memory retrieval as possible.

Cognitive psychology The psychological approach that focuses on mental processes, including learning, memory, perception, and attention.

Comorbidity The presence of more than one medical condition in a person at a time.

Compatibility The ability to get along well with someone due to shared interests and opinions.

Compliance A type of conformity in which a person behaves in a way that's appropriate to fit in and be accepted. It involves the individual's public but not private acceptance of the dominant group's beliefs and behaviours.

Computed tomography (CT) scanning A brain-scanning technique that uses X-rays and a computer to create cross-sectional images of body organs.

Concordance rate The proportion of pairs of individuals that share a trait, given that one already has this trait.

Conditioned response In classical conditioning, a response that is learned or becomes associated with a specific stimulus.

Cone cell A colour-sensitive receptor cell in the retina, used primarily for daytime vision.

Confederate A person who plays the role of a participant – unbeknown to other participants – in a research study but is actually part of the research team.

Conformity The tendency of people to adopt the behaviours, attitudes, and values of other members of a group or an authority figure.

Confounding variable An extraneous variable in an experiment that is not controlled and that may distort the results; *see also* extraneous variable *and* variable.

Congruence The state in which the perceived or real self is aligned with the ideal self.

Consciousness The state of awareness of the outside world and of inner thoughts and feelings that occurs when a person is awake.

Conservation The understanding that the quantity of something can stay the same despite its appearance changing.

Continence The ability to control your bladder and bowels.

Contralateral On the other side of the body or brain. Damage to the brain often leads to problems on the contralateral side of the body.

Control group A group of participants in a study who are not exposed to the conditions of that experiment.

Corpus callosum The thick band of nerve tissue that connects the left and right hemispheres of the brain and carries information between them.

Correlation A statistical term for the tendency of two data sets or variables to vary in a similar way in a certain set of circumstances. It is often mistaken for causation.

Cortex *See* cerebral cortex.

Cortisol A hormone made by the adrenal glands when the body is stressed. Cortisol has many effects, including raising the level of glucose in the blood and limiting the production of white blood cells.

Counselling Providing help and guidance to people with psychological problems.

Counterconditioning Behavioural therapy that uses classical conditioning to change an unwanted emotional or behavioural response triggered by a particular stimulus.

Cranium The rounded top part of the skull that protects the brain.

Criminality Behaviour that is against the law.

Critical period A period of time in a young person or animal's development when emotional attachment to a parent or caregiver forms.

Cross-sectional study A study that compares people of different ages at one point in time.

Cultural bias A failure to take into account differences between cultures or nationalities when undertaking psychological research.

Cultural relativism The view that there are no universal values and that behaviour can only be understood within the context of a particular culture.

Custodial sentence A prison sentence or confinement in a similar institute, such as a psychiatric hospital.

Delinquency Criminal acts, particularly those perpetrated by young people.

Delusion A false belief that is not easily eradicated by exposure to evidence that reveals its falsity.

Demand characteristics Unintended cues in an experimental setting that allow participants to work out the purpose of the study, which may then cause participants to answer in ways they think help or hinder the research. *See also* participant bias.

Dementia A loss of brain function due to degeneration through age or cumulative damage to the brain.

Dendrite A branch that extends from a neuron's cell body and receives signals from other neurons.

Dependence A physical or psychological need for a substance or a behaviour to which a person is addicted.

Dependent variable The variable in an experiment that is measured to find out if there has been an effect; *see also* variable and independent variable.

Depressant Any substance that reduces the activity of the central nervous system.

Depression A mood disorder characterized by feelings of hopelessness and low self-esteem.

Desensitize A process of weakening a strong response to an event or thing by repeated exposure to that stimulus.

Determinism The doctrine that all events, acts, and choices are caused by past events and not by free will.

Deterrence The idea that the fear of punishment such as imprisonment will discourage crime and therefore reduce the amount of offending.

Developmental psychology The branch of psychology that focuses on age-related behaviour and how that changes over time.

Diathesis A vulnerability to a psychological disorder.

Dilemma A tough situation in which a choice has to be made between two or more alternatives.

Directional hypothesis Also called a one-tailed hypothesis, an experimental hypothesis (prediction) that specifies a change in a particular direction.

Discrimination The act of treating people unfairly due to their characteristics.

Dishabituation The process of noticing a stimulus again after having been habituated (adapted) to it; *see also* habituation.

Disorder A problem or illness that affects a person's mind or body and may require medical treatment.

Dispositional To do with the way someone feels or behaves.

Dizygotic twins Twins that arise from two separately fertilized eggs. Dizygotic twins share about half of their genes. Also called nonidentical or fraternal twins; *see also* monozygotic twins.

DNA Deoxyribonucleic acid, the chemical that stores genetic material inside living cells.

Dopamine A neurotransmitter involved in motivation. Dopamine is released in the brain during anticipation of a reward or goal.

Double-bind theory The theory that proposes conflicting emotional signals from carers increases the risk of schizophrenia.

Drive A trigger that motivates people to satisfy physiological needs. For example, the drive of hunger encourages people to eat.

Drive reduction theory The theory that proposes behaviour is motivated by the need to reduce unpleasant states of tension (drives).

Drug A chemical taken into the body in order to alter the way the body works. Most drugs are taken to treat or prevent disease.

Dual-process theory The theory that people use two different systems of thinking – intuitive and slower, more analytical thinking – to make decisions.

Dysfunctional Abnormal or not working properly.

Ecological validity The extent to which the results of a psychological investigation can be generalized to real life.

EEG *See* electroencephalograph.

Ego In psychoanalysis, the conscious and rational part of the mind.

Egocentric bias The tendency to overinterpret external events as having personal relevance, leading to delusions.

Electroconvulsive therapy (ECT) A treatment for mental disorders, in which an electric current is passed through the brain to induce a fit.

Electroencephalograph (EEG) A graphic record of the electrical activity of the brain, made by attaching electrodes to the scalp that pick up the underlying brainwaves.

Emotions Feelings that you have, such as happiness when something good happens to you.

Empathy The ability to understand the feelings or emotional states of other people.

Empiricism A philosophical and psychological approach that assigns the attribution of all knowledge to experience.

Endorphins Neurotransmitters that cause a feeling of wellbeing.

Enzyme A protein made by living cells that speeds up a chemical reaction.

Epigenetics The study of environmental changes to genes.

Epilepsy A disorder marked by sudden seizures, associated with abnormal electrical activity in the brain.

Epinephrine *See* adrenaline.

Episodic memory The memory store that records events and experiences.

Equity The state of a relationship between two people in which there is equal give and take.

Ethics The moral rules and principles governing human behaviour.

Ethnocentrism The tendency to judge beliefs and behaviour of others relative to one's own cultural norms.

Ethology The scientific study of animal behaviour.

Event-related potential The neural activity recorded by an EEG machine in response to a specific stimulus.

Excitatory neurotransmitter A type of neurotransmitter that encourages neurons to fire; *see also* inhibitory neurotransmitter.

Experiment A scientific procedure carried out to test a hypothesis (prediction).

Experimental hypothesis A prediction of the outcome of a scientific procedure.

Explicit memory The memories that can be consciously retrieved and reported.

External validity The extent to which the results of a psychological investigation can be generalized to other situations.

Extraneous variable A variable in an experiment that isn't the independent or dependent variable. Extraneous variables need to be controlled to prevent them from affecting experimental results.

Extrinsic motivation The incentive for someone to do something because it has an external reward, such as money.

Extroversion The focusing of one's energy primarily towards the external world and other people; *see also* introversion.

Extrovert A person who directs their energy towards the outside world. Extroverts are often outgoing and talkative, and enjoy the company of other people.

False memory A recovered memory of an event that did not take place.

Fatuous Foolish or silly.

Field experiment Also called a real-world experiment, a study carried out in an everyday setting.

Fixation A mental obstacle that prevents a person from getting a fresh perspective on a new problem. Fixation also refers to obsessive behaviour, such as nail-biting, that originates from over- or under-gratification during the psychosexual stage of development.

Flashbulb memory A vivid memory associated with an emotional event.

Flooding A type of counterconditioning in which a person is exposed to a feared situation or object for a prolonged period until they eventually start to calm down and lose the phobia.

Fluid intelligence The capacity to solve problems through reasoning, independent of acquired knowledge.

fMRI *See* functional magnetic resonance imaging.

Forensic A term used to describe scientific work that helps solve crimes.

Free will The notional ability to consciously control behaviour.

Freudian slip An act or word that is close to but different from the one intended, and reflects unconscious thoughts.

Frontal lobe The area at the front of the brain, responsible for thinking, making judgments, planning, decision-making, and conscious emotion.

Functional imaging A range of techniques that allow neural activity to be measured and shown as visual images.

Functional magnetic resonance imaging (fMRI) A brain-scanning technique that detects increased blood flow, revealing which areas of the brain are most active.

Functional plasticity The brain's ability to re-map cognitive functions from one area of itself to another.

Fundamental attribution error The tendency to explain other people's behaviour by reference to personality traits rather than external situational factors.

GABA Gamma-aminobutyric acid, the major inhibitory neurotransmitter in the brain.

Gender The state of being masculine or feminine in relation to cultural norms.

Gender bias The exaggeration or disregard of differences between males and females in psychological research.

Gender dysphoria A mental health condition caused by a mismatch between a person's biological sex and gender identity.

Gender identity An individual's feelings about their own gender.

General intelligence An ability that underlies all intelligent behaviour, proposed by Charles Spearman.

Generalization The extent to which the results of a psychological study also apply to a wider population.

Genes A set of instructions that are encoded in DNA and are passed from parents to children. Genes control the way the body develops and works.

Genotype The combination of genes that influence a particular trait.

Geographical profiling Studying the locations of linked crimes to determine where the offender may live.

Ghrelin A hormone secreted by the stomach that increases hunger.

Glucose A simple sugar that is the body's main source of energy.

Glutamate The most common excitatory neurotransmitter in the brain.

Grammar The system of rules and structures for the formation of sentences.

Grey matter The darker tissues of the brain, made up of densely packed cell bodies, as seen in the cortex.

Groupthink A phenomenon that occurs in a group of people when the desire to conform overrides independent critical thinking, often leading to bad decision-making.

Habituation The process of becoming less responsive to a stimulus.

Hallucination A false perception that occurs in the absence of any sensory stimuli.

Halo effect The tendency to focus on one characteristic of someone (or something) to make positive judgments about their other characteristics.

Hedonic adaptation The tendency to quickly revert to a "happiness set point" after an emotional event, whether positive or negative.

Hemisphere One of the two halves of the brain.

Heritability The percentage of variation in a group of people for a trait that can be attributed to genes rather than environment.

Heterosexual A person attracted to people of the opposite sex.

Heuristic A "rule of thumb" or general guideline used as a mental shortcut to solve a problem.

Hindbrain The back part of the brain, adjoining the spine, that includes the cerebellum, pons, and medulla.

Hippocampus A part of the limbic system lying on the inside of each temporal lobe. It is crucial for spatial navigation and coding and retrieving long-term memories.

Holism The point of view that sees behaviour and its context as a whole rather than the sum of its parts.

Homeostasis The self-regulating maintenance of a constant environment inside the body.

Homosexual A person attracted to people of the same sex.

Hormone A chemical that is released into the blood to change the way a part of the body works.

Hostile attribution bias The tendency to judge ambiguous situations, or the actions of others, as threatening when they are not.

Humanistic psychology A psychological approach that emphasizes the importance of free will and self-actualization in determining good mental health.

Hypothalamus A small structure in the brain that controls many bodily functions, including feeding, drinking, and the release of many hormones.

Hypothesis A prediction or statement tested by experimentation.

Hypothetical reasoning A problem-solving approach that considers various outcomes to find the best result.

Id In the psychodynamic approach, the unconscious part of the mind that is associated with our instinctive drives and physical needs.

Identification A type of conformity in which a person changes their behaviour and opinions due to a desire to be part of the current dominant group.

Idiographic In psychological research, an approach that focuses on the person's unique subjective experience, motivations, and values; usually associated with research methods that produce qualitative data.

Illusion A false perception or distortion of the senses, often caused by unconscious brain processes.

Implicit memory The memories that cannot be retrieved consciously, but are activated as part of particular skills or actions, or in the form of an emotion linked to an event that cannot be made conscious. They underlie the learning of physical skills such as playing a ball game.

Imprinting An innate system of rapid learning that takes place in animals immediately after birth; it commonly involves developing an attachment to a specific individual or object.

In-group A group to which a person belongs. Members often view their own group more favourably than other groups (out-groups).

Incapacitation The act of taking an offender out of society by imprisonment in order to protect the public.

Independent variable The variable that is manipulated in an experiment.

Individual differences All the psychological characteristics that can vary between individuals, such as personality or intelligence.

Informational social influence The willingness to follow the guidance of others in order to conform.

Inhibitory neurotransmitter A type of neurotransmitter that stops neurons firing; *see also* excitatory neurotransmitter.

Innate Present from birth, rather than acquired through experience. It may or may not be inherited.

Inpatient A person who stays in hospital while receiving medical care or treatment.

Insight The sudden realization of the solution to a problem or, in psychodynamic therapy, why you might behave in a particular way.

Instincts Naturally occurring, innate behaviour patterns in animals or humans.

Institutionalization The process of becoming so accustomed to the norms and routines of life in prison or another institution that it becomes hard to return to normal society or life.

Insular cortex A part of the cerebral cortex of the brain that becomes active when we feel anger, fear, disgust, happiness, or sadness.

Intelligence The ability to learn from experience, solve problems, and adapt to new situations.

Intelligence quotient (IQ) A measure of intelligence based on a range of tests. The mean IQ is 100.

Interactionism The belief that genes (nature) and environment (nurture) are both important and intertwined in relation to personality and ability.

Internal validity The extent to which scientific studies are carried out under carefully controlled conditions.

Internalization A type of conformity in which a person accepts the dominant group's behaviours and opinions publicly, privately, and usually permanently.

Intersex Any condition in which a person is born with ambiguous genitals, has an abnormal number of sex chromosomes, or whose genitals do not match their chromosomal sex.

Intrinsic motivation The incentive to engage in an activity out of interest and satisfaction.

Introspection The examination of one's own inner state and thoughts.

Introversion A personality type that focuses energy primarily towards its own internal thoughts and feelings; s*ee also* extroversion.

Intuition The ability to make decisions without conscious thought.

IQ *See* intelligence quotient (IQ)

Irrational Not based on rational (logical) reasoning.

Ishihara test A test used to diagnose red-green colour blindness that involves trying to see numbers in patterns of coloured dots.

Klinefelter syndrome An intersex condition in which boys are born with an additional X chromosome, which may lead to infertility, reduced facial and body hair, and enlarged breasts in adulthood.

Lateral On or to the side.

Leptin A hormone produced by fat cells when they become large, in order to reduce hunger and help regulate body weight.

Libido A term invented by Sigmund Freud for a person's sex drive.

Limbic system A group of brain structures that are involved in emotions and memory, including the amygdala, hypothalamus, and hippocampus.

Linguistic determinism The idea proposed by Benjamin Whorf that language determines our thought processes.

Linguistic relativity The idea that language does not determine our thoughts but can influence them.

Lobe One of the four large regions of the cerebral cortex, consisting of the occipital, frontal, parietal, and temporal lobes.

Lobotomy An outdated, extreme form of psychosurgery that involves the removal or disconnection of certain brain regions.

Locus of control The amount of control a person believes they have over their own life and behaviour.

Long-term memory The final phase of memory, in which information storage may last from hours to a lifetime.

Long-term potentiation The strengthening of synapses between neurons in the brain following repeated stimulation, thought to be involved in memory and learning.

Longitudinal study A study that measures changes in the same people over a long period.

Magnetic resonance imaging (MRI) A brain-imaging technique that uses magnetism and radio waves to create images of soft tissues.

Mania A psychological disorder characterized by overactivity, elation, irritability, impulsive behaviour, or delusions; usually a part of bipolar disorder.

Maternal deprivation An extended separation between a young child and their mother or primary caregiver that may cause emotional and intellectual problems in later life.

Mean A measure of average found by adding up a set of values and dividing by the number of values.

Median A measure of average found by arranging a set of values in order and then selecting the middle one.

Medulla The bottom part of the brainstem, also known as the medulla oblongata or myencephalon. It is responsible for maintaining vital bodily processes, such as breathing and heart rate.

Melatonin A hormone that helps to regulate the sleep-wake cycle. It is produced by the pineal gland.

Menstrual cycle A monthly cycle of changes that take place in a woman's body, preparing her for a possible pregnancy.

Mental age The age at which children of average ability can perform particular tasks, as indicated by levels of performance in standardized tests.

Mental illness Any psychological disorder characterized by significantly distressing emotions, thoughts, or behaviour.

Mesolimbic pathway A part of the brain connecting the midbrain to the forebrain that is involved in motivation and reward.

Meta-analysis A statistical combination of data from multiple studies used to reach an overall conclusion.

Midbrain Also called the mesencephalon, the top part of the brainstem. It is involved in eye movement, body movement, and hearing. It includes the basal ganglia.

Milestone A major event in the life of a person, such as graduation.

Mind The thoughts, feelings, beliefs, intentions, and so on, that arise from the processes of the brain.

Mindfulness Focusing on the present, and being aware of yourself in body and mind.

Minimalization The downplaying of the significance of events, such as criminal acts.

Minority influence The ability of a smaller group (the minority) to change the beliefs and actions of a larger group (the majority).

Mode In statistics, the mode is the most common value in a group of data.

Monozygotic twins Twins that form by division of a fertilized egg cell, producing two individuals with the same genes. Also called identical twins.

Morality The set of values and beliefs held by a community about what is right and wrong.

More knowledgeable other (MKO) A person from whom a child gains knowledge during social interaction.

Morpheme The smallest unit of meaning in a language. For instance, the word submarine consists of three morphemes: sub (under), marine (sea), and s (more than one).

Motivation An internal state that propels a person to follow a course of action in pursuit of a goal.

Motivator Something that makes a person feel determined to follow a course of action in pursuit of a goal.

Motor cortex The region of the brain containing neurons that send signals, directly or indirectly, to the muscles. It stretches around the brain like an Alice band.

Motor neuron A neuron that infiltrates muscle and causes it to contract or stretch.

Motor skills Specific movements that are made by the body, such as walking and climbing.

Muscle A band of tissue that can shorten or lengthen to make parts of the body move.

Myelin A fat-rich insulating material that forms a sheath around the fibres of neurons, greatly increasing the speed at which nerve impulses travel.

Nativism The view that a person's abilities and personality are "hard-wired" into the brain from birth by their genes.

Need for achievement A person's desire for challenging tasks or goals that involve mastery of skills and lead to recognition.

Negative reinforcement In operant conditioning, the strengthening of a response through the removal of a negative stimulus.

Neocortex The wrinkled outer layer of the brain; also referred to as the cerebral cortex.

Nerve Long strands that are connected to the brain and run through the body; they sense the world around us and control muscles.

Nervous system The brain, spinal cord, nerves, and all connected nerve cells. The nervous system processes incoming sensory information and sends outgoing motor signals to the body to generate responses.

Neural Relating to nerve cells.

Neural network A network of neurons connected by synapses.

Neurodegenerative disease A disease that causes progressive damage to the brain or nervous system, usually through loss of neurons.

Neurodevelopmental disorder
Cognitive and behavioural disorders that develop early in life, such as autism and ADHD.

Neurogenesis The generation of new neurons in the brain.

Neurological Relating to the nervous system.

Neurologist A physician who specializes in the treatment of diseases affecting the nervous system.

Neuron A nerve cell. Neurons transmit information in the form of electrical signals.

Neuroplasticity The ability of the brain to adapt to changes by forming new neural networks.

Neuropsychology A subdiscipline of psychology and neurology that is concerned with the structure and function of the brain, and studies the effects of brain disorders on behaviour and cognition.

Neuroscientist A person who studies the brain or nervous system.

Neurosis A mental disorder that has no apparent physical cause.

Neuroticism A personality trait characterized by anxiety, irritability, and mood swings.

Neurotransmitter A chemical released by neurons in synapses to pass signals to other cells.

Nicotine An addictive compound in tobacco that acts as a mild stimulant and triggers release of the neurotransmitter dopamine in the brain.

Nociceptor Sensory receptor that detects tissue damage and triggers the sensation of pain.

Nomothetic approach A research style that aims to uncover general theories about human psychology, usually based on quantitative data collected in experiments.

Non-directional or two-tailed hypothesis An experimental hypothesis that predicts a change in the dependent variable without specifying an increase or decrease.

Non-rapid-eye-movement (NREM) sleep A stage of sleep when the muscles relax and brain activity, breathing, and heart rate slow down.

Norepinephrine An excitatory neurotransmitter, also known as noradrenaline; *see also* adrenaline.

Norm The rules and standards that govern the behaviour or attitudes of a community.

Normal distribution A bell-shaped curve obtained when plotting data on a frequency graph, with measurements on the x-axis and their frequencies on the y-axis. The curve is symmetrical around a central mean.

Normative Relating to a standard, such as a norm of behaviour.

Normative social influence The desire to be liked and accepted by society, leading to conformity.

Nucleus The control centre of a cell, where DNA is stored, or a cluster of nerve cells with a specialized function.

Null hypothesis In a scientific experiment, the null hypothesis is a statement that there is no causal relationship between the variables being studied.

Object permanence A stage in child development when infants understand that objects continue to exist when out of sight.

Observation A research method in psychology that involves watching subjects behave in a natural setting.

Obsession A constant and powerful thought that preoccupies the brain.

Occipital lobe The back part of the cerebrum, mainly dedicated to visual processing.

Occupational therapist A person who helps others develop or improve skills that are needed to carry out everyday activities.

Oedipus complex According to psychoanalytic theory, a developmental state that arises around the age of five, during which a boy experiences unconscious desire for his mother and the wish to replace or destroy his father.

Oestrogen A sex hormone produced by the ovaries of female animals. In humans, oestrogen regulates the reproductive cycle and prepares the body for pregnancy.

Offender profiling An investigative strategy used to identify suspects by inferring their psychological characteristics from evidence at a crime scene.

Olfactory Relating to smell.

Olfactory bulb A part of the brain just above the nose. The olfactory bulb processes smells and is connected to odour-sensing cells in the nasal cavity.

Operant conditioning A type of learning in which an animal's or a person's deliberate behaviour is modified by association with either a reward or a punishment.

Operationalizing Substituting an unmeasurable variable with a related variable that can be more easily quantified. For instance, socio-economic status might be operationalized by measuring income.

Opiate An addictive painkiller drug derived from poppy flowers.

Opioid A synthetic painkiller drug that acts in the same way as an opiate.

Optic chiasm Also called the optic chiasma, the location where the optic nerves from the eyes meet and cross.

Optic nerve A bundle of nerve fibres carrying signals from retinal ganglion cells into the main part of the brain for processing.

Optimism bias A tendency to underestimate risk. Optimism bias is a type of cognitive bias (a systematic error of reasoning).

Orbitofrontal cortex A part of the frontal lobe immediately above the orbits in which the eyes are situated.

Organ A group of cells that work together to do a job, such as the heart, eye, or brain.

Orgasm A moment of intense pleasure at the climax of sexual activity.

Ostracism Intentionally excluding someone from society or a social group, often due to disapproval or prejudice.

Out-group A group to which a person does not belong, and may, therefore, be viewed unfavourably.

Overgeneralization A stage of language development in which children apply inferred rules of grammar or word construction inappropriately.

Oxytocin A neurotransmitter involved in social bonding.

Paranoia A delusional belief that other people mean harm. Paranoia is associated with anxiety and is a symptom of some mental disorders, such as schizophrenia.

Parasympathetic nervous system A branch of the autonomic nervous system that has a calming effect on the body, conserving energy. It inhibits the sympathetic nervous system.

Parietal lobe The top-back subdivision of the cerebral cortex, mainly concerned with spatial computation, body orientation, and attention.

Parkinson's disease An illness characterized by tremors and slowness of action; it is thought to be caused by degeneration of dopamine-producing cells.

Participant bias A systematic error in data collection caused by participants acting in a way they think will please or displease the researcher; see also demand characteristics.

Pattern recognition Recognizing patterns in sensory information that match information stored in the memory, allowing categorization and predictions to be made.

Peer pressure Social pressure from friends or acquaintances to behave or think in certain ways.

Peer review The evaluation of research reports before publication by experts in the field.

Peptides Chains of amino acids that can function as neurotransmitters or hormones.

Perception The way that people organize, identify, and interpret information from the senses in order to understand their environment.

Peripheral nervous system (PNS) The part of the nervous system that includes all nerves and neurons outside the brain and spinal cord.

Personality A person's stable and enduring mental and behavioural traits and characteristics, which incline them to behave in a relatively consistent way over time.

Phenotype The observable trait controlled by a particular gene or combination of genes (genotype).

Phobia An anxiety disorder characterized by an intense, irrational fear of an object or situation.

Phoneme The smallest distinctive units of sound in a language.

Phonological loop A part of the working memory model proposed by Baddeley and Hitch, the phonological loop briefly stores sounds we have just heard or words we are about to speak.

Physiological Relating to physiology – the scientific study of how different parts of the human body function.

Pilot study A small-scale, preliminary study carried out to test the feasibility or design of a large or complex research project.

Pineal gland A pea-sized gland located near the thalamus that produces melatonin, which regulates the sleep-wake cycle.

Pituitary gland A hypothalamic nucleus that produces hormones, including oxytocin.

Place theory The theory that sounds of different pitch are detected in different locations in the cochlea of the inner ear.

Placebo An inert substance given to the control group in a drug trial, often in the form of fake pills.

Plasticity The capacity of the brain to change its structure and function.

Polygenic Controlled or influenced by many genes.

Pons The middle part of the brainstem. It helps coordinate facial movement, hearing, and balance.

Population validity The results of a research study have population validity if they can be generalized to the wider population from which the sample of participants was drawn.

Positive feedback A reward that reinforces a pattern of thought or behaviour, such as praise from a caregiver.

Positive psychology An area of psychology concerned with improving happiness and quality of life of all people, not just those with mental illness.

Positive reinforcement A key concept in behaviourism, this is the process of increasing the probability of a response by immediately following the required response with a reward or positive stimulus.

Positron emission tomography (PET) A brain-scanning technique that highlights active areas of the brain by detecting radioactively labelled glucose.

Post-synaptic neuron A neuron that receives messages from another; *see also* pre-synaptic neuron.

Post-traumatic stress disorder (PTSD) An anxiety disorder characterized by vivid, often intrusive memories (flashbacks) of a highly traumatic experience, such as a car crash, war, or life-threatening illness.

Posterior Towards the back or tail end.

Pre-synaptic neuron A neuron that releases a neurotransmitter to carry signals across a synapse to another neuron; *see also* post-synaptic neuron.

Preconceived An opinion or judgment that a person has already made before considering the evidence.

Preconscious One of Sigmund Freud's three levels of consciousness, the preconscious is said to store memories that can be retrieved with a little effort.

Prefrontal cortex The region of the brain in the forward-most part of the frontal cortex, involved in planning and other higher-level cognition.

Prejudice Preconceived, usually unfavourable, judgments towards people because of gender, social class, age, religion, race, or other personal characteristics.

Prevalence The proportion of a population affected by a medical condition.

Primary caregiver The person who takes responsibility for looking after another person who is unable to fully care for themselves.

Priming A form of learning in which exposure to a stimulus predisposes a person to respond in a particular way to a later stimulus, often unconsciously.

Prisonization Assimilation of a prisoner into inmate culture, which has a code of ethics different from that of the outside world.

Probability A branch of maths that deals with the likelihood of events occurring. Probability is used in statistical analysis of experimental data.

Procedural memory A form of memory relating to learned movements; for example, riding a bicycle.

Projective test A psychological test that uses ambiguous stimuli to reveal aspects of a person's subconscious mind.

Proprioception Sensory information relating to balance and the position of the body in space.

Prosocial Behaviour that is positive, constructive, and helpful (the opposite of antisocial).

Protocol A formal set of rules or procedures that should be followed.

Prototype A single mental image or best example that represents a broader category or concept. For example, a mental image of a simple, four-legged chair could serve as a prototype for the concept "chair".

Proximity Nearness.

Psychiatry The medical field dedicated to the study, diagnosis, and treatment of mental disorders.

Psychoactive Changing brain function, usually referring to drugs.

Psychoanalysis The theories and therapeutic methods, pioneered by Sigmund Freud, that aim to treat mental disorders by unlocking unconscious thoughts.

Psychodynamics The study of the psychological forces underlying a person's emotions, motives, and behaviour. The term was invented by psychodynamics pioneer Sigmund Freud.

Psychometric test A test that measures an aspect of psychology, such as intelligence or personality.

Psychomotor Relating to body movements and associated mental activity.

Psychopathology The area of psychology concerned with understanding, diagnosing, and treating mental illness. Also called clinical psychology or abnormal psychology.

Psychopathy A personality disorder, characterized by a lack of empathy or remorse, and antisocial behaviour.

Psychosexual stages In psychoanalytic theory, the developmental stages of childhood, centring on zones of the body through which pleasure is derived.

Psychosis A symptom of mental illness in which a person loses touch with reality and experiences delusions or hallucinations.

Psychosomatic disorder A medical disorder caused or aggravated by psychological factors.

Psychotherapy The treatment of a mental disorder using psychological rather than medical methods.

Puberty The developmental stage between childhood and adulthood.

Qualitative data Non-numerical data, such as interview transcripts and field observations.

Quantitative data Numerical data, such as measurements or counts. The data obtained by scientific experiments is usually quantitative.

Radio waves Invisible electromagnetic waves with long wavelengths, used for communication and other purposes.

Rapid eye movement (REM) A phase of sleep characterized by rapid eye movement and vivid dreams.

Reasoning Reaching a conclusion by thinking methodically and logically.

Receptor A tiny structure on a cell that detects sensory information, such as light and touch.

Recurring Occurring again.

Reflex action An automatic, involuntary movement, such as blinking when an object approaches an eye.

Rehabilitation Therapy to restore mental health and abilities, allowing normal life.

Reinforcement In classical conditioning, the procedure that increases the likelihood of a response.

Reliability The extent to which a test gives consistent results when repeated.

REM sleep The stage of sleep in which rapid eye movement occurs. Dreams tend to occur during REM sleep.

Replication Repetition of research or an experiment that lead to the same results. Replication is essential to establish validity of findings.

Repression In psychoanalytic theory, an ego-defence mechanism that pushes unacceptable thoughts, memories, impulses, or desires beyond conscious awareness.

Researcher bias Errors in the research process or in the interpretation of data resulting from the researcher's preconceived beliefs or expectations.

Retina The part of the eye containing light-sensitive cells, which send electrical signals to the visual area of the brain for processing into visual imagery.

Rod cell A sensory neuron located in the outer edge of the retina. It is sensitive to low-intensity light and specialized for night vision.

Sadistic Gaining pleasure from cruelty.

Sampling bias A sample that is not representative of the population from which it is drawn due to a failure of randomization.

Scenario A theoretical or imaginary situation.

Schema A mental framework that helps in understanding the world.

Schizophrenia A severe mental disorder characterized by a distorted sense of reality, with symptoms including hallucinations, erratic behaviour, and lack of emotion.

Secretion Production and release of a substance by cells or a gland.

Seizure A sudden attack of illness. An epileptic seizure is caused by excessive neural firing and can cause shaking and loss of consciousness.

Selection bias Selection of participants in a research study in a way that is not representative of the target population. Causes of selection bias include biased sampling and the dropout or non-response of some participants.

Selective serotonin reuptake inhibitor (SSRI) An antidepressant drug that works by slowing reabsorption of the neurotransmitter serotonin from synapses.

Self-actualization Achieving one's unique full potential. According to Maslow's hierarchy of needs, this is the most advanced human need.

Self-consciousness A heightened sense of self-awareness that occurs when a person feels they are being observed or judged.

Self-esteem How positively or negatively a person feels about their own worth, achievements, abilities, and value to others.

Semantic memory Memory of facts and knowledge.

Senses The faculties we use to perceive changes in our internal and external environments, including hearing, smell, sight, taste, and touch.

Sensory Relating to senses.

Sensory adaptation Reduced responsiveness of a sense organ or sensory cell after a repeated or sustained stimulus.

Serotonin A neurotransmitter that regulates many functions, including mood, appetite, and sensory perception.

Set point theory The idea that a person's body weight reverts to a stable point or range after weight loss or weight gain.

Short-term memory A memory store in which a limited amount of information may be held for several seconds to minutes; see also working memory.

Side-effect An unintended and usually unwanted effect of a drug.

Significance test A statistical technique used to assess whether the data collected in an experiment supports the hypothesis that the experiment is testing.

Situational Relating to the environment, circumstance, or social context a person is in.

Skewed Asymmetrical. A skewed distribution has a longer tail on one side.

Social construct Something that exists only by collective agreement and does not exist naturally or independently of human society, such as money.

Social influence Pressure to conform to the views and behaviour of other people living in the same society.

Social learning theory A theory of learning based on observing the behaviour of others and the consequences of that behaviour. Albert Bandura was the foremost proponent of this theory.

Social loafing The phenomenon in which people deliberately exert less effort to achieve a goal when they work in a group than when they work alone.

Social norms The rules and standards that govern the behaviour or attitudes of a community.

Society A group of people that are considered as one community, or who live together in a shared social system.

Socio-economic status A measure of a person's social position, based on their wealth, level of education, and profession.

Somatic Relating to the body. The somatic nervous system controls voluntary movement of the body.

Somatosensory cortex An area of the brain concerned with receiving and processing information about bodily sensations, such as pain and touch.

Spinal cord A major part of the nervous system that runs inside the spine, carrying information between the brain and body.

Spine A row of bones down your back. Also known as the backbone.

Split brain The result when the two hemispheres of the brain are surgically separated; originally used to treat epilepsy.

Standard deviation A measure of how widely dispersed a set of data is. In a normal (bell-shaped) distribution, 68 per cent of values are within one standard deviation of the mean.

Stereotype A fixed image or belief about a particular type of person or thing.

Stimulant A drug that increases activity in the central nervous system, raising arousal and alertness.

Stimulus Anything that is detected by sense organs and triggers a reaction in a human or animal.

Stress The physical and mental reaction to a challenging or threatening stimulus or situation, often involving the release of the hormones adrenaline and cortisol.

Stressor A stimulus that causes mental distress.

Subconscious Occurring without conscious awareness.

Subliminal stimuli Stimuli that are detected by sense organs but are barely noticed or not noticed.

Substance abuse The use of recreational drugs in ways that can cause harm or addiction.

Sulcus (pl. sulci) A valley or groove in the brain's surface.

Summation The process of adding excitatory and inhibitory signals from synapses, potentially leading to a new nerve impulse in the post-synaptic neuron.

Superego In psychoanalysis, the term for the portion of the psyche that is derived from internalizing parental and societal values and standards. It is governed by moral restraints.

Survey A method of collecting data from a representative sample of people, often by questionnaire.

Symbolic thinking A form of thinking that substitutes symbols, such as words or numbers, for ideas or objects.

Sympathetic nervous system A part of the autonomic nervous system that speeds up heart rate, among other things, in response to stimulation; see also parasympathetic nervous system.

Symptom A physical or mental problem that is experienced by a person and that may indicate a particular disease.

Synaesthesia Blending of the senses. For instance, sounds may be perceived as having specific colours.

Synapse The junction between two neurons across which neurotransmitters travel.

Synaptic pruning The removal of unused synapses (junctions) between neurons.

Temporal lobe A division of the cerebral cortex at the side of the head, concerned with hearing, language, and memory.

Tendon A band of tough connective tissue that anchors muscle to a bone.

Tension A feeling of unease, anxiety, or hostility.

Testosterone The male sex hormone, responsible for the development of secondary sexual characteristics such as body hair. Testosterone is produced by both sexes but levels are higher in males.

Thalamus A brain structure that is important for relaying sensory information from sense organs to the cerebral cortex.

Theory A scientific explanation or set of ideas that has been repeatedly tested and verified by experiments or observations.

Therapy Treatment for a medical condition.

Threshold A level or limit on a scale above which a change happens.

Tissue Cells that are similar and perform the same function.

Top-down approach An approach to offender profiling that categorizes murderers as either organized or disorganized, based on crime-scene analysis.

Trait A specific personal characteristic that occurs consistently and influences behaviour across a range of situations.

Transcranial magnetic stimulation (TMS) A method by which electrical activity in the brain is influenced by a magnetic field, usually generated by a wand held on the scalp.

Transduction The conversion of a sensory stimulus, such as light or sound, into an electrical signal by neurons in a sense organ.

Transference In psychoanalysis, the tendency for a patient to transfer emotional reactions from past relationships (particularly parental) onto the therapist.

Transgender Having a gender identity that differs from one's biological sex.

Trauma A very severe shock or distressing experience that can cause psychological damage.

Trend A pattern revealed when data is plotted on a graph, such as a rise or fall over time.

Trigger A stimulus that prompts traumatic feelings or memories.

Turner syndrome A condition in which females are born with only one X chromosome, leading to short stature and infertility.

Ultradian rhythm A biological cycle that is shorter than 24 hours.

Umbilical cord The tube that connects an unborn baby to its mother's body to provide nutrients and oxygen and remove waste.

Unanimity Complete agreement among a group of people.

Unconditioned response In classical conditioning, a reflexive or natural response elicited in reaction to a particular stimulus.

Unconditioned stimulus In classical conditioning, a stimulus that elicits a reflexive (unconditioned, natural) response.

Unconscious Not conscious. Or, in psychoanalysis, the part of the psyche that cannot be accessed by the conscious mind.

Unethical Immoral.

Universal Applies to all people irrespective of culture.

Validity The extent to which a test measures what it is supposed to measure.

Values A set of principles, standards of behaviour, or what people judge to be important in life.

Variable In science, a variable is a measurable quantity that can vary.

Ventricle A cavity within the brain containing cerebrospinal fluid.

Vesicle A membrane-bound compartment inside a living cell.

Vestibular system A system of sensory structures in the inner ear that detect motion and gravity and help us move and stay balanced.

Violation Infringement of an ethical principle or law.

Visual cortex The surface of the occipital lobe in which visual information is processed.

Visual field The whole extent of the image captured by the eye or both eyes.

Vivid Clear, detailed, or intense.

Vulnerable At risk of physical or emotional harm due to lack of protection, disability, or a mental health condition.

Waveform The shape of a wave when plotted as a graph, such as a sound wave depicted on a computer screen.

Wavelength A property of light or other form of energy that travels as waves. Different wavelengths of visible light are perceived as different colours.

Wellbeing The state of being contented, healthy, or successful in life.

White matter A type of brain tissue that is made up of densely packed axons that carry signals to other neurons. It is distinguished from cell bodies by its lighter colour. White matter generally lies beneath the grey matter that forms the cortex.

Working memory A process by which information is held "in mind" as active neural traffic until it is forgotten, or coded in long-term memory.

X-ray An invisible form of electromagnetic radiation that can pass through the human body and be used to create images of internal organs.

Zygote The single cell that forms when a sperm cell fertilizes an egg cell during sexual reproduction.

Index

Page numbers in **bold** refer
to main entries.

C

Cannon, Walter 148
Cannon-Bard theory 168
cardiovascular system 173
care 139
caregivers, attachment 122, 123, 124
case studies 13, **29**, 264
causation, correlation and **24**
cause and effect 14, 264
CDH13 gene 250
cell division 131
central control 201
central executive 93
central nervous system (CNS) 37, 38, 39
cerebellum 100, 131
cerebral cortex 44, 45, 169
cerebrum 44, 45, 48, 131
Chabris, Christopher 61
chance 33
children
    attachment 122, 123, 124, 126, 263
    brain development **133**
    cognitive development **134–5**
    developmental issues 132
    intelligence testing 116, 117
    language development **109**
    maternal deprivation **128**
    newborns **132**
    parenting style **125**
    prenatal development **131**
    psychosexual stages **159**
    see also babies
chloropromazine 181, 213
cholesterol 173
chromosomes 56, 141, 250
chronic pain disorder 216
chunking **95**
cilia 75
circadian rhythms 54, 138
civil rights movement 230
classical conditioning **81**, 85, 122, 184, 185, 205, 262
Cleckley, H.M. 193
client-centred therapy **209**
clinical psychology 35
    defining abnormality **182–3**
    history of **180–1**
closed questions 26, 27
comorbid conditions 197
cochlea 68, 70, 76
cochlear implants 71
cocktail-party effect 61
coding **89**, 91
    and recall 96
coefficient of correlation **23**
cognitive appraisal 168, 169
cognitive approach 11, 35, 90
cognitive behavioural therapy (CBT) 201, **206–7**, 255
cognitive bias 104, **106–7**, 195, 228

cognitive development **134–5**, 137
cognitive dissonance **227**
cognitive distortions 252
cognitive function, and ageing **140**
cognitive interview **99**
cognitive neuroscience 11
cognitive priming 239
cognitive process **102**, 108
    and technology **111**
cognitive restructuring 207
Cohen, Sheldon 172
cold viruses 172
collectivist cultures **127**, 145
colour blindness **64**
colour vision 62, **63**, **64**, 65
commitment
    investment model of 245
    minority influence 230
    romantic relationships 244, 245
communication **109**
community psychologists 35
companionate love 244
compassionate love 244
competence 139
competition
    and aggression 238, 262
    sexual **240**
complementarity 243
complex phobias 184
compliance 220, 221
compulsions 187
computers
    and brains **90**
    and cognitive processing 111
    computer games 239
COMT gene 187
conception 131, 141, 142
concepts **102**, 134
conclusions 14
concordance rates **57**, 250
concrete operational development stage 134
conditioned response 122, 185
conditioned stimulus **81**, 85, 122, 185
conditioning
    classical **81**, 85, 122, 184, 185, 205, 262
    contingencies of reinforcement **83**
    counterconditioning **205**
    extinction and spontaneous recovery **85**
    learning theory of attachment **122**
    nature versus nurture 261
    operant **82**, 83, **122**, 184, 185, 195, 211, 262
conduct disorder 196
conductive hearing loss 71
cone cells 62, 64
confabulation 97
confidentiality 34

conflict
    origins of **241**
    resolution of 259
    teenagers 138
conformity **218–19**
    explanations for **221**
    group influence **234**
    resistance to social influence **229**
    to social roles **222–3**
    types of **220**
confounding variables 15
congruence **146**
conscious mind 156, 157
    defence mechanisms **158**
consciousness, levels of 156
consequence, learning by 82, 83
consistence, minority influence 230
constancy theory (gender) 142
contact comfort **121**
contempt 167
context-dependent failure 96
contralateral organization 50
control
    perceived 210
    sense of 194, 229, 262
controlled observation 25
convergence (vision) 67
convergent thinking 108
conversion disorder 192
cornea 62
corpus callosum **51**, 131, 198
correlations 13, **23**
    and causation **24**
cortex **50**
cortical homunculus **72**
cortisol 149, 166, 172
Costa, Paul 161
counselling psychologists 35
counterbalancing **22**
counterconditioning **205**
countertransference **204**
covert observation 25
creative thinking **108**
creativity 50
crime/criminal behaviour 196, 238
    anger management **255**
    cognitive explanations **252**
    custodial sentencing **254**
    differential association theory **253**
    genetic explanations **250**
    and maternal deprivation 128
    moral development **256**
    neural explanations **251**
    offender profiling **248–9**
    psychology of custodial sentences **254**
crises (psychosocial turning points) 139
cross-sectional studies 17
crystallized intelligence 115

CT (computed tomography) scans 46
cue-dependent forgetting **96**
cultural bias 258, **260**
cultural difference 228, 242, 258, 260
cultural relativism **260**
cultures, comparing 127, 167
cumulative recorders 82
Cunitz, A.R. 92
custodial sentences, psychology of **254**
cyberbullying 152
cyclothymic disorder 191

D

danger 49, 75
dangerous behaviours 196
Darwin, Charles 165
data
    describing **30**
    visualizing **31**
    see also scientific research
Davis, Keith 243
deceitfulness 196
deception 34
decibel scale **69**
decision-making 49, 50, **105**, 106, 234
declarative memory 94
deep brain stimulation (DBS) 215
defence mechanisms **158**, 204
deindividuation **235**, 239
delayed reinforcement 211
delusions 197, 201
demand characteristics 15
dementia 140
dendrites 39, 41
denial 158
dependent variables 15
depression 160, 186, 191, 216, 254
    brain stimulation therapy 215
    CBT for **206**
    Ellis's ABC model of 208
    major depressive disorder **188–9**
    medication 213, **214**
depth perception **66–7**
desensitization
    media violence 239
    systematic 205
desirable behaviours 211
destructive obedience 224
determinism **262**
deterrence 254
developmental psychologists 35
diagnosis
    reliability 19
    schizophrenia **197**
Diagnostic and Statistical Manual of Mental Disorders (DSM) **177**, 181

Acknowledgments

The publisher would like to thank the following people for their assistance in the preparation of this book:
Sarosh Arif and Orso Publishing for editorial help; Smiljka Surla for design help; Steve Crozier for picture retouching; Manpreet Kaur and Aditya Katyal for picture research assistance; Victoria Pyke for proofreading; Helen Peters for indexing; Sreshtha Bhattacharya, Shreya Anand, Anastasia Baliyan, Neha Samuel, and Heena Sharma in the DK Delhi office for editorial and design work.

The publisher would like to thank the following for their kind permission to reproduce their photographs:
(Key: a-above; b-below/bottom; c-centre; f-far; l-left; r-right; t-top)

3 Alamy Stock Photo: The History Collection (bl, br). 9-288 Shutterstock.com: gabydesign. 11 Alamy Stock Photo: © Fine Art Images / Heritage Images (tr); Alfred Pasieka / Science Photo Library (bc/MRI scan). Dorling Kindersley: Egle Kazdailyte (cr). Shutterstock.com: piggu (bc). 15 Shutterstock.com: stas11 (cr). 22 Shutterstock.com: Leremy. 24 Lawrence, D., Mitrou, F. & Zubrick, S.R. Smoking and mental illness: results from population surveys in Australia and the United States. BMC Public Health 9, 285 (2009). : (br/Illustration adapted from). 27 Shutterstock.com: katsuba_art (crb/smileyx5). 29 Alamy Stock Photo: Everett Collection Historical (clb/skullx2); IanDagnall Computing (cr). Shutterstock.com: photastic (br); SKT Studio (cb/paperx2); David Smart (b); pics five (cra/crb). 33 Shutterstock.com: smx12 (cb/bottles). 34 Dreamstime.com: Rudmer Zwerver (br). Shutterstock.com: NVRs (cla); Yesaulov Vadym (clb); tatianasun (clb/Magnifying); tabako_ua (bl). 35 123RF.com: Mikhail Ryabtsev (bl). Shutterstock.com: Rauf Aliyev (cb/laptop); katsuba_art (cla); Icon Craft Studio (cl); Ps_Ai (clb/Home); Blan-k (clb); Vdant85 (cr); Arcady (cb); tatianasun (crb); Rvector (b). 37 Science Photo Library: PIXOLOGICSTUDIO (c). 39 123RF.com: Alfio Scisetti (bc). 46 Science Photo Library: Dr John Mazziotta Et Al (cr); LIVING ART ENTERPRISES, LLC (cl); SOVEREIGN, ISM (bl); Zephyr (br). 47 Science Photo Library: CENTRE JEAN PERRIN, ISM (br); Cordelia Molloy (tr/Illustration adapted from). 52 Alamy Stock Photo: Phanie - Sipa Press / BURGER (cr). 61 Simons, D. J., & Chabris, C. F. (1999). Gorillas in our midst: Sustained inattentional blindness for dynamic events. Perception, 28, 1059-1074.: (br). 64 Getty Images / iStock: Gal_Istvan (br). 65 Dorling Kindersley: The Flag Institute (b). 68 Science Photo Library: Steve Gschmeissner (cr). 74 123RF.com: petkov (clb). Dreamstime.com: Tonny Anwar (cb); Anatoliy Sadovskiy (clb/

Sugar); Christophe Avril (crb/Coffee); Elenadesigner (crb). 75 Dreamstime.com: Unique93 (cr). 90 Alamy Stock Photo: Jakub Krechowicz (cr). 97 Shutterstock.com: HSSstudio (cb/Butterfly); Na_Studio (cb). 99 123RF.com: pashabo (c). Alamy Stock Photo: Mikael Karlsson (br). Shutterstock.com: Lyudmyla Kharlamova (sticky notes); rvlsoft (cb/pins). 102 Dreamstime.com: Jedendva (cr). Getty Images / iStock: 3dalia (cl/chair); Azat_ajphotos (cla/bench); venusphoto (ca); shutswis (cl); MarkSwallow (c); AlexLMX (clb/wheelchair); E+ / dogayusufdokdok (clb). Shutterstock.com: Denis Polikarpov (cla). 105 Dreamstime.com: Yuri Arcurs (cr). 106 Dreamstime.com: Esviesa (cr); Konstantin Iuganov (clb). Getty Images / iStock: vladoskan (c). 111 Shutterstock.com: BaLL LunLa (clb); EgudinKa (cb). 116 Getty Images: Science & Society Picture Library (cr). London School of Hygiene & Tropical Medicine (cla). 117 National Archives (111-SC-387): (ca). © Science Museum / Science & Society Picture Library -- All rights reserved: (bc). Shutterstock.com: photolinc (ca/border). 118 Shutterstock.com: AnyaPL (crb/Stopwatchx3). 129 Alamy Stock Photo: Mike Abrahams (cra). 138 Gogtay, N., Giedd, J.N., Lusk, L., Hayashi, K.M., Greenstein, D., Vaituzis, A.C., et al., 2004. Dynamic mapping of human cortical development during childhood through early adulthood. Proc. Natl. Acad. Sci. U.S.A. 101 (21), 8174–8179. Copyright (2004) National Academy of Sciences, U.S.A.. : (cb). 140 Dreamstime.com: Elaelo (crb/cake). Shutterstock.com: macrojobs (br/heart); rehab-icons (br); maglyvi (crb/brain); Katerina Primula (crb). 145 Dreamstime.com: Leremy (crb/human Icons). 146 Dreamstime.com: Jovanmandic (br). 150 Shutterstock.com: Kolonko (cb/clock). 154 Myers/DeWall, Psychology in Everyday Life, 4e, © Worth Publishers: (br/Illustration adapted from). 157 Shutterstock.com: devankastudio (clb). 158 Dreamstime.com: Desislava Vasileva (br/Illustration adapted from). 160 Alamy Stock Photo: The History Collection (cb, cr). National Museum of American History / Smithsonian Institution: (br/x2). Shutterstock.com: Carolyn Franks (br/borderx2). 162 Shutterstock.com: Na_Studio (crb). 163 Shutterstock.com: katsuba_art (crb/smileyx2); James Weston (cra/silhouette); Irina Strelnikova (br); Sylverarts Vectors (cra/spot light). 165 Getty Images / iStock: GlobalP (br). 167 Getty Images / iStock: E+ / ozgurdonmaz (x5); ozgurdonmaz (cr/x2). 170 Shutterstock.com: IanL twerhsg ewges (b/Illustration adapted from). 175 Getty Images / iStock: borisz (br/Illustration adapted from - woman); lioputra (br/Illustration adapted from - man). 177 Getty Images: Premium Archive / MUUS Collection / Fred W. McDarrah (br). 180 Bridgeman Images:

© Archives Charmet (bl); Stanley B. Burns, MD & The Burns Archive (c). Getty Images: Bettmann (tr). Science Photo Library: NATIONAL LIBRARY OF MEDICINE (br). Shutterstock.com: photolinc (r/framex2); TR STOK (bl/frame). 181 Alamy Stock Photo: History and Art Collection (crb). National Museum of American History / Smithsonian Institution: (bc). Shutterstock.com: photolinc (crb/frame). 183 Shutterstock.com: lemono (br/x4). 185 Shutterstock.com: donatas1205 (cla/clb); Jjustas (crying babyx3, c); Rosa Jay (l/ratx3). 187 Shutterstock.com: NotionPic (clb). 192 Shutterstock.com: Knotnoi (crb). 200 Getty Images / iStock: Dumitru Ochievschi (bc). 204 Getty Images / iStock: undefined undefined (br). 207 Shutterstock.com: Mironov Konstantin (tc). 210 Shutterstock.com: IanL twerhsg ewges (bc); Katerina Primula (br). 212 Alamy Stock Photo: Elvira Gomolach (cb/TV frame). Getty Images: Moment / © Marco Bottigelli (cb); Westend61 (br). 216 Darren Leis / A-1 Medical Integration: (br). Reed Hutchinson: (cr). 221 Shutterstock.com: Marcelo Trad (c). 223 Getty Images: San Francisco Chronicle / Hearst Newspapers / Duke Downey (ca, cr). Shutterstock.com: photolinc (ca/frame). 226 Shutterstock.com: Alexandros Michailidis (cra). 228 Getty Images / iStock: Artis777 (cr/Illustration adapted from); S-S-S (cl/Illustration adapted from). 229 Getty Images / iStock: cherstva (b); undefined undefined (ca, cra). 230 Alamy Stock Photo: GRANGER - Historical Picture Archive (br). Shutterstock.com: photolinc (br/frame); WDnet Creation (bc). 231 Shutterstock.com: bsd studio (c/x2); Leremy (bc); IanL twerhsg ewges (crb). 232 Getty Images / iStock: undefined undefined (c). 233 Dreamstime.com: Dmitrii Luchinovich (cra/scales). Getty Images / iStock: cherstva (cra); DigitalVision Vectors / bubaone (ca); merteren (2.2/cb, 4/crb); E+ / Juanmonino (1.2/cb); Juanmonino (3/cb). Shutterstock.com: AYO Production (1/cb); Icon Craft Studio (cra/castle); Cookie Studio (6/br); oneinchpunch (1/bc); Lunov Mykola (3/bc); Daniel M Ernst (6.2/crb, 5/crb); MM_photos (br/paper); Fluke Samed (2/bc); Daxiao Productions (3.2/cb, 5/br, 2/cb, 4/br); Robert Kneschke (5.2/crb); lil-mo (4.2/crb); PeopleImages.com - Yuri A (6/crb). 234 Getty Images / iStock: undefined undefined (br). 235 Getty Images: Stefano Montesi - Corbis (br). 240 Alamy Stock Photo: Dominic Robinson (br). Dorling Kindersley: Rohan M. Brooker (cl). 242 123RF.com: Diana Johanna Velasquez (crb/ring). 245 Shutterstock.com: 4zevar (cl); Leremy (crb/couplex2, crb). 249 123RF.com: axsimen (cra). Dreamstime.com: Seventyfourimages (cla). 251 Adrian Raine: (br/x2). 252 Shutterstock.com: IKO-studio (cb/x5); katsuba_art (c/

smileyx5). 253 Shutterstock.com: bioraven (c); Leremy (cla); VoodooDot (cl); Sudowoodo (clb). 261 Alamy Stock Photo: A. Astes (br); Album / RAW (cb). Getty Images: DigitalVision / Thomas Barwick (br). 262 Dreamstime.com: Lefttime (crb). Shutterstock.com: maglyvi (crb/brain)

Cover images: Front: Alamy Stock Photo: ikonacolor l; Spine: Alamy Stock Photo: ikonacolor tl.